Study Commentary on John

A Study Commentary
on
John

Volume 1: John 1-12

Gordon J. Keddie

 EVANGELICAL PRESS

EVANGELICAL PRESS
Faverdale North Industrial Estate, Darlington, DL3 0PH,
England

Evangelical Press USA
P. O. Box 84, Auburn, MA 01501, USA

e-mail: sales@evangelicalpress.org

web: http://www.evangelicalpress.org

First published 2001

**British Library Cataloguing in Publication Data
available**

ISBN 0 85234 454 6

Printed and bound in Great Britain by Creative Print &
Design Wales, Ebbw Vale

Contents

Preface

The Gospel of John has been called 'the most amazing book that was ever written'.[1] Like no other book of the Bible, the Fourth Gospel contains the entire message of God's Word in microcosm. It takes us from eternity to eternity and shows the centrality of Jesus Christ to our lives, to human history and to the meaning of the cosmos itself. For that reason, it must be at the very core of the preaching and evangelistic ministry of the Christian church. People need to hear and understand the message of the cross as expounded in John.

This last concern is the reason for the present volume. It is not at all an academic commentary, but it nevertheless aims to be thoroughly expository and to keep the focus on the proclamation of Jesus Christ to the heart, mind and conscience of the reader. You will find that homiletics are never far from the surface here. As you read, you will find outlines within outlines, reflecting the fact that this commentary arises from preaching through John's Gospel several times in over a quarter of a century of pastoral ministry. It is my hope that this will prove helpful not only to other ministers of the Word of God, but to all who want to be gripped and moulded by the brilliance and clarity of this marvellous Gospel and the Saviour it so winsomely proclaims.

For detailed technical, controverted matters relative to the text, I would refer you to the standard

academic works. Of the current crop in that genre,
D. A. Carson's commentary, published in 1991, offers
one of the most sound, balanced and readable op-
tions.[2] Herman Ridderbos' 'theological commentary'
(published in 1997) provides a fine counterpoint to
Carson.[3] These give a more than adequate window on
the way John is being treated in the big wide world
today. For comment that addresses heart and conscience with pointed application, however, the old
writers have a virtual monopoly, and Matthew Henry,
John Calvin, George Hutcheson, together with forays
into Manton, Owen and other Puritans via the textual
indices to their works, are just goldmines of sage
comment and godly counsel. Set down your nets in
these waters and you cannot fail to haul in a bumper
catch! In such company, both ancient and modern,
my own efforts are certainly unworthy and arguably
unnecessary, but they will, I hope, be justified if,
with the blessing of God, they serve to whet an appetite for stronger stuff and warm the soul along the
way.

To the congregation of Grace Reformed Presby-
terian Church in State College, Pennsylvania, I offer
my heartfelt thanks for their encouragement and
forbearance through the process of completing these
rather lengthy volumes.

Gordon J. Keddie
State College, PA, USA
January, *Anno Domini* 2001

Introduction

Commenting on the contrast between the simplicity
of the church in the book of Acts and the elaborate
institutionalism of modern churches, Martyn Lloyd-
Jones has observed that people 'always make everything complicated... But the gospel always gets rid of
complications... Complications are man's doing,
simplicity ever characterizes the true gospel.'[1] This
applies equally to the making of commentaries on
Scripture and perhaps is never more obvious and
pervasive than in the handling of matters of 'introduction' to the study of books of the Bible. The reason for this is that 'introduction', as opposed to
'commentary', is often obliged to deal with matters
and lines of investigation quite removed from the text
itself. This thirst for answers can easily overwhelm
the absence of hard evidence and the constraints of
established exegetical certainties, and can breed a
bewildering array of ingenious and inventive theories.

The situation today is such that one writer can
admit that he has only seventy per cent confidence in
his view of the source of the text of John and expresses the hope that his readers will accept more
than half of what he offers![2] It is one thing to be
humble about one's opinions, but behind this is
something far more dangerous — namely, that the
underlying assumption and perspective for serious
study is that Scripture itself has ceased to be something in which we can ever have full confidence.

Under such an approach, it is no longer regarded in practice as a fully reliable word from God, to be believed for what it is (2 Tim. 2:13), but has been reduced to a mere collection of ancient religious texts of human provenance, over which we sit in judgement, and which we may, or indeed must, dismember, rearrange and reinterpret — even if we are only seventy per cent sure of our judgement! What is frequently missed, even by those who love Scripture and believe it to be the very Word of God, is that this *modus operandi* implies a retreat from the Bible's own doctrine of divine inspiration and effectively undermines the canonicity of Scripture, by eroding these foundational pillars of biblical authority under an ever-rising tide of competing and confusing speculation and scepticism.

The writers of Scripture often tell their stories without any great concern explicitly to identify authorship, place of writing, citation of sources, and the like. To the extent that they are vague, or even silent, on these matters, they provide fertile fields for the fabrication and elaboration of a multitude of theories and speculations. Over against that we must assert the Bible's own doctrine that it is the God-breathed Word that sufficiently, singularly and certainly reveals the mind of God to man. Arising from this, a couple of points are worthy of careful consideration.

The most important is that *John's Gospel is canonical Scripture*, whatever perplexities may exist as to its provenance, source materials, thematic purpose and the like, and that we are to treat it as such. We are therefore to receive it as the Word of God and bow before its teaching in submission of heart and consistency of life. Too many analysts of Scripture seem to sit over, rather than under, the text, so as, in effect, to decide what is acceptable about it and what is not. This is not evidence of being led into all truth by the Spirit of God (John 16:13). The perspective of this commentary is that here in the Fourth Gospel we have a divinely inspired text, infallible in its revelation of truth from God and inerrant in its original autographs.

This being the case, it follows that introductory studies do have an important, though limited, role in shedding contextual light on the book as a whole. We must constantly bear in mind, however, that the treatment of introductory matters must be the handmaid of what is actually taught in the text of Scripture. If this ever becomes attenuated by speculation into the thinnest of thin theories, which is certainly the case in many modern studies, then the time will have come to lay them aside and hasten to the Word itself. If John was not overly concerned that his authorship be pinned down with anything more than a reasonable certainty, then we need not be concerned to demand a higher level of evidence than that with which he and the Holy Spirit were satisfied.

Who wrote the Fourth Gospel?

The two main categories of evidence are those of the Scripture itself and that of history, in the form of references to the Fourth Gospel in the writings of the sub-apostolic period.

Biblical evidence

The authorial anonymity of this Gospel is more imagined than real (see the fifth point on page 13 below) and need not make us coy about identifying the author as John the son of Zebedee, one of the 'Sons of Thunder' (Mark 3:17) and, more touchingly, 'the disciple whom Jesus loved' (John 21:20; cf. 13:23). This is certified at the close — either by the elders of the church or, quite plausibly, by John himself under an editorial 'we' — in the words: 'This is the disciple who testifies of these things, and wrote these things; and we know that his testimony is true' (21:24). It is surely beyond question that John was the one who followed Jesus and Peter along the shore on that particular occasion. The text itself clearly intends that we should conclude that John the son of Zebedee was the author of the Fourth Gospel.

Some find it difficult to believe that the author could identify himself as 'the disciple whom Jesus loved' and not appear to be exalting himself over others. Did he think that Jesus loved him more and the others less? It seems to them more appropriate and plausible if someone else is describing John in this way, and so they cast around for an author other than the apostle. To this it can be said that there is no necessity to see John's self-identification as anything more than the effusion of a heart moved by a sense of Christ's unmerited grace towards him. He is not comparing himself favourably with other disciples but, if anything, is humbly acknowledging his greater need of grace and his amazement at being loved at all by Jesus. This was the man, after all, who in his younger days had pompously rebuked someone for casting out demons in Jesus' name because he was not one of Jesus' immediate band. He had also once argued about being the greatest, and on that occasion had been rebuked by Christ and pointed to the way of humility and self-effacement. Like every saved sinner, he had plenty of reasons to be modest, and the language he chooses to describe himself reveals him to be one who was happy to be a debtor to the love and mercy of the Lord Jesus Christ.

A number of other considerations support Johannine authorship.

Firstly, the author is an eyewitness of the events he describes: 'And he who has seen has testified, and his testimony is true; and he knows that he is telling the truth, so that you may believe' (19:35; cf. 1 John 1:1). See also 1:14: 'We beheld his glory.'

Secondly, the author was present at the Last Supper (13:23) and was therefore one of the Twelve, since only the Twelve were present with Jesus (Mark 14:17).

Thirdly, John, although a leading member of the Twelve, is never mentioned by name — except for a veiled reference in 21:2 — an omission that is difficult to explain, except in terms of Johannine authorship. Of the Twelve, which other disciple is a viable candidate for authorship of the Fourth Gospel?[3]

Fourthly, a more general consideration is that the text of the Gospel, on account of its 'multiple allusions to Jewish topography and history' and its parallels with the 'first-century ... thought-world' of the Dead Sea Scrolls / Qumran culture, shows that the author was a Jew and that this comports with Johannine authorship.[4]

Fifthly, authorial anonymity should not be seen as a problem. The absence of the name 'John' in a byline does not, in any case, conceal the identity of the author. It veils it to the degree necessary to achieve the particular purposes of the author.

For one thing, *the ultimate author is the Holy Spirit* (2 Peter 1:21; 2 Tim. 3:16) and, strictly speaking, the precise identity of the human agent is of secondary importance. The author of the Fourth Gospel understood this, as did the unknown writer of the Epistle to the Hebrews. To the extent that we believe in the divine inspiration of Scripture, we shall be less inclined to complain that the Holy Spirit has not given us as much information on the human author as we might desire to know (cf. Heb. 4:2).

Furthermore, from a literary point of view, *the absence of the identification of the author* at the beginning of the Fourth Gospel — in contrast to what would certainly be expected in letters, as we see in the New Testament epistles — *is something of a necessity*, given the character of the prologue to the Gospel. John begins with the eternality of Christ as the eternal Logos of God and majestically takes us to creation and incarnation and then, and only then, into the earthly ministry of Jesus. What a stylistic gaffe it would have been for John to precede this with his own name! The impact of beginning with eternity would hardly have been heightened! Indeed, might it not have seemed merely pedantic to insert his own name in such a blazing account of the self-revealing Son of God? In contrast, Luke begins his Gospel with a dedication to his friend Theophilus — but without any mention of his own name either — thereby most appropriately introducing his readers to what is clearly designed to be a historian's account of the life and ministry of Jesus.

Lastly, *John's modesty is such an obviously human touch.* It breathes something of the personality of the man. The Holy Spirit reveals God's Word through him, not as some robotic amanuensis, but as one of Peter's 'holy men of God' who was 'moved by the Holy Spirit' (2 Peter 1:21). We can see why Christ loved John. We are drawn to love him for the same reasons, precisely because he consistently withdraws himself behind the glory of Christ's person and work and points to his Saviour as the one to whom all are to give the pre-eminence.

Historical evidence

External evidence for Johannine authorship is found in a number of what we might call historical 'paper trails' leading back to the beginning of the second century A.D.

1. The earliest *manuscript* of John is a papyrus fragment from Egypt of John 18:31-33,37-38 (p 52). If, as is most probable, this is a copy and not an original autograph, then the origin of the Gospel is pushed back into the first century. Two other papyri (p 66 and p 75) date from the late second century and contain most of the Fourth Gospel.

2. The earliest *reference* to John's writings is to 1 John 4:2-3, by Polycarp of Smyrna, c. A.D. 120. Since this is by the same author as the Gospel and post-dates it, this too indicates a first-century provenance. A chain of personal acquaintance ties these together. Polycarp was a student of John's. Irenaeus (c. A.D. 130 – c. 200) knew him and testifies to hearing him speak of conversations with the apostle in which the latter talked of his memories of Jesus and his ministry.[5]

3. The earliest *quotation* of John's Gospel may be that of John 1:9 by Basilides (c. A.D. 130), referred to by Hippolytus (A.D. 160 – 235) in his *Refutation of Heresies*. Certain second-century Gnostic writers refer to John, and it is one of these, Heraclean, who wrote the earliest known commentary on the Fourth Gospel. This is known only from repeated references in Origen's third-century commentary.

4. The first *historical reference* to the provenance of John's Gospel comes from Irenaeus, who testifies that 'John the disciple of the Lord, who leaned back on his breast, published the Gospel while he was resident at Ephesus in Asia.'[6] Also in the late second century, Clement of Alexandria (d. A.D. 214) and Tertullian (d. after A.D. 220) bear a similar witness. Thereafter, the acceptance of the authorship of the Fourth Gospel was universal in the church until the rise of modern 'criticism' spawned a plethora of unconvincing alternatives.[7]

The most solid answer to the question of authorship, then, is that the author was John, the son of Zebedee, the some-time fisherman who became a disciple, the apostle and exile of Patmos, and writer of several canonical books of Scripture.

When and where was the Fourth Gospel written?

John was a Jew, who, with his father, was a fisherman by trade (Mark 1:19-20). His mother was Salome, who appears to have been a sister of Mary, the mother of Jesus (compare Mark 16:1; Matt. 27:56 and John 19:25). Accordingly John and Jesus were cousins — a circumstance that makes Jesus' later assignment of his mother to John's care not only intelligible but perfectly natural (19:26-27). John must have been a fiery character. He and his brother James — who is always mentioned first of the pair, presumably because he was older — were jointly known as 'the Sons of Thunder' (Mark 3:17). John was a follower of John the Baptizer before he was called to follow Jesus (Matt. 4:21-22). With his brother and Peter, he was one of a leadership triad among the disciples who were privileged to witness the transfiguration (Matt. 17:1-13). Later, he is named as one of the pillars of the Jerusalem church (Gal. 2:9). Beyond that, little is known of his career, except that he ministered in the province of Asia, was exiled to Patmos during Domitian's persecutions and died at Ephesus in the reign of Trajan at the very end of the first century.[8] The universal view of the Church Fathers was that the Fourth Gospel was written in Ephesus and there is no particular reason to doubt this. All attempts to place it somewhere else are no better than idle speculation.

Opinions as to the date of writing range from just before the destruction of the temple (A.D. 70) to close to the end of the first century. The arguments are densely labyrinthine and massively inconclusive. The conventional consensus favours a later date, some time after A.D. 80. An earlier date cannot be ruled out and is backed by John's lack of use of the other Gospels, the absence of any hint that the temple was past and gone, and curious little points like his mention of the Pool of Bethesda as if it still was there and in operation, which it was not after the Roman legions mopped up the Jews' rebellion.[9] Carson exemplifies the endless frustration of this quest felt by generations of commentators when he lays out the trail most meticulously and yet can only come 'very tentatively' to posit an A.D. 80-85 date.[10] John might have solved this so-called 'problem' at a stroke, but spent not one drop of ink on the subject — which surely tells us how important he, and the Holy Spirit who inspired him, thought it was.

Why is there a Fourth Gospel?

The basic reason for more than one Gospel is the biblical rule of evidence, which requires more than a single witness (Deut. 17:6). Matthew and John were eyewitnesses from within the Twelve. Mark and Luke represent the 'second-generation' witness, the former, according to tradition, recording Peter's remembrances of Jesus and presenting a fast-paced Gospel focusing on Jesus' redemptive activity for a Roman/Latin readership,[11] and the latter addressing the Gentile/Greek world with a Gospel of meticulous historical detail.

The first three Gospels are called by scholars 'the Synoptic Gospels', from the Greek σύν (*sun*) and ὄψομαι (*opsomai*), meaning 'a seeing together'. These differ in perspective and matters of detail, but nevertheless cover the same general narrative ground. All

of them were almost certainly in circulation prior to
A.D. 70. Is it likely that their content was unknown
to John before he wrote the Fourth Gospel?

This sheds some light on the fact that the Synoptics are more similar to one another than John is to
any of them. John's Gospel is largely new material.
This includes the accounts of the wedding at Cana,
the conversations with Nicodemus and the woman at
the well, the raising of Lazarus and the farewell discourses. The exceptions are a relatively few passages
which do have Synoptic parallels — namely, 4:43-45;
6:1-21; 12:1-8,12-19; 13:21,36-38; 18:1-9,25-40;
19:1-3,16-18,26-30,38-42; 20:1-10,19-23 — and
even then these parallels also have their differences.
There are, of course, passages in each of the Synoptics not found in John — e.g., the parables of the
Good Samaritan and the prodigal son, the raising of
Jairus' daughter, the transfiguration, the Lord's
Supper and Jesus' agony in the Garden of Gethsemane. John omits most of the parables and
records no healings of demoniacs, deaf mutes or
lepers. He uses previously published material spar-
ingly and only to make the points that are
particularly necessary to his purposes in writing this
additional Gospel — a selectivity that is perfectly
intelligible if we assume that he knew what Matthew,
Mark and Luke had recorded. Accordingly, of Jesus'
thirty-five recorded miracles, John mentions only
eight and, of these, six are unique to him.[12] John
clearly assumes the content of the Synoptics and
supplements this with a wealth of his own eyewitness
testimony, together with observations from the perspective of one who had lived to see the third generation of the New Testament church.

Several other features of John's Gospel are quite
distinctive from the other three.

1. The theme is that of believing in Jesus, the divine Son of God and the promised Messiah, for new life (20:31), rather than the Synoptic emphasis on the coming of the kingdom of heaven (cf. Mark 1:14-15). John is, as Gundry puts it, 'the gospel of believing'.[13]

2. The focus is largely upon Jesus' ministry in Judea at the time of the great annual feasts, whereas the Synoptics focus mainly on his ministry in Galilee and his final trip to Jerusalem.

3. Mention is made in John of at least three Passovers in Jesus' ministry, while the Synoptics speak of only one. In this way, John sets the context for a ministry spanning three years, while the others see no need to establish any point about the length of Jesus' ministry.

4. There is a 'highlight' feel to John, created by the recording of longer conversations and discourses, whereas the Synoptics more straightforwardly record incidents briefly, and more or less as they happened.

5. There is also a more 'theological' flavour to John. The other Gospels are fairly straight narrative (although, of course the 'Sermon on the Mount' in Matthew stands out as a vast theological and practical sermonic tour de force). From the eternality of the pre-incarnate Son, through such subjects as the new birth (3:1-21), the bread of life (6:22-71), the light of the world (8:12-59), the Good Shepherd (10:1-39), to the prospect of his departure and the promise of the coming of the Holy Spirit (13:31 – 16:33), we have a tapestry of basic doctrine necessary to both coming to faith in Christ and subsequently experiencing spiritual-mindedness and personal growth in grace in the Christian life. And like a string of beautiful pearls, our Lord's 'I am' sayings — 'I am ... the bread of life ... the light of the world ... the door of the sheep ... the good shepherd ... the resurrection and the life ... the way, the truth and the life ... the true vine' — trace an ever-larger Christological motif

across the Gospel, always evoking the essential deity of the 'I AM' of Jehovah's self-revelation in Exodus 3:13-14.

6. There are some differences of detail in which John illumines questions arising from the Synoptics' handling of the same subject. Bruce Milne notes, for example, that whereas the latter basically list the names of the disciples, leaving us to wonder why and how they were persuaded to follow Jesus, John gives lively anecdotal accounts of their calling that answer these questions. He also points out that the citation of Jesus' alleged remark about destroying the temple, raised at his trial (Mark 14:58), is fully elucidated in its original context in John 2:19, whereas it was never mentioned at all in the Synoptics.[14]

7. There are other differences that have required some efforts at harmonization, such as the cleansing of the temple and the date of the Last Supper. These will be discussed in the comments on the text.

The Fourth Gospel is the last eyewitness account of Jesus' earthly ministry by the last living member of the Twelve. It is not difficult to imagine why God determined to move the aged John to write his memoirs of Jesus then and not earlier. All the other apostles had, as far as we know, died martyr deaths. The last living trophy of the apostolic generation would soon pass into glory. How appropriate that he should pen a final, different, yet wholly consistent account of the good news about Jesus the Christ! If Mark and Matthew were a divinely inspired kind of journalism, and Luke an inspired history, then John is a magisterial piece of interpretation, with crisp theological exposition and searching personal application that brings the majesty and pathos of Jesus' dying for sinners to bear upon the hearts and consciences of his readers. Not only is this the work of the disciple whom Jesus loved, but it is the work of the disciple who loved Jesus and wants his readers also to love him.

For whom was the Fourth Gospel written?

By long-standing consensus, John has been regarded as the pre-eminently evangelistic Gospel. This rests on the comprehensiveness of its exposition of Christ as the Word made flesh, its vivid extended conversations and discourses and, not least, on the conclusion of the Gospel itself, which declares, 'And truly Jesus did many other signs in the presence of his disciples, which are not written in this book; but these are written that you may believe that Jesus is the Christ, the Son of God, and that believing you may have life in his name' (20:30-31).

On the face of it, these verses appear quite straightforward. Every non-Christian immediately understands that John wants him to believe in Christ as his Saviour, whereas every Christian hears a call to renewed faithfulness in personal devotion and discipleship to Christ. There is, however, a variant reading in some Greek manuscripts that raises a question as to what the expression 'that you may believe' actually means. Some manuscripts have the aorist πιστεύσητε *(pisteusete)*, while others have the present tense, πιστεύητε *(pisteuete)*. The division, by the way, crosses both main manuscript traditions (Byzantine/majority and Alexandrian/critical), so this is not one of these AV/KJV versus modern version controversies. Since the aorist refers to past completed action, it is argued that this must mean that conversion, or *first* believing, is viewed as in the past for John's readership, and his aim is therefore to encourage believers to continue in the faith already embraced. The present tense, in contrast, would indicate an appeal to believe *now*, addressed

to those who had not hitherto come to Christ. The
content of the Gospel as a whole comports with the
former viewpoint, without, however, necessarily
detracting from its intense evangelistic power. The
Fourth Gospel is hardly an 'evangelistic tract' in the
narrow, dedicated sense with which we are so famil-
iar today. John brings together at every point both
earnest appeal and weighty theology. The opening
words show how theology, in the right hands, can be
the perfect handmaid of evangelism. What could be
clearer in the prologue (1:1-18) than the implication
that this Word made flesh, this light that alone can
lighten any man, is the Saviour we need? The distinction between evangelism and edification is over-
played in our day, for doctrine rightly preached
cannot be anything other than evangelistic, and
evangelism rightly carried out must be edifying to
those already saved. The thematic emphasis is
clearly that of believing in Jesus for eternal life,
whether you begin today or are continuing on a
journey already begun.[15]

The debate over the precise purpose of John has
thrown up a variety of other suggestions. While
these may have a measure of substance, none can
claim primacy over the Gospel's own stated goal,
and, therefore, to the extent that they have any
validity, they must be regarded as distinctly secondary aims.[16]

Firstly, beginning with Clement of Alexandria,
many have suggested that John's leading motive was
the supplementation of the Synoptics with a 'spiritual
Gospel', as opposed to merely narrative accounts.
This smacks of the making of an invidious comparison, to say the least. When considering the distinctive perspectives of the various Gospels, it is surely
better to honour each one for the positive way in
which it contributes to the fulness of revelation in the
Scriptures as a whole. They are never to be set

against one another, as if the absence of this or that point or parable was a defect to made up for by a quasi-evolutionary 'development' of more satisfying material. John is not to be defined in terms of the alleged inadequacies of the Synoptics. The Synoptics and John need to be read for what they are and say, in their own right, as part of an unfolding mosaic of revelation concerning Jesus. The Synoptics are not inadequate because John alone records, for example, the conversation between Jesus and Nicodemus. The answer lies in the Bible's own doctrine of inspiration. The Gospel writers were led *by the Holy Spirit* variously to record this and not that. John may have been writing with an eye to what had already been written, but the Spirit led him to finish one piece in a uniformly brilliant mosaic of revealed truth.

More recently, John has been seen as addressing a raft of contemporary challenges facing the church at the end of the first century. These have included arming believers against Gnostic and Docetic teaching, and encouraging faithfulness in the face of the final break with the synagogue. Another, more speculative, notion involves correction of an alleged tendency among the followers of John the Baptist to deny Jesus' Messianic claims. While these were all aspects of the cultural and spiritual context for the Christians of the time, it does seem a little contrived to elevate any of them to the status of a major purpose for the Fourth Gospel. Carson deftly turns this approach on its head by observing that the fact that 'John's Gospel can be used to offer comfort to the bereaved' in our day 'does not mean that is why the Evangelist wrote it'.[17] It sometimes seems, however, in such matters that where scholarly inquisitiveness abounds, there strained speculations much more abound!

In the end, we return to John 20:30-31. The Gospel is 'good news' about Jesus, who will save all who come to him in repentance and faith, whatever heresies or

evils may currently dominate their thinking and conduct. 'That you may believe', and that in 'believing you
may have life in his name', is the unvarnished purpose
of the beloved disciple's Gospel.

Outline of John[1]

Prologue: the eternal Word comes to his world (1:1-18)

The Word is life (1:1-5)
The Word is light (1:6-13)
The Word is love (1:14-18)

I. The revelation to the world: Christ the life (1:19 – 12:50)

A. *Life announced* (1:19 – 2:11)

The Lamb of God identified (1:19-34)
The first disciples called (1:35-51)
The first sign: water to wine (2:1-11)

B. *Life acknowledged* (2:12 – 4:54)

1. In Judea (2:12 – 3:36)
The temple (2:12-22)
The new birth (2:23 – 3:15)
The salvation of believers (3:16-21)
The witness of John (3:22-36)

2. In Samaria (4:1-42)
The woman at the well (4:1-30)
Fields ready for harvest (4:31-42)

3. In Galilee (4:43-54)

A boy is healed (4:43-54)

C. *Life antagonized* (5:1 – 12:50)

1. Opposition emerges (5:1-18)

A lame man healed (5:1-18)

2. Opposition intensifies (5:19 – 10:42)

Son of the Father (5:19-47)
Bread of life (6:1-71)
Living water (7:1-52)
Forgiver of sin (7:53 – 8:11)
Light of the world (8:12-29)
Truth that liberates (8:30-47)
Before Abraham was (8:48-59)
Restorer of sight (9:1-41)
Good Shepherd (10:1-21)
Messiah (10:22-42)

3. Opposition solidifies (11:1 – 12:50)

The resurrection and the life (11:1-37)
The raising of Lazarus (11:38-57)
Anointed for burial (12:1-11)
The hour has come (12:12-36)
Rejected by men (12:37-50)

II. Revelation to the disciples: Christ the light (13:1 – 17:26)

A. *Light introduced and applied* (13:1-38)

Washing the disciples' feet (13:1-17)
Predicting his betrayal (13:18-30)
Explaining his departure (13:31-35)
Exposing Peter's pride (13:36-38)

B. Light imparted and explained (14:1 – 16:33)

Faith and confidence encouraged (14:1-4)
No other way (14:5-11)
The future fruit of faithful ministry (14:12-14)
The indwelling Spirit of truth (14:15-17)
Alone no more (14:18-31)
Branches of the true vine (15:1-8)
The claims and promise of his love (15:9-17)
Why the world hates (15:18 – 16:4a)
The advantages of Jesus' leaving (16:4b-15)
Sorrow turned to joy (16:16-24)
Peace through our overcomer (16:25-33)

C. Light interceded for and appropriated (17:1-26)

Jesus prays for himself (17:1-5)
Jesus prays for his disciples (17:6-19)
Jesus prays for the future church (17:20-26)

III. Revelation to the disciples and the world: Christ as love (18:1 – 20:31)

A. Love tried before the world (18:1 – 19:16a)

Arrest and trial (18:1-27)
Condemnation to death (18:28 – 19:16a)

B. Love tested to the ultimate (19:16b-37)

Delivered to death on a cross (19:16b-24)
Ministry from the cross (19:25-37)

C. Love triumphant in the end (19:38 – 20:31)

The empty tomb (19:38 – 20:9)

Resurrection appearances (20:10-18)
That you may believe (20:19-31)

Epilogue: the risen Saviour who calls us to follow (21:1-25)

Believing the risen Lord (21:1-14)
Loving the risen Lord (21:15-17)
Following the risen Lord (21:18-25)

1. Who is Jesus?

John 1:1-5

No portion of the Scriptures is used more frequently to introduce people to the Christian faith than the Gospel according to John. The reason is obvious. The Fourth Gospel distils the essence of the good news about Jesus Christ and presents it in a clear, concise and compelling way. It is straightforward and to the point. As an introduction to the whole depth and breadth of God's Word, it is user-friendly. John says as much towards the end of his account, when he tells us that 'These are written that you may believe that Jesus is the Christ, the Son of God, and that believing you may have life in his name' (20:31). His theme is nothing less than the transcendent glory of Jesus Christ, who is the very Word of God. And just as the words that we speak tell other people what we want them to know, so Christ has revealed the Father in his own person, being 'the brightness of his glory and the express image of his person' (Heb. 1:3). The apostle tells a world of ordinary people what they need to know about Jesus, so as to believe the good news about him and have new life through his name.

There is something of a paradox in this approach, for this 'easy' introduction to the gospel of Jesus Christ begins with the highest and most profound of truths. There is no gradual build-up to the idea that Jesus the man is God the Son, the Second Person of the Trinity made flesh. There is no painstaking development of a case for these assertions. We are thrown in at the deep end! Jesus is proclaimed, with unclouded simplicity and majestic profundity, to be the Word of God, the Creator of the world and the Light of men! We are taken immediately to eternity before the creation of the world and are given a vision in words of the pre-incarnate glory of the Son of God. Both faith and mind are challenged from the first syllables of the Gospel. Who was this Jesus, who ministered among us for a few years and was subsequently executed by the Romans? With breathtaking boldness, John affirms that he is God (1:1-2), Creator (1:3) and life and light (1:4-5).

Jesus is God
(John 1:1-2)

The first doctrine of John's Gospel is that Jesus is God. It is clear from 1:14 that this person whom John calls **'the Word'** (ὁ λόγος / *ho logos*) is none other than Jesus before his incarnation (which literally means 'enfleshment'): 'And the Word became flesh, and dwelt among us.' Three co-ordinate truths are presented in these verses: namely, that Jesus is the eternal Logos, or Word (1:1,14; 1 John 1:1; Rev. 19:13), that he is coequal with God the Father and that he is truly God.

In the beginning was the Word (1:1a)

1:1. In the beginning was the Word...

Jesus is the eternal Word of God. Two incontrovertible facts stand out. The first is that Jesus is the eternal wisdom and will of God, while the second is that he is — as the writer to the Hebrews puts it — 'the express image of [God's] person' (Heb. 1:3).

This means that Jesus *is* divine wisdom and he *communicates* something of that wisdom to the human race because he is the Son of God who took our flesh and lived among us. Both the prophecies of the Old Testament and the revelations of the New Testament confirm this with irrefutable clarity (Prov. 8:15-30; Micah 5:2; 1 Cor. 1:24; Heb. 1:3). Jesus is

'the Word' precisely because he eternally reflects the
mind of God and, in time and history, reveals that
mind to humankind. He is both *ratio* (thought) and
oratio (speech). He is the person in whom the wisdom
of God is pre-eminently revealed.

Note, too, that he was this Word **'in the beginning'**. The parallel with Genesis is deliberate and
unmistakable. The Word is uncreated and eternal. He
is deity himself. 'Genesis 1 described God's first
creation,' observes Leon Morris. 'John's theme is
God's new creation ... brought about through the
agency of the *Logos*, the very Word of God.'[1]

The Word was with God (1:1b)

1:1. ... and the Word was with God...

Jesus is coequal with God the Father. Not only did he
have a personal existence as eternal as that of God
the Father, but he bore a precise and intimate relationship with, or towards, God (πρὸς τὸν θεόν / *pros
ton theon*). 'He existed in the closest possible connection with the Father.'[2] He was with the Father, but a
distinct personality from the Father. John enlarges
on this in his first letter: 'That which was from the
beginning, which we have heard, which we have seen
with our eyes, which we have looked upon, and our
hands have handled, of the Word of life; (For the life
was manifested, and we have seen it, and bear witness, and show unto you that eternal life, which was
with the Father, and was manifested unto us)'
(1 John 1:1-2, AV).

The Word was God (1:1-2)

1:1-2. ... and the Word was God. He was in the beginning with God.

John is emphatic: the Word **'was God'**. Jesus is not 'a god', as the spurious New World Translation of the Jehovah's Witnesses has it.[3] The Greek text has no article — literally it reads: 'and God was the Word' (καὶ θεὸς ἦν ὁ λόγος). The absence of an article — definite or indefinite — in connection with 'God' (θεὸς / *theos*), notes Shedd, 'converts the word into the abstract, denoting the species "deity".'[4] That is to say, not only was Jesus the eternal Word (1:1a) and, therefore, coexistent 'with God' the Father (1:1b), but he is himself a divine person. Jesus is elsewhere variously called 'the true God' and 'the eternally blessed God', or just 'God' (1 John 5:20; Rom. 9:5; Heb. 1:8). There is simply no room for any fudging. There is no textual basis for denying the deity of Jesus Christ.

The Word is God: **'He was in the beginning with God.'** John wants us to be in no doubt as to his meaning. Jesus is the Word incarnate. Jesus is therefore God incarnate. This is at the heart of the gospel. Against all fudging and sceptical theological speculation, we must say with John Calvin, 'I am unwilling to carry the abstruseness of philosophy beyond the measure of my faith.'[5] Why? Because a Jesus who is no more than a personification of great wisdom (but is not wisdom himself), or is merely a good man and a marvellous teacher (as opposed to the light of the world), or is someone we think of as divine and inspiring to us subjectively (but is not actually God), is a man-made myth, powerless to save a single soul. To live and die and rise again for sinners in order objectively and definitively to remove their guilt and sin and give them new life requires that Jesus be the Son of God incarnate. The best example in the world could not actually save a flea! We needed real atonement cancelling real sins, not good advice, moral influence or myths that make us feel good. John was establishing the qualifications of Jesus the man to be the Redeemer of other men.

Jesus is Creator
(John 1:3)

1:3. All things were made through him, and without him nothing was made that was made.

What did the eternal, uncreated Son of God do 'in the beginning'? He made us! John's readers knew very well that the Scriptures taught that God created the world out of nothing in the space of six days, and that this constituted a clear identification of the man Jesus with the divine Logos as Creator. Just as he is the wisdom of God and the eternal communicator of that wisdom for God, so he was also active in the creative process that brought all things into existence.

Co-creator with God

'All things were made by him,' says John (1:3, AV). That is to say, 'Whereas you have always correctly assumed that God created all things out of nothing, now you must understand that the eternal Son of God was active with the Father as his co-worker in this creation.' Paul sets out the precise nature of this co-operation in 1 Corinthians 8:6: 'There is [but] one God, the Father, of whom are all things, and we in him; and one Lord Jesus Christ, by whom are all things, and we by him' (AV). All that exists has its ultimate source in God the Father, 'of whom' (ἐξ οὗ / *ex ou*) it came into being. This happened, however, with the co-ordinate creative act of the Son 'by [or through] whom' (δι' ου / *di' ou*) it was created. Together, they made all things (creation) and to this day they uphold all things (providence). 'My Father has been working until now, and I have been working ... for whatever he does, the Son also does in like manner' (John 5:17,19; cf. Heb. 1:3).

Creator of all things

Jesus, as the eternal Son, actually created 'all things': **'... without him nothing was made that was made.'** He had a hand in everything. 'For by him all things were created that are in heaven and that are on earth, visible and invisible, whether thrones or dominions or principalities or powers. All things were created through him and for him. And he is before all things, and in him all things consist [i.e. "hold together"]' (Col. 1:16-17). The Bible is abundantly clear that Jesus, the man from Nazareth — so contemptuously dismissed by some as 'the carpenter, the son of Mary' (Mark 6:3) — is the Creator and upholder of the universe (Ps. 119:73; Isa. 51:12-13; Rom. 4:17; 2 Cor. 4:6; Eph. 2:10; Heb. 1:2).

Why are we told all this? Because what is at stake is Jesus' qualification to be a real Saviour who can save real people from real sins and from the real and justified anger of a holy God. For the promised Messiah to be a true — and that means effective — Messiah, he must be powerful enough to secure redemption for lost people. The facts that Jesus was a good man, a profound teacher and a courageous exemplar of faithfulness unto death do not prove that he could save anyone, even himself. But his deity and his resurrection do afford the evidence we need to see that his claims are more than stirring words and personal nobility. John here provides the first part of the story. Jesus did not begin his life in Bethlehem. He was first the divine Son who created the world into which he came, in the fulness of his time, to be born of a woman, born under the law to redeem those that were under the law (Gal. 4:4-5). Hence, says Matthew Henry, 'He is appointed the author of our bliss who was the author of our being.'[6] He who came to make us new people is able to do so because he made us all in the first place.

Jesus is life and light
(John 1:4-5)

If Jesus is the incarnate Creator, he is qualified to make people into new creations (2 Cor. 5:17). This will later come to the fore in his encounter with Nicodemus and his teaching on the doctrine of regeneration by the Holy Spirit (3:1-8). The question at this point is: 'Given that the Creator can renew dead souls, what is it in him that effects such transformations?'

Jesus is life (1:4a)

1:4. In him **was** life...

John's words signify that Jesus is the source of all that is alive, physically or spiritually. The logic of the text is that the Creator of life must be the very essence and definition of life. He is the eternally self-existent life prior to, and creative of, our finite created existence. Later, Jesus tells his followers, 'For as the Father has life in himself, so he has granted the Son to have life in himself, and has given him authority to execute judgement also, because he is the Son of Man' (5:26-27). Life resides in the uncreated mystery of God — Father, Son and Holy Spirit. This puts our life in proper perspective.

Firstly, our life is *derived*. It is created, finite and
transient in nature. Human life was made in order to
reflect the uncreated life of God himself.

Secondly, our life is also *sustained* in its continuing
existence by 'the word of his power' (Heb. 1:3). It is not
self-existent. This is what Paul meant when he said to
the Athenian philosophers, in the words of their own
poets, that in God 'we live and move and have our
being' and 'are also his offspring' (Acts 17:28).

Furthermore, the inner life of the soul needs to be
regenerated through a spiritual rebirth effected by the
Holy Spirit in connection with the hearing of the gospel
— life fallen into spiritual deadness in sin is redeemed
to become new life through faith in Christ as Saviour
and Lord and to enjoy glorious fellowship with the
living God. Jesus is the source, for with him 'is the
fountain of life' (Ps. 36:9; cf. John 1:12-13; 3:3,7-8;
Titus 3:5).

Jesus is light (1:4b)

1:4. ...and the life was the light of men.

People are endlessly looking for answers. They want
'light' on the meaning and direction of life. In the mid-
twentieth century, science was the great source of light
for our dominantly non-Christian, secularist society. A
new generation has found that dry and unsatisfying —
not to say disillusioning, in view of the fact that 'science' has not solved problems like war, hunger, AIDS
and other diseases — and has turned to 'New Age'
gnosticism to fill its spiritual void. This is nothing new.
Speaking with the Greek philosophers in Athens, the
apostle Paul pointed out that God made man with a
constitutional need for the Lord — 'that they should
seek the Lord, in the hope that they might grope for
him and find him, though he is not far from each one

of us' (Acts 17:27). Of course, those who do not want to
have the true God rule over them look for gods of their
own, that is, for their own 'light'.

Nevertheless, it remains a fact that Jesus alone is
'the light of men'. This is true both in virtue of that
constitutional *sensus deitatis* (sense of God) in them by
nature, as those created in God's image and, most
pointedly, in the case of believers who have gospel light
through faith in Christ.

Light and life are inseparable: 'For with you is the
fountain of life; in your light we see light' (Ps. 36:9).
Light is just life made manifest. Later, Jesus will say it
right out: 'I am the light of the world. He who follows
me shall not walk in darkness, but have the light of life'
(8:12; cf. 9:5; 12:46).

For this reason, the unregenerate themselves neither
recognize such 'light' as they do have, nor accept it for
what it is: 'Men loved darkness rather than light,
because their deeds were evil' (3:19). Only in the conscious embracing of Christ in saving faith does a sinner
see the light that is Christ (Matt. 4:16, cf., Ps. 27:1;
36:9; 119:130).

Jesus dispels darkness (1:5)

1:5. And the light shines in the darkness, and the darkness
did not comprehend it.

What happens to this light in the real world? Jesus'
action is to illumine — even 'every man', at least in the
sense that he brings his 'light' to bear upon the minds
and consciences of lost people (1:9). The verb (φαίνει /
phainei) is in the present tense and denotes his ever-
present shining in the world, which is assumed to be
otherwise plunged into darkness. Consequently, the
darkness did not 'comprehend' it. This is generally
taken to mean that man, in spiritual darkness, cannot

understand the light. Another possibility, however, is that this should be read as 'overcome' — as in the NIV alternative reading: 'The darkness has not overcome it.' The idea then is that human darkness fails to overcome or extinguish the light — not at the Fall, when sin came into the world; not at Calvary, when Christ bore the sin of his people; and certainly not at the Great Day when man's rebellion against God will utter its last gasp under the final judgement of the returning Jesus.

The practical thrust of the revelation is that Jesus is God, Creator, life and light, and is to be received as the Saviour of lost, blinded and rebellious sinners that he proclaims himself to be. We are told these things that we 'may believe that Jesus is the Christ, the Son of God, and that believing [we] may have life in his name' (20:31). 'He came,' says George Hutcheson, 'to lead us through the veil of his flesh to this rock of his Godhead ... where it will get sure footing against all assaults.'[7]

What John wants us to grasp is that the man Jesus is the Lord from heaven — sent to save, and able to save, because, as Octavius Winslow so beautifully expressed it, 'The love of Jesus runs parallel with his being ... from all eternity to all eternity.'[8] 'Therefore I said to you,' says Jesus, 'that you will die in your sins: for if you do not believe that I am he, you will die in your sins' (8:24). Our Lord himself leaves no room for manoeuvre. It is life through saving faith in him, the Word made flesh, or it is death through ourselves remaining in our unbelief, unrepentant to the last. Those who deny Christ must reject him as a liar and a fraud, if only to justify to themselves their refusal to believe. They will have no excuse on the day they fly away to eternity. But while we live and hear the voice of Jesus calling in the gospel, the way to life is open for the repentant and believing: 'Believe on the Lord Jesus Christ, and you will be saved, you and your household' (Acts 16:31).

2. The true Light
John 1:6-13

Not so long ago, even in the industrialized West, the
setting of the sun left a darkness upon the land that
was only dimly punctuated by candles and gaslights.
The dawn and the daylight were all the more welcome
in a pre-technological age and vividly reminded
successive generations that the sun was God's great
gift to provide the energy which sustained our physical existence upon this planet. Today, in urban areas
at least, we take our well-lit nights for granted.
Perhaps only when we fly into a city like New York at
night and see a Manhattan etched in light, with a
bejewelled Statue of Liberty brightly guarding the
gate to the Americas, do we marvel at the brilliance
with which electricity has clothed our world and
ponder, too, the greater wonder of the light that does
not merely shine in the darkness, but dispels it
altogether in the brightness of the day.

This illustrates a more profound truth by far. God
is the light in whom there is no darkness at all
(1 John 1:5). He has sent his light into the world in
the person of his Son, Jesus, who is described in the
Scriptures as 'the light of the world' and 'the true
Light which gives light to every man coming into the
world' (John 8:12; 1:9). This is the basic thesis of
John's Gospel. The world is darkened and people's
hearts are dark. But into the Stygian reaches of

spiritually dead souls comes the light of God in Jesus the Saviour as he is offered in the gospel of redeeming grace.

People, of course, have their own ideas about what is 'light'. They have their own 'lights' — of their own preference or invention — and they live their lives according to these as it suits them, or not. They need to realize, as Isaiah put it to the Jews long ago, that if what they think of as 'light' does not speak according to God's Word, they actually have no light in them at all! (Isa. 8:20). John's assertion is that the true Light is God's Son, the Logos made flesh, Jesus Christ, without whom we shall do little better than whistle in the dark. The apostle makes three points about Jesus as the true Light: he was the light announced by John (1:6-8), rejected by his own (1:9-11) and received by all who believed (1:12-13).

Announced by John
(John 1:6-8)

1:6-8. There was a man sent from God, whose name was John. This man came for a witness, to bear witness of the Light, that all through him might believe. He was not that Light, but was sent to bear witness of that Light.

Whenever a head of state comes into an official gathering, he or she is preceded by a fanfare designed to prepare the people to offer respectful attention. Hence, the Queen has the brilliantly caparisoned trumpeters of the Household Cavalry, while the President of the United States has marine trumpeters and a band playing 'Hail to the Chief'. This is standard procedure. So we can have no difficulty in understanding that John the Baptizer was the herald of the King of kings, Jesus Christ. His ministry announced God's King and alerted the people of Palestine to the advent of the 'true Light' — the promised Messiah come to save his people from their sins. The apostle John accordingly sets out the salient points of the mission of John the Baptizer.

Sent by God (1:6)

To be a real herald, one has to be properly accredited. It is therefore perfectly proper to ask for John's credentials. Was he just another mad visionary, or a self-appointed prophet? The apostle wants us to be clear in this matter and so tells us, **'There was a man sent from God, whose name was John.'**

John was *sent from God* — objectively, really and according to the evidence. He was in fact the fulfilment of the last prophecy of the Old Testament period:

> Behold, I will send you Elijah the prophet
> Before the coming of the great and dreadful day
>   of the LORD:
> And he will turn
> The hearts of the fathers to the children,
> And the hearts of the children to their fathers,
> Lest I come and strike the earth with a curse
>   (Mal. 4:5-6).

That John is this second Elijah is confirmed by prophecies at the time of his remarkable birth (Luke 1:5-7,36). He would go before the Messiah 'in the spirit and power of Elijah' and would be called 'the prophet of the Highest: for [he would] go before the face of the Lord to prepare his ways...' (Luke 1:17,76). John was uniquely prepared by God to be the forerunner of the Messiah. The very choice of his name — against all tradition in his family (Luke 1:59-63) — accords with his calling. 'John' is the Greek version of the Hebrew *Jehohanan*, meaning 'God's favour', or 'the grace of God'. John was himself God's gift of grace declaring Jesus' imminent arrival. He proclaimed grace in his ministry because it prepared the way for the gospel of saving grace in Christ.

John, then, was the first New Testament prophet, the second Elijah and the forerunner of Jesus (Luke 1:76-79). He heralded the advent of the Messiah and the commencement of the present age, which will endure until the Lord returns.

Witness to the light (1:7)

John knew what he was doing. He knew that God
had raised him up (Luke 1:57-58). He also knew who
Jesus really was. 'We must not think that the Baptist
knew nothing about the pre-existence of the Logos
whom he saw in the person of Jesus,' observes
Lenski. 'This is a rationalistic assumption contradicted by the Baptist himself in v. 15 and v. 30.'[1]
John knew that he was called to stand at the cross-
roads of history and that he **'came for a witness'** to
point to the Son of God as **'the Light'** (1:7a).

He also knew that his ministry had the purpose of
bringing people to faith in Jesus as the Christ. He
preached so that **'all through him might believe'**
(1:7b). Lenski notes that '"believe" goes beyond the
figure of "light" to the reality meant by the figure,
which is truth'.[2] John's testimony was more than
imparting information about Jesus. He pointed to the
light that saves — Jesus the way, the truth and the
life (14:6).

Not that light (1:8)

The apostle John was careful to make clear that
John the Baptizer was **'not that Light, but was sent
to bear witness of that Light'**. For decades many
people followed John the Baptizer without fully
knowing about Christ and the Holy Spirit, and constituted a movement distinct from the apostolic
church. Apollos of Alexandria, for example, was a
disciple of John, as were the twelve who turned up in
Ephesus, to be baptized by Paul and inducted into
the church with a 'Pentecost' of their own (Acts
18:24-25; 19:1-7). The apostle accordingly took every
opportunity to emphasize that John himself meant

only to point people to Jesus (see 1:19-34; 3:22-36; 5:33-36).

It is easy to follow the wrong man, even if he is on the right track. Christ is neglected because of inordinate attention to his servants. Even denominational labels that serve the useful purpose of identifying churches and their distinctive doctrines have an implicit tendency to focus on the movements' founders rather than the believers' Saviour. True Christians who happen to be 'Calvinists' or 'Lutherans' do not worship Calvin or Luther, but can be tempted to lionize them to the diminution of Christ and the gospel. John's own word to his followers struck a decisive blow at any inclination to hero-worship they might have been indulging: 'He [Jesus] must increase, but I must decrease' (3:30; cf. 1 Cor. 3:1-9). The most faithful ministers of God only reflect the light of Jesus Christ, as the moon reflects the light of the sun. 'Following the man', however wonderful a preacher or warm a pastor he may be, is a sinful substitute for following Christ. He alone is the true Light!

Rejected by his own
(John 1:9-11)

1:9-11. That was the true Light which gives light to every man coming into the world. He was in the world, and the world was made through him, and the world did not know him. He came to his own, and his own did not receive him.

What, then, did the world do with the true Light? Even from the apostle's vantage-point — half a century of preaching the risen Christ — the world was still very pagan and often extremely hostile to the gospel. Proclaiming the advent of the true Light is one thing. Explaining the continuing darkness is another. Before that, however, came the personal rejection of Jesus of Nazareth by the generality of the Jews. Indeed, the very cross proclaimed as the salvation of sinners was to others the decisive proof of Jesus' rejection and failure as an alleged redeemer. John faces the issue squarely and records the true facts of the case.

The light was coming, and people have some already (1:9)

John begins with a remarkable assertion: Jesus was **'the true Light which gives light to every man coming into the world'.** The English here correctly reflects the order of the words in the Greek text, but obscures the true connection between its components, because the antecedent of the last clause ('coming into the world') is not 'every man', but 'the true Light'.[3] The NIV catches both the order and meaning clearly with the rendering: 'The true light that gives light to every man was coming into the world.' The 'true Light ... comes into the world' uniquely refers to the birth of the God-man. In Jesus, the eternally existent Light — the one who would say, 'Before Abraham was, I AM' (8:58) — took our nature and lived among us.

He is the one who **'gives light to every man'**. There is not the slightest case here for a universalistic salvation. To have some 'light' is not equivalent to being saved. This is a general statement about Jesus' relationship to such 'light' as there is in human lives. All real 'light' in the world is from Christ, whether in believers or unbelievers. Just as blind cave-fish, deep in subterranean streams, are ultimately sustained by the light of the sun, so even human beings have whatever light is theirs from him. This light is not the same as a saving knowledge of Christ — except, of course, in the case of those who have been converted. But it is light none the less and is sufficient to leave everyone without any excuse for unbelief towards God (Rom. 1:18-20; cf. Heb. 6:4-8). The point is that, even before his incarnation, the Son of God had seen to it that he had a witness in every human soul, however benighted.

The light was there, but not seen (1:10)

The apostle emphasizes his point by a triple reference to **'the world'**. Jesus was **'in the world, and the world was made through him, and the world did not know him'**. With each step, the scandal of Jesus' rejection is intensified.

First, we have the undeniable fact of history, attested by hundreds of thousands of witnesses.

Jesus was **'in the world'**. He became well known and crowds followed him. They saw his miracles and heard his words. The evidence had passed before their very eyes. Today billions of people know that Jesus was in the world about two thousand years ago.

Secondly, John asserts, **'The world was made by him'** (AV). The evidence pointed to Jesus as the Logos of God, by whom 'all things were made' (1:3). There is perhaps just the suggestion that the Creator cannot but be recognized by those he has made. Having been made in God's image, man retains an internal witness to the fact of his creation which responds to the Word of God — whether in faith or in unbelief. Darkness instinctively reacts to light.

Thirdly, John notes that **'The world did not know him.'** There is a quiet shift here in John's use of the word 'world' (κόσμος / *kosmos*). Up to now he has spoken of the world as created reality — the earth, and all that it contains (Ps. 24:1). Here he speaks of the world of *mankind in opposition to God*. Yes, crowds followed Jesus. But for the most part they did not really know who he was. People were amazed by his miracles and loved the idea of being led by him to greater glory as a nation, but in most cases they drew a blank on the real meaning of his mission and message. He was actually the source of their very life, but they would not see it. This heightens the scandal of his rejection. 'What can be more unreasonable', asks John Calvin, 'than to draw water from a running stream, and never to think of the fountain from which that stream flows?'[4]

The light was with them, but was not received (1:11)

As if that were not bad enough, John adds that **'He came to his own, and his own did not receive him.'** The first 'his own' is the neuter 'τὰ ἴδια' *(ta idia)*, which signifies property, or home territory. Whether this is applied restrictively to the Jewish homeland, or extensively to the world in general, the notion is that Jesus came to the arena of his authority, where he might reasonably expect to be welcomed, heard and received. The second 'his own' is οἱ ἴδιοι *(hoi idioi)*. This is masculine and relational, and refers to the people who, in the event, did not receive him. The Jews were his covenant people, those of whom the Lord said through Isaiah:

> I have nourished and brought up children,
> And they have rebelled against me;
> The ox knows its owner
> And the donkey its master's crib;
> But Israel does not know,
> My people do not consider
> (Isa. 1:2-4; cf. 65:2-3; Jer. 7:25-26).

George Hutcheson comments: 'As the great sin [outside] the church is ignorance, and not acknowledging and glorifying God, so the great sin within the church is contempt for Christ, and not embracing him nor his offer, for "the world knew him not", but "his own received him not".'[5]

While the unbelieving heathen may be an enemy towards the Lord, the hypocritical church member is a traitor. The former is 'without excuse', but the latter has 'provoked to anger the Holy One of Israel' (Rom. 1:20; Isa. 1:4). Christ still comes to his own — through the Scriptures read and preached in a million churches — and some of his own turn away from him in unbelief and disobedience. Jesus has been as firmly ejected from many modern churches as he was from the synagogue in Nazareth, where, you will remember, he identified himself as the promised Messiah (Luke 4:16-30).

Received by those who believe (John 1:12-13)

1:12-13. But as many as received him, to them he gave the right to become children of God, to those who believe in his name: who were born, not of blood, nor of the will of the flesh, nor of the will of man, but of God.

All this talk about the rejection that Jesus was to experience is not only not the whole story, but is really only the setting of the context in which the purpose of his mission would be fulfilled. Rejection of the gospel is only the natural entail of man's sinful condition and condemned state before God. Jesus did not come to condemn the world, 'but that the world through him might be saved' (3:17). Christ came to be **'received'**. As the 'true Light', Jesus came to be *seen* in a saving way by a people who would in this way enter into new life in him. The apostle John therefore ends his exposition of Jesus' status as 'the light' with a clear description of those who will receive him and how this will come about.

Who will receive him? (1:12)

To 'receive' Jesus is to 'believe in his name'. John tells us that **'As many as received him, to them he gave the right to become children of God,** [even] **to those who believe in his name.'** To modern ears, this may sound like poetic vagueness, but to those

attuned to the language of Scripture, it is heavy with
implications of profound commitment. The name *is*
the person. To believe 'in' the name is to trust in the
person represented by the name. The believing is
active.[6] It embraces by a living faith the one who is
believed and all that he is and represents. The New
Testament often refers to Christian baptism as baptism 'in [Gk. *eis* — "into"] the name of' ... 'the Father
and of the Son and of the Holy Spirit', or ... 'the Lord
Jesus' (Matt. 28:19; Acts 8:16; cf. 1 Cor. 1:13,15).
This expresses the union of the believer and his Lord,
signifying the former's 'passing into new ownership,
and loyalty, and fellowship'.[7] Faith in Christ's name,
says D. A. Carson, 'yields allegiance to the Word,
trusts him completely, acknowledges his claims and
confesses him with gratitude. That is what it means
to "receive" him.'[8]

Having received Jesus as their Saviour, believers
are granted **'the right to become children of God'**.
The text does not imply that someone can receive
Christ and then exercise an option *not* to become a
child of God. The thought is this: God gave them (by
sovereign grace) the 'right' (in the sense of privilege
and status) of sonship to him! That is simply to say
that they *actually become* children of God by adoption (Eph. 1:5). The *Shorter Catechism* asks, 'What is
adoption?' and answers: 'Adoption is an act of God's
free grace, whereby we are received into the number,
and have a right to all the privileges of the sons of
God' (Question 34).

How will they come to receive him? (1:13)

The power to receive Christ is not self-generated,
even if receiving Christ is an act of the human will.
Behind the movements of heart and mind, behind the
turning of the soul to Jesus in believing acceptance,

lies the mighty act of God's Spirit. John, therefore, proclaims that believers **'were born, not of blood, nor of the will of the flesh, nor of the will of man, but of God'**. His point is that people do not come to believe in Christ because of natural descent ('blood'), sexual desire ('the will of the flesh') or any human volition ('the will of man'), but because of the work of God in their hearts. This anticipates Jesus' later teaching on the necessity of a new birth by the Holy Spirit (3:3-8), but focuses on the simple point that 'It is not from any creature whatever that [believers] receive one spiritual blessing.'[9]

In practical terms, John is asking his readers a vital question about their true relationship to Jesus Christ. Are they born of God, or are they somehow depending on their ancestry or church connection? If they are born of God, then they know the power of a saving knowledge of Christ in their experience. Whether they were dramatically converted, like a Saul on the Damascus road, or came regenerate from the womb, like a John the Baptizer, they *know* Christ in the *power* of his resurrection — the power that regenerates dead souls. The Christian's experience of believing in Christ flows from something which 'no created power can effect'[10] — being 'born of God'. This is a felt reality for ever after in the hearts of the believers. There is nothing perfunctory or dead about saving faith in Jesus Christ. It is a living faith. It is the joy of mercies that are new every morning. It is sealed by the presence of the Holy Spirit in the Christian's heart (Eph. 1:13). This is deeply felt and exultantly confessed. Jesus is the true light of all who really know him, and they want to live for him. Charles Simeon reminds us that 'God had one only dear Son, whom he sent down from heaven to sojourn upon earth. And the Scripture fully informs us what dispositions he exercised, and what conduct he pursued. And everyone who is born of God will follow his steps, and "walk as he walked". He will "no longer walk according to the course of this world, according to the Prince of the power of the air, the spirit that now worketh in the children of disobedience"... In a word, he will not live unto himself, but unto God, making it his "meat and drink to do the will of his Saviour and Redeemer". Now then, brethren, this is the way in which you will live, if you are sons of God. "You will shine as lights in a dark world," and "Your light will shine brighter and brighter to the perfect day." ' [11]

The Lord's my light and saving strength;
Who shall make me dismayed?
My life's strength is the LORD; of whom
Then shall I be afraid? [12]

3. God became man

John 1:14-18

Under the battlements of Edinburgh Castle, there stands a church building with the words carved in the stonework over the door: 'For there is one God, and one mediator between God and men, the man Christ Jesus.' This text — 1 Timothy 2:5 — is quite appropriate for a church. What is remarkable about this instance of its use is that the church is Unitarian and that this Scripture is being used in support of their denominational assertion that Jesus was only a man. The implicit suggestion is that Paul was telling Timothy that 'the man Christ Jesus' is *not* God the Son come in the flesh. Jesus was a good man, to be sure, but no more than a man. It is a classic example of 'a text out of context becoming a pretext'. Serious examination of 1 Timothy 2 will reveal that Paul was not concerned at this point with Jesus' humanity as opposed to his deity. He was rather focusing on his status as the *new* man — the perfect man, the Son of Man of Daniel's prophecy and the last Adam — who dies in the place of old man, lost humanity in Adam. Paul's emphasis is on '*the* man Christ Jesus' as 'the ransom for *all* [men]' (1 Tim. 2:6). He is not the *Jew* Christ Jesus dying to save the old covenant people of God, but the *man* Christ Jesus who brings redemption to a people drawn from the whole human race, both Jews and Gentiles who become one in Christ Jesus (Gal. 3:28).

At the heart of this is the question as to *who* Jesus is. What is it about Jesus that is such a sticking-point with so many people? Surely it is the Scriptures' teaching that he is the God-man — God the Son who took a human nature and was 'born of a woman, born under the law' (Gal. 4:4). Already in John's day, the unitarian followers of the heretic Cerinthus were denying this cardinal truth. John, then, bears personal testimony to the person and work of Jesus. He was an eyewitness to the fact that Jesus is the Word become flesh: **'We beheld his glory'** (1:14). This is objective fact, the apostle is saying, and is not to be explained away as the product of a mad visionary's overwrought imagination. John writes with sober-minded precision about what he saw with his own eyes. It is important to remember this because the Christian faith is always presented in Scripture as a *historic* faith that is grounded on actual events, and not myths, legends and the hallucinations of mystics. These are God's mighty acts in history. John's testimony is developed along three lines: God became man in the person of Jesus (1:14); we have seen his glory (1:14); and the church has experienced his grace (1:15-18).

God became man
(John 1:14a,b)

1:14. And the Word became flesh and dwelt among us...

At the centre of the gospel of Christ is the fact of the incarnation. The efficacy of even the cross depends upon this as a historical reality. If a mere man, no different from any of us, died at Calvary, then Christians are kidding themselves and deceiving the world. The effect would be exactly the same as that which Paul says would result from there being no resurrection of Christ: '... then our preaching is empty ... your faith is futile; you are still in your sins!' (1 Cor. 15:14,17). But because the incarnate God died on that cross and rose again from the dead, it is death itself that died. Jesus was able, in Hugh Martin's apt phrase, to 'die death dead' precisely because he was the Son of God, with our human nature, but without our sin.

The Word became flesh (1:14a)

John's simplicity is breathtaking: **'And the Word became flesh.'** Christ is, says Paul, 'the seed of David according to the flesh' (Rom. 1:3). The Son of God was made 'in the likeness of sinful flesh' to be an offering for sin (Rom. 8:3). He was 'born of a woman' (Gal. 4:4), came 'in the likeness of men' (Phil. 2:7), 'was manifested in the flesh' (1 Tim. 3:16) and 'shared in [flesh and blood] that through death he might destroy him who had the power of death' (Heb. 2:14). That is why, as John Murray has put it, 'The Son of God was sent in that very nature which in every other instance is sinful.'[1] This 'flesh' is not just the body, but encompasses the whole of human nature. Christ took human nature, both body and soul. This was also why Jesus was born into the world by a *virgin* birth. It was to show beyond all doubt that he was the incarnate Son of God. Mary and Joseph, and those around them, could not but see that Jesus was supernaturally conceived by the power of God's Holy Spirit in her womb. In this way, we are shown how human nature and divine nature came to be combined in the one person of Jesus Christ — as the Council of Chalcedon (A.D. 451) defined it, 'inconfusedly, unchangeably, indivisible and inseparable'.

And dwelt among us (1:14b)

Everyone knew that Jesus had lived and died in Palestine. John says, literally, that he 'tented among us'. This language would have caught the attention of Jewish readers and taken their minds back to the tabernacle in the wilderness and the presence of God among his people (Exod. 40:34-38). This would say to them that all those earlier times when God was present with his people for particular periods of time were now fulfilled in the Word's becoming flesh.[2] Jesus *is* Immanuel — God with us. God thereby identifies with humanity in the most personal way possible: 'For God so loved the world that he gave his only begotten Son, that whoever believes in him should not perish but have everlasting life' (3:16).

We have seen his glory
(John 1:14c,d)

1:14. ... and we beheld his glory, the glory as of the only begotten of the Father, full of grace and truth.

What John goes on to say flows naturally from the truth that Jesus is the God-man who pitched his tent among us. **'Glory'** (δόξα / *doxa*) means 'brightness' or 'radiance'. As applied to the honour and reputation of God, it speaks of the majesty and dignity of God. Jesus' glory was a self-evidencing glory, says the apostle, which **'we'** — John and the other eyewitnesses — saw, both with the eyes and in the calm reflection of careful minds. How did they see this glory? They saw it in two ways.

The only begotten of the Father (1:14c)

First of all, what the apostles witnessed in Jesus was **'the glory as of the only begotten of the Father'**.

Jesus' 'glory' was intimately, inseparably and uniquely connected with his eternal sonship as the Second Person of the triune God. That is what John is saying. This does not mean that they usually saw a visible corona of glory emanating from Jesus — the so-called 'exception that proves the rule' being the transfiguration (Matt. 17:1-13). What they did see was a progressive unfolding of Jesus' prophetic self-revelation. All that he said and did flowed from his being the Son of God.

Jesus is the **'only begotten'** Son of God. The term μονογενής *(monogenes)* carries the idea of complete uniqueness, in his case from all eternity (1:18). Jesus is 'one and only' Son. This rules out spiritualizing the term to make it say he is merely a son begotten in the only way any and all Christians become children of God. Jesus is the only one of a kind and this reveals the glory of God.

The expression **'of the Father'** is something of a theme in John's Gospel. Because Jesus is 'of [or 'from'] the Father', he is the bread of life (6:46,48), the promised Messiah (7:26-29) and the victorious Mediator (16:26-27). When he performed miracles like the feeding of the five thousand or the healing of the blind beggar, or when he walked on the water, it all pointed to the glory of divine sonship. Jesus was infinitely more than a great teacher and a good man, John is saying. He is God with us.

Full of grace and truth (1:14d)

A second way in which Jesus' glory was witnessed was in the transparent perfection of his untainted righteousness. He was **'full of grace and truth'**. This describes the way he carried himself — what his behaviour conveyed to a watching world — in other words, his character. He is the 'impress' (χαρακτήρ / *charakter*) of God's nature (Heb. 1:3). His personal character was 'wholly without spot or blemish'; he was 'full of truth'; and 'in him was no sin', 'no guile' whatever.[3]

To say that he was **'full'** of grace and truth is to say that the 'grace' of God that seeks the good of lost people flowed from his innermost being. Like the Father, the Son was 'abounding in goodness and truth'

(Exod. 34:6) Whitacre points out that 'This *grace* answers to the *hesed* of the Old Testament — God's covenant-keeping, gracious love.'[4] With respect to his ministry towards that gracious goal, he declared the 'truth' of God with absolute accuracy and perfection.

Even the **'and'** is significant, because grace and truth are two sides of one coin. There is no grace without truth, and no truth without grace. Yet we are not infrequently the one without the other — either self-righteous (being 'righteous' at the expense of grace) or latitudinarian (being 'gracious' at the expense of truth). It is not truly gracious to be pleasant without principles; nor is it graciously truthful to be right without a loving spirit. In Christ, the two are perfectly conjoined.

We have all received of his fulness (John 1:15-18)

1:15-18. John bore witness of him and cried out, saying, 'This was he of whom I said, "He who comes after me is preferred before me, for he was before me." '

And of his fulness we have all received, and grace for grace. For the law was given through Moses, but grace and truth came through Jesus Christ. No one has seen God at any time. The only begotten Son, who is in the bosom of the Father, he has declared him.

John leads us a step further. God became man in Jesus Christ (1:14a,b). The apostles and eyewitnesses of his ministry saw his glory (1:14c,d). But there is more than that, for the church in the world ever since has also experienced his grace and truth. In other words, what God has done in Jesus Christ was not done in a corner and was not the exclusive province of a faithful core of initiates. From the perspective of the time of writing the Fourth Gospel, it was plain that Christ had been progressively proclaimed from the housetops and had burst upon the stage of human history in no uncertain way. In quick succession, a series of points drives the message home.

Christ superior to John (1:15)

John the Baptizer had testified to the superiority of Jesus: **'This was he of whom I said, "He who comes after me is preferred before me, for he was before me."'** This set the tone from the start. Chronologically, Jesus comes 'after' John — in modern terms we would say John had ministerial seniority over Jesus — but in status he is 'preferred' over John, because he was 'before' him in the sense of his absolute and eternal pre-existent primacy. Jesus was πρῶτός μου — 'first before me'. The uniqueness of Jesus resided in his being from eternity the Son of God. In receiving Jesus, we receive God himself. God has given to the church more than a prophet, more than a teacher, more even than a second Elijah. He has given a divine Redeemer, his only-begotten Son. This is crucial, for there could be no higher gift — indeed, no other Saviour. Until he came, all existed only in the form of a promise yet to be fulfilled. His coming is the hinge of history, for in Christ the actual accomplishment of salvation is realized.

Christ gives grace to believers (1:16)

And what did Christ do for his people? The apostle John, over half a century later, could testify that the church had received **'of [the] fulness'** of Christ. This 'fulness' consists in 'grace and truth' as these qualities are uniquely resident in the incarnate Son of God (1:14). In him 'dwells all the fulness of the Godhead bodily', for 'It pleased the Father that in him all the fulness should dwell' (Col. 2:9; 1:19). If we are to experience something of the fulness of God, it must be through Jesus Christ. John Calvin explains: 'The fountain of life, righteousness, virtue, and wisdom, is with God, but to us it is a hidden and inaccessible fountain. But an abundance of those things is exhibited to us in Christ, that we may be permitted to have recourse to him; for he is ready to flow to us, provided that we open up a channel by faith.'[5]

The expression **'grace upon grace'** (χάριν ἀντὶ χάριτος / *charin anti charitos*) evokes the image of the waves of the sea rolling gently over us again and again, repeatedly bestowing God's gifts and goodness upon us. The meaning hinges on the use of the preposition ἀντι / *anti.* The sense is that grace is received *in place of* grace. Over against grace we have more grace given. Had not Christians discovered his mercies to be new every morning? (Lam. 3:23). Is his grace not fully sufficient at all times? (2 Cor. 12:9). Are his commands not always mercy and truth? (Ps. 25:10). And will his truth not firmly stand to all generations? (Ps. 100:5). It is a fact of every believer's experience that life is filled with endless examples of God's goodness in the land of the living. Even in tragedy, grace and truth confirm their reality in our inner being. This is why Job could cry out from the misery of the dung-heap, 'Though he slay me, yet will I trust him!' and 'I know that my Redeemer lives!' (Job 13:15; 19:25).

Christ superior to Moses (1:17)

The fulness of the Christian salvation is further emphasized by a comparison of the gospel of Christ with the law of Moses: **'For the law was given through Moses, but grace and truth came through Jesus Christ.'** Clearly this cannot be taken to mean that there was no 'grace' and no 'truth' in the Old Testament. The point is that it had not yet fully revealed the grace that saves through the truth that is the promised Messiah. The law was good, as was the man through whom God revealed it, but it was still only 'our tutor to bring us to Christ' (Gal. 3:24). The law itself could not save sinners. It rather exposed our profound need of a Saviour and also pointed us to his coming according to the covenant promises of God set forth within its own pages. Christ fulfils these promises, so that in him the fulness of salvation by grace through faith in his finished work of atonement for sin comes to its decisive accomplishment. This is precisely the point of Hebrews 3:1 – 6:20, which is an extended exposition of the superiority of Jesus over Moses: 'For this one has been counted worthy of more glory than Moses, inasmuch as he who has built the house has more honour than the house... And Moses indeed was faithful in all his house as a servant ... but Christ as a Son over his own house, whose house we are if we hold fast the confidence and the rejoicing of the hope firm to the end' (Heb. 3:3,5,6).

Christ makes God known to believers (1:18)

Arching over everything is the truth that Christ has made known to us the God whom no one has seen: **'No one has seen God at any time. The only begotten Son, who is in the bosom of the Father, he has declared him.'** The *Textus Receptus* reading 'only begotten *Son*' (μονογενὴς υἱός / *mongenes huios*) is thought by many to be a scribal gloss in explanation of the 'only begotten *God*' (μονογενὴς θεὸς / *monogenes theos*) found in many manuscripts. As Carson notes, 'The nest of textual variants is rather complicated', and he can only say the latter is 'probably' the way to read it.[6] Suffice it to say that, whatever the reading, the deity of Jesus is central to the text. He *is* God the Son, eternally in the bosom of the Father and therefore uniquely qualified to make him known.

We have turned full circle to the seminal heresy of the Unitarians, with which we began this study. The 'man Christ Jesus' of 1 Timothy 2:5 reveals the invisible God to us *because,* and *only* because, he is the eternal Son made man through incarnation. Without having first been 'in the bosom of the Father', Jesus could not have been the Mediator and Redeemer of God's elect. Paul makes this connection in Colossians 2:9-10, when he says, 'In him dwells all the fulness of the Godhead bodily; and you are complete in him, who is the head of all principality and power.' The vital connection between God's 'fulness' and our 'completion' is Christ, the Son of God incarnate. Why did God the Son become man? To save us from our sin and present us faultless before the presence of God the Father with exceeding great joy. 'For there is one God and one mediator between God and man, the man Christ Jesus' (1 Tim. 2:5).

There was no other good enough
To pay the price of sin;
He only could unlock the gate
Of heaven, and let us in.

(C. F. Alexander)

4. The Lamb of God

John 1:19-34

Few of us today know the meaning of our own names. In years gone by, this was not the case: a 'Fletcher' made arrows, a 'Cooper' made barrels and a 'Smith' made horse-shoes. 'Cruikshanks' had bandy legs and 'Armstrongs' had strong arms! For many of us, myself included, that meaning is lost for ever in the mists of time. All that is left is a label — made up of little more than nonsense syllables — a code that singles us out from the crowd, but is totally devoid of content.

In Bible times names were never accidental. Mary, for example, was told by the angel to name her son 'Jesus', because he would 'save his people from their sins' (Matt. 1:21). Our Lord's name was the Hebrew *Yeshua* — Joshua — which means, 'Jehovah is salvation.' Applied to the son of Mary, it makes a very specific point. It identifies him as the Saviour of the world.

Apart from names, we also find epithets, titles and nicknames being applied to people to describe their distinctive attributes or character. James and John, the disciples of Jesus, were called 'Sons of Thunder', on account of their robust temperaments. In similar vein, but for an infinitely more profound purpose, Jesus is accorded many different descriptive titles — so many, in fact, that Philip Henry, the father of the commentator Matthew Henry, was moved to write a book explaining many of them![1] These titles tell us a lot about Jesus. Each of them highlights some aspect of his person and his mission. He is, to name but a few, the Bread of Life, the Light of the World, the Wonderful Counsellor, the Prince of Peace, the Gate for the Sheep, the Good Shepherd and the Man of Sorrows. At the inauguration of his public ministry, Jesus was given one of the most striking and frequently used of his titles. He was called **'the Lamb of God'** (1:29).

The identification of the Lamb
(John 1:19-29)

1:19. Now this is the testimony of John, when the Jews sent priests and Levites from Jerusalem to ask him, 'Who are you?'

It is significant that Jesus did not declare himself to be the Lamb of God. It fell to John the Baptizer, as the second Elijah promised in Malachi 4:5, to introduce Jesus to the world, not as the man from Nazareth — 'the son of Joseph, whose father and mother we know' (6:42) — but as the Saviour from God **'who takes away the sin of the world'** (1:29). The day before this happened, John had been confronted by a fact-finding committee from the ecclesiastical establishment in Jerusalem. They wanted to know who he was and what he was doing.

The identity of John (1:20-23)

1:20-23. He confessed, and did not deny, but confessed, 'I am not the Christ.'

And they asked him, 'What then? Are you Elijah?' He said, 'I am not.'

'Are you the Prophet?' And he answered, 'No.'

Then they said to him, 'Who are you, that we may give an answer to those who sent us? What do you say about yourself?'

He said: 'I am

The voice of one crying in the wilderness:
"Make straight the way of the LORD,"

as the prophet Isaiah said.'

Closely questioned about his identity, John denied
being the promised Messiah (**'the Christ'**) or **'Elijah'**
back from the dead, or **'the Prophet'**, i.e., the
Messiah as foretold in Deuteronomy 18:15-18. It is
true that the Synoptics identify him as the *second*
Elijah, but John, if he was aware of that, says
nothing about it (cf. Matt. 11:14; 17:12; Mark 9:13).

Pressed to give more than denials (1:22), John
does identify himself as **'the voice of one crying in
the wilderness, "Make straight the way of the
Lord"'** (1:23; quoting Isa. 40:3; cf. Matt. 3:3; Mark
1:3; Luke 3:4). He is not just another freelance
preacher! He is fulfilling the role of the prophesied
forerunner of the revival of God's people that would
come through the Servant of the Lord (Isa. 52:13 –
53:12). Isaiah's prophecy looked to the restoration of
exiled Israel not merely in terms of a return from
Babylonian exile, but in connection with the advent
of the Messiah. John's proclamation first of repentance — God's covenant people are in a spiritual
wilderness — and then his subsequent identification
of Jesus as the Saviour-Lamb is making straight the
way to the new era of the Messiah.

The activity of John (1:24-28)

1:24-28. Now those who were sent were from the Pharisees.
And they asked him, saying, 'Why then do you baptize if you
are not the Christ, nor Elijah, nor the Prophet?'

John answered them, saying, 'I baptize with water, but
there stands one among you whom you do not know. It is he

who, coming after me, is preferred before me, whose sandal
strap I am not worthy to loose.'

These things were done in Bethabara beyond the Jordan,
where John was baptizing.

John's eschatological self-identification did not move
his Pharisee enquirers to any follow-up along that
line. Perhaps they found it too vague to excite much
interest — possibly it was a 'generic' claim of many
erstwhile 'prophets' of the time. What did attract their
attention was John's practice of baptizing people. If he
was neither the Messiah nor Elijah come back to life,
then whence did he derive his *authority* to baptize
anyone — and to what end? (1:25).

John's answer is an almost poetic evocation of the
true stature of Jesus:

A		B
'I baptize with water'	versus	'There stands one among you whom you do not know.'
A		B
'It is he who, coming after me, is preferred before me...'	versus	'... whose sandal strap I am not worthy to loose.'

Whatever the status of one who may baptize repentant
sinners with water, this was well below that of the
'one' who was among them and whom they obviously
— and studiously? — **'do not know'**. John drives the
point home with a direct application of Isaiah's theme,
just quoted: Jesus *is* the 'Lord' whose 'way' John has
been making 'straight' (Isa. 40:3), the one who comes
after him and is 'preferred' before him. Then, to emphasize the difference, he declares himself with complete humility to be only Jesus' servant, and a servant
not even worthy to take off his sandals! (cf. 3:30-36).
These Pharisees were looking at the messenger and

missing the message. In their enthusiasm for what
were admittedly not unimportant matters of church
order, they were as yet oblivious to the advent of their
Messiah before their very eyes!

The testimony of John to Jesus (1:29)

1:29. The next day John saw Jesus coming toward him, and
said, 'Behold! The Lamb of God who takes away the sin of
the world!'

Accordingly, when Jesus arrived the very next day,
fresh from his temptation by Satan in the wilderness,
John hailed him with the words: **'Behold! The Lamb
of God...'**

1. Jesus is the final sacrificial Lamb

It is important to recognize that this title was something completely new. Plenty of lambs were sacrificed
in the Old Testament, but it remains a fact that there
was no identification of a personage called 'the Lamb
of God' in that period. Even when Isaiah describes
the 'Suffering Servant' of the Lord as being led 'like a
lamb to the slaughter', it is an illustration of the meek-
ness of Christ rather than an identification of his
person in its entirety. So when John identifies Jesus
as the Lamb of God, he is revealing from God a theology of the role of Jesus Christ in terms of the Lamb
— a theology into which the Old Testament data
about sacrificial lambs can be slotted.

Lambs were at the heart of the sacrificial system of
the old covenant. There was the *Passover lamb*,
offered once a year as a sin offering in the fullest
sense. This commemorated the exodus from Egypt,
the lamb's blood on the lintels of the doors representing atonement for the sins of the people (Exod.

12:12-13). There were also the *lambs of burnt offering* — the morning and evening sacrifices every day and twice on the Sabbaths (Lev. 1:4). Then there was the *lamb of the trespass offering*, which was offered as required when some particular defilement excluded a person from attending worship. In all these cases, lambs were sacrificed to provide legal purification for ceremonial defilement. They visibly demonstrated the need for an atonement in order to remove the pollution and penalty of sin and effect reconciliation between God and sinners.

All these sacrificial lambs were, however, only symbolic of what really needed to happen. They pointed to the one true and final Lamb — Jesus, the Lamb of God. In the person and work of Jesus Christ, the actual accomplishment of salvation burst upon the scene of human history. Jesus, the Lamb of God, is the substance of which the other lambs, from the substitute for Isaac on Mount Moriah (Gen. 22:8) down through all the Mosaic sacrifices in the temple, were merely the shadows.

2. Jesus takes away the sin of the world

Jesus is God's provision for the redemption of lost people and that is why John identified him as **'the Lamb of God, who takes away the sin of the world'**. This cannot mean that Jesus atones for all the sin in the world and therefore saves every human being in it. Jesus was not a universalist, as is made plain throughout his ministry (3:16-18; 10:11,27-28; 11:50-52; cf. 1:12-13). The intention of the atonement is the salvation of particular people, and it is for them that Christ dies (cf. 6:37,44,51). The wonder and mystery of this salvation is that all who come to Christ, believing in him and trusting him for salvation, will be saved (6:35; 10:9). This is the only 'truth' that will 'make you free' (8:32; cf. 8:42-47).

The mission of the Lamb
(John 1:30-34)

1:30-34. 'This is he of whom I said, "After me comes a man who is preferred before me, for he was before me." I did not know him; but that he should be revealed to Israel, therefore I came baptizing with water.'

And John bore witness, saying, 'I saw the Spirit descending from heaven like a dove, and he remained upon him. I did not know him, but he who sent me to baptize with water said to me, "Upon whom you see the Spirit descending, and remaining on him, this is he who baptizes with the Holy Spirit." And I have seen and testified that this is the Son of God.'

The mission of the Lamb of God was to take away 'the sin of the world'. Two aspects of this mission are set forth in this passage. The first is implicit in the very concept of a *Lamb* of God and is, as we have already mentioned, the substitutionary atonement for sin effected by the death of Jesus Christ. The second, testified to by John the Baptizer, is the baptism of the Holy Spirit which will issue from Christ's atoning work.

Substitutionary atonement for sin

The use of a lamb to define Christ's saving work is far more than a cute figure of speech. There is in this a theology conveyed in the image of a lamb that presents Jesus as the Saviour in precise and un-mistakable terms. The core significance of this is the idea that Jesus is *the sinless, self-sacrificing sin-bearer*. Lambs are the quintessence of unblemished innocence and therefore the perfect symbol for sub-stitutionary atonement. The participle translated 'takes away' (ὁ αἴρων / *ho airon* — 1:29) carries the notion of 'lifting up' and 'bearing away' its object (cf. 11:39) — in this case 'the sin of the world'.

> [Christ] was wounded for our transgressions,
> He was bruised for our iniquities;
> The chastisement for our peace was upon him;
> And by his stripes we are healed
>   (Isa. 53:5).

God, says Paul, 'made him who knew no sin to be sin for us, that we might become the righteousness of God in him' (2 Cor. 5:21). Christ has 'redeemed us from the curse of the law, having become a curse for us (for it is written, "Cursed is everyone who hangs on a tree")' (Gal. 3:13; quoting Deut. 21:23). Peter takes up the theme of the Lamb in his first letter when he tells us, '... you were not redeemed with cor-ruptible things, like silver or gold, from your aimless conduct received by tradition from your fathers, but with the precious blood of Christ, as of a lamb with-out blemish and without spot. He indeed was foreor-dained before the foundation of the world...' (1 Peter 1:18-20). John gives this last thought its final crowning expression when he describes Jesus as 'the Lamb [who was] slain from the foundation of the world' (Rev. 13:8).

These Scripture passages show that Jesus is the sinless sin-bearer who came to suffer that just wrath of a holy God that was due to sinners. Jesus places himself between God's justice and the condemned people he means to save. He takes away their sin by soaking it up in his own person: 'Christ was offered once to bear the sins of many' (Heb. 9:28). He paid the penalty and expiated God's just anger. This is what it meant for him to be made 'in the likeness of men' (Phil. 2:7). He felt the temptations we feel. He bore the guilt we bear. But he suffered punishment to free all he would redeem.

Baptism with the Holy Spirit

Having declared Jesus to be 'the Lamb of God', John went on to repeat in substance what he had said to the Pharisees the day before. Not himself the Messiah, John was rather his forerunner: **'After me comes a man who is preferred before me, for he was before me'** (1:30). Jesus is 'preferred' on the first and essential ground that he was 'before' John, which is to say, he was the eternal **'Son of God'**, as defined by the apostle John in the first sentences of his Gospel (1:34).

But how did John the Baptizer know that Jesus was the promised Messiah? He says, **'I did not know him'** — that is, 'I had no secret, personal knowledge of his Messiahship.' This needed to be **'revealed to Israel'**, to be the subject of revelation from God. To that end John was sent **'to baptize with water'**, with a word from God that the man on whom he saw **'the Spirit descending, and remaining'** was the one who would baptize **'with the Holy Spirit'** (1:31-33). The apostle assumes that his readers are acquainted with the accounts of that event in the other Gospels (Matt. 3:13-17; Mark 1:9-10; Luke 3:21-22). He wants us to understand that John's baptism served a double purpose: while baptism with water 'symbolized the impurity of sin, which gave John the opportunity to point to (or to speak about) Jesus as the Lamb of God who is taking away the sin of the world,[2] it also provided the occasion for the public unveiling of Jesus, at his baptism, as the Messiah who would pour the Holy Spirit out on his people.

John administered the outward sign (water), while Jesus would effect the inward thing signified (cleansing by the washing of regeneration through the Holy Spirit, Titus 3:5). This is not to say that John's baptism was merely an outward ritual. He baptized the repentant, and the assumption had to be that he conceived of his baptism as a sign of inward spiritual changes. But he did not see his baptism as *effecting* that change. This is still true of Christian baptism as administered in the church since the time of the apostles. God is the one who transforms. There is no baptismal regeneration of human nature in the mere act and fact of a minister's applying the water of baptism to a human being (as taught by Roman Catholicism and the Protestant 'Church of Christ', the so-called Campbellites). *Our* baptism is *meant* to be a sign and seal of what *Jesus* will do in those whom he saves. This is exactly what happens in and through Jesus' ministry as lives are changed and men and women are brought from darkness into his marvellous light. It was also Jesus' design for the ministry of the Word and Spirit after he had been crucified, buried, raised from the dead and instated in heaven as the risen Lamb of God. Hence his emphasis on that night of his betrayal in the Garden of Gethsemane upon the outpouring of the Holy Spirit on his people after his going to his Father (John 14:15-31; 16:5-33).

The claims of the Lamb

Neither John the apostle nor John the Baptizer, still less Jesus himself, revealed these things merely to provide information that might or might not interest some people. Their goal was radical personal reformation. Our response to the Lamb of God is simply our response to the gospel itself and the claims of God upon our lives. The Lamb *is* the good news of salvation for lost sinners. How, then, must we respond to the fact that Jesus is the Lamb of God?

First, *the Lamb is God's free-grace provision* to carry sin away and remake spiritually dead, lost and condemned sinners into new people, reconciled to God through the blood of the Son. The doctrine of Jesus as the Lamb of God calls you to throw yourself without delay and without reserve wholly upon the mercy of God in Christ, believing in him as your Saviour and the only Redeemer of God's elect.

Secondly, *the Lamb establishes the pattern of true discipleship*. We are called to have that attitude of heart in us 'which was also in Christ Jesus' (Phil. 2:5-8). And what are the Beatitudes but a transcript of the spirit of the Lamb of God? 'Blessed are the poor in spirit, ... those who mourn, ... the meek, ... those who hunger and thirst for righteousness, ... the merciful, ... the pure in heart, ... the peacemakers, ... [and] those who are persecuted for righteousness' sake' (Matt. 5:3-10).

Thirdly, *the Lamb is the Judge of everyone who will ever live upon this earth*. The Apocalypse portrays him as the Lamb who is slain, standing in regal majesty and surrounded by the redeemed. The Lamb has seven horns, these symbolizing the completed perfection of his work of salvation. This contrasts, by the way, with the seven points on the tiara of that bogus secular redeemer who promises new life in America to the 'wretched refuse' from the Old World's 'teeming shore', namely, the Statue of Liberty. The Lamb is the Ruler and the Judge in virtue of his completed sacrifice. He who is the gentle Lamb to those who believe and are saved is the Lion who will rise in judgement over the unbelieving who die in their sins (Rev. 5:5-6). That is why they will call upon the mountains and rocks to fall on them and hide them 'from the face of him who sits on the throne and from the wrath of the Lamb' (Rev. 6:16).[3]

Fourthly, *the Lamb is the glory of heaven*, 'for the glory of God illuminated it', and 'the Lamb is its light' (Rev. 21:23). It is in his priestly office, as the substitutionary sacrifice for his elect, that Christ is exalted in glory as the very light of heaven. As the Word, he is the Prophet who speaks for God. As the risen Saviour, he is the King of kings and Lord of lords. But in the midst of his people in glory, he is presented pre-eminently as the Lamb whose blood was shed for the remission of sins. And as in heaven he inhabits the praises of the Church Triumphant in his priestly character, so on earth it is the cross that is central to the witness of the Church Militant. Anne Ross Cousin's hymn based on the seraphic language of Samuel Rutherford gives fragrant expression to the deepest sentiments of the believer with respect to the eternal glory of heaven with Christ:

O Christ! He is the fountain,
The deep, sweet well of love;
The streams on earth I've tasted
More deep I'll drink above:

There to an ocean fulness
His mercy doth expand,
And glory, glory dwelleth
In Immanuel's land.

5. They followed Jesus
John 1:35-51

By the time John wrote the Fourth Gospel the Christian church had been in existence for over fifty years. The gospel was making a tremendous impact on the Roman world as ever larger numbers of people heard about Jesus and committed themselves to him as their Saviour and Lord. Well might people have asked, 'How did this all come about? Where did it start? Who is this Jesus who has made such changes in so many lives? Why do people follow him? What does it all mean?' The apostle does not say that he was bombarded by such questions. It seems clear enough, however, that he anticipated a perennial need for answers to them, because his first chapter addresses them all with remarkable directness and economy of expression.

The apostle begins with an open-and-shut statement of Jesus' deity, incarnation and redemptive mission to the world. He is God; he is God made man; and he came to make those who receive him into sons of God by a new birth (1:1-18).

John then moves to an account of four crucial days at the beginning of Jesus' public ministry (1:19-51), leaving to the other Gospels the record of our Lord's early life and the immediately preceding events of his baptism by John and the forty days in the wilderness when he was tempted by the devil.

These four days, the first two of which were covered
in the previous chapter, are as follows:

On *day one*, John the Baptizer, under the
questioning of some Pharisees, denied that he
was the promised Messiah, but declared that
the Messiah had indeed come and was among
them, although he was as yet not fully revealed
to Israel (1:19-28).

On *day two*, John hailed Jesus as 'the Lamb
of God' and described how the Holy Spirit had
descended upon him at his baptism, thereby
identifying him as the Messiah (1:29-34). (John
does not record the baptism of Jesus.)

On *day three*, Jesus called three men to be
his disciples: Andrew, an unnamed man (who is
surely the apostle John), and Simon, better
known as Peter (1:35-42).

On *day four*, Jesus calls two more disciples:
Philip and Nathanael (1:43-51).

In this way, Jesus launched his public ministry
upon an unsuspecting world. In a few sentences,
John takes us from the counsels of eternity,
through the incarnation to the baptism of Jesus and
the first gathering of his disciples. Jesus is uncompromisingly revealed as the Son of God made flesh,
come to seek and to save lost people. And no sooner
is he proclaimed as the Lamb of God who takes
away sin than converts are drawn to follow him. The
theme is well stated by the apostle: **'The two disciples heard him speak, and they followed Jesus'**
(1:37). This breathes the air of the dynamism of the
gospel and indicates something of what it means to
follow Jesus.

Three aspects of the experience of discipleship are
prominent in John's account of the encounters of
Jesus with his new disciples which took place on the

third and fourth days: firstly, the disciples recognize who Jesus is (1:35-39); secondly, they retell the message about Jesus to others (1:40-42); and finally, they receive the promise of future fellowship with Jesus (1:43-51).

Recognizing who Jesus is
(John 1:35-39)

1:35-39. Again, the next day, John stood with two of his disciples. And looking at Jesus as he walked, he said, 'Behold the Lamb of God!'
   The two disciples heard him speak, and they followed Jesus. Then Jesus turned, and seeing them following, said to them, 'What do you seek?'
   They said to him, 'Rabbi' (which is to say, when translated, Teacher), 'where are you staying?' He said to them, 'Come and see.' They came and saw where he was staying, and remained with him that day (now it was about the tenth hour).

On the third of the four days covered in John 1:19-51, John and two of his disciples encountered Jesus for the second day running. Once again, John hailed him as **'the Lamb of God'**, whereupon the two men **'heard him speak, and they followed Jesus'** (1:36-37). One is identified as Andrew (1:40), while the other is almost certainly the apostle John, modestly omitting mention of his own name.[1] The question is: why did Andrew and John leave John the Baptizer?

Christ is proclaimed (1:36)

The Word of God was proclaimed. The words were few on this occasion — **'Behold the Lamb of God!'** — but they were filled with the theology of salvation.

Andrew and John had been thoroughly taught by John the Baptizer about the promise of the Messiah/Christ. They knew the meaning of the law of Moses and the sacrificial system of the Old Testament. They had also been prepared in their hearts by God to hope most earnestly for the Christ to be revealed. They had *heard* the content of God's revelation. It is a simple truth of experience that we cannot believe something until we hear about it from someone or find it somewhere. No one can buy a product that has not somehow been advertised or displayed. The same is true with respect to faith to Christ. If anyone in our world is ever to know Jesus as his or her Saviour, then the gospel must be preached far and wide by God's messengers (Rom. 10:14).

Christ is believed (1:37-39c)

The hearers of the Word responded by turning in faith to Jesus. This was a physical as well as a mental and spiritual commitment. The two are inextricably bound up together. You cannot follow Jesus in your mind and not also follow him in your body. What you *do* expresses what you *are*: 'With the heart one believes unto righteousness, and with the mouth confession is made unto salvation' (Rom. 10:10). Living faith in Christ issues in willing obedience, notwithstanding the struggles within us between the flesh and the spirit (Rom. 7:23 – 8:1). It is precisely because we love the Lord that we will keep his commands (14:15). Faith without works is 'dead' (James 2:26). It is not a real faith. It is a self-deceived simulation. Real saving faith produces the fruit and evidence of its reality in the life of the one who professes true faith in Christ.

If it is protested that we are saved by grace alone, through faith and not by works, we say, 'Yes, we are

justified by faith alone, but not that faith which is
alone!' Andrew and John *followed* Jesus (1:37); they
enquired of him in such a way as to indicate their
desire to learn from him (1:38b); and they *remained*
with him, undoubtedly to sit under his teaching
(1:39a-c). These are the practical evidences that their
faith was real. They challenge us as to our devotion
to the Lord Jesus Christ. Do you have such an open-
faced, teachable spirit? Are you eager to be his disciple, to learn from him and to follow him in personal
godliness?

Christ transforms lives (1:39d)

We are also given a window here into the personal
experience of the apostle John. He records the time
of day when he began to follow Jesus. It was **'about
the tenth hour'** (1:39) — 4 p.m. according to the
Jewish reckoning.[2] The point is that John treasured
the moment when he met the Lord. Many Christians
can remember the hour of their conversion to Christ.
I, for one, can vividly recall the evening of Saturday,
20 May 1962, when, at a meeting in the southern
Scottish town of Galashiels, I believe I entered into
life in Christ. Others, not so dramatically converted,
remember warmly different milestones along their
spiritual pilgrimage — perhaps a church camp,
particular Scripture passages, or simply the happy
remembrances of a Christian home and a sound
church, where the gospel was always part of the warp
and woof of daily life.

When someone comes to a saving knowledge of
Jesus Christ, life can never be the same. There is no
road back (praise God!). The way is forward to ever
wider experiences of the love of the Lord and the joy
of being made a new creation by his transforming
Holy Spirit in our hearts.

Retelling the message about Jesus (John 1:40-42)

1:40-42. One of the two who heard John speak, and followed him, was Andrew, Simon Peter's brother. He first found his own brother Simon, and said to him, 'We have found the Messiah' (which is translated, the Christ). And he brought him to Jesus.

Now when Jesus looked at him, he said, 'You are Simon the son of Jonah. You shall be called Cephas' (which is translated, A Stone).

Whenever something good happens to us, it is the most natural thing in the world to pass on our news to others. What Andrew did offers us the simplest rubric for personal evangelism.

Seek out someone (1:40-41a)

The very same day that Andrew followed Jesus, he **'found his own brother Simon'**. The most natural impulse of a new believer is to seek out others for Christ. Andrew thought about his brother and took the time to track him down. He wanted him to know the good news. This was not the egotism of the Olympic victory lap, where the victor seeks the plaudits of the crowd, but an exultant desire for a loved one to experience the same grace and joy. In the Christian race, everyone who believes is a winner!

Pass on the message (1:41b)

Andrew then told Simon, **' "We have found the Messiah" (which is translated, the Christ).'** The message was not 'Come to church', even less 'Be good!' Jesus *is* the good news, precisely because he is the Saviour and we need to be saved. The disciples had a great deal to learn about Jesus, but they knew that the Messiah — the Christ, literally, 'the Anointed One' — was the only hope of Israel. Andrew made the vital connection between John the Baptizer's identification of Jesus as 'the Lamb of God' and the Old Testament teaching about the Messiah. He can hardly have had a developed doctrine of Christ's offices — i.e., Prophet, Priest and King — but he realized that Jesus was the one promised in the prophets.[3]

Bring people to Jesus (1:42a)

Andrew followed up on his message. He **'brought him** [Peter] **to Jesus'**. He took his brother to the source! In post-ascension terms, this translates into taking people to the Scriptures themselves and to the preaching and teaching of that Word. In our day, 'leading people to Christ' has come to mean a scripted methodology for eliciting a confession of faith rather than an ongoing experience of coming under the sound of the gospel, as proclaimed in and by the church, through the ordained ministers of the Word. Evangelism is more than personal witness. It moves on from the arena of personal contact to the church and her official heralding of the truth as it is in Jesus. It follows that all preaching should be evangelistic and not merely didactic. The gospel message must always be preached. Christ must always be proclaimed as the only one given under heaven by whom we must be saved. Sinners must be called to trust in him whenever God's people assemble for public worship.

Jesus welcomes those who come to him (1:42b)

It is remarkable that Jesus called Peter — a perfect stranger — by his name. **'You are Simon the son of Jonah.'** You would be impressed were a stranger to identify both your name and that of your father! Matthew Henry is correct in seeing this as 'a proof of Christ's omniscience'. It is surely as amazing as his later, better-known, revelation that he saw Nathaniel 'under the fig tree' (1:48). The general point is that the Lord knows those who are his — and does so *before* they come to him in faith (2 Tim. 2:19; cf. Eph. 1:4-5).

Also remarkable is his assignation of a new name to Simon: **'"You shall be called Cephas" (which is translated, A Stone).'** The designation 'A Stone' is, of course, 'Peter' — the name by which we know the apostle. Leon Morris points out that when God gives a name, it denotes his ownership (see 2 Kings 23:34; 24:17; Isa. 62:2; Rev. 2:17) and also 'speaks of a new character in which the man henceforth appears (e.g. Gen. 32:28).'[4]

Receiving the promise from Jesus
(John 1:43-51)

1:43-51. The following day Jesus wanted to go to Galilee, and he found Philip and said to him, 'Follow me.'

Now Philip was from Bethsaida, the city of Andrew and Peter. Philip found Nathanael and said to him, 'We have found him of whom Moses in the law, and also the prophets, wrote — Jesus of Nazareth, the son of Joseph.'

And Nathanael said to him, 'Can anything good come out of Nazareth?' Philip said to him, 'Come and see.'

Jesus saw Nathanael coming toward him, and said of him, 'Behold, an Israelite indeed, in whom is no deceit!'

Nathanael said to him, 'How do you know me?' Jesus answered and said to him, 'Before Philip called you, when you were under the fig tree, I saw you.'

Nathanael answered and said to him, 'Rabbi, you are the Son of God! You are the King of Israel!'

Jesus answered and said to him, 'Because I said to you, "I saw you under the fig tree," do you believe? You will see greater things than these.' And he said to him, 'Most assuredly, I say to you, hereafter you shall see heaven open, and the angels of God ascending and descending upon the Son of Man.'

On the **'following day'** — the fourth day since John the Baptizer had identified Jesus as the Lamb of God — Jesus **'found Philip and said to him, "Follow me."'** The counterpoint with the previous incident marks both the role of John the Baptizer as the forerunner of the Messiah and the transition from his

interim ministry to that of Christ himself and the
New Testament era. Now we see Jesus directly calling
a disciple to himself. As before, the disciple called in
this way immediately acts on his new-found relationship to the Saviour to call someone else to Jesus.
Here we also have some very definite pointers to what
is involved in the evangelistic process, although the
principal focus of the passage is on the character of
Nathanael and the way Jesus called him to be one of
the Twelve.

A call issued (1:43-44)

With the words to Philip, **'Follow Me'** (1:43), Jesus
defines the 'foundational challenge'[5] of the gospel of
the kingdom of God. People become Christians because Jesus *calls* them to himself. 'You did not
choose me, but I chose you and appointed you that
you should go and bear fruit,' Jesus would later
remind them (15:16). Jesus is not just another option
to be picked off the shelf of life's potential commitments, waiting for otherwise autonomous men and
women to spare him a thought and maybe join his
church. By nature, nobody wants to follow Jesus.
But he is sovereign and by his free grace transforms
human lives. The effectual call of the gospel of sovereign grace is first in the order of salvation. True
Christians are 'the called according to his purpose',
who are brought at length to glory through the
golden chain of foreknowledge, predestination, calling
and justification (Rom. 8:29-30).

What makes the call effectual is not the will of the
individual, but the power of God. The divine Spirit
accompanies the divine Word and draws the otherwise helpless sinner into a saving relationship with
Christ. 'Philip was brought to be a disciple,' says the
excellent Matthew Henry, 'by the power of Christ

going along with that word, "Follow me." See the nature of true Christianity; it is *following Christ*, devoting ourselves to his *converse* and *conduct*, attending his movements and treading in his steps.[6]

John mentions the detail that Philip came from **'Bethsaida'**, as had Andrew and Peter (although they later lived in Capernaum — Mark 1:29). Why are we told this? Surely as a counterbalance to Jesus' condemnation of the town as recorded in Matthew 11:20-21. It was not the kind of place from which one would expect great men of God to come. 'The work of the gospel and kingdom of Christ,' observes Hutcheson, 'may begin in very obscure places, and among mean persons, that so none may despise a day of small things ... for Bethsaida was a wicked place ... yet from thence [Christ calls] three eminent instruments.'[7]

A question answered (1:45-48)

Philip, like Andrew before him, immediately went off and found Nathanael and told him about **'Jesus of Nazareth'** as the one **'of whom Moses in the law, and also the prophets, wrote...'** (1:45).

This drew forth the question: **'Can anything good come out of Nazareth?'** (1:46). People are often subjected to prejudicial judgements based on their humble origins. The nineteenth-century American artist James McNeil Whistler came from a blue-collar town in Massachusetts. At a soirée in Boston, a society grand-dame asked him in a superior tone, 'Mr Whistler, what possessed you to be born in a place like Lowell?' Smiling broadly, he issued the deft riposte: 'I suppose, Madam, it was so that I could be near my mother.' D. A. Carson thinks Nathanael's question was 'scathing', but it is far more likely, as Leon Morris[8] and William Hendriksen[9] suggest, that this guileless Israelite was quizzically reflecting on the improbability of the Messiah's coming from a small town in Galilee that is 'never once named' in the Old Testament.[10] Had Jesus been known as 'Jesus of Bethlehem', with all the royal connections of that place, Nathanael's reaction might have been quite different. When we live and speak for Jesus, people will have their questions, and they are entitled to an honest answer. In this case, Philip did not argue the point, but gave the best answer possible: **'Come and see.'** He would let Jesus speak for himself — a function that the completed canon of Scripture fulfils in our day.

When Nathanael at length came to Jesus, the latter greeted him with a remarkable character assessment: **'Behold, an Israelite indeed, in whom there is no deceit** [or "guile"]**!'** (1:47). Nathanael was what Jacob — the first Israel(ite) — should have been but was not, on that occasion when he came to Isaac deceitfully (AV, 'with subtlety') and secured Esau's birthright for himself (Gen. 27:35). This receives further point when we notice the explicit reference to Jacob's dream of a ladder reaching from earth to heaven, with 'the angels of God ... ascending and descending on' it (1:51; cf. Gen. 28:12). Nathanael was consistently what the patriarch was only inconsistently — a thoroughly honest man.

Nathanael clearly knew that Jesus had the measure of him. Accordingly, in the ingenuous way that we react to surprising discernment in others, he asked Jesus how he knew, only to hear the answer to his first question as to the validity of Philip's claim that Jesus was the promised Messiah: **'Before Philip called you, when you were under the fig tree, I saw you'** (1:48). The fig tree, like the 'five husbands' in the case of the woman at the well (4:18), is a precise detail that leaves the hearer beyond all doubt as to what Carson calls 'Jesus' supernatural knowledge'.[11]

Answer to Nath question
Jesus who cansee
come from Naz

Nathanael knew that something good had actually 'come out of Nazareth'!

A confession made (1:49)

Nathanael was entirely disarmed. Philip was right! This man from Nazareth was the Messiah! His confession rings with the joy of an unexpected discovery of grace: **'Rabbi, you are the Son of God! You are the King of Israel!'**

The expression **'the Son of God'** repeats the testimony of John the Baptizer (1:34). This is important on two counts. The first is that, as Leon Morris points out, the inclusion of the article indicates 'a full, not a minimal content'.[12] In other words, it denotes the unique divine sonship of Jesus. He was not merely *a* son of God; he is the incarnate Son. The second consideration is that John the Baptizer certainly understood the divine origin of Jesus. John proclaimed that truth to which he had given mute prenatal testimony in the presence of the unborn Jesus (Luke 1:44). He knew the truth every bit as well as his relative Mary, the mother of Jesus. He baptized Jesus in the full awareness of his divine sonship. There is no reason to believe that Nathanael did not know what John had preached and what he was now confessing for himself. He did not need to have the full doctrinal clarity of the Athanasian Creed to understand that Jesus was the divine Son.

The expression **'King of Israel'** has respect to the particular focus of the Messianic expectation. Messiah would deliver his people. He would rule as their king. This theme recurs in the New Testament and has come to be understood in theology in terms of the threefold office of Christ as Prophet, Priest and King (see Mark 15:32; John 12:13; 18:36; cf. Rev. 1:5). The point for Nathanael was that *because* Jesus is the Son of God, he was *also* the King of Israel. As such, he was therefore Nathanael's sovereign Lord. He is also your Lord, either as the Saviour he was to Nathanael and to all who will believe in him, or as the Judge he will be to all those who persist in denying him till their last breath.

A promise given (1:50-51)

Jesus closes his exchange with Nathanael with a promise of greater things to come. He had believed on account of the miracle by which Jesus could see him under the fig tree. If he believed because of that, he should also know that he would see greater things by far. **'Most assuredly'** (literally, 'Amen, amen') says Jesus, he would see **'heaven open, and the angels of God ascending and descending upon the Son of Man'** (1:51). There is no question that Jesus is here employing the imagery of Jacob's vision at Bethel (Gen. 28:12). As Jacob saw the angels ascend and descend upon the ladder between earth and heaven, so Nathanael — and the other disciples, because the reference is plural[13] — would see the angels ascend and descend upon Jesus.[14]

There is no evidence that this was to be a single vision and there is no record of such an event. Rather, Jesus appears to be speaking in a 'durative sense ... "you shall see again and again." '[15] And what would they see? They would see that Jesus is the ladder spanning earth and heaven, that he is the Mediator between God and man. Everything that the disciples would see Jesus do and teach would demonstrate his Messiahship. Miracle after miracle and utterance after utterance, Christ would be to them a vision of mediation and reconciliation between God and sinners.

Furthermore, Christ does quite literally open heaven for those he saves, and he will bring them to glory in his time. Christ also gives believers, in this life, communion with God through the exercise of a living faith in him. 'Christ is to us as Jacob's ladder,' says Matthew Henry, 'by whom angels continually ascend and descend for the good of the saints'.[16]

Jesus' use of the term **'Son of Man'** reaches back to the vision described in Daniel 7:13-14, where:

> One like the Son of Man
> ... came to the Ancient of Days,
> And ... was given dominion and glory and a
>   kingdom,
> That all peoples, nations, and languages should
>   serve him.
> His dominion is an everlasting dominion,
> Which shall not pass away,
> And his kingdom the one
> Which shall not be destroyed.

The term 'Son of Man' appears more than eighty times in the Gospels and is used by Jesus in such a way as to transform it from the mysterious reference in Daniel 7 to a clear assertion of his Messiahship (see 3:13-14; 5:27; 6:27,53,62; 8:28; 9:35; 12:23, 24 and 13:31).[17] Lenski best sums up Jesus' identification of himself as the Son of Man when he notes that '[Daniel] 7:13,14 pictures the Messiah, yet the Jews had not drawn a title for the Messiah from it. This Jesus himself did.'[18]

Gives Jesus a un-used term to fill w/ his Messianic meaning)

Whom are we to follow?

What is clear from the calling of the disciples is that they did not merely follow a great man or a charismatic visionary. John's account is laced with the titles of divine Messiahship. Jesus is variously hailed as 'the Lamb of God' (1:36), 'the Messiah' (1:41), 'the Son of God' (1:49), 'the King of Israel' (1:49) and 'the Son of Man' (1:51). The miraculous discernment of Nathanael's character and the promise of the vision of the angels fill out a picture of Jesus of Nazareth as the Messiah promised in the prophets. He is Immanuel — God with us — come to save his people from their sins (Matt. 1:21).

Like the original disciples, we are called to follow none other than the Son of God. To that end we are given unmistakable views of his glory and promises of even more as we go on to live our lives with him as our Saviour and Lord. 'The sight of Christ's glory,' observes Hutcheson, 'is the great encouragement and ground of believers' confirmation, as being all for them and their good, and letting them see what excellency there is in him to be relied upon.'[19] The call and the promise of new life are still the same today. Jesus is still saying, 'Follow me' (1:43). What, then, is your response?

6. Water into wine

John 2:1-11

People want miracles all the time. They want their illnesses to disappear and their problems to evaporate into thin air. One American sweepstake, called 'Publishers' Clearing House', claims to be 'the place where dreams come true' and assures us that 'Miracles can happen; they can happen to you,' for you can have 'ten million dollars out of the blue'. At street level, so to speak, a great many people dream about the impossible happening to them. They thirst for 'miracles' that will free them from the drudgery of that dead-end job and their constant inability to live in the manner to which they would like to become accustomed.

The miracles recorded in the Bible bear very little resemblance to popular notions of the miraculous. Biblical miracles were specific acts of God in history — signs, wonders and mighty deeds attesting the validity of the messengers and their message (cf. 2 Cor. 12:12). These were not given just to be mind-boggling phenomena, too far off the statistical curve to be scientifically explicable. Neither were they designed merely to free some people from their personal miseries. They were certainly extraordinary events defying naturalistic explanations and they shine brightly as expressions of God's compassion for human need and suffering, but they were primarily signs and seals of the Lord's approbation of those through whom they were performed.

The first miracle of Jesus' public ministry demonstrates this very clearly. **'This beginning of signs Jesus did in Cana of Galilee, and manifested his glory; and his disciples believed in him'** (2:11). It attested the divine authority of Jesus as the promised Messiah and marked the establishment of a new order for the world. The kingdom of God had come in power in the person and work of Jesus Christ! The miracle at Cana began to reveal his glory to a world from which it had hitherto been largely concealed. His miracles confronted the world with his claims in a way that would change it for ever. It is worth noting, in passing, that the post-Cold-War assertion by former U.S. President George Bush that a 'new world order' was dawning was not only the illusion that the facts so soon proved it to be, but was a blasphemous parody of the biblical teaching on the kingdom of God. From Christ's first advent to his coming again there is a new world order, and this is not to be confused with the rhetorical inventions of political conceit.

Glory concealed
(John 2:1-5)

One of the most startling aspects of Jesus' ministry is that he kept it from the public for so long. For the first thirty years of his life, his glory was almost completely hidden. Even when it did break out at the wedding in Cana, it is almost as if it were an accident or an afterthought. Only quietly, behind the scenes, and in an obscure village in the hills, does Jesus launch the public phase of his road to the cross.

A challenge to take action (2:1-3)

2:1-3. On the third day there was a wedding in Cana of Galilee, and the mother of Jesus was there. Now both Jesus and his disciples were invited to the wedding. And when they ran out of wine, the mother of Jesus said to him, 'They have no wine.'

It was **'the third day'** after the calling of Nathanael and Philip. Jesus, his mother and his new disciples were invited to a wedding feast. All we are told is that the wine gave out. A wedding in those days was a community affair and no doubt more people arrived than were anticipated. There is no suggestion of excessive drinking of the kind so often indulged in at such gatherings today. Wine was, and remains, a staple in the Middle East, and according to the prevailing conventions it would have been extremely humiliating for the host to have failed to provide for his guests (2:1-2).[1]

When the wine was gone, Mary reported the fact to Jesus. The apostle highlights their relationship by not mentioning her name: **'The mother of Jesus said to him, "They have no wine"'** (2:3). The question is, of course, what exactly she meant by this. When I was a lad, we lived three floors above the shops in an Edinburgh tenement. My mother was always asking me to run down the stairs for a pint of milk or a loaf of bread. It is clear that Mary had something far more spectacular in mind. She was not looking for a message boy. She knew that Jesus had been born when she was a still a virgin. She had observed such glimpses as he had given of his uniqueness and she was sure he had the power to do great things. She must have believed that he was the Messiah promised to Israel (Luke 1:42-55; 2:25-35,51). Accordingly, she looked to him to do something decisive and was in a sense challenging him to act as the person she knew him to be. Like any normal mother, she wanted her child to make his mark and fulfil his destiny.

A caution against presumption (2:4-5)

2:4-5. Jesus said to her, 'Woman, what does your concern have to do with me? My hour has not yet come.'

His mother said to the servants, 'Whatever he says to you, do it.'

Jesus' reply reveals his understanding as to what his mother was requesting. Although it may not be obvious at first glance, these words strongly imply that Mary knew Jesus to be the Messiah and expected great things of him.

First of all, notice that even in the manner of his address Jesus puts a certain distance between himself and his mother. He calls her **'Woman'**. In modern English, this would be regarded as cold and demeaning, but the Greek γύναι *(gunai)* is the correct form of fond and respectful address to a lady. The NIV comes fairly close with its 'Dear woman'. Why such formality? Surely to emphasize to Mary that she must now think of him less as her son and more as her Lord! You know how difficult it is for mothers to let their children go and really treat them as adults. Mary's problem was infinitely more testing, for her son was also the Son of God. So it is as if Jesus were saying, 'Don't order me about, Mum. I am not your little boy any more. Neither am I your dial-a-miracle service. I am the Lord of glory, come to do the will of my Father in heaven' (cf. Matt. 12:46-50). It is worth noting, in passing, that giving due respect to Mary as 'blessed ... among women' (Luke 1:28) does not warrant the Mariolatry[2] promoted by Roman Catholicism. Calvin points out that Christ 'addresses his mother in this manner in order to lay down a perpetual and general instruction to all ages, that his divine glory must not be obscured by excessive honour paid to his mother'.[3]

Secondly, the body of Jesus' response makes clear that Mary, whether she knew it or not, was intruding into matters that were entirely beyond her. He asks, **'What does your concern have to do with me?'** (2:4; see also Matt. 8:29; Mark 1:24; Luke 8:28). The Greek expression is literally: 'What to me and to you?' (Τί ἐμοὶ καὶ σοι / *ti emoi kai soi*). This indicates the overstepping of a line, or the attempt to cross an uncrossable gulf. Mary was out of her depth and needed to recognize this and back off.

Thirdly, Jesus offers the reason for his caution: **'My hour has not yet come'** (2:4). This is a recurrent theme in the earlier stages of Jesus' public ministry (see 7:6,8,30; 8:20). He had a clear idea of the timetable for his mission as the Saviour of his people. At the beginning, Jesus took care to conceal his glory so as not to draw the unwelcome attention of his enemies until the time was ripe. There are times in everyone's life when it is best to keep out of sight. Jesus bided his time in accord with the eternal plan and purpose of God. Only later would he say, 'The hour has come that the Son of Man should be glorified' (12:23; 13:1; 17:1).

Finally, it is apparent that he was neither rejecting his mother nor dismissing her suggestion. Jesus did intend to do something about the wine shortage in Cana and thereby to begin to reveal his glory. Her *pas* was not entirely *faux*. What Jesus wanted Mary to grasp was that it was his work to do the will of his Father and that he would therefore act in God's time and on his own terms. He was quietly asserting his authority as the Messiah. Mary, for her part, accepted the point and left the matter in his hands, while clearly still expecting great things to happen. When she said to the servants, **'Whatever he says to you, do it,'** it was an act of faith in Jesus as the Lord and 'evidence of a truly gracious heart'.[4] Far from seeing his words as a snub, Mary saw in them something of the glory of Christ and trusted him to be himself and do his work.

Glory revealed
(John 2:6-11)

2:6-11. Now there were set there six water-pots of stone, according to the manner of purification of the Jews, containing twenty or thirty gallons apiece. Jesus said to them, 'Fill the water-pots with water.' And they filled them up to the brim. And he said to them, 'Draw some out now, and take it to the master of the feast.' And they took it.

When the master of the feast had tasted the water that was made wine, and did not know where it came from (but the servants who had drawn the water knew), the master of the feast called the bridegroom. And he said to him, 'Every man at the beginning sets out the good wine, and when the guests have well drunk, then the inferior. You have kept the good wine until now!'

This beginning of signs Jesus did in Cana of Galilee, and manifested his glory; and his disciples believed in him.

The account of the miracle is very straightforward, although that has not prevented it from suffering rather badly at the hands of some interpreters. The anti-supernaturalists reject it as the history of a real miracle. They variously write it off as a myth or heathen legend imported and adapted for the purpose of establishing the superiority of Jesus and Christianity over Judaism and paganism. Since all religions have their claims of the miraculous, it is difficult to see how this has any force at all. The issue is their validity, not their ubiquity or relative impressiveness. One commentator, Leslie Weatherhead, sees it as a joke, in which the water remains water, but is referred to as 'the best' wine, no doubt with a bartender's guffaw! How a joke could reveal Christ's glory and cause his disciples to have faith in him is not explained.

What happened — water into wine (2:6-10)

In the house, there were **'six water-pots of stone ... containing twenty or thirty gallons apiece'**. These would have provided water for ceremonial washings **'according to the manner of purification of the Jews'**. Jesus ordered them filled and **'They filled them up to the brim.'** Mention of 'up to the brim' emphasizes that there was no room left to sneak in some wine and fake a 'miracle'. This was real, not a ruse! He then ordered them to **'Draw some out and take it to the master of the feast'** (2:6-8).

When that gentleman tested the sample for taste, not knowing its provenance, he was impressed enough to tell the bridegroom, **'Every man at the beginning sets out the good wine, and when the guests have well drunk, then the inferior. But you have kept the good wine until now!'** (2:9-10). This was good quality wine and the statement is a mixture of surprise and compliment. All this emphasizes the fact of the miracle and its transparent credibility among the contemporaries of Jesus.

What it meant — glory revealed and faith deepened (2:11)

John describes this event at Cana as the **'beginning of signs'** in Jesus' ministry. This reminds us that 'It is characteristic of them not so much that they arouse wonder and are hard to explain, nor even that they are demonstrations of divine power, but rather

[handwritten: Magician→ How did you do it?]

[handwritten: Not the miracle, it is the person]

that they point us to something beyond themselves. They show God at work. They are meaningful.[5] What that meaning is the apostle now makes clear.

Most significantly, it was by this and other miracles that Jesus Christ **'manifested his glory'**. John had already defined the glory of Jesus when he testified, 'We beheld his glory, the glory as of the only begotten of the Father, full of grace and truth' (1:14). This glory is inherent in the fact that he was the eternal Son of God, the Word who 'became flesh and dwelt among us' and came to save his people from their sins. Jesus manifested glory in his person, as the incarnate Son of God, and in his work, as the Man of Sorrows who through his death and resurrection is exalted a Prince and a Saviour. The immediate question posed by the events at Cana concerns the extent to which this first miracle manifested Jesus' glory. Obviously, the 'beginning of miracles' could only mean a beginning to the manifestation of his glory. The effect of the miracle was bound to be limited. Indeed, it was designed to be so, since three years remained before Jesus would say that his 'hour' had truly arrived. Even allowing for this, there were at least four respects in which he did permit his glory to shine brightly enough for those who had eyes to see it.

First of all, *it really was a miracle*, and Jesus had performed it! People knew this was so. He was therefore marked out in many minds as a unique person. He became overnight someone to be watched. It does not matter how confused the views people had of Jesus were at this point. The reality is that he had given them something to think about — and that something was nothing less than a glimpse of his glory as 'the only begotten of the Father'. There was much more to come!

Secondly, it was the creation of richness and plenty (wine) out of a bare necessity (water), and was thus *emblematic of the new dispensation of God's grace in Jesus Christ*. This was the 'new wine' which could not be put in the 'old wineskins' of Mosaic rules and regulations (Luke 5:37-39). It heralded the fulness of God's provision for the redemption of a fallen world. It said that, in Christ, life would be more than merely existing. It would be a feast of fat things and refined wine (Isa. 25:6), a celebration of new and eternal life in a risen Saviour.

Thirdly, *it declared the compassion of Christ* for people in need. Providing wine for a wedding feast may not seem to us to be a case of alleviating poverty and distress, but this would be to misunderstand the situation. Weddings, then and now, cost a great deal. Failure to provide for the guests, then as now, might well issue in serious offence and lead to all sorts of problems in relationships. If nothing else, it might ruin a very important occasion in the lives of two young people, their families and their communities. It was therefore an act of the greatest kindness for Jesus to turn a potential disaster into an unforgettable pleasure. It must never become trite to say that Jesus cared about people. Jesus→ Power/Glory →7 Celebrate

Finally, *it announced the arrival of the coming of God's kingdom with power*. Later, in the parables of the wedding feast and the wise and foolish virgins, Jesus would use this figure of the wedding to explain further the nature of his kingdom. The miracle OT showed that Jesus was not a mere teacher, or a Israel visionary who dealt in high-sounding concepts and deppwis grand theories. He had the power to transform. of sin? Christ is not a 'paper tiger'. His miracles tell the → world that he will successfully complete the work he joy, has been given to do. The manifestation of his glory celebrate is proof of the certainty of his triumph. Kingdom

It is also significant that, as a result of the miracle(s), **'His disciples believed in him.'** We are told only about the disciples' response to the miracle.

What disciples do when glory shown

How others at the feast reacted, we do not know.
Those that did find out about it must have been
amazed, but we do not hear of any of them following
Christ as a result. The fact is that the best preaching
in the world and the most amazing miracles did not
convert the bulk of first-century Jews. Jesus 'came to
his own, and his own did not receive him' (1:11). But
his disciples were strengthened in their new faith in
him. Some three centuries ago, George Hutcheson
observed that 'A right sight of Christ in his glory is a
notable help to faith, and [calls] for it at our hands,
whereas narrow thoughts of him feed unbelief.'[6] What
the old Scots divine meant is simply that the more we
see of Christ, the larger will our heart become for
him. Just in the proportion that views of his glory fill
and expand the horizon of the eyes of our understanding, so will our faith in him be raised to exalted
appropriations of the assurance of hope and anticipations of joy in his presence for evermore. This will
be so for everyone who loves Jesus Christ.

> Sometimes a light surprises
> The Christian while he sings;
> It is the Lord who rises
> With healing in his wings:
> When comforts are declining,
> He grants the soul again
> A season of clear shining,
> To cheer it after rain.
>
> In holy contemplation,
> We sweetly then pursue
> The theme of God's salvation,
> And find it ever new.
>   (William Cowper, 1731-1800)

7. Cleansing the temple

John 2:12-22

The two so-called 'cleansings' of the temple are notable because they are the only recorded occasions in Jesus' earthly ministry when he employed physical force in the assertion of his authority. The first of these is recorded in our passage, while the second, much later in his ministry, is recorded in all the Synoptic Gospels (Matt. 21:12-13; Mark 11:15-17 and Luke 19:45-48). These expressions of righteous anger refute the popular notion that Jesus will forgive anything and everything that people do, irrespective of their attitudes or persistence in sin. Here is an indignant Jesus, incensed by the desecration of the house of worship and willing to flex his muscles to rectify the situation! This makes some folk uneasy. It does not sit well with the 'gentle Jesus, meek and mild' they sang about in Sunday School!

Jesus is, however, both the Lamb of God who takes away the sin of the world and the Lion of Judah who looses his wrath on the unrepentant (Rev. 5:5-6). His anger in the temple gives a glimpse of the wrath of the Lamb and serves notice that the one who keeps mercy for thousands will by no means clear the guilty (Exod. 34:7). He signals that he has authority to *judge* the living and the dead (2 Tim. 4:1). The very fact that God is holy and cannot look upon sin necessitates the exercise of perfect justice. So it is with the Son of God, who as the risen Christ will exercise all authority and power in heaven and earth (Matt. 28:18). He must rule until his enemies become his footstool (Heb. 10:13). His rule consists in both his judgements and his outpouring of gospel grace.

Herein lies the significance of the cleansing of the temple. In the first place, *it gives a glimpse of the wrath to come*, just as the miracle at Cana hailed the promise of future blessing. The fact that Jesus was angry with sinners and their desecration of God's house lends a pointed urgency to the necessity of heeding the gospel call to salvation. In the second place, *it highlights the love and mercy of a Saviour* who is willing to give himself in order to seek and to save the lost, in spite of the fact that they already, fully and otherwise irredeemably deserve his condemnation. John's account connects Jesus' cleansing of the temple (2:12-17) with the doctrine that Jesus *is* the true Temple (2:18-22), and in this way explains in a nutshell the true meaning of this temple that was at the heart of Jewish faith and life.

Jesus cleanses the temple
(2:12-17)

2:12-17. After this he went down to Capernaum, he, his mother, his brothers, and his disciples; and they did not stay there many days.

Now the Passover of the Jews was at hand, and Jesus went up to Jerusalem. And he found in the temple those who sold oxen and sheep and doves, and the money-changers doing business. When he had made a whip of cords, he drove them all out of the temple, with the sheep and the oxen, and poured out the changers' money and overturned the tables. And he said to those who sold doves, 'Take these things away! Do not make my Father's house a house of merchandise!'

Then his disciples remembered that it was written, 'Zeal for your house has eaten me up.'

After a few days in Capernaum, Jesus went up to Jerusalem for the Passover, that annual commemoration of the deliverance of Israel from Egypt of which Christ himself was soon to be revealed as the fulfilment (1 Cor. 5:7). This fell on 14 Nissan (our March-April), and the year was probably A.D. 27. He went to Jerusalem to observe the pattern of worship commanded in God's law.

What Jesus found in the temple (2:14)

The essential point is that the temple in Jerusalem had been turned into a market with **'those who sold oxen and sheep and doves, and the money-changers doing business'** (2:14). Specifically, the outer court, the Court of the Gentiles, had been turned into a bazaar where the worshippers could buy animals for the sacrifices and exchange money for paying the temple tax (a half-shekel in Jewish currency only).

Corruption or not, this arrangement had certain practical advantages. It was 'one-stop shopping' for the worshippers. It was so convenient, for everyone had to bring an animal and the correct currency, and this was a problem if you lived a good distance from Jerusalem. Now you could get everything you needed on the spot. There were also advantages for the ecclesiastical authorities. By selling approved animals, with guaranteed acceptability to the priests, they effectively cornered the market. Animals from other sources might be rejected. Seal your monopoly with such guarantees and almost any price can be asked. And, of course, it could all be justified in terms of the more effective working of the temple and the Mosaic sacrificial system!

Does this ring any bells for you? Think of the corruption of the pre-Reformation church, with its sale of indulgences, and the modern hucksterism of mail-order 'ministries' that will send you 'free' prayer mats for your 'freewill offerings'. And what of churches that prostitute the worship of a holy God on the Sabbath day with symphony concerts, art exhibitions, celebrity panel discussions and large-screen TV relays of sporting events? What does Christ discover in our churches? A house of prayer for all nations, or a **'house of merchandise'**? (2:16).

Why Jesus drove out the traders (2:15-16)

The Lord was angry, and his anger was fully justified. He had come to worship in perfect obedience to the law. But what did he find? He found an evil parody of what God — including himself as the eternal Son — meant to happen in that place. On the later occasion recorded in the other Gospels, he applied words of Jeremiah and Isaiah to the situation: 'Is it not written, "My house shall be called a house of prayer for all nations"? But you have made it a "den of thieves"' (Mark 11:17; quoting Isa. 56:7; Jer. 7:11). No doubt these same thoughts gripped his soul on this occasion. So, **'When he had made a whip of cords'** he drove men and animals from the temple and overturned the tables of the money-changers, declaring to those who sold doves, **'Take these things away! Do not make my Father's house a house of merchandise!'** (2:15-16).

But how did one man attack all these people and succeed in driving them out? Why did they not resist, and even overpower him? It was surely not mere physical force that ejected these people. Nor was it simply the force of personality. Christ certainly exercised the most commanding moral authority — what one commentator has called 'the blazing anger of the selfless Christ'.[1] No doubt this is true. But the true meaning of what happened, and why, resides in the fact that it was the fulfilment of a specific prophetic prediction: '"See, I will send my messenger, who will prepare the way before me. Then suddenly the Lord you are seeking will come to his temple; the messenger of the covenant, whom you desire, will come," says the Lord Almighty. But who can endure the day of his coming? Who can stand when he appears? For he is like a refiner's fire or a launderer's soap. He will sit as a refiner and purifier of silver; he will purify the Levites and refine them like gold and

silver. Then the LORD will have men who will bring
offerings in righteousness, and the offerings of Judah
and Jerusalem will be acceptable to the Lord, as in
days gone by, as in former years' (Mal. 3:1-4, NIV).

It was the power of God that cleared away the
merchants that day, as the Lord suddenly came to
his temple. This was a partial fulfilment of Malachi's
prophecy, pointing the discerning to the later completion of the prophecy that would take place in the
establishment of the New Testament church.

What the disciples made of it (2:17)

Seeing all this happen before their eyes, the disciples
were prompted to remember the words of Psalm 69:9:
'Zeal for your house has eaten me up.' This was
their thinking: what David experienced in his zeal for
God's house — the reproach of his detractors —
Jesus would come to experience some time in the
future. Jesus later would quote Psalm 69:4 as a
prophecy about himself and his treatment at the
hands of his enemies when he said, 'They hated me
without a cause' (15:25). He would also utter the
words, 'I thirst!', as he hung on the cross (19:28), in
fulfilment of Psalm 69:21. Indeed, this psalm is
quoted on no fewer than seventeen other occasions in
the New Testament. What this shows is that Psalm
69 is a Messianic psalm, and it suggests, although it
does not prove, that the disciples understood it in
these terms and saw it as clearly pointing to Jesus as
the promised Messiah.[2] The act of cleansing the
temple was a sign pointing to the coming of the
Messiah, every bit as clearly — and miraculously —
as the changing of water into wine at the wedding in
Cana.

Jesus is the true Temple
(John 2:18-22)

2:18-22. So the Jews answered and said to him, 'What sign do you show to us, since you do these things?'

Jesus answered and said to them, 'Destroy this temple, and in three days I will raise it up.'

Then the Jews said, 'It has taken forty-six years to build this temple, and will you raise it up in three days?' But he was speaking of the temple of his body.

Therefore, when he had risen from the dead, his disciples remembered that he had said this to them; and they believed the Scripture and the word which Jesus had said.

It was not long before Jesus was called to account for his outburst of righteous indignation. **'So the Jews answered and said to him, "What sign do you show to us, since you do these things?"'** (2:18). The question sounds so pious. Here were the guardians of the purity of the house of God, the upholders of God's law, demanding a 'sign' from Jesus, when his very action was a miraculous sign that gave the lie to their own desecration of God's house! Did they not know what Malachi had prophesied? Could they not see the significance of one man's prevailing over a veritable mob? They had seen one 'sign' already, but, as the saying goes, 'There are none so blind as those who will not see!'

In any case, they might have admitted that they should have kept the temple clear of all that merchandising in the first place. Their query as to Jesus'

authority betrayed their lack of a true commitment to
worshipping God as he had commanded in his Word.
They were shameless hypocrites! They had no conscience about the state of the temple, no thought
that God might be offended by their turning it into a
market! They merely objected to being challenged by
the righteous anger of Jesus of Nazareth.

The temple of his body (2:19-22)

Jesus did answer them, but with a riddle: **'Destroy
this temple, and in three days I will raise it up'**
(2:19). 'You want a sign? I'll give you one,' says
Jesus. 'Watch for the destruction and rebuilding on
the third day of this temple!' They were completely
confused, as Jesus intended them to be at this point.
They noted that it had taken forty-six years to build
the temple. And he was going to rebuild it in three
days? What a joke!

We know that the answer is in the double meaning. In referring to 'this temple', he **'was speaking of
the temple of his body'** (1:21). There was point to
the riddle. He was not merely playing with words, or
having fun being obscure. Jesus was planting a seed
that would later bear fruit in the minds of many who
were in the temple that day. He was in a veiled way
making a link between the temple and his body. He
was connecting the 'type' or shadow (the temple) with
the 'anti-type' or substance (the Messiah). He was in
effect saying, 'I am the true Temple. I am all that the
temple typifies. And the great sign of my authority
will be the raising of this temple, my body.'

The Jews were none the wiser. They could only
see Jesus' words as a threat against the temple and
much later, at his trial, they accused him of making
just such a threat (Matt. 26:61). The disciples did
not understand Jesus either. After his death and

resurrection, however, his words on this occasion came back to them and the penny dropped at last: **'And they believed the Scripture and the word which Jesus had said'** (2:22). Then they saw that he had been talking about himself as the true Temple. At the heart of the temple is the atonement for sin. And Christ is the one who gave himself as the ransom for many, the body which would be broken and the blood which would be shed as the once-for-all sacrifice for sin. This all fell into place for the disciples after the resurrection. Perhaps, too, they remembered some later words of Jesus in response to the perennial Jewish demand for a 'sign': 'An evil and adulterous generation seeks after a sign, and no sign will be given to it except the sign of the prophet Jonah.' And what was this sign? It was that Jesus would rise from the dead on the third day after his death! (Matt. 12:39-40). The resurrection of Christ is the final, once-for-all sign! *He* is the true Temple, crucified, dead and buried, who is raised up on the third day for the redemption of his people.

Responding to Jesus

What does the cleansing of the temple mean for us? Let me suggest three practical themes by way of application.

1. Jesus calls for reformation

He wants an end to greed and corruption and the secularizing spirit of the age in our lives, our churches and our communities and nations. He wants repentance from the worldliness, covenant-breaking and backsliding that in effect deny Christ and tell the world we really have no life-changing message, no powerful gospel, after all. The Court of the Gentiles in the Jerusalem temple was designed to allow non-Jews to approach God. It said to the world that there was a place for all peoples in the worship and fellowship of the living God. But the merchants encroached on that space and that was a symbol of the deadness of a religion that had no place for faithfulness to God and reaching out to lost people.

2. Jesus calls to us as the Judge of the living and the dead

He cleansed the temple because he had authority to do so (Mal. 3:1-4). He is coming again. He has authority meanwhile to subdue the kingdoms of this world and make them his footstool. Who will stand in the day of his coming? Not those who, by reason of their unbelief, will call for mountains to fall on them and hide them from the wrath of the Lamb! The certainty of final judgement calls for faith and repentance while it is still 'today' (Heb. 3:13,15).

3. Jesus calls us as the true Temple

The earthly temple disappeared for ever in A.D. 70. There is no temple building in heaven, because 'The Lord God Almighty and the Lamb are its temple' (Rev. 21:22). In Jesus Christ 'The dwelling of God is with men' (Rev. 21:3, NIV). Christ is priest and sacrifice, temple and altar. He is the all-sufficient atonement for sin. He is our Passover and all that the temple foreshadowed. He is able to save you, because his blood can make the foulest clean. Will you not then come to him and trust in him, and receive eternal life through faith in him as your precious Redeemer?

8. 'You must be born again'

John 2:23 – 3:15

2:23-25. Now when he was in Jerusalem at the Passover, during the feast, many believed in his name when they saw the signs which he did. But Jesus did not commit himself to them, because he knew all men, and had no need that anyone should testify of man, for he knew what was in man.

It is certain that the third chapter of John, considered as a block of self-contained teaching, ought to begin at John 2:23 rather than John 3:1. John 2:23-25 is clearly the introduction to the account of Jesus' nocturnal conversation with the Pharisee, Nicodemus. It defines the context for all that passed between the two men.

We are told, for example, that Jesus had been making a tremendous impact on the people in Jerusalem during Passover week. We have already seen that he had dramatically cleared the temple of the merchants and money-changers (2:13-22). He had also performed other miraculous signs. Many people had witnessed these and **'believed in his name'** (2:23). Jerusalem was in a ferment over Jesus. This intrigued, and perhaps worried, Nicodemus — so much so that he was moved to seek out the Lord and speak to him face to face.

There is something else in this passage that we should note. It is a startling fact that Jesus distanced himself from those who saw his miracles and 'believed'. We are told that **'Jesus did not commit himself to them, because he knew all men'** (2:24-25). He knew what was in their hearts. He knew what their real spiritual condition was. And because of that, his head would never be turned by his popularity with the crowds. He neither depended upon them, nor entrusted himself to them. He was not going to let them make him king (6:15). Jesus had not come into the world to ride to the heights of earthly kingship on the backs of the mob. He had come as Immanuel — 'God with us' — to confront the basic problem of the human race, namely, the fact of the universal fallenness of human nature. The plaudits of the multitude were, he knew, utterly illusory. His public support was ephemeral. Why? Because the *hearts* of the people needed to be changed by the power of God!

This sets the scene for the precise focus of our Lord's encounter with Nicodemus. There is a deliberate connection between Jesus' knowledge of the human condition in general and his meeting with the Pharisee in particular. He had come to effect radical inward change — nothing less than a new birth — in people who, if left to themselves, can only blunder blindly into perdition. We are taken, then, from Jesus' knowledge of **'all men'** to **'a man'** named Nicodemus (2:24-25; 3:1). In this juxtaposition of 'all men' and 'a man', John is signalling that Jesus was about to diagnose a problem and propose the remedy. Successively, the passage addresses the necessity of the new birth (3:1-3), the author of the new birth (3:4-8) and the focus of the new birth (3:9-15).

The necessity of the new birth
(John 3:1-3)

3:1-3. There was a man of the Pharisees named Nicodemus, a ruler of the Jews. This man came to Jesus by night and said to him, 'Rabbi, we know that you are a teacher come from God; for no one can do these signs that you do unless God is with him.'

Jesus answered and said to him, 'Most assuredly, I say to you, unless one is born again, he cannot see the kingdom of God.'

Nicodemus opened the conversation with what looks like an approving statement, but is in fact a loaded question. Nicodemus saw something in Jesus, but it is certain that he did not see him as the promised Messiah. Compare Nathaniel, who did, and on far less evidence (1:49). Nicodemus was courteous and evidently sincere. He respected Jesus as **'a teacher come from God'**, and was intrigued by the message conveyed by his miracles (**'these signs that you do'**) (3:2). He was ready to listen to what Jesus had to say, as one theologian to another. Significantly, he went to Jesus under cover of darkness. He was not yet ready to accept Jesus, in the full light of day, as 'the true Light' who had come 'into the world' (1:9). He was really asking, 'Who are you, Jesus?', but he was not sure what answer he was looking for.

Jesus, for his part, was not interested in some mild-mannered theological debate. In one fell swoop, he blew away the fog in Nicodemus' question. He did so by simply stating the radical claims of the kingdom of God: **'Most assuredly, I say to you, unless one is born again, he cannot see the kingdom of God'** (3:3).

The heart of the matter is the matter of your heart

You will notice that whereas Nicodemus had come to discuss the validity of Jesus' ministry, Jesus had decided to discuss the reality of Nicodemus' faith! So instead of having a quiet chat about Jesus, Nicodemus found himself confronted by a challenge that focused on the very basics of personal salvation! The words, **'unless one is born again,'** cut right across the Pharisaic credo, with its painstaking attention to the minutiae of external righteousness. Jesus served notice on the Pharisee that the heart of the matter was the matter of his heart. He wasted no time in getting to what really mattered — the true spiritual state of the human race in general and, by implication, Nicodemus in particular, and the consequent necessity of inward spiritual rebirth for anyone to see the kingdom of God. From the start, Jesus drove a theological stake into the hearts of those who think their so-called 'good works' will keep them right with God. His uncompromising insistence on a new birth dealt a body blow to external works-righteousness as the way of salvation.

John Calvin is surely correct when he observes that Nicodemus, for all his learning, had a mind 'so full of thorns and choked with noxious weeds that there was scarcely room for spiritual teaching'.[1] It was to this that Jesus threw down the gauntlet. It is as if he says, 'Nicodemus, let us talk about how we know God. Do you see that being right with God is an *inward, spiritual matter of the heart*? Do you see that sinners need nothing less than rebirth to have a new nature altogether?'

These same questions apply to us right now! Do we see what Jesus is saying to *us*? And if we know what the new birth is and are willing to search our hearts before the Lord, are we then willing to press these claims upon others? It is easy to hide from Jesus' challenge behind the protective shell of outward religion. What Jesus wants is your heart. He wants the real you!

Seeing the kingdom of God

The personal, experiential, heart emphasis is confirmed by what Jesus says about seeing **'the kingdom of God'**. Clearly, he was not thinking of a geopolitical entity to be established some time later in his earthly ministry, a kind of 'national home' for Christians on this side of heaven. What he means by this 'kingdom' is the rule of God, particularly as it is personally experienced and enjoyed by those who love him. This rule — the lordship of Christ in believers' lives and the world in which they live (see Eph. 1:22) — is nothing less than a new order of things established by the Lord.

This has its most visible manifestation in the body of Christ in the world — the church (1 Cor. 12:27). It is in the church that God gathers the folk who welcome the rule of Christ and seek to serve him day by day. Even though hypocrites masquerade as Christians in the church, and whole visible churches apostatize and become 'synagogue[s] of Satan' (see Rev. 2:9), it remains a fact that the true church of God in the world is the company of the Lord's redeemed people. They profess him as their Saviour and Lord and declare in word and life that their citizenship is in heaven.

There is another, wider sense in which the rule of God is exercised. That rule extends beyond the borders of the church and the personal commitment of his obedient followers. He actually rules the whole world. Indeed, he rules the whole of creation! (Eph. 1:22; Heb. 1:3). He brings lost, unconverted people to saving faith in Christ. If the kingdom of God were merely coextensive with the church, this would not happen and the church would never grow by conversion from the world.

> He does according to his will in the army of
>   heaven
> And among the inhabitants of the earth.
> No one can restrain his hand,
> Or say to him, 'What have you done?'
>   (Dan. 4:35).

A common misconception is that God is only an interventionist in the general affairs of human history. People will pray for God to 'intervene' and 'overrule', as if he were far away and uninvolved in the events that happen on, and beyond, the perimeter of the lives of his own people. And so miracles, providences and answers to prayer come to be thought of as little more than God's fighting patrols foraying into no-man's-land. We lose sight of the truth that the earth is still the Lord's, and everything in it (see Ps. 24). He is active in the lives even of his enemies. He is the Lord of history, the ruler over the kings of the earth (Rev. 1:5). The kingdom of God is constantly at work everywhere, rolling back the spiritual darkness, even when the Lord's people feel as if Satan is having things his own way.

Born from above

All this tells us why it is that unrenewed human nature **'cannot see the kingdom of God'**. What was Jesus telling Nicodemus? And what does he continue to say today? 'We are taught by this,' says Calvin, 'that at birth we are exiles and complete strangers to the kingdom of God, and there is perpetual opposition between God and us until he changes us by a second birth.'[2] We are dead until made alive, blind until given sight; we are at war with God until we are reborn as his adopted children of faith.

The statement that we must be **'born again'** to see the kingdom of God leaves no room for doubt as to the profound depth in personal experience that spiritual rebirth must involve. The ambiguity of the Greek γεννηθῇ ἄνωθεν / *gennethe anothen* — it may be rendered 'born from *above*' — intensifies the point. It hints at what is later explicitly stated by Jesus — namely, that God in all his sovereignty reaches down unilaterally into the darkened souls of the helplessly hopeless and the hopelessly helpless and brings forth new life where there was only spiritual death.

The author of the new birth
(John 3:4-8)

3:4-8. Nicodemus said to him, 'How can a man be born when he is old? Can he enter a second time into his mother's womb and be born?'

Jesus answered, 'Most assuredly, I say to you, unless one is born of water and the Spirit, he cannot enter the kingdom of God. That which is born of the flesh is flesh, and that which is born of the Spirit is spirit. Do not marvel that I said to you, "You must be born again." The wind blows where it wishes, and you hear the sound of it, but cannot tell where it comes from and where it goes. So is everyone who is born of the Spirit.'

Jesus' answer set Nicodemus thinking. And the more he thought, the more perplexed he became. **'How can a man be born when he is old? Can he enter a second time into his mother's womb and be born?'** (3:4). Now it may be true that there is no fool like an old fool, but Nicodemus, however old he was, was not one of them. He was not so naïve as to think that Jesus was speaking about a physical rebirth. He understood perfectly well that Jesus was talking about spiritual regeneration. He just could not cope with the concept. Hence his words about re-entering his mother's womb. What did he mean? Just this: that to him, Jesus' idea of a spiritual rebirth was as crazy as a physical rebirth! In his urbane way, he was saying in effect, 'You are having me on, Jesus! This is impossible! It just won't hold water!'

That, of course, is the way people can be expected
to react if they know nothing of their own spiritual
need, or if, like the Pharisees of old and the nominal
'Christians' of today, their whole religious life has
been lived on the plane of ritual form and works-
righteousness. To accept the need of a new birth,
Nicodemus would have had to admit the bankruptcy
of his religious life hitherto. And it is the same with
everyone who does not know the Lord. We would
have to confess to God, 'I have been all wrong. Save
me, or I am lost!' This Nicodemus could not see — or
should we say, would not see?

To this rebuff, Jesus replied with the most gracious earnestness. The characteristic preface, **'Most
assuredly'**, solemnly calls Nicodemus to pay the
closest attention (3:5).[3] From there, the Lord builds a
case that issues in the challenge: **'Do not marvel
that I said to you, "You must be born again"'**
(3:7). He makes three points in quick succession.

The absolute necessity of the new birth (3:5)

Jesus is emphatic: **'Unless one is born of water and
the Spirit, he cannot enter the kingdom of God.'**
His mention of water and the Holy Spirit connects
new birth with all that water signified in the religious
life of the Jews, ties it to the activity of the Holy Spirit
and thereby underscores the point that *spiritual*
rebirth is absolutely essential. Nicodemus knew that
there was a symbolic connection between water and
purification in the teaching of Scripture.[4] He was
bound to be aware of the baptism of John and would
have known that this had been rejected by the Pharisees (Luke 7:30). He would also have known that
John testified that his baptizing with water — the
sign — was a preparation for Jesus' baptizing with
the Holy Spirit — the substance (1:33). Hendriksen

hits on the central point when he comments, 'The *sign* is valuable, indeed. It is of great importance both as a pictorial representation and a seal. *But the sign should be accompanied by the thing signified*: the cleansing work of the Holy Spirit. It is the latter that is absolutely necessary if one is to be saved.'[5] In connecting water baptism with the Holy Spirit, Jesus relentlessly pressed the need of inward, Spirit-driven change upon the hapless Pharisee (cf. Ezek. 36:25-27; Luke 3:16).

The Holy Spirit effects the new birth (3:6-7)

Not only is spiritual rebirth essential, but it can only be effected by the work of the Holy Spirit. **'That which is born of the flesh is flesh, and that which is born of the Spirit is spirit.'** The kingdom of God is not of this world (18:36). Nothing that defiles can enter into that kingdom (Rev. 21:27). But by natural birth a person becomes a 'natural man', who 'does not receive the things of the Spirit of God, for they are foolishness to him; nor can he know them, because they are spiritually discerned' (1 Cor. 2:14). Without new birth by the Holy Spirit, the flesh remains flesh, the natural person remains what he or she is by natural birth. The mind is set 'on the things of the flesh' and this entails 'death' and 'enmity against God' (Rom. 8:5-7). Sin is, however, a curable condition. Sinners may enter the kingdom of God, but they must first be born again by the work of the Holy Spirit. Why, then, asks Jesus, should Nicodemus **'marvel'** at his doctrine of regeneration? New birth is the most obvious need of men and women in this world!

The coming of the new birth (3:8)

Jesus' next step was to explain *how* the new birth comes to a person. He used the illustration of the blowing of a zephyr — those lightest breathings of the wind on a quiet summer day. **'The wind blows where it wishes, and you hear the sound of it, but cannot tell where it comes from and where it goes. So is everyone who is born of the Spirit.'** His meaning is clear. The new birth is a secret work of God, in which the Holy Spirit works according to his hidden power and secret will. The new birth is not predictable, because it is a sovereign work of God's grace. It is not an act of the human will, because it is effected by the Holy Spirit in a heart that is opposed to the very idea. It is *all* the work of God. Dead people cannot raise themselves to life. Stones cannot change themselves into bread. In the new birth, God regenerates dead, stony hearts and makes them hearts of flesh, beating with new life — a renewed nature, with which they may *subsequently* embrace Jesus as their Saviour in a conscious act of faith (Ezek. 36:26). Notice what this means.

First of all, it means that being born again is not something that you *do*. When Jesus said, 'You must be born again,' he was stating a fact, not uttering a command. He was not saying, 'You must give birth to yourself again.' The new birth is not something we can induce or produce. It is God's work from beginning to end. It is a subconscious work initiated by God in the hostile territory of spiritually dead hearts and dispositions. It is the supernatural renewal of souls that are captive to sin.

Furthermore, Jesus was not equating this prior act of the Holy Spirit in new birth (regeneration) with the subsequent act of the reborn person in believing in Christ (conversion to Christ). The distinction made in theology between *regeneration* and *conversion* must be maintained. John 3:3-8 is about regeneration, while John 3:14-21 is about conversion. The former is what God does; the latter flows from this and is where we come consciously to respond to the gospel. This shows us that salvation is rooted in God's free grace alone. Being born again — regeneration — is God's sovereign *act*; our coming to Christ in faith and repentance — conversion — is our *activity*.[6]

It is obvious, therefore, that the new birth, though itself to us a subconscious act of the Holy Spirit, must immediately have the effect of breaking through into the consciousness of the one who has been regenerated. The renewing breath of the Holy Spirit is felt *after* it has passed and done its work. Like the zephyr, we have no sense of whence it came or where it is going. Conversion to Christ follows. It can be dramatic or gradual, but it begins to flow instantaneously from the Holy Spirit's act of regeneration. We are awakened to the gospel of Christ and soon discover a new view of ourselves and of the truth of God. We find a new conviction of sin, a new willingness to respond to the claims of Jesus Christ. It is in this that we experience the evidence of the reality of the new birth. We do not choose to be born again; we choose Christ because we are already born again. We do not feel the new birth itself, but we do feel the new life that comes through believing, precisely because we were first reborn by the Holy Spirit in the innermost reaches of our being.

The focus of the new birth
(John 3:9-15)

Jesus Christ is the focus of the new birth. This is why Jesus turned the spotlight upon himself as the only Saviour of sinners. The new birth does not come in abstraction from hearing the gospel and coming in faith to Christ. You cannot be 'born again' and *not* come to confess Christ as your Saviour and Lord.

In our day, this term 'born again' is applied promiscuously to all sorts of human experiences and often means no more than an enthusiasm for some activity. Hence, people who love the television series *Star Trek* call themselves 'born-again Trekkies'. What is more to the point is that the term 'born-again Christian', by analogy with the secular usage, often signifies little more than a generalized experience of religious enthusiasm, with little or no specific reference to personal faith in Christ and consistent commitment to a life of personal godliness.

The point to be grasped is this: everyone who loves the Lord Jesus Christ with heart, soul and mind was first born again by the Holy Spirit. On the other hand, anyone who claims to be born again as a result of some dramatic religious experience, but does not confess Christ in word and deed as the focus of a holy life, has not so far given evidence of the new birth. If we abstract our personal experiences from Christ, we will trust in *them* rather than *him*! The real evidence of being born again is *knowing Jesus Christ as your Saviour and living for him as your Lord*!

This is why our Lord did not leave Nicodemus with a bare assertion of the necessity and authorship of the new birth. Jesus was determined to show how the new birth related to himself as the Saviour who alone could take away the sins of sinners and so effect the basis upon which sinners could be born again and saved by grace through faith in him.

Listen to the Word of God! (3:9-11)

3:9-11. Nicodemus answered and said to him, 'How can these things be?'

Jesus answered and said to him, 'Are you the teacher of Israel, and do not know these things? Most assuredly, I say to you, we speak what we know and testify what we have seen, and you do not receive our witness.'

Nicodemus just did not grasp what Jesus was saying (3:9). This drew from Jesus what has become the classic rebuke of spiritually blind leaders of the spiritually blind (3:10-11). The use of the plural, '... **you do not receive ...**', takes in the Pharisees as a class. They should have had no difficulty under-standing the need for spiritual renewal by a new birth. The Scriptures abounded with passages on the subject (cf. Ps. 51:1-12; Jer. 31:31-33; Ezek. 36:25-27). The evidence of human sin was all around them. Even a modicum of Bible knowledge, not to mention self-knowledge, would have proved the need of personal renewal. But they could not see it. As the Americans would say, in baseball parlance, Nico-demus did not make it to 'first base'. He did not see how dead he was, even in a world that was filled with death on every side.

Believe in the Saviour of sinners! (3:12-15)

3:12-15. 'If I have told you earthly things and you do not believe, how will you believe if I tell you heavenly things? No one has ascended to heaven but he who came down from heaven, that is, the Son of Man who is in heaven. And as Moses lifted up the serpent in the wilderness, even so must the Son of Man be lifted up, that whoever believes in him should not perish but have eternal life.'

The implication of this was far-reaching, to say the least. These, said Jesus, are **'earthly things'** — matters that fall within human observation and experience. There is nothing mysterious about the need for spiritual renewal in human beings in this world, even though the solution requires the sovereign power of God. Even so, Jesus says to Nicodemus, **'You do not believe'** (13:12). In this way, Jesus demonstrates afresh that Nicodemus needed to be born again. Could he not see that his failure to understand 'earthly things' — basic truths revealed in the Scriptures he professed to believe — was a powerful argument for the need of spiritual rebirth?

This being the case, what would Nicodemus make of the even more profound truths that remained to be revealed? **'How will you believe if I tell you heavenly things?'** asks Jesus (3:11-12). But what were these 'heavenly things'? In explanation, Jesus sets out two basic facts at the heart of the gospel.

The first fact that Nicodemus needed to grasp is that *God has spoken through his Son.* Jesus declares that **'No one has ascended to heaven but he who came down from heaven, even the Son of Man who is in heaven'** (3:13). This is the basis of his claim that he will teach 'heavenly things'. Jesus boldly asserts that he is the Word, or Logos, of God, who has come in order to be the light of the world (cf. John 1:1-9; Heb. 1:1-3). He is not just another prophet; he is *the* Prophet promised in the Scriptures (Deut. 18:15).

The second fact is that *he is the Son of Man who came to give eternal life to all who believe in him*: **'And as Moses lifted up the serpent in the wilderness, even so must the Son of Man be lifted up, that whosoever believes in him should not perish but have eternal life'** (3:14-15). He is the Messiah, come to save his people. Jesus points to the way that salvation will be accomplished. He refers to the incident in the desert wanderings of Israel, as recorded in Numbers 21. Israel had rebelled against God. He sent poisonous snakes among them, so that many people were killed. When the people confessed their sin, the Lord had Moses make a brass snake. This was set on a pole in full view of the people, so that any who had been bitten by a snake might look to it and be healed. This, says Jesus, is a picture of redemption through the Messiah. The Son of Man must be lifted up, so that all who believe could, **'in him'**, have eternal life. In the language of prophecy, he is alluding, of course, to his death on the cross. He is the answer to the human predicament. He is the Saviour who gives new life (cf. p.98 above).

There are two textual variants in 3:15 which ought to be noted.

1. The 'critical text' behind most modern Bible versions does not include the words 'not perish, but' (μὴ ἀπόληται, ἀλλ'). The conventional wisdom of the critics is that this is a scribal insertion emphasizing what is explicit in 3:16. Those preferring the 'Received Text' would see it as an alteration, perhaps removing a perceived redundancy.

2. More significant is the fact that **'believes in him'** is backed in the 'Critical Text' by πιστεύων ἐν αὐτῷ (*pisteuon **en** auto*), while the

'Received Text' has πιστεύων εἰς αὐτὸν (*pisteuon* **eis** *auto*n).

If the latter *(eis)* is the uncorrupted text, then the rendering should be 'believes in him' as in the NKJV — that is, believes in Jesus as the ground of receiving eternal life. John uses εἰς after πιστεύων thirty-four times, always making this point.

If, however, the former *(en)* is the correct variant, it is generally agreed that it ought not to be connected with 'believes', but rather with 'eternal life'. The verse would then read, 'Whoever believes shall have eternal life *in* [*i.e.*, in union with] him.'

The question with which Jesus confronts Nicodemus — and confronts us all today — is this: 'What will be your response to me? I am the *only* Saviour of sinners!' Yes, you *must* be born again! You cannot save yourselves by your own best efforts to keep the Law of God. You certainly cannot give birth to yourself again and recreate your corrupted human nature into one that is fit for heaven. You must depend upon the grace of God and the breath of the Holy Spirit for that. Does this bother you? It should! You are helpless! You cannot save yourself! But there is a way to new life. Sin is not an incurable condition.

You may well ask, however, why Jesus first tells us that we need to be 'born again' and then goes on to inform us that it is wholly a work of the Holy Spirit, something that we cannot do for ourselves? Does he mean to depress us, to have us give up and go away feeling doomed? And how do we square this with his subsequent exhortation to look to the Son of Man lifted up — to the crucified Christ — and in believing in him receive eternal life? What is the connection between our total inability to make ourselves 'born again', and our evident responsibility to believe and be saved? The answer — and the logic of Jesus' argument — is this, I believe. When Jesus shows us

that we are utterly helpless to change our nature and
disposition by a self-induced new birth, his design is
to provide a vehicle by which the Holy Spirit may
make us feel our helplessness, so that in a rising
sense of desperate need we would flee to him for
salvation. What sinner will ever look to Jesus for salvation, unless he feels his helplessness to save himself? The key, of course, is that the Holy Spirit accompanies the proclamation of the Word at every
point. He sovereignly works in human hearts. As he
persuades us of our helplessness, he also shows us
that God is able to help us. And the call to look to
Christ, to believe in him as our Saviour, is also
accompanied by the power of the same Holy Spirit
who regenerates dead souls. When the call of the
gospel is made *effectual* by the accompanying power
of the Holy Spirit, *regeneration* and *conversion* (faith
and repentance) follow in its train.[7] Christ closes in
on sinners from all sides. Even as the Word comes to
our ears or eyes from outside, the Holy Spirit is doing
his work on the inside, in our hearts and minds. The
power of God to save bridges the gap between our
total inability to save ourselves and our responsibility
to believe the gospel so that we will be saved. In our
personal experience of the Word and Spirit, the
doctrine of our helplessness becomes the handmaid
of our conversion to Christ.

Consequently, the last word for Nicodemus and for
us is not 'Give up, because only God can change
you,' but 'Believe in Christ and you will discover that
God has saved you in the very act of believing.' Jesus
Christ is able to give eternal life to all who trust
themselves to him in saving faith. In him, and in him
alone, we discover what it means to be born again
and to see the kingdom of God.

9. Amazing love

John 3:16-21

When Nicodemus went to speak with Jesus, we can be sure he did not expect to be told that he needed to be born again. What he thought would be a quiet theological discussion turned into a personal challenge that reached behind his great learning and knocked on the door of his heart. But apart from the very brief record of what Nicodemus said to Jesus, we are told nothing of the thoughts that must have coursed through his mind as he listened to the Lord talking about the doctrine of the new birth. He was a Pharisee, and all that Jesus said cut right across the kind of religion the men of that school had developed for themselves over the years. They tended to see salvation in terms of the punctilios of outward rules and rituals. Now the Lord confronted their religion, in the person of Nicodemus, with the radical claims of the gospel of the kingdom of God. People have to be regenerated in their innermost being by the Holy Spirit. They cannot save themselves, however impressive their efforts! They *must* be born again! (3:3-8).

Jesus realized how difficult it was for Nicodemus to cope with what he was saying. He knew that in laying on the Pharisee's conscience the necessity of an *inner* rebirth by the Holy Spirit, he was overturning the convictions of a lifetime. But he did not

intend to leave Nicodemus confused and without a
message of real hope. Jesus therefore pointed him to
the gospel, to the good news that would be the means
of bringing him to see the kingdom of God. He reminded Nicodemus of the incident of the bronze
snake in the desert (Num. 21) and pointed to its
contemporary fulfilment in the lifting up of the Son of
Man as the way in which God would bring salvation
to lost people (3:14-15). He was, of course, referring
to his own death as the once-for-all atonement for
the sins of his people (cf. Matt. 1:21). He was telling
Nicodemus that the way to be saved is to look to the
Son of Man — that is, to believe in Jesus as his
Saviour and Lord, the promised Messiah come to give
himself as a ransom for his people.

Even this could only have left Nicodemus wondering what on earth was going on. After all, he
might have asked, 'Who is this "Son of Man"? How
and when will he be "lifted up"? How does this relate
to salvation and my personal destiny? How, indeed,
does it relate to God himself?'

The answer to such questions as these is set forth
in 3:16-21. We are told successively of the love of the
Father (3:16), the light of the Son (3:17-20) and the
life of the believer (3:21). Whether these are the
words of Jesus or the reflections of the evangelist is
not altogether clear. The passage reads well as either,
but it seems forced, on the face of it, to sunder the
text between verses 15 and 16 in this way. However,
even if Nicodemus never heard these words from
Jesus' lips, they are certainly the words of Christ to
the church. It is no accident that these words have
powerfully touched the hearts of millions of people in
the two thousand years that have passed since they
were first uttered.

The love of the Father
(John 3:16)

3:16. 'For God so loved the world that he gave his only begotten Son, that whoever believes in him should not perish but have everlasting life.'

The origin of the gospel is the eternal love of God for the world that he is determined to save out of the world that he made good at the beginning, but which had fallen into sin in Adam. Calvin's comment so beautifully catches the heart of the matter: 'Christ opens up the first cause, and, as it were, the source of our salvation, and he does so, that no doubt may remain; for our minds cannot find calm repose, until we arrive at the unmerited love of God.'[1] Why is there a plan of salvation involving regeneration by the Holy Spirit and faith in the lifted-up Son of Man? For the answer, let us go back to the source, namely the love of God for the world he had made.

Hrard so often don't connect w/ 3.1-15

The character of God's love

John says, **'For God so loved the world that he gave his only begotten Son...'** The greatest gifts spring from the deepest love. Therefore, when the gift is the only begotten Son — that is, the Son of Man lifted up (3:14) — we can surely understand that behind it lies the most amazing love. Parents know how to give good gifts to their children. So, argued

Jesus, 'How much more will your Father who is in heaven give good things to those who ask him?' (Matt. 7:11). The nature of the gift says something about the character of the giver. And in this instance the giver is the God who 'is love' (1 John 4:16). Three aspects of the gospel display the character of God's love: its source, its sacrifice and its scope.

1. The source of the gospel

God so **'loved'** the world that he gave his Son. The verb here is ἀγαπάω / *agapao*, the word most commonly used in Scripture of the love of the Father for the Son, and of God for his people. It is a love based upon choice and consideration, and with reference to the Lord it reaches to his eternal will and purpose. Here is a point beyond which we cannot go. We are brought to the very limits of God's revelation of himself to us. We stand before a great wall of light, beyond which we are not given to see. It is the frontier of his secret will. It is the visible side of the eternal counsel of the Father, Son and Holy Spirit. We cannot reason our way through that light, or speculate our understanding into the heart of the eternal. God *is* love! And he **'so'** loved that **'he gave...'** Why did he send Jesus to save sinners? We are in the end told no more than this. 'In love he predestined us to be adopted as his sons through Jesus Christ,' says Paul (Eph. 1:5, NIV). 'Love so amazing,' writes John Murray, 'we cannot scale its heights nor fathom its depths.'[2]

2. The sacrifice in the gospel

God 'so' loved — loved in such a way, in such a character, and to such an extent — that he **'gave his only begotten Son'**. He gave him away. He gave him over to death. He gave him as the substitute for sin.

God's love for sinners was such that he was willing
for his Son to bear the penalty of the full weight of
the divine justice that was due to them. God knew
that only Jesus could, to use Hugh Martin's phrase,
'die death dead', and he was accordingly willing to
give him up. The sacrifice of the Son was as great as
it was necessary. It was the greatest that could be
made. We should not forget that the Son was also
willing to lay down his life, and so shared the love of
the Father for those he would save (John 10:15-18).
He was the Lamb of God 'slain from the foundation of
the world' (Rev. 13:8).

3. The scope of the gospel

Only the Son of God could take on himself our human nature and take away the sin of sinners in his
own person. Only he could effect the intended redemption. 'There was no other good enough to pay
the price of sin, wrote C. F. Alexander.[3] It would not
have escaped Nicodemus' attention that God's redeeming love was directed to otherwise lost and
hostile people. God gives his Son for the sake of
enemies, not friends! 'In this is love,' says John, 'not
that we loved God, but that he loved us and sent his
Son to be the propitiation for our sins' (1 John 4:10).
'God demonstrates his own love toward us', writes
Paul, 'in that while we were still sinners, Christ died
for us ... when we were enemies we were reconciled
to God by the death of his Son...' (Rom. 5:8). This is
simply the explicit statement of what is implicit in
the very provision of a Saviour. It is axiomatic that
those who need to be saved are at war with God. This
illumines the scope of God's love for sinners. He gave
his Son to die for people who were dead to him and
did not want to be saved by him. Jesus noted once
that 'Greater love has no one than this, than to lay
down one's life for his friends' (15:13). But the love of

God the Father and God the Son surpasses even
that, for Jesus laid down his life for enemies, in order
to make them what they could not be by themselves
— his friends.

All of this teaches us how precious to God the
salvation of his elect people really is. Consider the
depth of the Father's love for his Son. Yet he loved
lost people with a love that would deliver up his only
Son for their redemption. He gave because he was
determined to save. The cost *to God* tells us how
profound his love is — and from before the foundation of the world (Eph. 1:4). Speaking to the Roman believers, Paul sums up the character of God's
love when he asks, 'He who did not spare his own
Son, but delivered him up for us all, how shall he not
with him also freely give us all things?' (Rom.
8:32).

This cannot but be precious for Christians. Knowing the love of God, the forgiveness of sin and new life
in Jesus Christ, the believer knows what it is to be
saved, and saved for ever! And, with that, we understand something of how great the Lord's love had to
be to climb over the mountain of our sin and rebellion against God. How much sweeter still will this be
in heaven when we enjoy the fulness of our salvation
in Christ and marvel all the more at how he loved us
when we did not love him![4]

The purpose of God's love

God loved **'the world'** so that **'whoever believes in
him should not perish but have everlasting life'**.
The question is: what 'world' (κόσμος / *kosmos*) did
God so love that he deemed it necessary to send his
Son?

What God does *not* love is clear enough. God does
not love the world of evil. God hates sin. He also
hates sinners who unrepentantly sin their way into a

lost eternity (e.g. Rom. 9:13). He takes no pleasure in
the death of the wicked, but his love is particularly
directed to the world he will redeem through the
power of the everlasting gospel in Christ Jesus his
Son.

The answer to the question, then, is defined by the
goal of his love, namely the everlasting life of **'whoever believes in him'**. He loved the world of the
fallen humanity he was determined to redeem by the
blood of his Son. Birds and bees and sticks and
stones require no redeemer, even if the creation may
be said to be subject to futility and meanwhile groans
and labours along with the redeemed as they await
the redemption of their bodies (Rom. 8:20-23). The
creation is affected by man's fallen state, to be sure,
and will be renovated as a result of the salvation of
the elect, but it is for sinners that Christ made atonement, not their earthly environment. God determined
to redeem a people, and with them his creation, from
the ashes of the Fall.

God's purpose of love was also directed to sinners
in the *whole* world — not just to the Jews, the people
of the Old Testament, but to both Jews and Gentiles
under the New Testament. The elect are to be gathered from the four winds — that is, the whole earth
in all its generations (Mark 13:27).

The result of God's love

God will save **'whoever believes in [Jesus]'**. True
believers will **'not perish but have everlasting life'**.
God's saving grace is personal and particular. Unbelievers will 'perish', but believers will 'have ... life'. In
Christ, God plans to save a people who will be the
new, redeemed humanity that will one day fill the
new heaven and the new earth (Rev. 21:1). Jesus
actually saves sinners. The purpose of God's love

was, and is, to bring lost people, one by one, to saving faith in Christ. The outstanding thing about faith, observes Calvin, is 'that it frees us from everlasting destruction'.[5] Faith embraces Christ. Faith receives his victory over death. Faith is the means by which we come to know and experience the power of Christ's resurrection. And this is the purpose of God's love: to pour the life of heaven — everlasting life — into spiritually dead souls.

The light of the Son
(John 3:17-20)

3:17-20. 'For God did not send his Son into the world to condemn the world, but that the world through him might be saved. He who believes in him is not condemned; but he who does not believe is condemned already, because he has not believed in the name of the only begotten Son of God. And this is the condemnation, that the light has come into the world, and men loved darkness rather than light, because their deeds were evil. For everyone practising evil hates the light and does not come to the light, lest his deeds should be exposed.'

The urgency and earnestness of God's loving purpose in sending Jesus is now made clear: **'For God did not send his Son into the world to condemn the world, but that the world through him might be saved'** (3:17). This has to be understood in the context of Jesus' instruction of a Jew. It is a clear statement that the Jewish Messiah had not come to save the Jews only and condemn the rest of the world. No one was to be allowed to think of the Messiah's mission with God-on-our-side self-righteousness, as if rescuing us consisted in destroying everybody else! Christ's mission was not to condemn, but to save! Unless we repent, we shall all perish (Luke 13:3,5). To make this absolutely plain, two arguments are advanced: the first, that the world is actually condemned already; and the second, that people really love darkness.

Didn't send to condom, already was

Condemnat is implied by need for Salvation

Condemned already (3:18)

Christ did not need to come in order to condemn anyone, for the simple reason that all who do not believe **'in the name of the only begotten Son of God'** are **'condemned already'**. The unconverted are in the condition of being under condemnation. This is what it means to be spiritually dead, blind and lost. It is to be in danger of a lost eternity. Condemnation is like junk mail — you don't need to do a thing in order to receive it. It goes with the territory!

Jesus did not need to be born to Mary to make sure that the world was properly condemned. In fact, he came precisely because the world was *already* condemned and in desperate need, not of a judge, but of a saviour! Christ Jesus came to save sinners (1 Tim. 1:15). Why do we preach Christ? To tell people they are doomed and have no hope? Of course not! It is to call people to saving faith in Christ, to new life and to the hope of glory. Christ's call in the gospel is one hundred per cent positive: he came that sinners might have life, and have it abundantly (10:10). He came that we might declare to the world through all the generations to come, 'Believe on the Lord Jesus Christ, and you will be saved!' (Acts 16:31).

Men loved darkness (3:19-20)

Why is the world 'condemned already'? What has the human race done to deserve this condemnation? **'And this is the condemnation, that the light has come into the world, and men loved darkness rather than light, because their deeds were evil'** (3:19). Jesus is the light of men, who 'shines in the darkness', the 'true Light which gives light to every man coming into the world' (1:4,9). Men and women have no excuse (Rom. 1:18-20). Confronted, however, by the contrary claims of light and darkness, many people prefer the latter. Jesus is the manifestation of the love of God for sinners who are lost and dwelling in darkness. He is light and life. In him there is no darkness at all. He calls us to freedom and the eternal love that casts out fear. But we will not have him as our Saviour and Lord. We prefer our present state and will not change our allegiances and our ways.

Why? The answer is that people **'loved darkness ... because their deeds were evil'**. The verb, incidentally, is the same word, ἀγαπάω / *agapao,* that is used of God's love in sending Christ to save us. The problem is not primarily one of ignorance of the claims of the gospel, or of the difference between light and darkness. It is an inner disposition, a love — in this case for darkness. This is evidenced by the fact that their deeds are evil. What people do, how they choose to live — all as measured against the standard of God's revealed will — tells the story of their deepest commitments. Opposition to the light, not ignorance of it, is why people do what they do. They act out of their (un)beliefs. However sophisticated their defence of behaviour that God deems evil, they do what they do because deep down they **'[hate] the light'** and they will not come to it for the fully justified fear that their **'deeds should be exposed'** (3:20).

Now we can see what Jesus was getting at with Nicodemus. It is the question of his, and our, heart-response to Christ as the true Light, come to save a people that walk in darkness (Isa. 9:2). Here is the cutting edge of the gospel message. There are many ways to resist the call of Jesus Christ. You can knock it around in your mind as an intellectual problem and repeatedly debate the pros and cons of it, but never come to a decision. You can even call that agnosticism and persuade yourself you are more high-minded than those who do decide one way or

the other. You can go away, like that famous unbeliever of the apostolic age, Felix, and wait for a
more convenient time to give attention to the things
of God (Acts 24:25). Or you can claim you are too
busy with your work, like the man who wanted to
build bigger and better barns for the storage of his
wealth (Luke 12:18-21).

But all this is a smokescreen. These are all excuses and exercises in self-deception. Why? Because
the real issue is: what have you done with the light
that is shining in the person of Jesus Christ? Beetles
know what to do with sunlight, when you lift a stone
and expose them to its rays. They scuttle for darkness as fast as they can. It is their nature to do so.
They react to the light as a danger to their way of life.
That is the way it is with godless human beings. They
intuitively shrink back into the darkness. They resist
the light and seek to suppress it. This shows itself
very vividly in the sleazy underside of modern society
in, say, London's Soho or New York's Times Square,
but is in truth the way of life of secular-humanist
man.

In the suburbs and the high places of the land, sin
is constantly being redefined as good and justified as
normal, when all the real evidence is that it is ruin-
ous to the fabric of human life. Thus governments
and apostate churches tell us that homosexual
behaviour is to be accepted as a normal, healthy
alternative lifestyle, when the graveyards are filling
up with its practitioners. The madness of loving the
darkness is only too obvious on every hand. But
there are none so blind as those that do not want to
see, so the madness goes on. AIDS, drugs, pornog-
raphy, child abuse, crime, abortion and the break-up
of the family — the list is endless — are all addressed
by biblical morality, in terms of real answers and
with the promise in Christ of happy solutions. But we
will not go to the Lord that we might have life! God's

light is studiously avoided by our policy-makers and academics, and we are obliged to conclude that they have made a covenant with death and are in agreement with hell (Isa. 28:15). At the personal level, this phenomenon is exhibited in refusing to read the Scriptures and to attend public worship, in prayerlessness and a myriad of other ways of putting out the light of God from one's life.

The real issue, as we have already noted, is what you will actually do with Christ, the true Light, when he confronts you with that light. Will you choose his way, or hold to your own course? Will you choose light, or cling to the darkness? Will you choose death, or life through faith in Jesus Christ? We have reason to believe that Nicodemus did eventually come to embrace Christ as his Saviour (7:50-51; 19:39). What have you done? What will you do?

The life of the believer
(John 3:21)

3:21. 'But he who does the truth comes to the light, that his deeds may be clearly seen, that they have been done in God.'

Coming to Christ in faith is life-transforming. Embracing the light issues in living the truth. Christians are a bit like house plants. They have to live in a relatively darkened place. The sun shines in, but only through the windows. The plant, however, can turn its leaves towards the window. It is drawn towards the light and derives its sustenance from the light. In this way it is possible to grow beautiful plants in what is a rather hard and hostile environment for them. And so it is with the Christian in this less than perfect world. Darkness abounds in the world, but there is light for sinners in Jesus Christ. Believers reach for that light. They walk in the light. The light of Christ shines in their hearts. They love that light. It is their life and it is natural for them to bear that light in the sincere obedience of a happy discipleship to their Saviour, Jesus.

The standard by which the believer measures his life is Christ, the true Light — not other people's lives, not public opinion, and not any vague notion like the 'basic human values' which politicians trot out but never define. Christ is the light, and the Word of God is the only infallible rule of faith and practice. The combination is light, life and truth, and it all centres on the Lord Jesus Christ. 'For God so loved the world that he gave his only begotten Son, that whoever believes in him should not perish but have everlasting life' (3:16).

One day in the 1820s, a Scottish schoolboy named James Simpson saw a man being dragged through the streets of his home town, his back torn and bleeding from a public flogging, the last instance of such a punishment in Scotland. The man bore that penalty alone and for one offence. A few years later, by now a university student, Simpson witnessed a public execution. 'The man's arms were pinioned,' he records. 'His face was already pale as death, while thousands of eager eyes gazed on him as he came up from the gaol.' Simpson then asks, 'Did anyone ask to die in his place? Did any friend come and loose the rope and say: "Put it round my neck and let me die instead?" No, he underwent the sentence of the law. For many offences? No, for one offence. He had stolen a parcel from a stagecoach. He had broken the law at one point and must now die for it. It was the penalty of a changing human law in this case too; it was also the last instance of capital punishment being inflicted for that offence.' Reflecting on this, he testifies, 'I saw another sight — it matters not when — myself a sinner, standing on the brink of ruin, deserving nought but hell. For one sin? No, for many sins committed against the unchanging laws of God. But again I looked and saw *Jesus*, my Substitute, scourged in my stead and dying on the Cross for me. I looked and cried and was forgiven.' Towards the end of his life, now Sir James Young Simpson, famed as the pioneer of anaesthesia, he was asked what was his greatest discovery, and he replied without hesitation, 'That I have a Saviour.'[6]

Jesus' words to Nicodemus surely resound with the clearest urgency for our time. The time is short. We must soon appear before the judgement seat of Christ (Rom. 14:10). Believe on the Lord Jesus Christ, and you will be saved (Acts 16:31).

10. A witness for Christ

John 3:22-36

A perennial charge laid at the door of Christians and the church is that they are so riven by division and disagreement that their message has lost all credibility. 'There are so many interpretations of the Bible,' you will hear people say. 'So which one are we to believe?' They will argue, in effect, that the existence of a plethora of denominations and controverted interpretations of Scripture is reason enough for being altogether sceptical of any and all of the claims of Christianity! The illogical nature of this approach is not particularly difficult to prove. We can point out that it simply does not follow that the existence of contrary, and mutually exclusive, viewpoints even implies, far less proves, that no one position can be correct and that all can therefore be discounted. We can rightly say that this is no more than a pretext for ignoring the truth.

Christians must nevertheless face the fact that disunity between believers *is* a practical stumbling-block to many people. Differences and disagreements, whether doctrinal or practical, personal or denominational, can, and do, hinder the witness of the gospel in the world. Our Lord wants his followers to be united in the faith 'which was once for all delivered to the saints' (Jude 3). On the night he was betrayed, he prayed that his followers 'all may be one, as you, Father, are in me, and I in you; that they also may be one in us, that the world may believe that you sent me... I in them, and you in me; that they may be made perfect in one, and that the world may know that you have sent me, and have loved them as you have loved me' (17:21,23). In other words, the visible, practical unity of believers in Christ will have such a powerful evangelistic witness that the world will thereby *know* that Jesus came from glory to save sinners, and will also know that God loves his people even as he loves his Son!

Hindrances to Christian witness (John 3:22-26)

3:22-26. After these things Jesus and his disciples came into the land of Judea, and there he remained with them and baptized.

Now John also was baptizing in Aenon near Salim, because there was much water there. And they came and were baptized. For John had not yet been thrown into prison.

Then there arose a dispute between some of John's disciples and the Jews about purification. And they came to John and said to him, 'Rabbi, he who was with you beyond the Jordan, to whom you have testified — behold, he is baptizing, and all are coming to him!'

An argument that might have done great damage to Jesus' ministry broke out because of some disciples of John the Baptizer. After the Passover was finished (2:13,23), Jesus and his disciples went out into the country, where the latter engaged in a ministry of baptism, apparently after the pattern of John's ministry (3:22; 4:2). The net effect was that more and more people turned to Jesus' ministry, while fewer attended that of John (3:26). It was at this time that **'There arose a dispute between some of John's disciples and the Jews about purification'** (3:25). The gist of this seems to have been that John's followers were jealous of Jesus' greater popularity and were insisting that John's baptism was superior to that of Jesus. They were beginning to think of Jesus as a rival to John.

This was a potential root of bitterness, which, were John to agree with them, would have driven a wedge between him and the Lord and completely compromised the whole prophetic preparation for the advent of the Messiah which was really the heart and soul of John's ministry. John's response was therefore vitally significant. He had formally identified the Messiah. Should he retract this, Jesus' credibility would have been seriously compromised. Far from denying Jesus, however, John showed his disciples why he, they and all Christians are to bear witness to Christ as the Lord from heaven. He shows us the 'what' (3:27-30), the 'who' (3:3:31-35) and the 'why' (3:36) of Christian witness.

The character of Christian witness (John 3:27-30)

The 'what' of Christian witness is its character. In illustration of this, John explained the significance of his ministry as the herald who had been preparing the way for the Lord.

Answering God's call (3:27-28)

3:27-28. John answered and said, 'A man can receive nothing unless it has been given to him from heaven. You yourselves bear me witness, that I said, "I am not the Christ," but, "I have been sent before him."'

God had given John his ministry. He had a deep sense of the sovereignty of God and of his place in God's eternal purposes. God had made him what he was and God had given him the message that he proclaimed. Had it not **'been given to him from heaven'**, he would have had and been nothing.

Notice that *John was what he was because of God's appointment*. He had the unique calling to be the forerunner of Jesus (Mal. 3:1; 4:5; Luke 1:16-17). He therefore reminded his followers of his consistent testimony: **'You yourselves bear me witness that I said, "I am not the Christ," but, "I have been sent before him."'** John knew he was the last prophet of the Old Covenant and the herald of the New.[1] His role could never be repeated. He was a living milestone along the path of God's revelation of his purposes and promises for human history and destiny. He knew *from God* who he was and what he was to do, and nothing could budge him from that divinely given assurance.

Even though John had an utterly unique role in God's unfolding plan of redemption, the certainty that he knew as to his own relationship to God is, in principle, that which the testimony of the Holy Spirit will secure for every child of God. The Holy Spirit, as 'the Spirit of adoption', is received in the believer's heart, so that the latter is enabled to 'cry out, "Abba, Father!"' with a settled assurance of faith (Rom. 8:15). With that comes a deepening self-knowledge: a knowledge as to who we are before the Lord, a knowledge of our gifts and our limitations, of our place in his plans for our life and of our personal destiny in his redeeming love. This is what being assured of being saved and knowing Christ has to mean. We know who we are in God's great universe. Most of all, we know him in the power of his resurrection! (Phil. 3:10).

Secondly, we should note that John also knew that his message was from God. *He preached revealed truth.* He did not make it up as he went along, like so many self-appointed visionaries before and since. 'The word of God came to John the son of Zacharias in the wilderness,' and he preached 'a baptism of repentance for the remission of sins', and fulfilled his prophesied and prophetic role as the one who was to prepare the way of the Lord (Luke 3:2-6).

Notwithstanding the unique aspects of John's ministry, this also encapsulates a basic principle that applies to us as much as it did to him. Our witness is also to the Word which God has given. We have the full and sufficient revelation of God in the Scriptures of the Old and New Testaments. That is the church's

message to every generation today. Furthermore, as
Paul said to the Corinthians, we are not to go 'beyond
what is written, that none of [us] may be puffed up'
(1 Cor. 4:6). We have the fulness of the Word of God
to rest upon as the only rule of faith and life.

Pointing to Christ (3:29-30)

3:29-30. 'He who has the bride is the bridegroom; but the
friend of the bridegroom, who stands and hears him, rejoices
greatly because of the bridegroom's voice. Therefore this joy
of mine is fulfilled. He must increase, but I must decrease.'

John illustrated his position from everyday experience. In marriage the bride belongs to the bridegroom, not to the 'best man'. The joy of the groom's
friend was to see everything come to happy fruition
for the groom himself. John's point is obvious. In the
Old Testament Israel was the bride of Jehovah (Isa.
54:5; 62:4-5, Jer. 2:2; 3:20; Ezek. 16:8; Hosea
2:19-20). Jesus is Immanuel — God with us — come
for his bride, the people of God! This theme surfaces
later in the New Testament, where the church is
clearly identified as 'the bride of Christ' (2 Cor. 11:2;
Eph. 5:32; Rev. 21:2). John bears witness to the
fulfilment of the promises of God with respect to the
Messiah (Isa. 40:3-5). He therefore can only rejoice in
the coming of the Messiah: **'Therefore this joy of
mine is fulfilled'** (3:29). His mission had already
succeeded. Jesus was his joy.

Consequently, John is content to recede into the
shadow of history, as Jesus shines ever more brightly
upon the scene: **'He must increase, but I must
decrease'** (3:30). John's message was transitional in
nature, and had already become obsolescent. In this
sense it was inevitable that he would 'decrease'.

Candles are put out after the electricity comes back on.

In another sense, any witness for Christ involves the decrease of the witnesser and the increase of the one to whom witness is borne. The Queen's brilliantly caparisoned heralds blow glorious fanfares to announce her arrival at the House of Lords for the State Opening of the British Parliament, but the more they blow, the less are they the focus of attention, until at length they stop and everyone waits upon the monarch to enter the chamber and read the speech from the throne. John's preaching heralded the advent of Jesus and, the more John preached, the more he magnified the importance of Christ. John pointed *away* from himself. He did not even mention what God had done for *him*. Everything pointed to the Lord. He did not begin by saying, as we so often do, 'Well, I think this ...' He went straight to what God had said, what God had given, what God had done and what he would yet do in the person of his Son, Jesus Christ. Everything John said and did magnified Jesus, while he faded himself out from the picture. This has its echo, surely, in all Christian witness. To what do we testify, but to the grace of God in Jesus Christ? The more we witness for Jesus, then, the less prominent should we ourselves be in the equation, and the more should Christ be lifted up as the Saviour of the world.

It is not only relative to John that Christ must increase. He must increase in the devotion of his people. Speaking of the church's love for her Saviour, Charles Simeon remarks that 'The language of her heart will be, "Whom have I in heaven but thee? And there is none upon earth that I desire in comparison of thee," and "All other things will be counted but dross and dung in comparison of the knowledge of him" (Ps. 73:25; Phil. 3:8).'[2]

He must also increase in the eschatological impact of his rule in human history as the mediatorial King who rules as head over all things to the church, for 'Of the increase of his government and peace there will be no end' (Isa. 9:7; Eph. 1:22). Then 'comes the end, when he delivers the kingdom to God the Father, when he puts an end to all rule and all authority and power. For he must reign till he has put all enemies under his feet' (1 Cor. 15:24-25). What begins with John's self-effacement will end in the consummation of Christ's kingdom on the last great day of the present era of human history.

The subject of Christian witness
(John 3:31-35)

31-35. 'He who comes from above is above all; he who is of the earth is earthly and speaks of the earth. He who comes from heaven is above all. And what he has seen and heard, that he testifies; and no one receives his testimony. He who has received his testimony has certified that God is true. For he whom God has sent speaks the words of God, for God does not give the Spirit by measure. The Father loves the Son, and has given all things into his hand.'

It is warmly debated by the commentators as to whether these words were spoken by John the Baptizer, or whether they are an explanatory reflection by the apostle John.[3] They do seem to have the ring of a reflective comment, but, whatever their provenance, they show that the 'who' of Christian witness is Jesus Christ, and no one else.

Jesus' unique character (3:31-33)

First and foremost, *Jesus is unique*. **'He who comes from above is above all; he who is of the earth is earthly and speaks of the earth. He who comes from heaven is above all'** (3:31). John the Baptizer is 'of the earth', while Jesus is the Lord from heaven, the 'only begotten Son' of verse 16. There is, so to speak, no comparison. The Messiah is in a class of his own. John was not merely being humble. He was recognizing the divine and incarnate Son of God.

Furthermore, *there is sufficient evidence that this is indeed the case.* It is true that Jesus came and bore testimony to what he had **'seen and heard'** (cf. 3:11), and **'No one receive[d] his testimony'** (3:32; 1:11) — not literally 'no one', of course, but a large enough number to indicate that plenty of people were clear as to what Jesus had proclaimed as truth and did not like what they heard.

Many, however, had **'received his testimony'** and had **'certified that God is true'** (3:33). The point is that all those who had believed Jesus' testimony about himself thereby accepted God's testimony about Jesus, which was: 'You are my beloved Son; in you I am well pleased' (Luke 3:22; cf. John 1:34). William Hendriksen notes that this is the positive statement of what the apostle John states negatively in 1 John 5:10: 'He who does not believe God has made him a liar, because he has not believed the testimony that God has given of his Son.'[4] John, says Calvin, 'exhorts and encourages the godly to embrace boldly the doctrine of the Gospel, as if he had said that there was no reason why they should be ashamed or uneasy on account of their small number, since they have God as the Author of their faith... If we are not harder than stones, this lofty title by which faith is adorned [i.e., the truth of God, GJK] ought to kindle in our minds the most ardent love of it; for how great is the honour which God confers on poor worthless men, when they, who by nature are nothing else than falsehood and vanity, are thought worthy of attesting by their signatures the sacred truth of God?'[5]

Jesus' relationship to God the Father (3:34-35)

Believing in Jesus is not merely following a good man, or embracing a philosophy of human invention. Jesus is God the Son. He is one with the Father. To know him is to know the Father. John confirms this by laying out five salient truths with respect to the relationship between Jesus and God the Father.

Jesus was **'sent'** by God. He was not self-appointed. He was not a man on the make, a man with dreams of making a name for himself. Neither was he an altruistic visionary bent on making the world a better place through social engineering. He was an ambassador from heaven, sent by the God who made this world and plans to redeem it.

As God's ambassador, Jesus **'speaks the words of God'**. Unlike every other religion or philosophy that ever saw the light of day, Jesus' message was the very Word of God. We should hang on his words, not because he was a 'great teacher', but because he was the Logos, or Word, of God (1:1,14).

This, in turn, is proof that Jesus was filled with the Holy Spirit, **'for God does not give the Spirit by measure'**. Prophets had spoken for God throughout the history of his dealings with people. They had a measure of the Spirit, as indeed do all believers (Eph. 4:7), but what we see in Jesus is the limitless endowment of the Spirit — something to which John the Baptizer had borne witness at Jesus' baptism (1:32-34).

Jesus is loved by the Father: **'The Father loves the Son.'** Behind the observable character of Jesus lies an eternal bond of love. This is a unique bond. Jesus is not merely a man sent from, and gifted by, God. He is the divine Son. The mediatorial, incarnate sonship rests upon the essential, trinitarian sonship, and everlasting love is the bond that joins them in perfect unity.

Finally, **'all things'** have been **'given into [Jesus']
hand'**. As Leon Morris puts it, 'The love of the Father
for the Son guarantees the Son's plenipotentiary
powers.'[5] He has been given all authority as the God-
man, who is the only Mediator between God and
man. Consequently, it is through Jesus that 'all
things' — the benefits of sovereign grace — will flow
to those whom he redeems as his own people (1 Cor.
3:21,23).

This Jesus is the very heart of Christian witness,
because he is the Son of God made flesh and the
Saviour of the world. A Christless Christianity is no
Christianity at all. It is social work without a soul —
a little false comfort on the road to a lost eternity. In
Jesus Christ, however, there is comprehensive redemption. As the *Heidelberg Catechism* so beautifully
puts it, 'What is your only comfort in life and in
death? That I am not my own, but belong — body
and soul, in life and in death — to my faithful Saviour Jesus Christ. He has fully paid for all my sins
with his precious blood, and has set me free from the
tyranny of the devil. He also watches over me in such
a way that not a hair can fall from my head without
the will of my Father in heaven: in fact, all things
must work together for my salvation. Because I
belong to him, Christ, by his Holy Spirit, assures me
of eternal life and makes me wholeheartedly willing
and ready from now on to live for him.'[7] True Christians are truly 'Christ's ones'. They love to say so,
and they love to commend him to others that they too
might receive him as their Saviour.

The reason for Christian witness (John 3:36)

3:36. 'He who believes in the Son has everlasting life; and he who does not believe the Son shall not see life, but the wrath of God abides on him.'

The final verse of this section rounds out the discussion of the significance of John's testimony by proclaiming once more the teaching of John 3:16-21. This answers more precisely the question as to *why* Christians witness to Christ at all. Why can these Christians not keep their faith to themselves? You will hear this complaint constantly today. 'Faith is a private matter,' we are told. 'It is between me and God. Therefore, I am entitled to be left alone by you and your zeal for what you believe!'

That would be all very well if what people believed had no real cosmic consequences. Faith is personal, to be sure, but it is not merely an individual matter. God is not indifferent as to what people do with his claims. The bottom line is that the world is lost and going to hell. Each and every unbeliever in the Son of God **'shall not see life, but the wrath of God abides on him'**. There is no annihilationism here — to be deprived of seeing 'life' is not equivalent to the oblivious non-existence which so many in this world hope will follow their godless lives. Neither is there any capricious vindictiveness. God's wrath is not a supercharged version of apoplectic human rage. His anger is the perfectly holy response of our Creator

God to the transgressions of his rebellious creatures. This wrath **'abides'** on those who die in their unbelief. The verb is the present of μένω (*meno*, remain) and evokes the unending experience of the lost in hell, giving force and urgency to Jesus' words on another occasion: 'And do not fear those who kill the body but cannot kill the soul. But rather fear him who is able to destroy both soul and body in hell' (Matt. 10:28). This is the endless destruction of the death that never dies.

It is a measure of God's gracious purposes that he does not leave the world to go on its way, leaving everybody to find their own individualistic validation and self-fulfilment as they please, with its inevitable terminus in a lost eternity, but proclaims the good news of salvation through Jesus Christ, his Son. The world needs the gospel message. There are precisely two alternatives: 'genuine faith and defiant disobedience', to use D. A. Carson's words.[8] There is a basic antithesis between God and Satan, light and darkness, and life and death. Certain and just judgement awaits every soul, and Jesus Christ alone is the way to eternal life.

John highlights the contrast between belief and unbelief and implicitly challenges every reader to believe the gospel. Why is this witness necessary? Why must people *never* be left to a privatized, individualistic view of what they are pleased to call 'faith'? Because Jesus Christ is the *only* Saviour of sinners, and sinners are just plain lost when left to themselves. The Christian witness in the world is a witness for God's revealed truth. It is a witness to Jesus as the only Redeemer of men and women. It is a witness to the provision of new and everlasting life for a lost and perishing humanity. It is a witness to the God who loves enough to give his only begotten Son, and the Son who loves enough to give himself to death on a cross as the substitute who bears the penalty for the sin of otherwise helpless people.

11. The living water

John 4:1-29

The biblical truth that God is sovereign over everything that happens in life has tremendous practical implications for his people. Believers can face every day with the fully justified conviction that the one who knows the end from the beginning will surely do all things well in the interests of his people and his kingdom, even when circumstances have taken a turn for the worse (Isa. 46:10; Mark 7:37). This means in practice that they will very frequently see God turn bad things to good effect. Just as Joseph could say to his brothers concerning their earlier murderous intentions towards him, 'You meant evil against me; but God meant it for good in order to bring it about as it is this day' (Gen. 50:20), so many a Christian has seen a personal disaster issue at a later date in new blessing from God's hand. God will not have his grace-driven, love-filled plans for his people thwarted by the evils that come upon them from time to time. His enemies may do their worst, but the Lord will outflank them when his time is ripe and gain the victory.

So it was with Jesus. We cannot be sure that the Pharisees had begun to plot against Jesus at this early stage of his ministry, but it is certain that they had John the Baptizer in their sights. It would not be long before the latter was thrown into Herod's dungeon

(Luke 3:19-20). The evidence of popularity swinging to Jesus from John had not escaped their notice, and Jesus could therefore expect trouble from them before too long. To forestall any unwelcome attention, he **'left Judea and departed again to Galilee'**.[1] This apparent retreat was, however, to issue in a real advance, for on the way to Galilee, Jesus felt compelled[2] **'to go through Samaria'** and so came to meet a woman at a well and to bring the gospel to the people of Samaria (4:3-4).

The significance of this is that Jesus here encounters his first non-Jew, **'a woman of Samaria'** (4:7), who evidently comes to believe in him (4:29) and is the means of bringing her whole village to confess Jesus as **'the Christ, the Saviour of the world'** (4:42). Here is a concrete fulfilment of the promise of John 3:17: 'For God did not send his Son into the world to condemn the world, but that the world through him might be saved.' We have in all this a (but not *the*) paradigm for personal evangelism and a wonderful example of how the Holy Spirit can draw someone to Christ. The former is our invariable duty; the latter is the sovereign work of God in human hearts. As the narrative unfolds, Jesus is successively revealed as the seeker of the lost (4:1-15), the searcher of hearts (4:16-20) and the Saviour of the world (4:21-29).

Seeker of the lost
(John 4:1-15)

The fundamental truth that God sent his Son 'to seek and to save that which was lost' is being suppressed 'in unrighteousness' by many in our day, and a cultural amnesia about the true claims of Jesus Christ has descended upon vast numbers of people in so-called 'Christian' countries (see Luke 19:10; Rom. 1:18). Between the doctrinal vagaries of theological liberalism and the maudlin sentiments of the modern Christmas, the popular perception of Jesus' mission, even in many churches, has effectively been reduced to pious wishes of universal 'peace and goodwill', with just a touch of a good example of self-sacrifice. Jesus is the personification of 'being nice' and if you are nice to people, then God (if he is there at all) will be nice to you. Among the unchurched, 'Jesus' means little more than childhood Sunday School memories, or, more often, the compulsive expletive of foul mouths. The real Jesus has vanished in a fog of popular myth, inhabited by plastic nativity scenes, idolatrous crucifixes and plaster saints, all sinking fast into a miasma of casual blasphemy.

Jesus is the Christ (4:1-4)

4:1-4. Therefore, when the Lord knew that the Pharisees had heard that Jesus made and baptized more disciples than John (though Jesus himself did not baptize, but his disciples), he left Judea and departed again to Galilee. But he needed to go through Samaria.

In sharp contrast to all this, the Jesus who trudged along that dusty Samarian road reveals himself as the Saviour-evangelist who reaches out to lost people. In so doing, he provides us with a paradigm for the primary task of the church in the world — to proclaim the gospel message of salvation to a lost world. Jesus meets someone in the normal course of life, opens a conversation, turns it to spiritual things, then follows through against all attempts at evasion and insists on keeping the focus on the central issues of life. There is nothing vague about the real Jesus or his teaching. Although it may not be obvious at first reading, this is confirmed in John's passing observation of the fact that Jesus **'did not baptize'** anyone (4:2). This is usually glossed over by the commentators as no more than an incidental detail. But it surely serves to emphasize the significant theological and practical truth that Jesus came expressly to baptize with the Holy Spirit, and not with water — that is, with the *substance* of which the water of baptism is the *symbol*. Hence the juxtaposition, in his encounter with the woman at the well, of drinking water (4:7) and 'living water' (4:10) for the soul. No one could dismiss Jesus as merely another 'baptizer', like either his forerunner, John, or the many other 'baptizers' of that time. In this way, Jesus carefully maintained his position as the Messiah heralded by John.

We should also note two features of the context of this event that clothe it with particular significance.

The first concerns *the general attitude of Jews to Samaritans*. The Samaritans were descended from the intermarriage of Assyrian colonists and the remnant Jewish population of the northern kingdom of Israel in the years after its destruction in 722 B.C.

These adopted a truncated form of the Old Testament religion, recognizing only the Pentateuch as the Word of God. They 'feared the LORD', but also served their idols (see 2 Kings 17:24-41). When, after 586 B.C., the Jews returned from the exile (of the southern kingdom of Judah) in Babylon, the Samaritans opposed the rebuilding of the temple (Neh. 4:1-2). They subsequently built their own temple on Mt Gerizim and, although this was later destroyed in 108 B.C. by the Maccabean rulers of Israel, they have continued to offer annual sacrifices on that mountain to this very day. The essential point is that the Jews regarded the Samaritans as heretics (which they were) and despised them as inferior beings (which they were not). It is this, of course, that gives such dramatic power to Jesus' parable of the Good Samaritan (Luke 10:25-37).

The second feature of this event, as it is related in the Fourth Gospel, is its juxtaposition with the account of Jesus' conversation with Nicodemus. It is clear that John means us to catch the contrast between the two. They represent diverse extremes. Nicodemus is the insider, the Jew, the theologian, morally upright and a man. The woman is the outsider, the Samaritan heretic, the unlettered peasant, of easy virtue — and, of course, a woman! In the last analysis, their differences count far less than what they have in common — namely, spiritual lostness and need of a Saviour! In both cases, Jesus has to peel away layers of resistance to truth — the calluses of hardened, uncomprehending souls — to drive home his claims to their allegiance. If anything, the loose woman of Samaria comes out better than the urbane moralist from Judea.

Opening a conversation (4:5-9)

4:5-9. So he came to a city of Samaria which is called
Sychar, near the plot of ground that Jacob gave to his son
Joseph. Now Jacob's well was there. Jesus therefore, being
wearied from his journey, sat thus by the well. It was about
the sixth hour.

A woman of Samaria came to draw water. Jesus said to
her, 'Give me a drink.' For his disciples had gone away into
the city to buy food.

Then the woman of Samaria said to him, 'How is it that
you, being a Jew, ask a drink from me, a Samaritan woman?'
For Jews have no dealings with Samaritans.

There are many ways to make evangelistic contacts.
The easiest of all is to have the opportunity dished up
on a platter through being approached by someone
who is looking for answers, such as a Nicodemus or a
rich young ruler. All that is needed is the readiness
to give 'a reason for the hope that is in you' (1 Peter
3:15). The easiest form of *initiating* a contact is simply to talk to people you happen to meet along life's
way. Jesus came to **'Sychar'**, probably the modern
Askar, some thirty miles north of Jerusalem and the
site of **'Jacob's well'** (cf. Gen. 48:22). It was **'the
sixth hour'** (about 12 noon) and Jesus, weary from
the journey, sat alone by the well. The disciples had
meanwhile gone into the village to buy food.

A Samaritan woman came up to draw water from
the well and **'Jesus said to her, "Give me a
drink."'** She could not believe her ears! **'How is it'**,
she expostulated, **'that you, being a Jew, ask a
drink from me, a Samaritan woman?'** Jesus broke
the mould of Jewish-Samaritan relations. She knew
it in an instant. This was an extraordinary Jew, the
like of whom she had never encountered in her life.

Turning to spiritual things (4:10)

4:10. Jesus answered and said to her, 'If you knew the gift of God, and who it is who says to you, "Give me a drink," you would have asked him, and he would have given you living water.'

Jesus' reply was even more mind-boggling. He quietly reversed the direction of the conversation. The irony is that whereas he in his need had gone to her for help, the true need was on her side and he was the one who could provide the help! Notice three things here.

First of all, notice how *Jesus directed the conversation to spiritual things*. This had already half happened when she noted how the Lord had broken with the conventional Jewish attitude to Samaritan women.[3] He did not get bogged down in an answer to her question, but took the opening it afforded to tell her something about himself and what he could do for her. He did not retreat, as we often do, from opportunities to press the claims of the gospel, but boldly focused on the central issues of his ministry and her need.

Secondly, *Jesus identifies himself as the gift of God and the giver of* **'living water'**. The **'gift of God'** in the text is frequently identified as eternal life,[4] but it seems more in accord with the flow of the text to see the second clause (**'who it is who says to you'** — i.e., the Christ) as descriptive of the first (**'If you knew the gift of God...'**).[5] George Hutcheson's comment beautifully catches Jesus' meaning: 'Christ is then known rightly and savingly when he and all that he hath are looked on as freely gifted to the world by the Father (as well as by himself), and made theirs by offer to be embraced in the due order; for therefore is he named "the gift of God".[6] There are two gifts in this verse. Christ is the first 'gift of God' (cf. 3:16), who, as Mediator between God and man, gives the second gift of the 'living water', which is eternal life, to all who believe in him.

Thirdly, the **'living water'** plays on the distinction between the standing water in the well and the spring that feeds it from deep in the earth. *Christ is the fountain from which all new life flows for believers:* '"He who believes in me, as the Scripture has said, out of his heart will flow rivers of living water." But this he spoke concerning the Spirit, whom those believing in him would receive' (7:38-39). Jesus is the prophesied 'fountain ... opened for the house of David and for the inhabitants of Jerusalem, for sin and for uncleanness' (Zech. 13:1). This is the central theological theme running through the whole encounter. The woman needs this gift of living water, and Christ is the one who can, and does, give it to her.

Following through (4:11-15)

4:11-15. The woman said to him, 'Sir, you have nothing to draw with, and the well is deep. Where then do you get that living water? Are you greater than our father Jacob, who gave us the well, and drank from it himself, as well as his sons and his livestock?'

Jesus answered and said to her, 'Whoever drinks of this water will thirst again, but whoever drinks of the water that I shall give him will never thirst. But the water that I shall give him will become in him a fountain of water springing up into everlasting life.'

The woman said to him, 'Sir, give me this water, that I may not thirst, nor come here to draw.'

The woman immediately went on the defensive. Her reply might seem to suggest that she understood Jesus to be talking of literal 'living' (i.e., spring) water — the deep and hidden source of the still water in

Jacob's well. How could Jesus supply her with such water, seeing that he had **'nothing to draw with'** and did not obviously seem to be **'greater than our father Jacob'** who made the well (4:11-12). By any normal canons of conversation this is surely thinly veiled mockery, not crass literalism. 'She understands quite well,' observes the ever-perceptive Calvin, 'that Christ is speaking figuratively, but she throws out a jibe by a different figure, intending to say, that he promises more than he can accomplish... She proceeds to charge him with arrogance in exalting himself above the holy patriarch Jacob.'[7] She was no more literalistic about the living water than was Nicodemus on the doctrine of the new birth. Thus, when Jesus offers further explicit explanation, her response has the ring of a certain unwillingness to entertain what she realizes only too uncomfortably is a challenge to her spiritual condition.

Yes, the water he will give means no more thirst, for the reason that it is an internal **'fountain of water springing up into everlasting life'** (4:13-14). Now we can understand that she might be puzzled as to what he meant in precise theological terms, but would anyone with even a rudimentary acquaintance with the religion of the Jews miss the point that Jesus is making about the well-springs of spiritual life in human beings? Even a Samaritan might know that God was called 'the fountain of living waters' in the Jewish Scriptures (Jer. 2:13). Any sinner would realize immediately that Jesus was aiming for the soul in some way and had not the slightest interest in local water resources. She got the point. And the best she could do was fob the Lord off with a ridiculing conversation stopper: **'Sir, give me this water, that I may not thirst, nor come here to draw'** (4:15).

If we pause at this point in the 'evangelistic process', we must surely be struck by the boldness of the Lord. Jesus reaches out to someone who had not sought him. 'I was found by those who did not seek me' (Isa. 65:1). If Jesus' dealings with Nicodemus exemplify the way the church is to minister to those who enquire after the truth, then his conversation with the woman of Samaria shows us how to touch the lives of lost people. Notice, too, the loving way in which Jesus reached out to her. He did not treat her as part of the scenery and move on. He noticed her. He spoke to her. He asked a favour. He was prepared to drink from her cup. He listened to her. He answered firmly, but never put her down. And he persisted in showing her the truth, in spite of her initial resistance. He was earnest, positive, gracious and respectful. He did not write her off as a poor evangelistic prospect because of her social status. He made an effort to face her squarely with the issues of life. He called her to a new life.

Searcher of hearts
(John 4:16-20)

At this point, however, the woman became uneasy with the drift of Jesus' conversation. That is why she did her best to put a stop to what he was saying about the 'living water'. But like a good general on the battlefield, Jesus sought to outflank her defences (her words) and overrun her headquarters (her conscience). He therefore changed the subject to get her off her balance and so, paradoxically, keep her focus on the main point. He began to make her search her heart.

Changing the subject to get to the point (4:16-18)

4:16-18. Jesus said to her, 'Go, call your husband, and come here.'

The woman answered and said, 'I have no husband.'

Jesus said to her, 'You have well said, "I have no husband," for you have had five husbands, and the one whom you now have is not your husband; in that you spoke truly.'

To hear Jesus abruptly say, **'Go, call your husband, and come here'** (4:16), may seem out of place at first reading, but it is yet another instance of our Lord's brilliant flexibility in diverting faltering conversations into fruitful channels. The obvious question is: 'What is the connection between this and what has gone before?' What relevance does this have to the 'living

water'? What is the logic, if any, of Jesus' sudden
change of tack?

Jesus' dual subject was his gift and her need. She
would never understand his gift until she acknowledged her need. Therefore, she must be shown her
need. He discerned that the quickest way to do that
was to ask her to call her husband! Why? Because,
as she had to confess, she did not have a husband!
True, said Jesus, **'for you have had five husbands,
and the one whom you now have is not your
husband'** (4:18). Her life was a sad string of broken
relationships — the serial adulteries that pass for
'marriage' in the lives of people to whom fidelity is a
synonym for infatuation. What is new? Behind the
divorces and the 'live-in boyfriends' lie oceans of
emotional bruising, broken trust, bitter feelings and,
not least, aching fears of more of the same in the
future. 'The way of the unfaithful is hard' (Prov.
13:15). She knew it. And Jesus wanted her to face it
honestly and be inwardly convicted of her need to be
saved from her sad, hurting, shameful life.

We do not know the secrets of people's hearts as
Jesus did, but we can know human nature and
human sin well enough to bring the challenge of
God's Word home to the consciences of men and
women. Essential to biblical preaching and evangelism is the faithful emulation of Jesus as he, to use
Carson's words, 'drives home to the individual's
greatest sin, hopelessness, guilt, despair, need'.[8] Lost
people do not need to be massaged with false gospels
of self-esteem and health and wealth — 'if they just
trust Jesus'. That is just psychotherapy in God-
language. No! Lost people need to convict themselves
of their lostness and cry to the real Jesus for redemption through his blood, and the forgiveness of
sins. Jesus' approach to the woman at the well
showed her that she needed heart surgery, not a
bandage! Evangelism is not the peddling of vitamins

and health food. It is a trip to the hospital's emergency department for life-saving care by the best doctor in the world.

You will also notice that Jesus' change of subject was chosen in order to keep the woman from getting away from the point. Sinners are experts at evading the real issue. We shall see still more of this in a moment. Suffice it to say for the present that evasion can be expected and must not silence Christian witnessing. Lives are at stake and eternal destinies are at issue.

Changing the subject to get away from the point (4:19-20)

4:19-20. The woman said to him, 'Sir, I perceive that you are a prophet. Our fathers worshipped on this mountain, and you Jews say that in Jerusalem is the place where one ought to worship.'

The woman reeled under the impact of Jesus' revelation. We can imagine her thoughts racing as she grasped for something to say. She rather weakly replied, **'Sir, I perceive that you are a prophet'** (4:19). Even if, as some have suggested, the language is reminiscent of the prophecy of the Messiah in Deuteronomy 18:15-18,[9] it is doubtful whether she meant any more than a simple acknowledgement of Jesus' apparent ability to read her life. In any event, she soon recovered any loss of composure, for she promptly changed the subject! She began to talk religion also, but not on Jesus' terms. She was uncomfortable with subjects like 'living water' and serial divorce and fornication, so she retreated into the broad and less personally threatening subject of denominational differences over worship. She talked about church: **'Our fathers worshipped on this mountain, and you Jews say that in Jerusalem is**

the place where one ought to worship' (4:20).
Carson suggests that the interpretation that she
changes the subject to divert Jesus' attention from
'the sin-question she finds so embarrassing' may be
'guilty of too greatly "psychologizing" the text'. His
alternative is to see her raising the Samaritan-Jewish
controversy 'as much to demonstrate her religious
awareness as to set the stranger a testing challenge'.[10] To that it may be said that Carson's view is
no less a 'psychologizing' of the text than the other, if
either view may rightly be so characterized. This is,
after all, a passage about a mind in turmoil, bobbing
and weaving to cope with the blows of Jesus' revelatory statements. Besides, the universal reason for
openly ungodly people trotting out their feeble and
unconvincing 'religious awareness' in the context of
moral and spiritual challenges is precisely their
desire to escape the searchlight of God's Word. The
woman was trying to fob Jesus off and it stretches
credulity to believe she had suddenly discovered a
detached interest in the difference between Jewish
and Samaritan worship.

Is this not typical, even today? How much easier it
is to discuss denominational differences, or the
number of members in the church, or when the choir
meets, or whatever! Anything that can be used as a
smokescreen to cover a determination to avoid facing
the real spiritual and practical issues of the gospel
and a serious personal faith-relationship to the Lord
is fair game. People will talk about anything but sin,
anything but personal faith, anything but the practice of truth, anything but the claims of Christ. And
how 'pious' it sounds to cover it all by 'talking
church'!

Saviour of the world
(John 4:21-29)

Our Lord was not to be denied by such a stratagem. Little did the woman know that she had handed him the opportunity for further serious teaching and personal challenge. He swiftly moved from her external chatter about places of worship — the 'denominational differences' between Mt Gerizim and Jerusalem — to focusing on the essential nature of true worship and its implications for her life. This is the defining moment in the conversation. Jesus seizes on the very point that she hoped would take the heat off her beleaguered conscience and invests it with the Word that is 'sharper than any two-edged sword, piercing even to the division of soul and spirit, and of joints and marrow, and is a discerner of the thoughts and intents of the heart' (Heb. 4:12), and this will lead to the healing of her soul and renewal of her life before the day is done.

Spiritual worship (4:21-24)

4:21-24. Jesus said to her, 'Woman, believe me, the hour is coming when you will neither on this mountain, nor in Jerusalem, worship the Father. You worship what you do not know; we know what we worship, for salvation is of the Jews. But the hour is coming, and now is, when the true worshippers will worship the Father in spirit and truth; for the Father is seeking such to worship him. God is Spirit, and those who worship him must worship in spirit and truth.'

She first had to understand that something *new* was about to happen. The days of worshipping the Father either on Mt Gerizim (**'this mountain'**) or Mt Zion (**'in Jerusalem'**) were fast drawing to a close (4:21). Old loyalties and prejudices needed to be reviewed in the light of what God was doing as **'the hour'** approached — that is, as the time of the promised Messiah dawned.

She also needed to grasp that **'Salvation is of the Jews.'** The Samaritans had all along worshipped what they did **'not know'**. They were a essentially a cult based on a perverted view of the Scriptures. The Jews, however, had truly been God's covenant people and had received his whole revealed will (Isa. 2:3; Micah 4:2). Consequently, Jesus could say, **'We know what we worship'** (4:22). She could therefore expect that the Messiah would come from the Jews and definitely not be the *Taheb* (or 'Restorer') of Samaritan lore.

Finally, she needed to realize that the *true worshippers* are those who **'worship the Father in spirit and truth'** (4:23-24). The emphasis that **'God is Spirit'** (not merely *a* spirit) indicates not only the non-material essence of true worship as a transaction of the soul, but points to the truth, later explicitly set out in the New Testament, that it is in the Spirit of God that we must worship. This would not be obvious to the woman, although she could well understand the notion of worship as a deeper, inward, spiritual exercise in communion with an incorporeal God. The inclusion of **'truth'** ensures that worship is not reduced to whatever feels right subjectively. Truth is the Word of God, and true worship is truth-driven, according to the regulative prescription of the Scriptures, received and obeyed with profound inward gratitude and joyous conviction.

Promised Saviour (4:25-26)

4:25-26. The woman said to him, 'I know that Messiah is coming' (who is called Christ). 'When he comes, he will tell us all things.'
Jesus said to her, 'I who speak to you am he.'

This seems to remind the woman about the promise of the Messiah (Deut. 18:15,18), although as yet she does not appear to see any connection between Jesus and the Messiah. She knew the **'Messiah [was] coming'** and expected that he would **'tell [them] all things'** (4:25). Calvin sees this as a three-part acknowledgement: firstly, that she accepted the imperfection of the Mosaic law and the superiority of the Messiah; secondly, that she expected Messiah to interpret the will of God to his people; and, thirdly, that she could therefore desire nothing higher than the Messiah's teaching.[11] This is all wonderful application to the way *we* ought to think, but it is most unlikely that she had it all so precisely and theologically in its place. It is more likely that was still trying to cope with the overwhelming revelations pouring over her mind and heart as she tried to understand this incredible Jewish stranger.

If her comment was, on her part, a hoped-for end to the conversation, Jesus' reply more than kept it alive by shining a brilliant beam of divine light on her soul. **'Jesus said to her, "I who speak to you am he"'** (4:26).[12] Here was an explicit self-disclosure of his being the Messiah! The promised Saviour was the man who had said so mysteriously that he could give her the 'living water'! Christ was nearer than she had known! This remains true in the experience of those

who come to him in faith today. Believing in him is
always a surprising discovery of free grace, unmerited, undeserved and unsought. There is something
very touching in the fact that before his trial Jesus
never revealed himself so clearly as the Messiah to
anyone else, with the exception of the man born
blind (9:37) — not even to John the Baptizer, and
certainly not to the Jews — as to this woman of
Samaria.

Saving faith (4:27-29)

4:27-29. And at this point his disciples came, and they
marvelled that he talked with a woman; yet no one said,
'What do you seek?' or, 'Why are you talking with her?'
    The woman then left her water-pot, went her way into the
city, and said to the men, 'Come, see a man who told me all
things that I ever did. Could this be the Christ?'

When the disciples arrived, they **'marvelled that he
talked with a woman'** — for reasons already stated
— although they did not dare to question Jesus
(4:27). The conversation thus interrupted, the woman
laid aside her water-pot and went off to the village,
where she shared her glorious confession: **'Come,
see a man who told me all things that I ever did.
Could this be the Christ?'** (4:29).
    She testified to *the way in which Jesus had re-
vealed his character to her.* He had knowledge of her
secrets. Her **'all things that I ever did'** voices, with
hyperbole, her conviction that what Jesus knew
about her marital and sexual shenanigans proved
there was nothing he could not know about her. She
saw that Jesus was no mere man, but one with the
attributes of divinity — in this case, omniscience.
    She testified to *Jesus' convicting her of sin.* The
scales fell from her eyes and she ceased to be defensive

about her messed-up life. She openly admitted the exposure of her sin, with all the relief of someone who has faced herself honestly before God for the first time. Conviction of sin is the end of the concealing of sin.

She testified to *Jesus as the Christ*. Her tentative-sounding **'Could this be the Christ?'** may express a hesitant apprehension that the man Jesus really is 'the Prophet' and Messiah (Christ) promised in the Scriptures, but it is wholly consonant with the drift of her confession to see it as a tactful way of approaching her fellow Samaritans with the idea. No one truly believes in Jesus Christ until he, or she, is persuaded in his own heart that Jesus is the Christ. Pointing people to Jesus is our task. Convincing them to trust in Christ is the work of the Holy Spirit in the heart.

She testified *with urgent excitement* to the prospect of coming to Jesus. She left her water-pot. She spoke to her neighbours. She wasted no time. She was a changed person, and that transformation showed in her enthusiasm for Jesus. That caught the interest of the people in Sychar, for they **'went out of the city and came to him'** (4:30).

She is a testimony for all time to *the power of God* to convict us of our sins and bring us with open faces to his mercy seat through Jesus Christ his Son. For many a lost soul, coming under the preaching of the gospel will mean that 'the secrets of his heart are revealed; and so, falling down on his face, he will worship' (1 Cor. 14:25). Then he will in his turn call others to 'Come, see a man who told me all things that I ever did.' He who had asked for a mere drink of water from the well had given her the 'living water' which would forever be 'springing up into everlasting life' in her heart and life.

12. Fields white for harvest

John 4:31-42

People in a hurry have no time to eat or drink. The woman of Samaria was so powerfully affected by all that Jesus had said to her that she completely forgot why she had come to the well. She left her water jar and rushed off to tell the villagers about the man who had told her 'all things' that she had ever done (4:28-29). She neither drew her water nor provided Jesus with the drink he had asked for at the beginning. Jesus, too, had become preoccupied with the conversation. He made no further mention of his request for a drink of water, and when his disciples arrived from Sychar and offered him something to eat, it is clear that he had other things on his mind. **'My food'**, he said, **'is to do the will of him who sent me, and to finish his work'** (4:34). Eating and drinking may be important, but they are not the be-all and end-all of life. We eat in order to do what is really important in life. Jesus is saying that eating and drinking illustrate something about his relation-ship — and ours — to the work of the kingdom of God. Our real food has to do with living for God. Our real food has to do with a heart for God, with the very meaning of our lives. We love the Lord and so it is our food and drink — our life itself — to keep his commandments. We say with the psalmist, 'I delight to do your will, O my God, and your law *is* within my heart' (Ps. 40:8).

And so, just as Jesus took the woman of Samaria from an ordinary drink of water to the gift of the living water of eternal life, he also took the disciples from the food they had just bought in the village to the spiritual food that filled his heart and life, and was to fill theirs too. The parallelism is quite deliberate. It emphasizes that the true realities in life are spiritual and concern our *personal relationship to God.* For the woman this was the need of new life in Christ. For the disciples, it is a deepening commitment to the ministry of the gospel of the kingdom of God.

At this point in the story, Jesus and the disciples are soon to be surrounded by Samaritans earnestly enquiring about Jesus and all that he had said to the woman. Jesus therefore wastes no time giving the disciples a crash course about their calling to proclaim his message of saving grace to a very needy world. What he tells them meshes perfectly with the conversion of the people of Sychar, so as to teach them the basics of the mission of the church of the New Testament era. Three major features of that mission are emphasized as the passage unfolds. These are: the church's motive — a desire to serve God (4:31-34); the church's mission — harvesting lost people for Christ (4:35); and the church's means of achieving this goal — sowing and reaping through faithful ministry (4:36-42).

Motive — desiring to serve God
(John 4:31-34)

4:31-34. In the meantime his disciples urged him, saying,
'Rabbi, eat.' But he said to them, 'I have food to eat of which
you do not know.'

Therefore the disciples said to one another, 'Has anyone
brought him anything to eat?' Jesus said to them, 'My food is
to do the will of him who sent me, and to finish his work.'

Jesus is speaking here specifically of his own earthly
ministry, most of which was yet in the future. Yet,
from what follows in 4:35-38, it is clear that what he
says about himself also applies to the church as she
follows him.

His food

We have already noted that the disciples urged him
to have a bite to eat, only to have him decline the
offer out of an obvious preoccupation with the subject of his conversation with the woman of Samaria.
'I have food to eat of which you do not know,' he
says. When he sees that they are completely baffled
by this, since he had no literal food that they knew
of, he further explains, **'My food is to do the will of
him who sent me, and to finish his work'**
(4:31-34). What does he mean by this? Just that his
mission is that of the Messiah promised in the
Scriptures and that he is so absorbed with this task

that it can be called his 'food'. D. A. Carson sees here
an echo of Deuteronomy 8:3, which teaches that
'Man shall not live by bread alone; but man lives by
every word that proceeds from the mouth of the
LORD.'[1] The will of God is of the essence. It is why he
came. It is vital to him. It is his food. There is a
twofold aspect to this.

First of all, *Jesus was committed to doing the will
of his Father* (see also 5:36; 6:38; 9:3-4; 10:25,32-38;
14:10; 17:4). In his 'human and mediatorial capacity', observes Simeon, Jesus 'was the Father's servant'.[2] The same writer notes that Jesus 'was filled
with joy at the least prospect of success, 4:35, and he
grieved and wept when he could not succeed, Mark
3:5, Luke 19:41'.[3] His Father's will was his winning
post and the consuming motive for running the
course. The unwavering motto of his humanity was
'Not my will, but yours, be done' (Luke 22:42).

Secondly, *Jesus was determined to finish the work
he had been given to do.* 'I have a baptism to be
baptized with', he said in prospect of his death, 'and
how distressed I am till it is accomplished!' (Luke
12:50). The cross was the finish of his work of *accomplishing* salvation (19:30) and that is what is in
view here, but it should not be forgotten that Christ
continues in the work of the *application* of redemption in his mediatorial rule and heavenly intercession
until that day 'when he delivers the kingdom to God
the Father, when he puts an end to all rule and all
authority and power' (1 Cor. 15:24).

Jesus was absorbed in his mission as the Messiah. Like food, it was so vital to him that he could
not do without it. A deep and abiding inner compulsion flowing from the eternal decree of God bound
him lovingly and unswervingly to his redeeming
work.

Our calling

Christ is, of course, unique in his person and work, but, in our very imperfect way, our calling is to mirror him in our discipleship. 'God, indeed', writes R. C. H. Lenski, 'gives us spiritual life and powers in order to serve Him.'[4] Surely our food ought also to be the doing of our heavenly Father's will and the completion of the work he has given us to do. John Calvin, as usual, has an intriguing comment. He says that we must not 'lose the causes of life on account of life itself'.[5] What the Reformer means is that *the purpose of living is more than merely keeping alive.* The Lord is the strength of our life (Ps. 27:1). Living for him is to be our food. And that may sometimes mean missing our meals because we have a pressing opportunity to serve the Lord — perhaps in talking to someone about the gospel, or helping someone out in a material way. We may even be called to face death for Christ! The point is that the purpose of life is more than living till you die. We may eat to live, but we must not live to eat! The Lord's will must be our consuming passion. And his will is the furtherance of the gospel in the world, as the succeeding verses amply demonstrate. What, then, is your first concern in life? Is it to serve God and win a world for Christ? Professing Christians, is your 'food' to do the will of the Lord who bought you?

Mission — harvesting lost people for Christ (John 4:35)

4:35. 'Do you not say, "There are still four months and then comes the harvest"? Behold, I say to you, lift up your eyes and look at the fields, for they are already white for harvest!'

Jesus frequently speaks of the church's mission as a 'harvest'. On one occasion, he looked on the crowds and, seeing them as 'sheep having no shepherd', he told his disciples, 'The harvest truly is plentiful, but the labourers are few. Therefore pray the Lord of the harvest to send out labourers into his harvest' (Matt. 9:36-38). Then there is the parable of the sower, in which the true converts are called 'the ones sown on the good ground, those who hear the word, accept it, and bear fruit: some thirty-fold, some sixty, and some a hundred' (Mark 4:20).

The harvest was in the middle of April, so, with **'four months'** to go, it would have been December and the crops, planted in November, would only have been showing a short green growth above the soil. But Jesus says, 'The harvest is *now!*' The inclusion of 'already' (ἤδη / *ede*) in reference to the harvest is redundant to the support of this point and, more properly belongs with 4:36, of which it is really the first word.

The **'fields'** Jesus wanted them to look at were **'white for harvest'**. What fields? What does he mean? Clearly, he is referring to the approaching people from Sychar. They are the 'field'. They are the harvest to be reaped! He means that the present generation will quickly be lost, unless they are savingly reached through the faithful preaching of the gospel by the church of Jesus Christ. The harvest-time of souls is the lifetime of each and every generation. Just as the pale yellow fields tell the farmer to reap, or the grain will rot where it stands, so the very presence of men and women who must soon die and go to eternity must spur the church to reap before they perish. 'The harvest of souls', said Robert L. Dabney, 'awaits no man's sluggishness. Death is afield with his flashing scythe mowing down the nations and gathering his sheaves for hell-fire; so that the work of redeeming love must be done at once, or never. In this is the point of our Saviour's reasoning. This is obviously true of each generation of sinners as to its own generation of Christian labourers, on the supposition that the world is indeed subject to condemnation.'[6]

We do not need to get bogged down in unprofitable discussions on the fate of the 'unreached' heathen, or the ability of God to save sinners who never heard the gospel. God will do all things well. He is sovereign and not one of his elect will be plucked out of his hand. The Bible, however, offers not the slightest comfort to the devotees of either the non-Christian religions of the world or the 'churchianity' of the pseudo-Christian West! The Scriptures are clear that, for all practical purposes, there is one great fact facing all who do not hear the gospel, or who, having heard, do not believe in Christ as the only Saviour of sinners — and that fact is a lost eternity away from the face of God! The church must reap, or the people will die. Reap, or the world perishes! Hence the urgency of the apostle Paul in writing to the Roman Christians: 'For there is no distinction between Jew and Greek, for the same Lord over all is rich to all who call upon him. For, "Whoever calls on the name of the LORD shall be saved." How then shall they call on him in whom they have not believed? And how shall they believe in him of whom they have not heard? And how shall they hear without a preacher? And how shall they preach unless they are sent? As it is written: "How beautiful are the feet of those who preach the gospel of peace, who bring glad tidings of good things!"' (Rom. 10:12-15; quoting Joel 2:32, Isa. 52:7; Nahum 1:15).

Means — sowing and reaping the gospel (John 4:36-42)

4:36-42. 'And he who reaps receives wages, and gathers fruit for eternal life, that both he who sows and he who reaps may rejoice together. For in this the saying is true: "One sows and another reaps." I sent you to reap that for which you have not laboured; others have laboured, and you have entered into their labours.'

And many of the Samaritans of that city believed in him because of the word of the woman who testified, 'He told me all that I ever did.'

So when the Samaritans had come to him, they urged him to stay with them; and he stayed there two days. And many more believed because of his own word. Then they said to the woman, 'Now we believe, not because of what you said, for we ourselves have heard him and we know that this is indeed the Christ, the Saviour of the world.'

The means by which the harvesting of lost people will be accomplished is the faithful sowing and reaping of the gospel by the church of Jesus Christ in every generation. The gist of Jesus' argument is that we are to be diligent in the work of God's kingdom. It will be done, but we must do it. The God who has sovereignly decreed the end has also appointed the means. 'You did not choose me,' says Jesus years later, 'but I chose you and appointed you that you should go and bear fruit, and that your fruit should remain' (15:16).

Your reward is 'fruit for eternal life' (4:36a)

We must understand what is at stake here. It is the gathering of a people to be God's people — **'fruit for eternal life'**. Indeed, this was already happening. When, as already noted, the last word of 4:35 is given its more probable place as the first word of 4:36, that verse reads: **'[Already] he who reaps receives wages, and gathers fruit for eternal life.'**[7] Lives were being changed. The woman and the approaching Samaritans were the visible evidence. This work is still in progress.

You are part of a team effort (4:36b-38)

Jesus did not, however, want his followers to be puffed up. The work of the church is a team effort. One man 'reaps' — that is, he is the instrument of someone's conversion to Christ and actually sees that person's entrance into eternal life — while another sows the seed of the Word. Both **'he who sows and he who reaps'**, will **'rejoice together'** in the common fruit of their several labours (4:36). This is confirmed by two major encouragements.

The first is that *sowing and reaping are complementary tasks*. The proverb, **'One sows and another reaps,'** does not glumly suggest that the reapers get all the glory, but that, whoever does what, they are fulfilling God's plan to complete his work of redemption. Therefore, we have no cause to be discouraged because we have not seen the results we hoped for. If we do see success, then we should humbly thank God for those who sowed and watered the seed for Christ before we ever came on the scene.

The second encouragement arises from *their own calling*. Jesus was sending the disciples to enter into the labours of others (4:38). This most probably refers to the ministry of John the Baptizer, who had preceded them in Samaria (3:23). Indeed, Andrew and the author of this Gospel were themselves fruit reaped by Jesus after it had been sown by John (1:37).

You can see people already coming to Christ (4:39-42)

The greatest encouragement of all is always the sight of people coming to Christ. The testimony of the woman had persuaded **'many'**, and they **'believed in him'** (4:39). What reality or depth was there to this new-found faith? With Charles Simeon, we surely 'cannot regard this faith in any other light than as a speculative assent, grounded upon human testimony'.[8] There is a difference between being impressed by Jesus' ability to read the secrets of a stranger's life and trusting him from your heart as your Saviour. Saving faith in Christ is more than warm curiosity and a desire to meet the great man.

In any event, whatever might have been lacking in their faith was supplied in the two days Jesus stayed in Sychar. It did no disservice to the woman's testimony for them to tell her, **'Now we believe, not because of what you said, for we ourselves have heard him and we know that this is indeed the Christ, the Saviour of the world'** (4:42). They now knew Jesus with respect to his purpose in coming into the world. The Samaritans confessed that 'Salvation is of the Jews' (4:22). Jesus' death on the cross was yet in the future, as was the outpouring of the Holy Spirit at the Pentecost that followed. Nevertheless, they received him with a saving faith and declared him to be the 'Saviour of the world'.

A double challenge

The conversion of the Samaritans of Sychar offers us a double challenge. The primary challenge is a call for us to reflect on *our own relationship to Jesus Christ*. Is your faith second-hand — less than personal, more habit than conviction, a nod towards the Lord, but nothing that really moves and motivates you? Do you *know* Christ as *your* Saviour? Have you acknowledged your sins and your lost condition and *fled* to Christ for mercy, forgiveness and new life?

The second challenge concerns *the church's calling to sow and reap for Christ* in a lost and perishing world. Are you gripped by a sense of the need of lost people? Do you pray for them? Do you seek to reach them for Christ? The fields really are white for harvest; they always are. Every generation is there to be harvested. Where I live in Pennsylvania, white-tail deer abound and the 'deer season' in late November sees 1.2 million hunters — 10% of the entire population of the state — take to the woods to bag their quota for both trophy wall and table. This happens every year. Every year there is a harvest and these have been increasing (the white-tails double their numbers in a season). Jesus has made his disciples 'fishers of men' — harvesters of a dying race that will multiply in number and will be lost if we do not reap. And the Lord's promise is that we *shall* reap, if we do not faint (Gal. 6:9).

> Though bearing forth the precious seed
> The reaper sowing grieves,
> He doubtless shall return again
> And bring with joy his sheaves.[9]

13. Prophet without honour

John 4:43 – 5:18

One day in 1956, we eleven-year-olds were shunted into the school hall and shown a film about the evils of smoking and the danger of lung cancer. Blackened lungs and dire predictions of failing health paraded past our eyes and ears for half an hour. We duly returned to our classes, at once fascinated by the miseries that come upon human beings and convinced that it wouldn't happen to us, even if we did smoke cigarettes! Apart from one or two sensitive souls, most of us thought that lungs that looked like kippers were a great laugh!

Why does hard evidence of the terrible consequences of foolish behaviour make so little impression on most of us? Reflect, for instance, on the devotion of our secular age to the proposition that the solution to crime, poverty, AIDS, and all the ills of society, lies in 'better education'. Of course, ignorance is not the answer to anything, but the problem is that even the best of education has proved to have severe limitations when it comes to changing people's attitudes and behaviour. It is obvious that the facts — evidence, truth, call it what you like — bounce off the surface of minds that are bent on having things their own way. So the prisons continue to overflow, the toll from AIDS mounts and smoking remains the primary cause of lung cancer and heart disease!

Christians, too, can get caught up in this idea that a few good facts are all we need to build a better world. Some think that if you scientifically prove that miracles could, or did, happen, many more people would become Christians. It has even been suggested that if we could only find the remains of Noah's ark on Mt Ararat, people would believe the Bible and come to faith in Christ. 'Evidence' would persuade! That is the underlying assumption. In this view, our only real problem, then, is marshalling the facts and presenting them effectively to the watching world.

Background to rejection
(John 4:43-45)

4:43-45. Now after the two days he departed from there and went to Galilee. For Jesus himself testified that a prophet has no honour in his own country.

So when he came to Galilee, the Galileans received him, having seen all the things he did in Jerusalem at the feast; for they also had gone to the feast.

The realities of human nature, however, paint a somewhat different picture. The principle was stated by our Lord in his parable of the rich man and Lazarus. You will recall that the rich man, in hell, wanted someone to go and warn his five brothers, so that they might escape his 'place of torment'. Abraham's answer was: 'They have Moses and the prophets; let them hear them... If they do not hear Moses and the prophets, neither will they be persuaded though one rise from the dead' (Luke 16:29,31). There was evidence and to spare, but it was insufficient by itself to overthrow the commitment of hearts that were not inclined to accept it. The problem of a hostile disposition to the truth (i.e., presuppositions) is not vanquished by mere facts, or even miraculous signs and wonders (i.e., evidence).

Nothing exhibits this truth more vividly than the way some people responded to the miracles that Jesus performed before their very eyes. After two days in Samaria, Jesus returned to Cana, in Galilee, where he had performed his first recorded 'sign' —

that of changing the water into wine (4:43,46; 2:1-12).

John notes, in connection with this, that **'Jesus himself testified that a prophet has no honour in his own country'** (4:44). This has attracted some attention from the commentators,[1] because the expected dishonour is not immediately obvious in the statement immediately following: **'So when he came to Galilee, the Galileans received him, having seen all the things he did in Jerusalem at the feast; for they also had gone to the feast'** (4:45). If Jesus' 'own country' was Galilee, and a prophet has 'no honour' there, then why was he 'received' on this occasion? How do these two verses square with one another?

The best answer in this case is also the simplest. For three reasons, we can conclude that what actually happened in Galilee proved Jesus' prediction to the letter.

First of all, although Jesus was welcomed, it does not mean that he was either believed or held in great honour. The word 'received' *(endexanto)* carries no more than the implication that the Galileans were cordial and had their interest roused by what Jesus had done in Jerusalem.

Secondly, when the passage is read as John meant it to be read — as a flowing narrative of Jesus' 'signs' together with the people's response to them — it is clear that the generality of the inhabitants of both Galilee and Judea never really honoured him (cf. 4:48; 5:10,16,18,40-41,47).

Finally, the other three passages that record this proverb all refer to Jesus' rejection in Galilee (Matt. 13:57; Mark 6:4; Luke 4:24). Galilee certainly qualifies as 'home territory' for Jesus. It is every bit as clear, however, that Judea held the same role in Jesus' life and ministry.

A straightforward reading of the *whole* narrative reveals, with brilliant dramatic development, how Jesus' first welcome in Galilee soon degenerated into lack of comprehension (4:48) and how, in Judea, it issued in widespread rejection (5:18). This is in fact the key to understanding what was going on in Jesus' ministry at this juncture. The theme is unfolded from his observation in 4:44 that a prophet has no honour in his own country, to his declaration in 5:34-40 that he receives no honour from men, as evidenced by their unwillingness to come to him that they might have life.

A boy healed in Capernaum
(John 4:46-54)

4:46-54. So Jesus came again to Cana of Galilee where he had made the water wine.

And there was a certain nobleman whose son was sick at Capernaum. When he heard that Jesus had come out of Judea into Galilee, he went to him and implored him to come down and heal his son, for he was at the point of death.

Then Jesus said to him, 'Unless you people see signs and wonders, you will by no means believe.'

The nobleman said to him, 'Sir, come down before my child dies!'

Jesus said to him, 'Go your way; your son lives.'

So the man believed the word that Jesus spoke to him, and he went his way. And as he was now going down, his servants met him and told him, saying, 'Your son lives!'

Then he enquired of them the hour when he got better. And they said to him, 'Yesterday at the seventh hour the fever left him.' So the father knew that it was at the same hour in which Jesus said to him, 'Your son lives.' And he himself believed, and his whole household.

This again is the second sign Jesus did when he had come out of Judea into Galilee.

The healing of the dying boy in Capernaum, and when Jesus was at a distance in Cana, is the second of Jesus' 'signs' recorded in John, the first being the water-to-wine miracle at Cana itself. The boy's father was a *basilikos* — an official of the king *(basileus)*, in this case Herod Antipas. Having heard of his miracles, he sought Jesus out and **'implored him to come down and heal his son, for he was at the point of death'** (4:47). The subsequent exchange between Jesus and this man further develops the tension hinted at in 4:44-45.

Jesus did not specifically answer the man, even if his words were clearly meant to be a challenge to his faith. He first commented on the general attitudes of the people to his ministry: **'Unless you people see signs and wonders, you will by no means believe'** (4:48). The word 'people' is inserted by the translators to make clear that the 'you' is a plural, so there was no churlish or grudging tone here, as when we might say, with a groan, 'You people...!' to those whom we regard as unappreciative of all we have been doing for them. Jesus was simply inviting all who were present to engage in some solemn reflection on their prevailing attitude to his miracles. In general, they 'looked for the spectacular, and were linked to him only by a love of the sensational'.[2] Jesus was probing their consciences and gently rebuking their shallowness.

The father was not put off. He begged Jesus to go with him to Capernaum before it was too late. Jesus assured him that the child would live, and he **'believed the word that Jesus spoke to him, and he went his way'** (4:49-50). Subsequent events confirmed that the lad was healed at the very time Jesus had spoken these words. As a result, not only the father **'himself believed'**, but also **'his whole household'** (4:51-54). They thereby joined the minority of Jews who honoured Jesus in his own country. We should not miss the healing behind the healing. The nobleman first believed 'the word' that Jesus told him about his son's recovery, but only subsequently believed 'himself' — that is, in his heart, that Jesus was really the promised Messiah, heralded by John and attested by the miracles he performed. The contrast between this family's faith and the general attitude of the majority underscores the truth of the proverb to which Jesus had earlier testified (4:44). It also offers an encouragement to those who love the Lord, for, as Matthew Henry observes, 'Somewhere or other Christ will find a welcome. People may if they please shut the sun out of their own houses, but they cannot shut it out of the world.'[3]

A man healed at the Pool of Bethesda (John 5:1-15)

The healing of the blind man in Jerusalem is the third of the 'signs' performed by Jesus as recorded by John. Some time after the healing of the nobleman's son in Galilee, Jesus went to Jerusalem for some unspecified **'feast of the Jews'**.

The Bethesda phenomenon (5:2-4)

5:1-4. After this there was a feast of the Jews, and Jesus went up to Jerusalem.

Now there is in Jerusalem by the Sheep Gate a pool, which is called in Hebrew, Bethesda, having five porches. In these lay a great multitude of sick people, blind, lame, paralysed, waiting for the moving of the water. For an angel went down at a certain time into the pool and stirred up the water; then whoever stepped in first, after the stirring of the water, was made well of whatever disease he had.

At the pool called 'Bethesda' (meaning 'house of out-pouring*'), it was customary for sick people to gather in anticipation of a miraculous healing effected, they thought, by an angel. The question here is as to whether this is an account of genuine divine and angelic activity, or merely the popular view of the time as to what was happening at the pool. Most commentators regard these verses as having been imported into the text over a period of time by overzealous copyists and see them as representing the popular view. The manuscript evidence certainly is very mixed.[5]

The real issue remains as to whether the text (i.e., 5:3b-4, as in the NKJV) should be read as a history of what *God* was doing at Bethesda, or as an account of what *people* mistakenly attributed to him. That the latter would seem to be the case is confirmed by the fact that Jesus' healing of the man took place apart from the water of the pool. Jesus' true miracle exposed the Bethesda phenomenon for what it was — a grotesque lottery that offered bogus healing to the first and fastest into the water, and so perennially preyed on the desperation of the chronically ill. The parallels with the expectations of healing fostered in the unfortunate clients of modern so-called 'healing ministries' are not too difficult to discern. As Bethesda was in Jesus' day, these are pools that today become parched ground (cf. Isa. 35:7).[6]

A real miracle (5:5-9a)

5:5-9. Now a certain man was there who had an infirmity thirty-eight years. When Jesus saw him lying there, and knew that he already had been in that condition a long time, he said to him, 'Do you want to be made well?'

The sick man answered him, 'Sir, I have no man to put me into the pool when the water is stirred up; but while I am coming, another steps down before me.'

Jesus said to him, 'Rise, take up your bed and walk.' And immediately the man was made well, took up his bed, and walked.

Jesus singled out a man who, having suffered an infirmity for thirty-eight years, believed that he had missed being healed only because he was too slow in getting to the water. Having enquired as to his desire to get well, and having elicited from him a public testimony to the facts of his case, Jesus told him to take up his bed and walk, whereupon **'The man was made well, took up his bed, and walked'** (5:9). This was a real miracle and, as such, was a massive attestation of Jesus' person and mission, of his compassion and power to heal, all sealed by the proof of the man's obedient response in taking up his bed and walking away from the dead-end hoax of the Bethesda phenomenon. The miracle certainly attests and encapsulates the very essence of gospel grace. It was sovereignly given, it was attended by the exercise of faith on the part of the recipient and it issued in a radically new life for him.

There is no reason to speculate about some supposedly hidden symbolism in this event. Some draw parallels between the man's thirty-eight years of illness and Israel's thirty-eight years of wandering in the wilderness of Sinai (Deut. 2:14). Others view the man as symbolic of the state of the Jews at that time. Still others regard the Pool of Bethesda as a picture of the impotence of the law as a means of salvation.[7] John simply records the essential facts, and these prepare us for the account of what followed, the heart of which is the deep-seated opposition of the Jewish leadership to Jesus and his message of the gospel of the kingdom of God.

The legalists object (5:9b-15)

5:9-15. ... And that day was the Sabbath. The Jews therefore said to him who was cured, 'It is the Sabbath; it is not lawful for you to carry your bed.' He answered them, 'He who made me well said to me, "Take up your bed and walk."'

Then they asked him, 'Who is the man who said to you, "Take up your bed and walk"?' But the one who was healed

did not know who it was, for Jesus had withdrawn, a multitude being in that place.

Afterward Jesus found him in the temple, and said to him,
'See, you have been made well. Sin no more, lest a worse
thing come upon you.'

The man departed and told the Jews that it was Jesus
who had made him well.

Many Christians assume that 'signs and wonders',
whether charismatic healings, prophecies and
strange tongues, or Roman Catholic relics or appearances of the Virgin Mary, will somehow produce more
followers for Jesus. Why they imagine this to be a
biblical expectation is by no means clear, because
from the Bible's record of Jesus' performance of *real*
signs and wonders, it is clear that he definitely
garnered more opposition than anything else. At first,
people clamoured for more miracles, but the more
miracles he did, the more they turned against him!
Why was this so? The answer is that the more Jesus
revealed of *himself* — and the miracles were dramatic
supernatural attestations of his *authority* — the more
he challenged the deeper convictions of his hearers.
He went beyond their fascination with the amazing
and inexplicable and reached into their souls, confronting them with the claims of his truth. Many of
them did not like that. As long as people could treat
Jesus' ministry as a kind of do-gooder's show-time,
they gathered in their thousands. As soon as their
consciences were challenged and they were made to
feel uncomfortable about their fundamental life-
commitments and their sins, they began to back
away from him.

1. A reproach vented (5:10)

The miracle took place on **'the Sabbath'**. Whatever
joy and amazement they may have felt at the cripple's

return to health, **'the Jews'** wasted no time in informing him, **'It is not lawful for you to carry your bed.'** Nothing could more clearly demonstrate the bondage of the legalist mind-set than this juxtaposition of a cripple healed after almost four decades and his contravention of an extra-biblical rabbinical rule.[8] They should have been praising God and acknowledging Jesus as the promised Messiah, but their consuming passion was to maintain a standard of behaviour that God had never required, and all on the false presupposition that they had authority to apply the Sabbath principle in ways of their own devising. In fact, the Scripture prohibition on carrying burdens on the Sabbath was related to doing so for commercial gain (Jer. 17:19-27; Neh. 13:15). It was not inconsistent with the sanctity of the Sabbath (Exod. 20:10), as defined by Scripture, for the man to take his bed home with him.

You see the same kind of thing today in churches that make rules about things like skirt length, teetotalism and owning television sets. The legalist's eye is always, in football parlance, 'off the ball'. The rule is the thing, and any conception of grace is completely overwhelmed by concern for the punctilios of invented righteousness. When we begin with the idea that what God has *said* is not enough, and persuade ourselves we must develop additional rules and regulations of our own, it is a short step to becoming incapable of seeing what God is doing when he pours out his love and his grace under our very noses! Jesus healed the man from a life of misery, and all they could think of was their outrage that he was carrying his bed on the Sabbath!

2. A response expressed (5:11-13,15)

The man's reply is wonderfully fresh and down to earth: **'He who made me well said to me, "Take up**

your bed and walk" ' (5:11). It is as if he says, 'Give
me a break! A man who can heal me can surely tell
me what to do!' The cripple understood the real
issue. He did not yet know Jesus' name (5:12-13),
but he understood the implication of the miracle,
namely, that this was a man with special authority
from God. In due course, he found out who Jesus
was and told the Jews, thereby inadvertently trig-
gering the plot against his life (5:15). D. A. Carson
sees this as the man merely 'blaming' Jesus for his
bed-carrying, and regards his later going to them to
tell them Jesus' name as an attempt at 'ingratiating
himself with them'.[9] This is a dark view of evidence
that, more persuasively, suggests the man's elation
with his new freedom and his joy in the one who
healed him. He saw Jesus do in a moment what
neither the legalists nor the Bethesda waters had
achieved in almost forty years. Why should he be
impressed by the legalistic carping of the powerless
proponents of Phariseeism?

3. A responsibility enjoined (5:14)

Jesus' healing miracles were never ends in themselves, as if health was everything in life. Jesus
sought the man out and enjoined him, **'Sin no more,
lest a worse thing come upon you.'** In harmony
with Jesus' teaching in John 9:3 and Luke 13:1-5,
this should be taken as a call to believe and repent,
and so escape, in time and eternity, the righteous
judgement of God, rather than as connecting the
man's particular condition with some specific sin
committed thirty-eight years before. It is certainly
and universally true that going on sinning will issue
in worse things happening in our lives. It is also true
that specific sins can have specific and tragic consequences (1 Cor. 11:28-32). There are, however, worse
things even than being crippled for a lifetime. There

is a lost eternity ahead for the unrepentant! 'Sin no more' does not merely mean, 'Be good,' or 'Do some good deeds,' or 'Give up one particularly heinous sin.' It is not a call for 'goodness' in an abstract external sense. It is a call for comprehensive reformation, from the heart, in terms of a new relationship to the Lord.

The plot to kill Jesus
(John 5:16-18)

5:16-18. For this reason the Jews persecuted Jesus, and sought to kill him, because he had done these things on the Sabbath. But Jesus answered them, 'My Father has been working until now, and I have been working.' Therefore the Jews sought all the more to kill him, because he not only broke the Sabbath, but also said that God was his Father, making himself equal with God.

Having discovered Jesus' identity, **'The Jews persecuted Jesus, and sought to kill him.'** This marks a transition as startling as any in Scripture. From Jesus' act of supreme kindness (5:15), we are taken directly to the Jews' decision to put him to death! (5:16). This at first seems rather overstated. Did they really mean to *kill* him? What follows makes plain the reasons for this hardening of opposition to Jesus and his ministry.

Charge one: Sabbath-breaking (5:16)

The first charge was that **'He had done these things on the Sabbath'** (5:16; cf. Mark 2:23-28; Luke 13:10-17; 14:1-6). Jesus had not carried any beds on the Sabbath, but as the one who told the man to do so, he incurred the legalists' displeasure. This was, however, no more than a pretext, for such a relatively trivial infringement of a rabbinical punctilio does not

remotely justify their lethal intentions. There had to
be a deeper layer of resentment behind their huffing
and puffing over a bed!

The only intelligible explanation is that they had
concluded that Jesus was a fundamental threat to
their Pharisaic religion and way of life, and that he
therefore had to be nipped in the bud. Three centuries ago, George Hutcheson pinpointed the issue
when he observed that 'Sound doctrine meets oft-
times with corrupt hearers, who are more enraged
thereby... The rising and spreading of Christ's glory is
an eyesore to corrupt teachers and people, who are
thereby discovered to be what indeed they are, and
their seeming glory obscured; and persecution is the
ordinary entertainment that Christ, manifesting his
glory, may look for at the hand of such; for "therefore", upon the report, "did the Jews persecute Jesus",
by their reproachful tongues, and devising how to
take his life, either in a tumult or judicially.'[10]

Many faithful followers of Jesus Christ have been
on the receiving end of the same treatment that their
Master faced before them. And, always, the persecution is justified by trumped-up charges that are
no better than a smokescreen to hide the accusers'
hatred for the truth of God.

Charge two: blasphemy (5:17-18)

How, or in what context, Jesus answered the Jews is
not clear. What he says has the air of an official
communiqué, conveyed through an intermediary
rather than face to face on the street. It is a stunning
reply, which could only have sent shock waves
through the Pharisaic community: **'My Father has
been working until now, and I have been working'**
(5:17).

The *major premise* is that, notwithstanding God's Sabbath rest from the work of the six days of creation week, God is still at work in his creation. This was disputed by no one, and was an important and necessary distinction, with the obvious implication that the cessation of *all* that can be called 'work' is not the point of the law of Sabbath. Rather, the Sabbath was a rest from specific labours that would otherwise obtrude upon a focused attention to the worship and the glory of God. Jesus' healing of the man on the Sabbath was not the kind of work that was inconsistent with either the principle or the practical goal of worshipping God. It was the work of God, and therefore invulnerable to divine censure. We would properly say the same for our caring for the sick on the Sabbath today. 'The Sabbath was made for man, and not man for the Sabbath,' Jesus pointed out on another occasion (Mark 2:27).

The *minor premise* is: 'I [Jesus] am doing the kind of work now that the Father has been doing all along.' In other words, Jesus' defence is not couched in terms of the ethics of Sabbath-keeping as such, but is rooted in the uniqueness of his relationship to his Father. His argument is: 'My Father works all the time (which you all agree is true), and I have been working too.' Hutcheson completely misses the point when he comments that Christ was not subject to the law and could command the man to carry his bed.[11] Jesus was always consistent with his own law, and did not break or modify the Sabbath law here or anywhere else. What he did do, however, was to expose the Jews' erroneous accretions to the law, and bring out its true scope and spiritual focus — and what he did in fact brought honour and glory to God.

The *conclusion* is as obvious as it is unstated. The one who stands in 'the closest possible relationship' to his Father God can only be engaged in the same

'work of preservation and redemption'.[12] The implications of this were not lost on the Jews, for they
**'sought all the more to kill him, because he not
only broke the Sabbath, but also said that God
was his Father, making himself equal with God'**
(5:18). He claimed deity for himself and was, therefore, in their reckoning, a blasphemer of the first
rank. They correctly perceived that in claiming God
as his Father, Jesus was claiming equality with God.
Sonship does not imply any essential inferiority, even
if it required a certain submission to paternal
authority for a season. This is true even in our
earthly father-son relationships. How much more
must it be true of the heavenly Father and his eternal
Son?

The precise relationship of Jesus to the Father is
set out in 5:19-47, and will be examined in our next
study. Suffice it to say at this point that what made
for Jesus' being so quickly rendered a 'prophet' with
'no honour in his own country' was the accurate
perception on the part of the Jewish leadership that
he claimed to be the divine Son of the God of Israel.
Far from being persuaded by Jesus' miracles to
receive him for who he really was, the Jews recoiled
with all the hardened determination of people resolved to deny their clear implications. The same
people who had seen the impossible happen — water
changed to wine, a dying boy healed, and a lifelong
cripple made to walk again — refused to acknowledge
that the hand of God was in these events, and dismissed their author as a blasphemer worthy only of
death.

Why was Jesus a prophet without honour to his
own people? Why is it that the clearer and more
winsome the presentation of the gospel message is,
the more fierce the opposition that the Lord's people
have to face? Matthew Henry pinpoints the problem:
'Those that will not be enlightened by the word of

Christ will be enraged and exasperated by it, and nothing more vexes the enemies of Christ than his asserting his authority.'[13] Authority is the issue! The psalmist had prophesied the rejection of the Messiah centuries earlier:

Why do the nations rage,
And the people plot a vain thing?
The kings of the earth set themselves,
And the rulers take counsel together,
Against the LORD and against his Anointed,
    saying,
'Let us break their bonds in pieces
And cast away their cords from us'

(Ps. 2:1-3).

This was to be the issue when Pilate surrendered Jesus to the judgement of the chief priests. 'Pilate said to them, "Shall I crucify your King?" The chief priests answered, "We have no king but Caesar!"' (19:15). It remains the issue for everyone who is confronted with the claims of Jesus Christ, and the same psalmist who recorded the rejection of our Lord holds out the way of life — and the way of death:

Kiss the Son, lest he be angry,
And you perish in the way,
When his wrath is kindled but a little.
Blessed are all those who put their trust in him
(Ps. 2:12).

14. Jesus and the Father

John 5:19-47

It was not for lack of evidence that Jesus' claims were roundly rejected by the Jews. Scripture itself and Jesus' teaching and miracles all attested to his Messiahship. Yet, the more the Lord said and did, the more the opposition to him stiffened, and the closer drew the final crisis that would nail him to the cross. It all illustrates the power of the presuppositions and predispositions of the unregenerate human heart to overthrow the most satisfactory levels of proof.[1] Modern psychological parlance calls this 'denial'. It is as common as dirt in everyday human life. People will look the facts in the face and say, with a straight face, 'I just don't see things the way you do!' The facts become matters of opinion, wrong is redefined as right and the ultimate appeal is made to what is true 'for me'.

In a world of such studied subjectivism and relentless commitment to the invisibility of plain evidence, the tendency of the Christian is often to give up the active promotion of biblical truth and assume a passive stance — being ready to give 'a reason for the hope that is in you' (1 Peter 3:15), but only if backed against the wall! Well, the fact that his hearers were predisposed to reject the evidence did not prevent our Lord from telling people who he was and what he had come to do. His ministry on earth saw a progressive unfolding of his person and work as the promised Messiah. In the face of rising opposition, he revealed more of himself and his claims. He challenged consciences and rebuked pride. He commanded repentance and offered consolation. He uttered sentences of the most condign punishment upon the unbelieving, and proclaimed the kingdom of heaven for all who would follow him in heartfelt discipleship.

After the setback of being rejected over the healing of the man at the Pool of Bethesda, Jesus did not retreat from the scene, but addressed himself to the charge of blasphemy brought against him by certain Jews. He set out an account of his relationship to his Father and his relationship to lost humanity itself, at once vindicating his earlier defence of healing on the Sabbath day and issuing a ringing denunciation of the unbelief of his accusers, together with a call to come to him in faith so as to enter into everlasting life.

Jesus and the Father
(John 5:19-30)

It is not clear as to how, or in what context, Jesus answered the critics. His statement has the ringing tones of a public declamation. He still moved about in public, and taught the people who attended his ministry, and the fact that others plotted to kill him did not inhibit him from doing so, even to the last week of his life. Whatever the chosen means of delivering his response, his first concern was to make clear his relationship to God, his Father.

Jesus is one with the Father

5:19. Then Jesus answered and said to them, 'Most assuredly, I say to you, the Son can do nothing of himself, but what he sees the Father do; for whatever he does, the Son also does in like manner.'

Jesus' reply begins with an even stronger statement than that reported before. Not only does Jesus continue to do his work on the Sabbath, as does God the Father (15:17), but he also works in imitation of the Father and in the exercise of the Father's power. Calvin catches the significance of this when he notes that 'The Jews beheld him [Jesus] in nothing higher than human nature, and, therefore, he argues that, when he cured the diseased man, he did it not by human power, but by Divine power which was concealed under his visible flesh. The state of the case is this. As they, confining their attention to the appearance of the flesh, despised Christ, he bids them rise higher and look at God.[2]

Here, too, is an insight into the economic triunity of God. This is the way in which the Son, having assumed our human nature, subordinates himself to the Father in his work as the incarnate Mediator. The initiative lies with the Father, whereas the Son, as the incarnate Mediator, does the will of his heavenly Father.

Jesus is loved by the Father (5:20)

5:20. 'For the Father loves the Son, and shows him all things that he himself does; and he will show him greater works than these, that you may marvel.'

How can the Son do whatever the Father does? The connection is between love and self-revelation. The union between the Father and the Son is one of communicating love, something that is in pointed contrast with the hatred so many people were exhibiting towards Jesus. And the implication of this is: 'You ain't seen nothin' yet!' Why? Because God will show the Son still greater works, commanding widespread amazement. What these **'greater works'** will be, he now proceeds to explain.

Jesus is empowered by the Father (5:21-23)

5:21-23. 'For as the Father raises the dead and gives life to them, even so the Son gives life to whom he will. For the Father judges no one, but has committed all judgement to the Son, that all should honour the Son just as they honour

the Father. He who does not honour the Son does not
honour the Father who sent him.'

Marvellous as healing miracles are, they pale into
relative insignificance beside the future works of the
triumphant Messiah, for he will both give life to the
dead and be the Judge of the living and the dead.
The Old Testament had attributed to God alone the
power to raise the dead to life (2 Kings 5:7; Ezek.
37:13)[3] and to be the Judge of all the earth (Gen.
18:25). These powers are now declared as being given
to the Son, who **'gives life to whom he will'** and has
'all judgement' committed to him (5:21-22). The
unspoken implication throughout is that Jesus is
God. Of course, as the eternal (pre-incarnate) Son,
the Logos of John 1:1, he exercised all the preroga-
tives of God, because of his coequality with the
Father and the Spirit in the essential triunity of God.
The focus here, however, is the exercise of that same
power by the incarnate Son, who in order to be the
Mediator between God and man 'humbled himself
and became obedient' to the Father (Phil. 2:6-8). In
one sweeping sentence, we are given an outline of the
threefold mediatorial office of Jesus Christ as
Prophet, Priest and King. As the eternal Logos (Word)
made flesh, he speaks the very words of God; as the
great High Priest of his people he gives them life from
the dead; and as mediatorial King, he sits in final
judgement over the human race.

Christ, as the only Mediator, raises the dead and
sovereignly gives life to those he intends to save. This
is true both spiritually and physically and includes
both their present experience and their eternal destiny. He is 'head over all things to the church' (Eph.
1:22), and consequently judges everyone, both now
and on the Day of Judgement. He is Lord of human
history as a whole. He is 'Lord of all' (Acts 10:36;
Rom. 14:9). We must therefore deal with him, because

he is appointed to deal with us. No one comes to the Father except through Jesus (John 14:6).

The purpose of this empowerment of the Messiah is that **'all should honour the Son just as they honour the Father'**. Since there is solidarity and unity between the Father and the Son, both as to their essence and their works, therefore they must be accorded the same honour. So intimate and inseparable is this unity that **'He who does not honour the Son does not honour the Father who sent him.'** John expresses a similar thought elsewhere when he says that 'Every spirit that acknowledges that Jesus Christ has come in the flesh is from God, but every spirit that does not ... is not from God' (1 John 4:2-3, NIV). Unless Christ is acknowledged, received and trusted as Mediator, 'God' is only a three-letter word. God reveals himself in Jesus Christ. So when people talk about believing in 'God' and have not the slightest commitment to Christ, or even explicitly reject the claims of Christ, Jesus himself is telling them, 'You do not know my Father!' 'God' in abstraction from the Son he sent to be the Saviour is not the living God, but the construct of a combination of wilful ignorance and wishful thinking in the minds of the spiritually blind and lost. Hence the need, of course, for the preaching of Christ to the ends of the earth.

Jesus has life in the Father (5:24-29)

5:24-29. 'Most assuredly, I say to you, he who hears my word and believes in him who sent me has everlasting life, and shall not come into judgement, but has passed from death into life. Most assuredly, I say to you, the hour is coming, and now is, when the dead will hear the voice of the Son of God; and those who hear will live. For as the Father has life in himself, so he has granted the Son to have life in himself, and has given him authority to execute judgement also, because he is the Son of Man. Do not marvel at this; for the hour is coming in which all who are in the graves will hear his voice and come forth — those who have done good, to the resurrection of life, and those who have done evil, to the resurrection of condemnation.'

Why are we to take this so seriously? Because the life that the Son gives is for all who will hear him and believe. This is why the Messiah has come, why the Son has been revealed, why the Father has given him the power to give life. The implications could not be more personal, or more far-reaching. Jesus' repeated use of the words, **'Most assuredly, I say to you,'** emphasizes that he is addressing hearts and consciences and is looking for a response from his hearers.

1. Jesus indicates who will receive life from him (5:24)

This answers the question raised by his earlier statement that 'The Son gives life to whom he will' (5:21). It is true that, at the point when these words were spoken, the cross, the resurrection, the ascension and the coming of the Holy Spirit upon the church still lay in the future. Even so, the rudiments of the gospel way of salvation are set forth in these words of our Lord. There are four basic elements in the sinner's experience of being saved by Jesus Christ.

Firstly, *we must listen to what Jesus is saying*. Who enters into new life? The one, says Jesus, **'who hears my word'**. In context, that means the aggregate message of his earthly ministry. For us today, it extends to the whole canon of Scripture, which is the final and full Word of God for the present age.[4]

Secondly, *we must respond to Jesus' word by believing* **'in him who sent'** *him*. We come to the Father through Jesus the Son. We come in faith, believing Father and Son, believing that Jesus is

truly 'Immanuel' (God with us — Isa. 7:14; Matt.
1:23), and that God has truly sent him to 'save his
people from their sins' (Matt. 1:21).

Thirdly, *we shall thereby come to possess* **'everlasting life'**, both as a present reality and a future
prospect. Believers in Christ, notes Hutcheson, 'get
spiritual life, and not only shall they have, but they
already have, eternal life by covenant-right, in the
bud and earnest [down-payment] of it, Eph. 1:13,14;
1 John 5:11, and in their head Christ, Eph. 2:5,6 ...'[5]

Fourthly, *we therefore* **'shall not come to judgement'** *since we have* **'passed from death to life'**. It
should be obvious that 'everlasting' life, once gained,
can never be lost. Whatever their trials, believers will
persevere. They will never perish. Faith that fades
was never true faith, however credible it may have
seemed at the time to those who observed it. Saving
faith goes one way only, even on this side of heaven.

2. Jesus explains why he can give life (5:25-27)

Even though Christian faith is 'the substance of
things hoped for' and 'the evidence of things not
seen', it is never a *blind* faith. Reasons for believing
are set down plainly. Even glimpses of the mysteries
of eternity and the mind of God are opened to our
view, to inform, encourage and deepen our attachment to the Lord and his revealed truth. Jesus
wanted his hearers to understand why he could
make the claims he did, and he never left them with
naked assertions that they would have to take or
leave without question or explanation. Jesus offers
three reasons.

The time had come (5:25)

The Lord declares that **'The hour is coming, and
now is, when the dead will hear the voice of the
Son of God; and those who hear will live.'** There is

a sense of movement in this. The time is 'not yet', but it is 'now'. The advent of the new (i.e., New Testament) age of the Messiah is coming to fruition, is in process of being unfolded and is coming to a climax when all will be made plain. The spread of the gospel and the conversion of millions lies as yet in the future, as does the cross and resurrection, but it is at hand. The 'Son of God' is with us, and the voice that countless dead souls will hear to their eternal vivification and joy is already heard in the world. The 'last days' (the *eschaton*) have come and the promises of God are being fulfilled before our eyes.[6]

Jesus has 'life in himself' (5:26)

Just as the Father is self-existent, self-sufficient and inherently and essentially possessed of eternal life — 'infinite, eternal and unchangeable, in his being ...', as the *Shorter Catechism* so lucidly expresses it (Answer to Question 4) — so the Son likewise possesses such life. This is said to be **'granted'** by the Father, not because Jesus was given 'life in himself' after his incarnation, but because in eternity, and in terms of the inter-trinitarian relationship (what theologians call 'the eternal generation of the Son'), it is the Father who gives and the Son who receives. Jesus possesses, says John, 'that eternal life which was with the Father and was manifested to us' (1 John 1:2).[7] This is why 'those who hear will live' (5:25). Jesus has life to give, in virtue of his being the divine Son of his divine Father.

Jesus has 'authority to execute judgement ... because he is the Son of Man' (5:27)

In this case, his authority is said to reside not only in his deity as the eternal Son of God, but in his mediatorial ministry as the Son of Man. **'Son of Man'** is not a mere reference to his humanity, but a title for the divine-human Messiah (see comments on p.98 above). He who, having taken our human nature, dies in order that sinners might live, also secures the right to judge those who have rejected his supreme sacrifice and proffered salvation.

3. Jesus exhorts them not to respond to his teaching with uncomprehending amazement (5:28-29)

There will indeed be a day of general resurrection: **'those who have done good, to the resurrection of life, and those who have done evil, to the resurrection of condemnation'**. There is no salvation by works here, for Jesus consistently teaches that 'the work of God' is 'that you believe in him whom he sent' (6:29). The idea is rather that in the Great Day, what we are and what we did in our lives will come to the light. The godly, saved by grace through faith in Christ, will be acquitted, while the wicked, steadfast in a reprobate mind, will be condemned from the mouth of the Jesus whom they so determinedly rejected. There will be no exemptions from attendance at the last assize. **'Do not marvel at this'** means, 'Do not persuade yourselves it is too far-fetched to be believed, or too weird to be a possibility! Do not go on kidding yourself! Rather hear and live!'

Jesus does the will of the Father

5:30. 'I can of myself do nothing. As I hear, I judge; and my judgement is righteous, because I do not seek my own will but the will of the Father who sent me.'

Jesus here returns to the thought of 5:19 and sums up his whole argument with a restatement of the character and scope of his mediatorial ministry. The argument is straightforward:

1. What he does: he does not act independently;
2. How he operates: he judges as he hears and he judges righteously;
3. Why he is unimpeachable: he does the Father's will.

We must not forget the occasion that precipitated this defence of his ministry. Jesus had healed the man at the Pool of Bethesda, and for this wonderful act of love and compassion he had been accused first of Sabbath-breaking, and then, having declared that he was doing his Father's work, of blasphemy. His last word is to reaffirm that he does his Father's work, and is in perfect unity with him and submission to him. The implication for his persecutors is clear: in their dealings with him, they must answer to the Father. Furthermore, they must face the reality that they must either hear his words and receive eternal life in him, or, if they persist in their present course, be condemned in the judgement by the very one they reject as a blasphemer!

Jesus and history
(John 5:31-47)

What Jesus has said thus far about his relationship to God the Father might be dismissed as no more than his opinion. 'Where is the corroborative testimony?' someone might ask. 'How does it integrate with other, independently obtained evidence? How does it square with the wider witness of history?' To answer concerns of this kind, Jesus proceeds to discuss several lines of evidence. They are all appeals to God's revelation of himself in the course of human history. Jesus' life and ministry, although self-interpretive, are also interpreted by what God has done and is doing in the experience of the human race. What Jesus says and does squares with what is in plain view in the world in which we live.

Jesus' testimony is not uncorroborated

5:31-32. 'If I bear witness of myself, my witness is not true. There is another who bears witness of me, and I know that the witness which he witnesses of me is true.'

He first acknowledges that even his testimony does need to be corroborated (5:31). The fact that all that Jesus says cannot but be true is beside the point. He is simply saying that mere self-attestation does not in itself establish the truth of that attestation in the public arena. Just think how quickly, how frequently

and how furiously we become offended when someone insists on corroborative testimony for something
we have asserted. 'Are you calling me a liar?' is the
common response. Yet here is Jesus unreservedly
pointing 'to the impossibility of a man's being accepted on the basis of his own word'.[8]

The most obvious application of this principle is to
be found in the legal system. For anything to be
admissible in court, there has to be more than one
witness. The witnesses may be people, or they may
be physical or forensic evidence of various kinds. Old
Testament law demanded two or three witnesses
(Deut. 19:15); that principle has never been revoked,
and where it has not been observed — as, at one
time, in Northern Ireland in convicting alleged IRA
terrorists — justice has inevitably suffered. In the
New Testament church, the same principle is invoked
(Matt. 18:16; 2 Cor. 13:1; 1 Tim. 5:19).

Well, said Jesus, **'There is another who bears
witness of me, and I know that the witness which
he witnesses of me is true'** (5:32). This is clearly a
reference to the Father, of whom he has just been
speaking, but Jesus is vague enough to leave the
Jews wondering exactly what he means, and this
provides the springboard for the survey of the other
witnesses that follows. The immediate import of this,
however, is that Jesus' own testimony is not to be
dismissed as if it were uncorroborated. His testimony
is valid, and if people will reflect further, they will
soon discover how well attested it actually is. An echo
of this in our own day is to be found in the proper
way to handle the Bible. We listen to the Word and
the Holy Spirit, who testifies of Christ and guides us
into the truth (John 15:26; 16:13). We compare
Scripture to Scripture. We give attention to the
multiple testimonies of the Scriptures — witnesses
from Moses and Job to the New Testament writers,
spanning a millennium and a half — and discover

how they attest to the unitary truth they were given to reveal to us.

The testimony of John the Baptizer

5:33-35. 'You have sent to John, and he has borne witness to the truth. Yet I do not receive testimony from man, but I say these things that you may be saved. He was the burning and shining lamp, and you were willing for a time to rejoice in his light.'

Jesus reminds the Jews that they had **'sent to John'** and he had **'borne witness to the truth'** (cf. 1:19-36; 3:22-36). He hastens to add that he was not citing John in his support — i.e., relying on human, as opposed to divine, testimony (cf. 5:32). This was certainly very important testimony because John was the second Elijah promised centuries earlier by the prophet Malachi, sent to herald the coming of the Messiah. Jesus only mentions him so that they **'may be saved'** (5:33-34).

John had been a **'burning and shining lamp'** and they had been willing **'for a time'** to **'rejoice in his light'** (5:35). In other words, although not *the* light, John was a lamp (λύχνος/ *luchnos*). He had shed light on the meaning of Jesus' mission. Nevertheless, just as a lamp attracts moths for a while, they had only paid attention to him for a short time, and then wheeled off again into the darkness. They had only dabbled with John's testimony. This implies the rebuke that they had no excuse for not recognizing Jesus as the very Messiah for whom they, as God's covenant people, were professedly waiting.

The testimony of Jesus' works

5:36. 'But I have a greater witness than John's; for the works which the Father has given me to finish — the very works that I do — bear witness of me, that the Father has sent me.'

In contrast even to the remarkable witness of John, Jesus can say that his ministry has had a greater impact. The verse begins with the emphatic, **'But I'** (ἐγὼ δέ / *ego de*). 'There is all the majesty of his person in it,' observes Morris.[9]

What is that greater witness? It consists in the works his Father has given him to do. This is very pointed, for the **'very works'** that Jesus has done include the healing of the man at the Pool of Bethesda on the Sabbath day — the ground of their charges of blasphemy and the original cause of their desire to kill him!

These miracles do have evidential value. Jesus will later call on his faltering disciples to at least believe on the evidence of the miracles themselves (14:10-11). They speak volumes concerning the one who performed them. Do they even remotely suggest that Jesus was a blasphemer? Do they merely demonstrate that he was a gifted human being — a prophet, as Islam will admit? No, they prove that he was the Lamb of God, as heralded by John, the Messiah promised in Scripture and revealed in Jesus' own teaching about himself! The point is that Jesus' ministry as a whole — teaching and miracles as integrated ministry — is solid evidence of the validity of his claims. He himself later cites his death and resurrection as the ultimate 'sign' and witness of the character of his person and the validity of his claims (Matt. 12:39-41). To reject the resurrection is to reject the risen Saviour!

The testimony of Jesus' Father (5:37-38)

5:37-38. 'And the Father himself, who sent me, has testified of me. You have neither heard his voice at any time, nor seen his form. But you do not have his word abiding in you, because whom he sent, him you do not believe.'

In fact, says Jesus, the Father has **'testified'** of him (μεμαρτύρηκεν / *memartureken* from μαρτυρέω / *martureo* — whence our English 'martyr'). The perfect tense of this verb indicates that the Father's testimony is not new, but an established reality in the history of his people. Some commentators think this refers to the witness of the Old Testament, but that seems precluded by the explicit references in the verses that follow. What is more likely is that Jesus is referring to the other ways in which God had spoken to Israel — 'at various times and in various ways ... in time past to the fathers by the prophets ...' (Heb. 1:1).[10] Not every word from God had been written down as Scripture. Neither every true prophecy, nor even every true prophet, was recorded for posterity. Down the centuries God had manifested himself in all sorts of ways that his people had witnessed with their own eyes and ears, and much of it, one way or another, pointed to the Messiah and the deliverance he would secure for them. Some, like Moses, Abraham, Jacob, Samuel, Elijah and others, had experienced remarkable encounters with God. They had variously heard his voice and seen theophanic appearances. Israel had sought guidance from a God who had manifested himself as a glory-cloud in the tabernacle in the wilderness, and answered their enquiries through the ministry of the priests and the mysterious Urim and Thummim.

These latter-day Jews, however, were blind to all this. Jesus underscores that fact by rebuking their threefold ignorance. They had never heard God's

voice (5:37b). They had never seen God's form
(5:37c). They had never had God's Word in their
hearts (5:38a). And the reason for this was that
'Whom he [God the Father] **sent, him** [Jesus his
Son] **you do not believe'** (5:38b,c). The voice and
form of God were before them in the person of Jesus,
the incarnate Son of God. They did not believe Jesus,
and so were incapable of seeing what was otherwise
remarkably clear and wonderfully supported by the
evidence. Their unbelief meant they had no meaningful relationship with God. Consequently, 'The
Father's witness is accessible only to those who
believe on the Son.'[11]

The testimony of the Scriptures (5:39-44)

5:39-44. 'You search the Scriptures, for in them you think you
have eternal life; and these are they which testify of me. But
you are not willing to come to me that you may have life. I do
not receive honour from men. But I know you, that you do not
have the love of God in you. I have come in my Father's
name, and you do not receive me; if another comes in his
own name, him you will receive. How can you believe, who
receive honour from one another, and do not seek the
honour that comes from the only God?'

The incomprehension of Jesus' critics is nowhere
more profoundly evident than in their failure to
understand the very Scriptures of which they
thought themselves the most masterly interpreters.
The AV renders the opening words of this passage as
an imperative: **'Search the Scriptures'** (5:39). Accordingly, generations of Christians have regarded
this as one of the great commands of Christ relative
to personal piety and spiritual growth. We should
indeed search the Scriptures, as did the Bereans
after hearing from Paul (Acts 17:11), but the context

here suggests that it should be rendered as an indicative: 'You search the Scriptures.' Jesus is simply
describing what they did.

Their problem was *not* that they did not diligently
'search the Scriptures' (5:39). They studied the texts
meticulously. If you go to the Catskill resorts in
upstate New York in the summer, you will see devoted orthodox Jews sitting in the heat of the after-
noon — on their holidays — poring over the Scriptures and the rabbinic commentaries, hour after
hour! In stark contrast, what passes for 'Bible study'
among Christians today — a few people sitting in a
circle for half an hour, sharing their uninformed
responses to a cursory reading of the text — would
have been greeted with utter stupefaction by these
Jews, ancient and modern!

The problem was that they had a fatally flawed
view of what their searching was achieving. **'You
search the Scriptures,'** says Jesus, **'for in them
you think you have eternal life'** (5:39). The Scriptures certainly teach about eternal life, but the study
of Scripture does not confer eternal life, *ex opere
operato*, as the rabbis appear to have taught.[12] They
had a superstitious view of their study. They were,
formally, pursuing the right goal, but in a completely
misguided and ultimately counter-productive manner.

The tragedy of the problem was highlighted by the
fact that these very Scriptures are, as Jesus puts it,
'they which testify of me' (5:39; *cf.* 1:45; 2:22;
3:10; 5:45-46; 20:9). Carson's comment is excellent:
'What is at stake, is a comprehensive hermeneutical
key. By predictive prophecy, by type, by revelatory
event and by anticipatory statute, what we call the
Old Testament is understood to point to Christ, his
ministry, his teaching, his death and resurrection.'[13]
They stared all this in the face and could not, or
would not, see it.

In spite of all that clear Scripture testimony, Jesus
tells them, **'You are not willing to come to me that
you may have life'** (5:40). They could not admit that
'this' (the Messiah promised in the Old Testament)
was 'that' (the Jesus revealed in the New Testament
and now speaking to them). Like the Ethiopian
eunuch, they did not understand what they were
reading (Acts 8:30-35), but unlike him, they were not
willing to listen to the explanation, far less believe in
Jesus Christ. This is the universal condition of lost
mankind, for 'There is none who seeks after God'
(Rom. 3:11). The human will is free within the borders of its predispositions, and its war with God continues to be reflected in its decisions, until and
unless the Lord graciously subdues it by the power of
the gospel.

Finally, Jesus points out that their rejection of him
arises from their not having **'the love of God'** in
them (5:42). He establishes this point by presenting a
fairly elaborate argument.

They could well dismiss this assertion about not
loving God by arguing that Jesus was just angry
because they had not praised him, as he had expected. Perhaps anticipating such a rejoinder, Jesus
asserted that he was not interested in receiving
'honour from men' (5:41) 'Honour' is the Greek
doxa, meaning 'glory'. He did not seek to be glorified
by the praise of men. The issue was not that he was
personally offended that they had not lauded him to
the skies.

The fundamental issue was their relationship to
the God they professed to serve. Yet they appeared
convinced that their devotion to God demanded their
rejection of Jesus as a blasphemer. In that way, of
course, they could hold on to their assurance that
they were right with God, and dismiss Jesus as the
man with the problem. That would effectively drive a
wedge between Jesus and the Father. This Jesus

would not allow. He pointed out, **'I have come in my Father's name, and you do not receive me; if another comes in his own name, him you will receive'** (5:43) They would accept a false messiah on his own testimony, but had rejected Jesus, who had come in the name of his Father God!

Here he touches on the problem with his critics and the kind of religion they represented, and pinpoints the reason why they would not accept him. They were praise-seekers, and utterly self-centred. **'How can you believe,'** he asks, **'who receive honour from one another, and do not seek the honour that comes from the only God?'** (5:44). Later, he was to describe them as those who 'loved the praise of men more than the praise of God' (12:43).

The testimony of Moses (5:45-47)

5:45-47. 'Do not think that I shall accuse you to the Father; there is one who accuses you — Moses, in whom you trust. For if you believed Moses, you would believe me; for he wrote about me. But if you do not believe his writings, how will you believe my words?'

Jesus now introduces a final witness. But first he emphasizes that, notwithstanding the fact that he is the one who was despised and rejected by them (i.e., the Jews), he will not be the one to accuse them before the Father. He had not come 'into the world to condemn the world, but that the world through him might be saved' (3:17). Rather, they will be accused by **'Moses, in whom [they] trust'** (5:45).

Why would 'Moses' accuse them? For the reason, Jesus tells them, that if they really believed Moses, they would believe him. They 'trust' Moses, but do not believe what Moses really says, namely, the law to which they were so attached in their deluded way. In their attention to the precise commands of the law, and their rabbinical elaborations, they were completely missing the actual meaning and import of the Mosaic revelation, which was to point ahead to the Messiah who would deliver his people, once and for all, from a bondage of which Israel's sojourn in Egypt was itself only a shadow — and that Messiah had now come! They had missed the wood on account of the trees!

The Lord's challenge to them could hardly be more pointed. He, in one sense, was lifting Moses up above himself, in that he was holding them accountable to the one human being they revered more than any other — and that before any accountability they had even to him as the Messiah. What could be more startling than the warning that the very same law, the one with which they felt themselves to be so safe, would be the measure of their condemnation!

The ranks of the deluded have still been swelling in the gospel era, for Jesus himself tells us, 'Not everyone who says to Me, "Lord, Lord," shall enter the kingdom of heaven, but he who does the will of my Father in heaven. Many will say to me in that day, "Lord, Lord, have we not prophesied in your name, cast out demons in your name, and done many wonders in your name?" And then I will declare to them, "I never knew you; depart from me, you who practise lawlessness!"' (Matt. 7:21-23).

The challenge that these words afforded at the time they were uttered, and still do today, is nevertheless pre-eminently one of grace and an invitation to life. It is too late for those who, having resisted the Lord to their last breath, at this very hour contemplate the truth of these warnings from the other side of divine justice. But for those with ears to hear, there is newness of life in the Lord Jesus Christ for all who will believe his testimony of himself, his herald John, the testimony of his Father, his miraculous works, and the Scriptures themselves, including the law of Moses. Will you come to him, that you might have life?

15. The food that lasts
John 6:1-34

We human beings have a tremendous capacity for missing the point. For example, a recent American poll identified the 'evangelizers' in the so-called Christian community. These are the people in the churches who say they believe in spreading their faith. Apart from the fact that this was only a proportion of the 'church people', the most astounding revelation was that almost half of the Southern Baptist 'evangelizers' believed in salvation by good works! That is to say, millions of people in America's largest putatively evangelical and Bible-believing denomination have missed the whole point of the evangel (the gospel) and think that being good will get you to heaven!

The truth is that most people missed the point of Jesus' miracles, even though they happened before their very eyes. They all had *opinions* about what Jesus was doing. The church leaders didn't like what was happening and plotted to do away with Jesus (5:16-18). The ordinary people, on the other hand, flocked to see Jesus **'because they saw his signs which he performed on those who were diseased'** (6:2). Yet, for the most part, they treated these miracles as if they were stunts. Relatively few saw beyond the miracles themselves to the real meaning of what Jesus was doing. Most of the people never bridged the gap between sign and substance. They were merely dazzled by the effects.

It is no accident, then, that Jesus offers explanations of the significance of his ministry, in the form of fairly lengthy discourses, in close proximity to the miracles he performed. John's account begins with the miracles of the feeding of the five thousand and Jesus' walking on water, and concludes with the Lord's teaching on the bread of life. He takes us from vivid representations of human need to the abundant provision of divine grace. The fact that this did not exactly win over the masses only serves to underline the points being made. Christ alone is the Saviour of sinners, and we need him as the true bread that alone can sustain our life — 'the food which endures to everlasting life'.

In his sixth chapter, John unfolds five aspects of the 'bread of life': the need for it (6:1-24), the source of it (6:25-31), its nature (6:32-34), its identity (6:35-40) and the various responses to it (6:41-71). We shall examine the first three of these in our present study.

The need for the bread of life
(John 6:1-24)

The reason why Jesus' miracles were such effective signs attesting his mission as the promised divine Messiah is that they invariably addressed real needs in a way that unmistakably revealed the love, compassion and mercy of God.

The feeding of the five thousand (6:1-15)

6:1-15. After these things Jesus went over the Sea of Galilee, which is the Sea of Tiberias. Then a great multitude followed him, because they saw his signs which he performed on those who were diseased.

And Jesus went up on the mountain, and there he sat with his disciples. Now the Passover, a feast of the Jews, was near. Then Jesus lifted up his eyes, and seeing a great multitude coming toward him, he said to Philip, 'Where shall we buy bread, that these may eat?' But this he said to test him, for he himself knew what he would do. Philip answered him, 'Two hundred denarii worth of bread is not sufficient for them, that every one of them may have a little.'

One of his disciples, Andrew, Simon Peter's brother, said to him, 'There is a lad here who has five barley loaves and two small fish, but what are they among so many?'

Then Jesus said, 'Make the people sit down.' Now there was much grass in the place. So the men sat down, in number about five thousand. And Jesus took the loaves, and when he had given thanks he distributed them to the

disciples, and the disciples to those sitting down; and likewise of the fish, as much as they wanted.

So when they were filled, he said to his disciples, 'Gather
up the fragments that remain, so that nothing is lost.' Therefore they gathered them up, and filled twelve baskets with the
fragments of the five barley loaves which were left over by
those who had eaten.

Then those men, when they had seen the sign that Jesus
did, said, 'This is truly the Prophet who is to come into the
world.'

Therefore when Jesus perceived that they were about to
come and take him by force to make him king, he departed
again to the mountain by himself alone.

Even if a segment of the Jewish leadership was
plotting to kill Jesus, he remained very popular with
the mass of the people. Drawn by his healing miracles, rather than by any discerning devotion to him,
they followed him to the east side of the Sea of Galilee (6:1-3; cf. Luke 9:10-11).

'Now the Passover ... was near' (6:4). Mention of
the feast sets the scene for the two miracles that
follow and, not least, the 'bread of life' discourse, for
the pointedly theological reason that the Passover,
with its sacrificial lambs, commemorated God's
provision of a sacrifice for the sin of his people and
Israel's deliverance from Egypt. Since Jesus had
already been heralded by John as the Lamb of God
who takes away the sin of the world (1:29), and had,
at the previous Passover, indicated, albeit in a veiled
manner, that he was the 'temple' who would be
destroyed and in three days be rebuilt — a statement
remembered by the disciples after his resurrection
(2:19-22) — we are here given a further indication
that Jesus himself is the final Passover Lamb, who
effects the redemption only foreshadowed in the
lambs sacrificed over a period of a millennium and a
half (1 Cor. 5:7).

The story of the feeding of the 5,000 is well known. Jesus saw the people coming and asked Philip how they would feed them all. This was **'to test him [Philip], for he himself knew what he would do'**. The latter clause is presumably the clue to the 'test'. This must have been along the line of seeing if Philip would trust Jesus to supply the need, when it was obvious that nothing could be done, if it depended on the disciples' resources — a point Philip brought out with transparent realism. Even six months' wages — **'two hundred denarii'** — could not have provided them with more than a snack! By human calculation, the numbers could not work. Philip must have passed the test, for no more is said on the matter (6:5-7). Andrew, meanwhile, had found a boy with **'five barley loaves and two small fish'**, and these by a miracle of replication became sufficient to feed the whole crowd and leave enough to fill **'twelve baskets'** (6:8-13).

The significance of this miracle is not difficult to discern, although the Jews misinterpreted it at the time. The filling of everyone present proclaims, as Leon Morris puts it, that Jesus is the 'supplier of man's need'. [1] The baskets of leftovers — one for each of the tribes of Israel — stress the covenant faithfulness of God towards his people into the future. There is no warrant to view this as an anticipation of the Lord's Supper — the words of institution and the occasion of the Last Supper properly indicate the only sure and certain inception of that sacramental meal. The point here is the more general one of the fulness of God's provision of Christ as the bread from heaven who gives life to the world, and the need of men and women for his redemptive provision (6:33).

The Jews, for their part, misinterpret the event. They see Jesus as **'the Prophet who is to come into the world'** (6:14) — a reference to the promise of the second Moses in Deuteronomy 18:15. This was correct in part, the only trouble being that few at that time among the Jews viewed this as a prophecy of the Messiah.[2] The tainted character of this interpretation is confirmed by the inclination of the people **'to come and take him by force to make him king'** (6:15). They saw their future deliverance in political terms, and looked for an earthly kingdom, when Jesus' kingdom was to be 'not of this world' (18:36). This snare lives on in modern Christian yearnings for political influence and in those churches whose clergy affect the trappings of earthly power and style themselves 'princes of the church'. Jesus accordingly withdrew **'to the mountain by himself alone'** (6:15).

Jesus walking on the water (6:16-21)

6:16-21. Now when evening came, his disciples went down to the sea, got into the boat, and went over the sea toward Capernaum. And it was already dark, and Jesus had not come to them. Then the sea arose because a great wind was blowing.

So when they had rowed about three or four miles, they saw Jesus walking on the sea and drawing near the boat; and they were afraid. But he said to them, 'It is I; do not be afraid.' Then they willingly received him into the boat, and immediately the boat was at the land where they were going.

The disciples, meanwhile, left by boat for Capernaum without Jesus. After about three miles of rowing in a rising gale, **'They saw Jesus walking on the sea and drawing near the boat'** (6:19). The sceptics dismiss this as a hallucination, a mistake (was Jesus really just paddling along a sandbank?), or a scribe's way of making him look more godlike. Miracles, however, come in a single package. Walking on water is arguably easier than raising someone from the dead, and certainly no more difficult than feeding a large crowd from a few loaves and fishes. 'Let God be true but every man a liar'! (Rom. 3:4). The God who made the world and its natural laws is hardly bound to sink into the waves when he has a point to make!

The disciples **'were afraid'** — 'more ... of an apparition (for so they supposed him to be),' remarks Matthew Henry, 'than of the winds and the waves'.[3] But Jesus said to them, **'It is I; do not be afraid'** (6:20). They received him into the boat, and **'immediately the boat was at the land where they were going'** (6:21). The landfall has long been regarded as a miracle, evocative as it is of the central theme of Psalm 107:23-32, but that is by no means certain on the face of the narrative. Matthew records that Peter, after faltering a little, walked on the water to meet Jesus, after which 'the wind ceased' (Matt. 14:28-32; Mark 6:51). The Lord stilled the fears of his disciples and sustained them through an experience of threat and uncertainty. The central point in both miracles is that they had fundamental needs which they could not meet from their own resources, physical and spiritual, and Jesus made plain to all who had eyes to see that he was able to supply all the needs of his people (Phil. 4:19).

The source of the bread of life
(John 6:22-31)

6:22-24. On the following day, when the people who were standing on the other side of the sea saw that there was no other boat there, except that one which his disciples had entered, and that Jesus had not entered the boat with his disciples, but his disciples had gone away alone — however, other boats came from Tiberias, near the place where they ate bread after the Lord had given thanks — when the people therefore saw that Jesus was not there, nor his disciples, they also got into boats and came to Capernaum, seeking Jesus.

These miracles provide the context for Jesus' teaching about 'the bread of life'. It is clear that the crowd who had been miraculously fed also surmised that Jesus' departure had something of the miraculous about it, so their curiosity was doubly whetted and they followed him to Capernaum.

What should people want most in life? (6:25-27)

6:25-27. And when they found him on the other side of the sea, they said to him, 'Rabbi, when did you come here?'
　　Jesus answered them and said, 'Most assuredly, I say to you, you seek me, not because you saw the signs, but because you ate of the loaves and were filled. Do not labour for the food which perishes, but for the food which endures to

everlasting life, which the Son of Man will give you, because God the Father has set his seal on him.'

The first question the people ask Jesus seems unexceptionable: **'Rabbi, when did you come here?'** (6:25). They had not seen him embark at Bethsaida and knew that only one boat had left on that previous evening. It had to be a miracle. What other explanation was possible? Jesus could have answered them directly, and told them how he walked on the water, stilled the wind and brought the boat to land. Had he done so, he would only have reinforced their appetite for the dramatic and their interest in him as a miracle-worker. Jesus did not, however, want mere 'fans'. He was not promoting a 'career', and he was certainly not interested in being part of the entertainment business. He therefore ignored their question and came straight to the real point of what he had done, and what he had come to do for people, if they would only listen to him and receive him for who he really was.

Jesus first challenges the character of their interest in him and his miracles: **'You seek me, not because you saw the signs, but because you ate of the loaves and were filled'** (6:26). Their interest was thoroughly superficial. They were missing the real point. They were drawn to Jesus on account of what the miracles had done and could do for them — in this case something no higher than a free lunch! Mark notes that even the disciples 'had not understood about the loaves, because their heart was hardened' (Mark 6:52).

What they needed to do, Jesus charges them, was to labour **'not ... for the food which perishes, but for the food which endures to everlasting life, which the Son of Man will give you, because God the Father has set his seal on him'** (6:27) This is the thesis of Jesus' entire 'bread of life' discourse.

What they had to grasp was that Jesus' mission is to do with eternal life, and his kingdom is not of this world. All materialistic notions miss the point. We may eat to live, but we do not live to eat. The food we really need is that which will save us both for now and for ever. The ephemeral phenomena of miraculous signs — in this case, healed people and filled stomachs alike — are not that food, but rather are pointers to the real food, which is Christ himself. We are to 'labour' for that real food. That ought to be our priority.

The paradox is that the thing which we are to 'labour' for is essentially a gift of God's grace. Working for the enduring food is a matter of seeking the gift of eternal life through the Son of Man. The thrust of the verse can be set out as follows:

...enduring food (*which is the gift of* ...)
...the Son of Man (*who is the gift of...*)
...God the Father.

Last but not least, we are told that Jesus is the one upon whom the Father has **'set his seal'** (ἐσφράγισεν). This is rendered 'certified' in John 3:33: 'He who has received his testimony has certified that God is true.' The idea is of an official seal or certification. Jesus is the approved agent of God and the seal of God rests constantly upon him in his person and work, although it may properly be seen as particularly connected with his baptism and public ministry. He alone is, we might say, 'the genuine article', and no substitutes should be accepted, for he is the only way to new and eternal life.

From what follows, it is clear that Jesus *is* that 'food which endures to everlasting life'. Everything else is at best secondary, at worst diversionary, to the achievement of this great goal. That is why what people do with Jesus is the great watershed of their present experience of life and their eternal destiny.

What should people do to please God? (6:28-31)

6:28-31. Then they said to him, 'What shall we do, that we may work the works of God?'

Jesus answered and said to them, 'This is the work of God, that you believe in him whom he sent.'

Therefore they said to him, 'What sign will you perform then, that we may see it, and believe you? What work will you do? Our fathers ate the manna in the desert; as it is written, "He gave them bread from heaven to eat."'

The people did not grasp what Jesus had said. They asked two very revealing questions.

First, they asked, **'What shall we do, that we may work the works of God?'** (6:28). The legalistic cast of mind shines through: 'What shall we *do*, that we may *work*...?' The rich young ruler came from the same stable (Mark 10:17-22). Jesus' answer is to point out that **'the work of God'** is to **'believe in him whom he sent'** (6:29). Our work is to respond in faith. That work of faith is, to be sure, a gift of God, and the receiving of the gift of life, but it is something *we* must do. It is God-given faith, as opposed to man-generated works!

The second question is even more crass than the one which preceded it. **'What sign will you perform then, that we may see it and believe you?'** they ask. **'What work will you do?'** (6:30). It takes the breath away! Feeding the crowd and crossing the lake on foot were not good enough signs! They needed something bigger and better before they were prepared to believe Jesus! They even gave an example — from Scripture, no less — to help Jesus out. Remember the manna in the wilderness? God '**gave them bread from heaven to eat**' (6:31; quoting Ps. 78:24). You can see the reasoning behind this. Feeding 5,000 people with one meal of earthly bread on one day was impressive, but does it not seem insignificant beside God's feeding some two million people for forty years with bread 'from heaven'? Could Jesus really be said to be greater than Moses? On this ground, the people held Jesus at arm's length, and challenged him to persuade them that he was who he claimed to be. That is still the way it is! The evidence itself is overwhelming, but does not in itself compel people to trust themselves to Jesus.

The nature of the bread of life
(John 6:32-34)

Though the Son of Man was the source of the bread
they needed, and faith in him the way to receive
everlasting life, Jesus' auditors could not see beyond
the very signs that pointed to these truths. Having
failed to acknowledge the true character of their
need, they were totally incapable of understanding
the true source of its alleviation. It is at this point
that Jesus delivers yet another lesson on the meaning of grace. Far from dismissing them, as we might
do, the Lord patiently explains himself to them.

Jesus' explanation (6:32-33)

6:32-33. Then Jesus said to them, 'Most assuredly, I say to
you, Moses did not give you the bread from heaven, but my
Father gives you the true bread from heaven. For the bread
of God is he who comes down from heaven and gives life to
the world.'

They needed to understand, first of all, that his
Father 'is giving' — present tense — them the **'true
bread from heaven'** (6:32). Moses did not give them
the manna; God did. In any case, the manna was not
the 'true bread', and that was past and done. Manna,
like the multiplied loaves and fishes, fed their bodies.
The 'true bread' is in a different class, for it pertains

to 'everlasting life' and was in process of being given even as he spoke!

They also needed to realize that this 'true bread' is *a person*: **'For the bread of God is he who comes down from heaven...'** (6:33). The term 'bread of God' is used in the Old Testament of the showbread (literally, 'bread of the presence'), twelve loaves of bread which were placed before the Lord in the temple, symbolizing the dependence of God's people on his life-giving presence with them (Lev. 21:21-22). This clause, notes Carson, 'serves as a transition from the thought that Jesus *provides* the true bread from heaven (vv. 27ff.) to the thought that Jesus *is* the true bread from heaven (vv. 35ff.)'.[4] The connection Jesus makes here would have been unmistakable to a devout Jew. The 'bread of God' is the Son of Man, the promised Messiah. He is the bread who was now present with them. '*Bread-corn* is *bruised* (Isa. 28:28),' observes Matthew Henry; 'so was Christ; he was born at Bethlehem, the *house of bread*, and typified by the *show-bread*.'[5]

Furthermore, this person, Jesus the Messiah, **'gives life to the world'** (6:33). 'In him was life, and the life was the light of men' (1:4). This new life is for 'the world' — not merely the Jews, but people of all kinds, provided they come to him, believe in him and are 'taught by God' (6:35,45).

The hearers' incomprehension (6:34)

6:34. Then they said to him, 'Lord, give us this bread always.'

Their response is palpably weak. There is no need to read any sarcasm into this. They just could not get their minds round what Jesus was saying. Physical food and prolonged longevity they could understand. But, like the woman at the well (4:15), they had not

grasped the spiritual dimension of what Jesus had
said. As the saying goes, 'They just didn't get it!' The
penny had not dropped. They did not see the point,
even when it stared them in the face. That should
surprise no one. It is not easy to learn that 'Our
bodies could better live without food than our souls
without Christ.'⁶ Such things, indeed, are 'foolishness' to 'the natural man' who 'does not receive the
things of the Spirit of God ... nor can he know them,
because they are spiritually discerned' (1 Cor. 2:14).
Revelation is more than imparting of information. It
requires a renewing and revivifying work of God in
the heart and the mind.

We need the bread from heaven because, left to
ourselves, we are both dead and dying.

> Break thou the bread of life,
> Dear Lord, to me,
> As thou didst break the loaves
> Beside the sea...
>
> (M. A. Lathbury, 1841-1913)

16. 'I am the bread of life'

John 6:35-71

The obvious is not always so obvious. The common proverb hits the nail on the head: 'There are none so blind as those that will not see.' We indulge a superior attitude in such matters at our peril. 'Denial', as has already been noted,[1] is a common refuge of people who cannot face up to realities that are apparent to all but themselves. This is more than the strictly intellectual problem of not being able to grasp something because it is difficult or obscure, or because of some mental handicap. At its root it is an anguished and aching 'No!' that cannot, and will not, accept plain facts.

The acknowledgement of the claims of Jesus often runs into this problem. More than the obstacle of mere ignorance, he faces the intransigence of presuppositions that allow no room for a Messiah like him. When, in his earthly ministry, Jesus pointed to himself as the true bread from heaven — a thinly veiled allusion to his being the promised Son of Man — he faced stiffening resistance from more and more people that seemingly no amount of evidence could budge.

This sense of deep-seated opposition — of minds so made up that they did not want to be confused by the facts — intensifies as John unfolds the account of Jesus' teaching on the 'bread of life'. In the first half of John 6, the need for it (6:1-24), its source (6:25-31) and its nature (6:32-34) are expounded. In the second half, which now commands our attention, the apostle unfolds the identity of the 'bread of life' (6:35-40) and describes some of the responses that those present made to the claims of Jesus (6:41-71). It is in this latter section that we see the crystallization of the opposition that eventually would nail the Lord to the cross of Calvary.

The identity of the bread
(John 6:35-40)

6:35-40. And Jesus said to them, 'I am the bread of life. He who comes to me shall never hunger, and he who believes in me shall never thirst. But I said to you that you have seen me and yet do not believe. All that the Father gives me will come to me, and the one who comes to me I will by no means cast out. For I have come down from heaven, not to do my own will, but the will of him who sent me. This is the will of the Father who sent me, that of all he has given me I should lose nothing, but should raise it up at the last day. And this is the will of him who sent me, that everyone who sees the Son and believes in him may have everlasting life; and I will raise him up at the last day.'

Jesus took the incomprehension of his hearers with regard to his words about the 'true bread from heaven' (6:32) as his cue to press the matter further. He accordingly identified the 'bread' with an explicitness that they would have to face for what it was. He offered them three main points of teaching.

Jesus is the bread of life (6:35a)

The great metaphor, **'I am the bread of life'**, allows no escape. It is a Messianic self-revelation, and it blows away the confused materialism that looked for a kind of New Testament manna 'from now on' that people could pick up and eat (6:34). The majestic 'I am' is the first of seven in the fourth Gospel.[2] It has, as Morris notes, 'distinct overtones of divinity',[3] echoing as it does the language of divine self-revelation in Exodus 3:14: 'And God said to Moses. "I AM WHO I AM." And he said, "Thus you shall say to the children of Israel, 'I AM has sent me to you.'"' Jesus is the food for eternal life. Jesus is the giver and sustainer of new redeemed life. The illustration is so simple, yet eternally profound. As bread is the staple of daily life, so Christ is the staple of eternal life.

Jesus will fully meet the need of all who come to him (6:35b-36)

How is this life received? **'He who comes to me shall never hunger,'** says Jesus, **'and he who believes in me shall never thirst.'** The language illumines the metaphor. We are to 'come to', and 'believe in', Christ, in order that our spiritual hunger and thirst may be assuaged. This puts in proper perspective his later charge to 'eat the flesh of the Son of Man and drink his blood' (6:53-57). It explodes in advance any tendency to literalize this process and define it in terms of the physical ingestion of bread and wine, conceived of as the literal flesh and blood of Jesus (as in the Roman Catholic doctrine of transubstantiation). Partaking of the bread and wine in the Lord's Supper is indeed symbolic of spiritual feeding upon Jesus, and has the promise of his presence for the already believing and confessing communicant.

What Jesus is talking about here, however, is how one becomes a Christian. Carson[4] points up a link with Isaiah 55 and its theme of 'the dawning of eschatological salvation' and 'of a new and everlasting covenant':

> Ho! Everyone who thirsts,
> Come to the waters;
> And you who have no money,
> Come, buy and eat.
> Yes, come, buy wine and milk
> Without money and without price
>
> (Isa. 55:1).

Put more practically, this means, 'The promised Saviour has come into the world. I, Jesus, am he. Come to me, believing in me for salvation, and I will fill your emptiness and heal your miseries.' Jesus had called for faith some moments before, but they had still insisted that he give them another miraculous sign as a condition of believing him (6:29-30). The Lord returns to this and rebukes their unbelief: **'But I said to you that you have seen me and yet do not believe'** (6:36). They had no excuse. They wanted to be filled with a different food from that with which Christ would fill them.

Jesus will certainly save all who come to him (6:37-40)

The unwillingness and apparent incapacity of the crowd to believe in Jesus suggests the obvious question as to whether his mission was in any sense failing. The perennial prevalence of unbelief in the world is often hailed as evidence of the impotence of the gospel, if not indeed even of the so-called 'death of God'. There are times when the 'big battalions' are rather obviously not on the Lord's side. To this, Jesus gives a three-part answer.

1. God chooses (6:37a)

Who will come to Jesus? He answers, **'All that the Father gives me will come to me.'** The responsible commitment of coming to, and believing in, Christ is preceded by a decided intention on God's part to save particular lost people. God gives before people come. The 'all' that God gives to Jesus are first chosen in his eternal mind and purpose (Eph. 1:4; 1 Peter 1:2). His sovereign choice (election) is the root of our willingness to believe.

2. Jesus saves (6:37b-39)

When he says, **'The one who comes to me I will by no means cast out'** (6:37b), he means, not merely that he will welcome whoever comes to him, but that he will save, keep, or preserve all who do so. This emphasis is confirmed by what follows. Jesus came **'from heaven'** to do **'the will of the Father'**, which is that **'Of all he has given me I should lose nothing, but should raise it up at the last day'** (6:38-39). Human unbelief will not thwart God's intention to save a people. From the decree of God 'from heaven', to the resurrection of the precise number of the elect on the 'last day', the purpose of God in salvation will be perfectly fulfilled. None will be lost. All who come to Jesus in faith will be kept. These will then persevere in the faith. God in his sovereignty sent his Son, gave him particular sinners to save, brought them to faith, keeps every single one in his hands and will raise them all to glory.

3. You must believe (6:40)

What ought to be our response to Christ, and the revelation of his sovereignty in salvation? He who **'believes in him'** will receive **'everlasting life'** and be raised up **'at the last day'**. The responsibility to come to Christ is laid squarely upon every one of us. Human responsibility operates within the sphere of the overarching sovereignty of God. Human beings are accountable to God and are not ignorant of the difference between believing and not believing in the Son of God. No one believes or disbelieves against his will. We will what we want to will. The human will acts freely, albeit within the bounds of its own character and predispositions. Jesus therefore addresses the consciences of wilful people, and calls for faith as the absolute prerequisite for entering into eternal life. The fact that it takes the power of God to regenerate our human nature (cf. 3:7) and draw us to Jesus in a living faith (6:44), far from diminishing the element of responsibility, actually serves to underscore the necessity of a genuine heart-commitment to the Lord.

Responses to the bread
(John 6:41-71)

It is hardly surprising that the Jews were baffled by
Jesus' identification of himself as 'the bread of life'.
Even a full-blown conviction that he was the Messiah
would have left them full of questions. So impenetrable was their incomprehension, however, that any
sense of wonder they might have had at his miracles
soon gave way to outrage that he should claim to
have come down from heaven. Even among those
who had come to attend on his ministry, he faced a
stiffening opposition of the very kind that had already
induced the Jewish leadership to plot his death. Four
responses are recorded by the apostle: three negative
and one positive.

Response no.1: 'We know where you came from' (6:41-51)

6:41-51. The Jews then complained about him, because he
said, 'I am the bread which came down from heaven.' And
they said, 'Is not this Jesus, the son of Joseph, whose father
and mother we know? How is it then that he says, "I have
come down from heaven"?'

Jesus therefore answered and said to them, 'Do not
murmur among yourselves. No one can come to me unless
the Father who sent me draws him; and I will raise him up at
the last day. It is written in the prophets, "And they shall all be
taught by God." Therefore everyone who has heard and
learned from the Father comes to me. Not that anyone has

seen the Father, except he who is from God; he has seen
the Father. Most assuredly, I say to you, he who believes in
me has everlasting life. I am the bread of life. Your fathers
ate the manna in the wilderness, and are dead. This is the
bread which comes down from heaven, that one may eat of it
and not die. I am the living bread which came down from
heaven. If anyone eats of this bread, he will live for ever; and
the bread that I shall give is my flesh, which I shall give for
the life of the world.'

The first objection came from **'the Jews'**, those
hearers who could not be described as his followers.
The objection is that Jesus was **'the son of Joseph'**,
and a man **'whose father and mother we know'**
(6:41-42). This is a variation on the earlier theme
that 'A prophet has no honour in his own country'
(4:44). Those who rise to any kind of prominence
always tend to be regarded as 'too big for their boots'
by those who remember their humble beginnings —
especially if the latter want to find a reason for rejecting them. If you claim to have come down from
heaven, but have parents on earth that everybody
knows, you can expect some serious questions! The
irony, in Jesus' case, is that had they really known
Jesus' parents and the incarnational significance of
his parentage, they would have seen it as confirming
his claims of a heavenly provenance! They could not,
and would not, lift their eyes beyond the naked
observation that Jesus had an earthly father and
mother, just like everybody else.

Jesus' answer to this seemingly impenetrable
blindness is that they needed to be **'taught by God'**
(6:43-51). He sets out five truths that they needed to
understand and face squarely.

1. Why people cannot see (6:43-44)

For a start, they were murmuring among themselves. Jesus' rebuke emphasizes their responsibility. Instead of receiving the truth of God from the Son of God, they immediately went into a huddle to discuss and dispute it, as if they were the arbiters of truth! Let them look at themselves and face the fact that wilful unbelief, and not any lack of evidence, was their real problem!

Behind that, however, lies a mystery, which, if they could understand plain language, should have driven them to their knees, to cry out to the Lord for mercy: **'No one can come to me unless the Father who sent me draws him,'** said Jesus, **'and I will raise him up at the last day.'** This is God's sovereign grace in action. God wills and God draws. That drawing is evidently the irresistible power of grace. It is, you notice, set over against the unwillingness of the unbelieving to believe. So great is the resistance of the human will that it takes divine power to bring it to brokenness before God and a readiness to hear and believe. Carson points out that 'The combination of v. 37a and v. 44 prove that this "drawing" activity of the Father cannot be reduced to what [Arminian, GJK] theologians sometimes call "prevenient grace" dispensed to every individual, for this "drawing" is selective, or else the negative note in v. 44 is meaningless.'[5]

Let no one think, then, that he can feel secure in God (the Father), while despising his Son. As orthodox Jews, Jesus' complaining auditors would not deny that the Father was active in drawing people to himself, and therefore needed to grasp the fact that no one comes to the Father except through the Son. They were responsible to Jesus, as the only Mediator between God and man, and needed to reckon with their own depravity and their need for the free and sovereign grace of God.

2. How will people come to see? (6:45-46)

Jesus answers this question by quoting Isaiah 54:13: **'And they shall all be taught by God.'** The meaning is that in the day when the Messiah comes faith will be constrained by the work of God in human hearts. Here is the new covenant of Jeremiah 31:31-34 come to fruition. Notice, also, the juxtaposition of divine initiative and human response. God teaches, and **'Therefore everyone who has heard and learned from the Father comes to me'** (6:45). The thrust of this is experiential. As Hutcheson puts it, 'No light nor illumination of the mind, nor any other change, will prove a man taught of God unless he be convinced of his own misery and of Christ's mercy, and brought to close with him, and daily to come unto him, and practise this lesson of coming; for this is the evidence of a man that he heard and learned — he "cometh to me".[6] This completely gives the lie to all the nominal religion that passes itself off as Christian. Where there is no love for the Lord, no broken spirit and contrite heart, no commitment to biblical teaching, no life of prayer and no continuing discipleship, there is no living faith, no saving knowledge of Christ, or reconciliation to God.

When Jesus adds, **'Not that anyone has seen the Father, except he who is from God; he has seen the Father'** (6:46), he identifies himself as the one who *alone* has seen the Father. Some commentators think that Jesus was here refuting a potential objection that he was (blasphemously) saying that those who come to God will *see* him with their own eyes. This is, however, simply without foundation (cf. 5:37).[7] While the statement does disavow such a viewpoint, it can hardly be the Lord's main point. He is laying down another piece of the mosaic of Messianic character and office.

3. Why people must see (6:47)

There is exactly one way to everlasting life. **'Most assuredly'** — the emphatic *amen amen* allows no misunderstanding of Jesus' point — **'I say to you, he who believes in me has everlasting life.'** 'Has' *(echei)* is a present active indicative — meaning that the believer is constitutionally in possession of eternal life, even on this side of eternity. Salvation is not locked up in some 'sweet by-and-by, when we meet by the beautiful shore'. It is as really 'now', even if its consummation is 'not yet'.

4. What people must see (6:48-50)

Jesus returns to his earlier assertion: **'I am the bread of life'** (6:35), and again that he is the bread that alone gives eternal life, whereas the manna in the wilderness did no such thing (6:30-33).

5. What people must do in order to gain eternal life (6:51)

Prattling about the manna, and looking for a repeat performance of what was, however miraculous and symbolic of God's power to give life, a remarkable material boon, was entirely misplaced. Jesus is **'the living bread'**. There is nothing here of the Roman Catholic eucharistic transubstantiation that claims to dispense the literal body of Christ, which the faithful receive by ingesting bread that has been miraculously transformed into actual flesh. The bread, which remains bread, is a simple, yet profound, metaphor for the life-giving Saviour of the world, and a particularly appropriate symbol and vehicle for Christ's making his presence known to his people, as they feed upon him by faith.

The focus, in any case, is not upon the yet to be instituted sacrament of the Lord's Supper, but has to do with the sacrificial death of the Son of God to save his people from their sins. In a very few words, our Lord outlines the theology of his mission: first, he is the *incarnate* bread **'from heaven'**; secondly, he is the *life-giving* bread, so that anyone who receives him **'will live for ever'**; thirdly, he is the voluntary *sacrifice* offered for sin, for his **'flesh'** is the bread; and finally, he is the *atonement* who gives himself **'for the life of the world'**.

The thrust of this is a call to faith. The 'bread' we need is not the manna of the wilderness wanderings, but the Lord from heaven, who, having taken our flesh, gives himself as the substitute for all who will commit themselves to him in saving faith.

Response no. 2: 'How can he give us his flesh to eat?' (6:52-59)

6:52-59. The Jews therefore quarrelled among themselves, saying, 'How can this man give us his flesh to eat?'

Then Jesus said to them, 'Most assuredly, I say to you, unless you eat the flesh of the Son of Man and drink his blood, you have no life in you. Whoever eats my flesh and drinks my blood has eternal life, and I will raise him up at the last day. For my flesh is food indeed, and my blood is drink indeed. He who eats my flesh and drinks my blood abides in me, and I in him. As the living Father sent me, and I live because of the Father, so he who feeds on me will live because of me. This is the bread which came down from heaven — not as your fathers ate the manna, and are dead. He who eats this bread will live for ever.' These things he said in the synagogue as he taught in Capernaum.

The hearers drew a blank. The fact that they did not quite understand what Jesus was saying does not imply they were so uncomprehending as to think he was talking about the literal cannibalization of his flesh. They knew he was talking figuratively, theologically and spiritually — that this was a *maschal*, or veiled saying.[8] They just could not, or would not, grasp the implications of what he was saying. Their demurral, **'How can this man give us his flesh to eat?'** poses the question as to whether he can do so in any sense — figurative or physical — for the one seems as impossible as the other!

Jesus replies by repeating essentially what he has already taught, but with greater intensity — with language that could only be calculated to shock and stir his hearers, and make them face the real issue. They must eat his flesh, so to speak, for several very pressing reasons.

First of all, *this is absolutely indispensable* to their personal salvation and resurrection to life in the last day, for **'unless'** they feed on Jesus, they will have **'no life'** in them. The heart of the matter is therefore **'eternal life'** and resurrection to salvation on the Last Day (6:53-54). There is no other way.

Secondly, *Jesus is the Mediator* through whom new life may be received. Feeding on Jesus is necessary to abiding in him, and that in turn is the sole means of receiving new life from his **'living Father'** (6:55-57). Notice that Jesus identifies himself as **'the Son of Man'** (6:53) — something he made plain to Nathanael when he first called him (1:51), and which links him both with Jacob's vision in Genesis 28:12 and Daniel's prophecy of the Messiah in Daniel 7:13-14.

Thirdly, *the death of Jesus*, and with it the element of sacrifice for sin, is emphasized by the graphic repetition of the necessity of eating his **'flesh'** and drinking **'his blood'** (6:53,54,55,56). Again, let it be

said that this is not to be construed as a reference to
the Lord's Supper in advance of its institution, even
though the Lord's Supper is obviously a symbolic
partaking of Christ's flesh and blood, and none of
John's readers would miss that connection. Neither
are we to understand the Jews as concluding that
Jesus was advocating the ingestion of his own flesh
and blood, in direct contravention of the Mosaic law
(Lev. 3:17; 17:10-14). The spiritual nature of the
transaction is, if anything, implied in the contrast
between Jesus' self-identification as **'the bread
which came down from heaven'**, who conveys
eternal life, to the manna eaten by their long departed fathers (6:58). Given the inherent difficulty,
and indeed ambiguity, in Jesus' language, it is small
wonder that his hearers were perplexed by what he
said. But they did at least realize that he was talking
about himself as the promised deliverer, the Son of
Man, and that eternal life was to be found in accepting him as such and being committed to him in
terms of an intimacy of which the language of eating
and drinking his flesh and blood was somehow
expressive. The one is shadow and the other is
substance.

Response no. 3: 'This is too hard to understand' (6:60-66)

6:60-66. Therefore many of his disciples, when they heard
this, said, 'This is a hard saying; who can understand it?'
    When Jesus knew in himself that his disciples complained
about this, he said to them, 'Does this offend you? What then
if you should see the Son of Man ascend where he was
before? It is the Spirit who gives life; the flesh profits nothing.
The words that I speak to you are spirit, and they are life. But
there are some of you who do not believe.'
    For Jesus knew from the beginning who they were who
did not believe, and who would betray him. And he said,

'Therefore I have said to you that no one can come to me unless it has been granted to him by my Father.'

From that time many of his disciples went back and walked with him no more.

The third response came from his own disciples — his wider group of followers, as distinct from 'the Twelve' (cf. 6:67). These said among themselves, **'This is a hard saying; who can understand it?'** (6:60). In this context, 'hard' means 'disturbing' or even 'offensive', as in 'hard to accept'. The problem was more than a merely intellectual one. It was more to do with a predisposition — call it theological or religious — not to accept that any Messiah of theirs could involve himself in anything as revolting as the drinking of blood, however figuratively conceived and applied! 'Professions of visible interest in Christ,' notes Hutcheson, 'will not always prove sound to the end, but the most part of such professors will, sooner or later, when their trial and temptation comes, stumble at him, his way and truth; for "many of his disciples" did here miscarry.'[9]

Jesus knew what was going through their minds (cf. 2:24; 4:18; Luke 6:8), and challenged them directly.

First he *calls them to account*: **'Does this offend you?'** (6:61). The word rendered 'offend' is the Greek *skandalizei*, from which we have our English 'scandalize'. The Greek root referred to the stick with the bait that, once knocked, would trigger the trap and capture an animal. The import here is that these people were caught and embarrassed in a difficulty they had not anticipated. Jesus' question allowed them no escape from facing the implications of their own scepticism.

Secondly, Jesus seeks to *dispel any nagging notion that he might be advocating a literal ingestion of his flesh and blood*. He does this in a most interesting

way, at every point searching their minds and prick-
ing their consciences (6:62-63).

He first *asks what they would think* if they **'should
see the Son of Man ascend where he was before'**.
He has already said that he is the living bread *from*
heaven. This has scandalized many of them. But they
really had not seen anything yet! What if they actually saw him ascend *to* heaven? Would they be more,
or less, scandalized? What if they actually witnessed
that event, which would be proof positive of his deity
and of his claim to be the prophesied 'Son of Man'?[10]
He is inviting them to think through what he has told
them. What do they expect of Daniel's promised 'Son
of Man'? What do they expect the Messiah to do?
Why are they so evidently uninterested in understanding what is meant by eating his flesh and
drinking his blood? Why do they now recoil from him,
as if there could be no truth to his claims?

He then *sets out the spiritual character* of what he
had been teaching them: **'It is the Spirit who gives
life; the flesh profits nothing. The words that I
speak to you are spirit, and they are life.'** It is as if
Jesus says, 'Look, I am talking about a new life that
is born of the Spirit of God. This is not going to come
from eating manna, or miracles of multiplying loaves
and fishes, or from eating physical flesh of any kind.
I am talking about a spiritual eating and drinking. It
is to do with my words, which are spirit (because
they come from the Spirit) and life! (because the
Spirit gives life). Banish materialist conceptions from
your mind. The flesh counts for nothing!' It is indeed,
'hard', as Carson says, 'not to see in the last clause
an allusion to Jeremiah 15:16, where the prophet
addresses God: "When your words came I ate them;
they were my joy and my heart's delight" (cf. also
Ezek. 2:8 – 3:3; Rev. 10:9ff.).'[11] Did they not remember God's word through Moses: 'Man shall not live by
bread alone; but man lives by every word that proceeds

from the mouth of the LORD'? (Deut. 8:3). And Jesus
is the divine Word, the Word made flesh! (1:1,14).

Finally, he *challenges their unbelief* (6:64-65). It is
not for lack of evidence that people reject Jesus
Christ. It takes more than schooling to make a
Christian. It takes a work of God's sovereign grace.
Reminding them of earlier statements (6:37,44),
Jesus says, **'Therefore I have said to you that no
one can come to me unless it has been granted to
him by my Father.'** The question arises as to why
Jesus should reach beyond their own unbelief to the
sovereignty of God. Might they not turn around and
say, 'Well, if that's the case, you can't blame us!'

To that, we would have to say that it is a strange
logic that draws comfort from being condemned in
this way, and imagines that this somehow conveys
the kind of innocence that should promise an exactly
opposite fate! The realization that God could well be
passing me by ought to send me fleeing in desperation to his mercy, rather than comforting myself
with a false excuse. When Jesus reminds them of the
sovereignty of God's grace, he is serving notice on the
danger of their deciding against him. Our relationship to Jesus is neither an option, like choosing our
friends, nor a matter of indifference to his holy and
just Father God. Even a coolness towards Jesus may
be evidence of rejection by his Father. Not all that is
called 'faith' proves that there is grace in the heart.
What Jesus says ought to dampen any enthusiasm
for unbelief, and cannot by any stretch of the imagination be made to absolve the sinner of his responsibility to come to Christ. The true cause of unbelief is in
the unbeliever. Mercy is optional with God.[12] It is therefore a fearful thing to be left to a wilful determination
not to heed the warnings and invitations of both law
and gospel. The very possibility ought to drive us to
our knees before the Lord, there to apply to him for
the mercy that he has promised to all who will come

to him. Sovereign grace is found in the context of a broken spirit and a contrite heart (Ps. 51:17).[13]

This was evidently a watershed, for thereafter many of Jesus' erstwhile disciples **'went back and walked with him no more'** (6:66; cf. Gal. 3:3; 4:15). There is every indication that he was abandoned by virtually all but the Twelve (cf. 6:67).

It was at least an honest apostasy, if anything wicked can be said to be honest. Many of their modern descendants are perhaps less straightforward. They will reject the teaching of Jesus and still claim to be his followers. They preach sermons, write commentaries and instruct the church and the world about what Bible doctrines need no longer be believed, and why such things as homosexual 'marriage' and killing unborn babies are perfectly acceptable morality for our day! At the turn of the twenty-first century, it is in the corridors of ecclesiastical power and theological seminaries that the self-professed disciples of Jesus will all too frequently be found to walk with him no more!

Response no. 4: 'To whom shall we go?' (6:67-71)

6:67-71. Then Jesus said to the twelve, 'Do you also want to go away?'

But Simon Peter answered him, 'Lord, to whom shall we go? You have the words of eternal life. Also we have come to believe and know that you are the Christ, the Son of the living God.'

Jesus answered them, 'Did I not choose you, the twelve, and one of you is a devil?' He spoke of Judas Iscariot, the son of Simon, for it was he who would betray him, being one of the twelve.

If Jesus knew what the murmuring ex-disciples were thinking, he certainly was not unaware of what was in the minds of the Twelve. His question was less for his own information than for their reflection and response. **'Do you also want to go away?'** he asks, the very form of words offering an opportunity for them to say 'No'.

With his characteristic enthusiasm, Peter blurts out a confession of faith unequalled in its eloquence and power: **'Lord, to whom shall we go? You have the words of eternal life. Also, we have come to believe and know that you are the Christ, the Son of the living God'** (6:68-69). This 'Majority Text' rendering (i.e., the Greek textual tradition behind the AV and the NKJV) has Peter identify Jesus as 'the Christ, the Son of the living God', in the words he used at Caesarea Philippi on another occasion (Matt. 16:16). The modern critical texts follow manuscripts that have Peter saying on this occasion, 'You are the Holy One of God.' Most commentators regard the former rendering as an importation from the Synoptics to remove any ambiguity from the expression 'Holy One', which is not so explicitly Messianic.[14]

Whatever the case, this is a verbal crescendo issuing in a glorious affirmation of Jesus as the true bread from heaven, indicating that Peter warmly embraced the very truths that so many others had found offensive. The order of expression itself is almost a four-point sermon outline on the person and work of Christ, for he is, firstly, the unique Lord; secondly, the giver of life; thirdly, the promised Messiah; and, fourthly, the divine Son of God.

The earnestness of Peter's confession did not tell the whole story, either for Peter or the other eleven. There was a great deal of water to pass under the bridge for them, and the future was to see their faith severely tested. If Peter, or any of them, entertained any superior feelings towards those who had abandoned Jesus, these were immediately dampened by

Jesus' answer: **'Did I not choose you, the twelve, and one of you is a devil?'** (6:70).

Even being chosen by Jesus did not insure against hypocrisy and betrayal! *Diabolos* means 'slanderer' or 'accuser'. Satan is *the* accuser and the father of lies. He and his agents — demons are fallen angels — are at work seducing and suggesting, easing sinners to their ruin, and trying to deceive even the very elect (Matt. 24:24). Jesus would call none other than Peter by the name 'Satan' when he dared to deny that Jesus should suffer and die in fulfilment of his mission (Mark 8:33).

John adds the commentary that **'Judas Iscariot'** was the one who would betray Jesus (6:71), but as the devil was yet to enter into him (13:2), it is not very likely that he recognized himself in Jesus' words. We are not told what the disciples made of Jesus' warning but, if their later confusion over other things that Jesus told them is any indication, it is most probable that they just shrugged their shoulders in bewilderment and hoped that such a thing would never happen.

All the more reason, then, that we should come to Christ and feed on him as the life-giving Saviour. He is the bread of life. The alternative is spiritual starvation, with, as its end, eternal death.

17. Indications of need

John 7:1-36

The events of John 6 occurred at the time of the Passover of April A.D. 29 (6:4). John 7 takes us to the Feast of Tabernacles in October of the same year. During that spring and summer, Jesus engaged in what is called his 'retirement ministry' (see Mark 7-9 for a full account). Of that time, John says only that **'Jesus walked in Galilee; for he did not want to walk in Judea, because the Jews sought to kill him'** (7:1).[1] Jesus was not ready to precipitate the final crisis that would take him to the cross, but he could not very well avoid Jerusalem altogether. So the approach of the feast was bound, once again, to draw him into the cockpit of controversy, simply because his attendance, as a devout Jew, could not but put him on a collision course with those who already had him marked for death. In John's record of the run-up to that confrontation we are provided with some vivid sketches of the attitudes and responses of different people to Jesus, all of which indicate the need of God's ancient people for the good news of Jesus their Messiah.

The chapter recounts the way in which Jesus came to be at the Feast of Tabernacles, how he took occasion from this to teach the people about the 'living water' that he would give them, and how this was the true fulfilment of the promise encapsulated in the feast itself. John first describes the indications of the spiritual neediness of the people (7:1-36) and then, as we shall see in our next study, records Jesus' invitation to them to come to him, as the living water, for a new life (7:37-52).

Unbelief at home
(John 7:1-9)

7:1-9. After these things Jesus walked in Galilee; for he did not want to walk in Judea, because the Jews sought to kill him.

Now the Jews' Feast of Tabernacles was at hand. His brothers therefore said to him, 'Depart from here and go into Judea, that your disciples also may see the works that you are doing. For no one does anything in secret while he himself seeks to be known openly. If you do these things, show yourself to the world.' For even his brothers did not believe in him.

Then Jesus said to them, 'My time has not yet come, but your time is always ready. The world cannot hate you, but it hates me because I testify of it that its works are evil. You go up to this feast. I am not yet going up to this feast, for my time has not yet fully come.'

When he had said these things to them, he remained in Galilee.

Jesus did not just face problems in the big wide world 'out there'. Even his own **'brothers'** — the other sons of Mary — **'did not believe in him'** (7:5). They had a superficial notion of his significance, and while they were all for his going to the feast, they did not remotely understand who he really was, far less trust in him as their Saviour and Messiah. Their concern was for him to promote himself by doing miracles where they could be seen by the widest audience (7:2-4).

The Lord's explanation must have set them thinking. They could go to Jerusalem at any time (7:6), but
his **'time [had] not yet fully come'** (7:8).[2] The reason for this, Jesus told them, was that whereas **'the
world'** did not hate them, **'It hates me, because I
testify of it that its works are evil'** (7:7). Jesus
highlights his uniqueness and the antithesis between
his message and the status quo. His brothers go to
the feast simply as worshippers. He goes as the one
who has come to change the world. The central issue
is *who* Jesus is!

Seen in this light, it is quite beside the point to
expound this, as most commentators do, in terms of
the theological and experiential distinction between
the regenerate (believers) and the unregenerate
(unbelievers), even though that is a necessary assumption of the passage. It is true that the brothers
were not believers, and that this is why they missed
the point Jesus was making. This certainly points up
the need for lost people to be converted to Christ. He
came to his own, and his own did not receive him
(1:11). The principal concern here, however, is to
assert the uniqueness of Jesus as the promised
Messiah, against the background of the incomprehension of Jesus' relatives. He was not just anybody
going to the feast. He was the Christ, whose hour
would come some six months later, and not before.
He was not willing to precipitate the crisis by undue
exposure to the Jewish leadership on this occasion.
This was one of those vital, unrepeatable moments in
the course of redemptive history — in this case, on
the road to the cross — in which timing was of the
essence. But it was lost on the brothers.

Questions on the street
(John 7:10-24)

It is clear that **'the Jews'** — in this context, the Jewish authorities (7:11,13) — were looking for Jesus, and not without malicious intent. His arriving **'in secret'** in **'the middle of the feast'** (7:10,14) was suitably prudential in the light of his previously stated aims and their known designs upon him. The thrust of this section, however, is directed not at the attitudes of the leaders of the Jewish church, but those of the 'man in the street'.

Looking for answers

7:10-15. But when his brothers had gone up, then he also went up to the feast, not openly, but as it were in secret.
   Then the Jews sought him at the feast, and said, 'Where is he?' And there was much complaining among the people concerning him. Some said, 'He is good'; others said, 'No, on the contrary, he deceives the people.' However, no one spoke openly of him for fear of the Jews.
   Now about the middle of the feast Jesus went up into the temple and taught. And the Jews marvelled, saying, 'How does this man know letters, having never studied?'

The mass of the people were very divided in their assessments of Jesus. Some thought him **'good'**, others that he **'deceive[d] the people'**. No one **'spoke openly of him for fear of the Jews'**, but all were amazed that a man who had taken no formal training with a rabbi was possessed of the magisterial grasp of the Scriptures (**'letters'**) that he had demonstrated in his public ministry.

Finding correct answers

7:16-18. Jesus answered them and said, 'My doctrine is not mine, but his who sent me. If anyone wills to do his will, he shall know concerning the doctrine, whether it is from God or whether I speak on my own authority. He who speaks from himself seeks his own glory; but he who seeks the glory of the one who sent him is true, and no unrighteousness is in him.'

Jesus' answer affords us a marvellously compact explanation of his authority, and sketches succinctly the way in which his message will be properly received by those who have ears to hear.

First, we must realize that *Jesus' message is not the word of one man* (7:16; cf. 1 Thess. 2:13). He did not make it up himself. He therefore says, **'My doctrine is not mine.'** Even God the Son, as the incarnate God-man, exercises a ministry with a derived character and authority. 'The Rabbinical method was to cite authorities for all important statements.[3] It was — and remains — the height of arrogance to invent one's own 'truth'. Every scholarly paper and doctoral thesis, however brilliantly innovative, must cite its sources. Jesus claims no sole origination for his teachings. Compare this with the doctrinal fictions of cults like Mormonism and the equally unfounded inventions of theologians who have rejected the inspiration and authority of Scripture in favour of their own speculations.

Secondly, we must realize *it is the Word of God* (7:16). His message was from God — it is **'his who**

sent me'. He might have added that his grasp of Scripture was the proof of that fact. His doctrine was demonstrably divine in origin. 'To the law and to the testimony! If they do not speak according to this word, it is because there is no light in them' (Isa. 8:20). 'God is light and in him is no darkness at all' (1 John 1:5).

Thirdly, we must respond to this message with *a commitment to do God's will* (7:17). **'If anyone wills to do his will'** challenges the heart and its attitude towards God and says, 'Without faith it is impossible to please [God], for he who comes to God must believe that he is, and that he is a rewarder of those who diligently seek him' (Heb. 11:6; cf. 1 Cor. 2:14-16; Heb. 4:2). The eye of faith will see the self-authenticating character of God's Word, as opposed to the bogus authority of the word of men.

Fourthly, we can see, in Jesus' own ministry, *the evidence that he is true and faithful to the living God* (7:18). He clearly was not seeking his own glory, but rather **'the glory of the one who sent him'**. For that reason, he is **'true, and no unrighteousness is in him'**. The criticisms of detractors and the doubt of the unconvinced are without foundation, for the evidence is incontrovertibly before their eyes — and still is through the window of the completed canon of Holy Scripture.

Making sound judgements

7:19-24. 'Did not Moses give you the law, yet none of you keeps the law? Why do you seek to kill me?'

The people answered and said, 'You have a demon. Who is seeking to kill you?'

Jesus answered and said to them, 'I did one work, and you all marvel. Moses therefore gave you circumcision (not that it is from Moses, but from the fathers), and you circumcise a man on the Sabbath. If a man receives circumcision on the Sabbath, so that the law of Moses should not be broken, are you angry with me because I made a man completely well on the Sabbath? Do not judge according to appearance, but judge with righteous judgement.'

The Jews certainly believed that God had given Moses the law at Sinai. On that point there was no dispute, whatever their doubts about Jesus. 'Very well,' Jesus is saying, 'let us apply the authoritative Word of God to what is going on in your minds as you assess me and what I have done, and let us see how sound your judgements really are.' He poses three practical questions.

1. Do you keep God's law? (7:19)

Talk is cheap. Keeping the law is different from accepting that it comes from God. The Jews in fact did not keep the law. The proof of this was to be found in the fact that they were seeking to kill Jesus, in blatant contradiction of the Sixth Commandment! (Exod. 20:13). They were guilty of the very impurity of motive and practice of which they accused Jesus!

2. Do you discern the work of God? (7:20-23)

The people present denied that anyone was seeking to kill Jesus and basically told him he was crazy to think any such thing: **'You have a demon.'** In response to this, Jesus refers them to his well-known miracle of healing the man at the Pool of Bethesda on a Sabbath day (5:1-9). They marvelled at the miracle (7:21), but objected to the fact that he did it on the Sabbath (5:16). At the same time, they did not feel they were breaking the law of Moses — i.e., God's revealed will — by circumcising covenant children on the Sabbath, when the eighth day after a child's birth fell on that day.[4] So why did they charge him with breaking the law by making a man **'completely well on the Sabbath'**? (7:23). The point is that they had earlier missed the true point of the Sabbath by imposing their legalistic punctilios upon it. Accordingly, they had wrongly cast Jesus in the role of an anti-sabbatarian who intended to liberalize the Sabbath law (see the exposition of 5:16-18, pp.217-21).

3. Do you make sound judgements? (7:24)

Their doubts about Jesus were wholly unfounded. Their judgement had been unsound. It had been superficial. They needed to **'not judge according to appearance, but judge with righteous judgement'**. This recalls something of the contrast in 1 Samuel 16:7: 'The LORD does not see as man sees; for man looks at the outward appearance, but the LORD looks at the heart.' Jesus had no time for judgementalism (Matt. 7:1), but called for spiritually discerning moral judgements, informed by the righteousness of God rightly understood.

Hostility in high places
(John 7:25-36)

Some of the local people knew the authorities wanted to kill Jesus and noticed that, though he spoke **'boldly'**, they said nothing to him. Their remark about the rulers possibly regarding Jesus as **'truly the Christ'** (7:26) is a lightly disguised jibe, as if to say in a mocking tone, 'Do they know something we don't know?' The local people were sure of what they knew: Jesus could not be the Messiah, for the reason that they knew where he came from (7:25-27). After all, they expected the Messiah to come from Bethlehem, and Jesus was associated with Galilee (Matt. 2:6 [quoting Micah 5:2]; John 7:41-42).[5] It was an easy question to answer, was it not? So why should the rulers be so coy?

Sent from God (7:25-31)

7:25-31. Now some of them from Jerusalem said, 'Is this not he whom they seek to kill? But look! He speaks boldly, and they say nothing to him. Do the rulers know indeed that this is truly the Christ? However, we know where this man is from; but when the Christ comes, no one knows where he is from.'

Then Jesus cried out, as he taught in the temple, saying, 'You both know me, and you know where I am from; and I have not come of myself, but he who sent me is true, whom

you do not know. But I know him, for I am from him, and he
sent me.'

Therefore they sought to take him; but no one laid a hand
on him, because his hour had not yet come.

And many of the people believed in him, and said, 'When
the Christ comes, will he do more signs than these which this
man has done?'

Jesus did not enlighten them about his true birth-
place. But with a loud, impassioned exclamation, he
rebuked their pettifogging prejudice with a stinging
challenge and followed up with an explicit declaration
that he had come from God: **'You both know me,
and you know where I am from'** (7:28a,b) is
equivalent to, 'So you think you know it all, do you?'
They thought they knew, but were actually profoundly ignorant of the facts.

1. Truths about Jesus (7:28-29)

What were the facts? Jesus lays out the essentials
with masterly simplicity: **'I have not come of myself, but he who has sent me is true, whom you do
not know'** (7:28c). The material point is that had
they really known God, they would have recognized
that he, Jesus, was indeed sent by God! Jesus is the
test and the measure of truly knowing the living God.
That they 'do not know' the God they so proudly and
exclusively boast as theirs is proved by their failure
to acknowledge Jesus for who he really is!

In contrast, says Jesus, **'I know him, for I am
from him, and he sent me'** (7:29). His origin 'from',
or with, God, and his divine commission, endow him
with a unique knowledge of God. This is a clear claim
to an exclusive and thorough intimacy with the Father.
It implies, albeit in a muted way, Christ's role as the
only Mediator between God and man. 'I know him
and you do not,' Jesus is saying, 'and, furthermore,

knowing me is the only way to knowing him' (cf. 5:19; Matt. 11:27; Luke 10:22). The claim to be the Messiah may not be explicit in these words of Jesus, but it was not lost upon his hearers. They had been backed against a wall, and were forced to choose between accepting Jesus as the one he claimed to be, or rejecting him as an impostor.

2. Responses to Jesus (7:30-31)

The revelation of God in Jesus Christ always divides its hearers. The preachers of the gospel are, says Paul, 'the fragrance of Christ among those who are being saved and among those who are perishing. To the one we are the aroma of death leading to death, and to the other the aroma of life leading to life' (2 Cor. 2:15-16). Both responses were forthcoming on this occasion.

Opposition is inevitable

John's emphatic **'Therefore they sought to take him'** (7:30a) conveys the air of the expected, as if to say, 'What else would you look for from people?' Christians, especially the inexperienced, are often shocked and dismayed by the virulence of the opposition that sometimes bursts upon them from the world, as if it is somehow incomprehensible that anybody should react with offended fury to such a benign and helpful message as the gospel of Jesus Christ. They miss the vital point, however, that the gospel calls for unconditional surrender from sinners and, furthermore, commands their sincere repentance and pervasive reformation! This is bound to be the most threatening message in the world to a person who is determined to deny God's claims upon his life. It strikes at the citadel of human autonomy from God. It requires the confession from the heart that God is right and I am wrong, that I am lost and only Jesus can save me, and it commands my immediate personal commitment to him as Saviour. The wickedness of the world and its determination to resist the gospel of Jesus Christ should come as no surprise to any servant of the Lord. No servant is above his master; and if they hate Jesus, they will also hate faithful Christians. This is not a martyr complex, but Jesus' own test of reality for his followers! (Matt. 10:24-26; John 15:18-21).

The opposition is not omnipotent

The enemies of the gospel are on a leash! No one laid a hand on Jesus **'because his hour had not yet come'** (7:30b). The hour of Jesus' death was decreed by God, notwithstanding the wilful determination of men to kill him (Acts 2:23). How he escaped on this occasion is immaterial. The point is simply stated to underscore the sovereignty of God. The moment for the cross had not yet come.

There is an absolute principle in this event and it is universal in its application. Calvin's comment is matchless: 'And hence we ought to infer a general doctrine; for though we live from day to day, still the time of every man's death has been fixed by God. It is difficult to believe that, while we are subject to so many accidents, exposed to so many open and concealed attacks both from men and beasts, and liable to so many diseases, we are safe from all risk until God is pleased to call us away. But we ought to struggle against our own distrust; and we ought to attend first to the doctrine itself which is here taught, and next, to the object at which it aims, and the exhortation which is drawn from it, namely, that each of us, *casting his cares on God* (Ps. 55:22; 1 Peter 5:7), should follow his own calling, and not be led away from the performance of his duty by any fears. Yet let no man go beyond his own bounds; for

confidence in the providence of God must not go
farther than God himself commands.[6]

Some, however, were open to Jesus' teaching

**'And many of the people believed in him, and
said, "When the Christ comes, will he do more
signs that these which this man has done?"'**
(7:31). They thought, on the basis of the miracles he
had performed, that he might well be the promised
Messiah. Their question rebukes the scepticism of
their own leadership. What could 'the Christ' do to
convince such people? The question is apropos to all
modern unbelief. What more could Jesus do to
convince the world of sin, righteousness and judgement to come? On the day of his appearing, every
cavil will be confounded and every sceptic silenced.

This is not to say that these people had a true and
living faith in Jesus Christ. Their 'believing' in him
would appear to have been limited to a general acceptance of his having a reasonably credible claim to
Messiahship — one that, at the very least, should not
be summarily dismissed. For all that, they 'depended
more on miracles than they relied on doctrine', notes
Calvin, 'and were not convinced that Jesus was the
Christ'.[7] Millions today 'believe' in Jesus in the same
kind of detached way. They accept the notion that
Jesus was a special kind of person — maybe even
(who knows?) the Son of God. As to *knowing* him and
the power of his resurrection and the fellowship of
his sufferings, they have not the slightest clue (cf.
Phil. 3:10-16). They have no experience of saving
faith and the transformation this would have
wrought in their deepest being. There is no *heart* for
the Lord, only an intellectual recognition of the
possibility that he might be who he claims to be.

Returning to God
(John 7:32-36)

Even the most tentative sympathy for Jesus was enough to spur an already hostile and worried Jewish establishment to some decisive action. This united these otherwise warring factions — **'the Pharisees'** and **'the chief priests'** (i.e., the Sadducees) — in the common cause of preserving their privileged positions and, no doubt, their cherished heresies, and they **'sent officers to take him'** (7:32). As has often been the case ever since, Christ and his following were viewed as a greater danger than any other single rival group. A world estranged from God clings to its own received orthodoxies and instinctively closes ranks against the unsettling, and therefore unwelcome, advent of the Lord of glory and his righteousness (1 Cor. 2:8).

The counsel of God

7:32-34. The Pharisees heard the crowd murmuring these things concerning him, and the Pharisees and the chief priests sent officers to take him.

Then Jesus said to them, 'I shall be with you a little while longer, and then I go to him who sent me. You will seek me and not find me, and where I am you cannot come.'

The officers duly went to arrest Jesus. For the result of the encounter, we shall have to wait until verses

45-52, but it is clear enough that the Jewish authorities are in for a disappointment on this occasion! Jesus gives his erstwhile captors a lesson, theological and practical, in the doctrine of the divine decree and the consequent impossibility of men's thwarting the sovereign purpose of God. Jesus' saying is clothed in mystery, but in it can be discerned the most solemn of truths.

In the first place, *they will not take him now,* for, he declares, **'I shall be with you a little while longer'** (7:33a). When questioned later as to why they had not arrested Jesus, the officers answered, 'No man ever spoke like this man!' (7:46). They had been disarmed by the power of Jesus' words, that is to say, by the power of God. We are reminded here of the way in which Jesus, at the very commencement of his public ministry, escaped being thrown from a cliff by the irate people of Nazareth: 'Then passing through the midst of them, he went his way' (Luke 4:30). The invisible hand of God was at work in the hearts and minds of his enemies, so that in spite of themselves they could not alter the Lord's timetable!

Secondly, *they will never make an end of him,* for, he says, **'... then I go to him who sent me'** (7:33b). It was the conceit of the enemies of the gospel that by killing Jesus, and later his followers, they could terminate their influence in the world. But they could only cut off what was visible above the ground. The root would remain to sprout with new life. In any case, Jesus was going to God, who sent him; he was not despatched by the will of his murderers. That was their delusion. Even the death they were later to inflict on Jesus had been decreed by God for the very purpose which they, in their blindness, believed they were thwarting!

Thirdly, *the reprobate lost will cry in vain for redemption:* **'You will seek me and not find me'** (7:34a). In due course, Jesus was indeed found, arrested, condemned, crucified and buried. But the tomb emptied on the third day. Jesus appeared to the apostles over forty succeeding days and then ascended into the heavens before their eyes. Above 500 were witnesses of his resurrection! (1 Cor. 15:6). At the very least, then, this statement means that the Jews were left with no more than an empty tomb for all their malicious pains. They could not find his body.

There may be an even more sombre thought here, however, for the Jews still sought their Messiah, even though they had rejected the real one! In rejecting Jesus, Israel had denied the very hope of Israel (Jer. 17:7; Acts 28:20), but still looked for him elsewhere. That 'messiah' they could never find, simply because he was a figment of their own imagination! 'Many [professed Christians] will say to me in that day, "Lord, Lord, have we not prophesied in your name, cast out demons in your name, and done many wonders in your name?" And then I will declare to them, "I never knew you; depart from me, you who practise lawlessness!"' (Matt. 7:22-23). 'Hence let us learn,' pleads Calvin, 'that we ought to receive Christ without delay, while he is still present with us, that the opportunity of enjoying him may not pass away from us; for if the door be once shut, it will be vain for us to try to open it, "Seek the Lord," says Isaiah, "while he may be found; call upon him, while he is near" (Isa. 55:6).[8]

Finally, *they will go to a lost eternity*, for **'Where I am you cannot come'** (7:34b). Jesus was going to the Father. Here he slams the gate of heaven in the face of all who finally reject him as the Son of the Father. And yet, to any who will hear him, this is a plea to think again.

Do not harden your hearts, as in the rebellion
[says the Lord through the psalmist]

As in the day of trial in the wilderness,
When your fathers tested me;
They tried me, though they saw my work.
For forty years I was grieved with that gener-
   ation...
So I swore in my wrath,
'They shall not enter my rest'

(Ps. 95:8-11).

You mock the Lord at your peril! But turn to him,
and you will live!

The confusion of men (7:35-36)

7:35-36. Then the Jews said among themselves, 'Where
does he intend to go that we shall not find him? Does he
intend to go to the Dispersion among the Greeks and teach
the Greeks? What is this thing that he said, "You will seek
me and not find me, and where I am you cannot come"?'

The men did not understand Jesus at all. Their reply
appears to indicate that they thought he was merely
talking about escaping their jurisdiction as police-
men. Where could Jesus go where they could not
arrest him? Why, to **'the Dispersion among the
Greeks'**! Hendriksen, following the lead of Calvin,
thinks they were mocking Jesus,[9] but a judicious
assessment of this context and verses 45-47 suggests
that they were simply dumbfounded. It is just the
kind of lame response that people will blurt out
because they cannot think of anything intelligent to
say.
   Could there be a more pathetic indication of their
spiritual blindness and their need of the Saviour they
could not see, even when he was under their very
noses? Here is the real world — our world as much
as that of the first century — a world in desperate

need, that will not see the Saviour who is holding his hands out all day to their own generation. It is no accident that Jesus now goes on to proclaim himself as the living water who can assuage the deepest thirst of souls who will come to him, believing, and receive the Holy Spirit. Oh, pray that the Lord would revive us in these days!

18. Invitation to life

John 7:37-52

Every October, the Jews went up to Jerusalem for the Feast of Tabernacles, a feast in which they remembered and celebrated how God had sustained them in the wilderness wanderings in Sinai, and gave thanks for the harvest of the past year.[1] 'You shall keep ... the Feast of Harvest, the firstfruits of your labours which you have sown in the field' (Exod. 23:15-16; cf. Lev. 23:33-43 for the details of this observance). For a whole week, they lived in booths made from tree branches and palm fronds.

On each of these seven days, the high priest filled a flagon with water from the Pool of Siloam and processed up to the temple, where this water and some wine were poured out at the altar in commemoration of God's provision of water in the wilderness (Num. 20:2-13), and prayer was offered for God's future provision for his people. Isaiah 12:3 was associated with this ceremony: 'With joy you will draw water from the wells of salvation.' In Jewish thought, notes Carson, 'These ceremonies were related ... both to the Lord's provision of water in the desert and to the Lord's pouring out of the Spirit in the last days. Pouring at the Feast of Tabernacles refers symbolically to the messianic age in which a stream from the sacred rock would flow over the whole earth.'[2]

The invitation given
(John 7:37)

7:37. On the last day, that great day of the feast, Jesus stood and cried out, saying, 'If anyone thirsts, let him come to me and drink...'

With this statement, Jesus puts himself squarely into the context provided by the Feast of Tabernacles and, especially, the ritual of the water of Siloam and its evocation of the promise of the outpouring of the Spirit of God (Isa. 12:3). In doing so, he issues one of the great invitations of the gospel to come to him as the giver of new life — 'Christ's sweet sermon' as George Hutcheson calls it.[3] Now he reveals himself without the reserve that kept him from going to the beginning of the feast (7:6-9).[4] The implication is that his time had come, and events would swiftly unfold to the climax of his earthly ministry.

To whom must we come?

The unvarnished simplicity of Jesus' invitation allows no room for misunderstanding. He commands us, **'Come to me...'** He had said as much to the woman of Samaria when he declared that he could give 'living water' (4:10), and that whoever received this water would 'never thirst', but would discover it to be 'a fountain of water springing up into everlasting life' (4:14).

Just as God provided for Israel in the desert, so Jesus will give the life-giving Spirit of God to thirsty souls. Carson has suggested that Jesus had in mind Nehemiah 9:15,19-20, where manna, water and God's Spirit are connected (the only place in the Old Testament where this happens), and the context in which it is set — the reading of God's law to the people at the Feast of Tabernacles (Neh. 8:8-15; Deut. 31:10-11).[5] If this is so, then, argues Carson, 'The gift of the law/Spirit is symbolized by the provision of manna/water' and Jesus is putting himself at the centre of it as the promised Messiah.[6] *He* gives the living water — the gift of the Holy Spirit! To receive it for ourselves, we must go to *him*!

Who is to come?

Anyone who **'thirsts'** is to come to Jesus. The emphasis is upon felt need. The same focus on the personal and the experiential is also found in Jesus' words in Matthew 11:28: 'Come to me, all you who labour and are heavy laden, and I will give you rest.' The gospel is always addressed to the anxious heart that deeply feels the need of a Saviour. The Lord explicitly declares that he did *not* come to call 'the righteous, but sinners, to repentance' (Matt. 9:13). It is not that there were any righteous people who did not need to be called. Jesus' point is that those who believe themselves to be righteous already will not feel the need of his salvation. The only people who will come to him are those who first admit to themselves and to God that they are sinners and need a Saviour.

Furthermore, **'anyone'** who is thirsty is called to come. No one is excluded from the duty of coming to Christ. No one is too guilty, too miserable, too unhappy. If they thirst, they may come, and must come,

to Jesus. The call is universal. The target is dry,
parched, thirsty souls:

> Ho! Everyone who thirsts,
> Come to the waters;
> And you who have no money,
> Come, buy and eat.
> Yes, come, buy wine and milk
> Without money and without price
>
> (Isa. 55:1).

What are we to do?

In the first place, *when Jesus calls, we are to go to
him.* He says, **'Come...'** That is the command we
must heed and obey. This coming to him is not a
speculative mechanical response, as if following up a
potentially advantageous option, without any knowledge of who or what is involved. Coming to Jesus
involves an explicit faith, for 'Without faith it is
impossible to please him, for he who comes to God
must believe that he is, and that he is a rewarder of
those who diligently seek him' (Heb. 11:6). We come
to Jesus believing that he is from God, that he is the
incarnate Son of God and that he is able to save lost
people, dead in sin, in virtue of his substitutionary,
atoning death upon Calvary's cross. There is a great
deal of content in the matter of coming to Christ for
salvation. It is a coming that comprehends the content of the gospel. He is understood to be the fountain opened for sin and for uncleanness (Zech. 13:1).

In the second place, *when we go to Jesus, we are
to* **'drink'**. We are to act on that first faith that trusts
him. We are to go on to feed on him, so to speak. We
are to follow him and become his disciples. When
children are called to the dinner table, they go willingly when they are hungry, and they go because

they believe that their mother has actually put a meal on the table. They go, firstly, because they are called and commanded; secondly, because they believe there will be food there for them; and, thirdly, with the desire and intention of eating the meal.

The Christian life is eating and drinking Christ, or it is nothing at all. He is the bread of life (John 6:35). He is the giver of life and living water. Life in Christ is likened to the enjoyment of a feast (1 Cor. 5:8). The imagery of the Lord's Supper — eating bread and drinking wine that are the symbols of Christ's broken body and shed blood — vividly enhances that practical trust, devotion and discipleship that cannot but flow from a living faith in the crucified and risen Redeemer. As our Redeemer, Christ fulfils the offices of Prophet, Priest and King. As Prophet, he reveals the will of God and the knowledge of God (Acts 3:22; 2 Cor. 4:6). As Priest, he offered himself as a sacrifice for sin, his blood cleansing his people from their sin and reconciling them to God, and he continues to make intercession for them with the Father (Heb. 8:1-3; 9:28; 7:25). As King, he subdues us to himself, rules and defends us, and restrains and conquers his enemies and ours (Ps. 2:6; John 18:36; Acts 15:14; Isa. 33:22; 31:2; 1 Cor. 15:25, see also *Shorter Catechism,* Questions 23-26). The whole Christian life is subsumed under the ministry of Jesus Christ received and enjoyed as a personal Saviour. It is he who calls sinners to come to him, with the assurance that whoever believes in him will not perish, but have everlasting life (3:16).

The invitation received
(John 7:38-39)

7:38-39. 'He who believes in me, as the Scripture has said, out of his heart will flow rivers of living water.'
But this he spoke concerning the Spirit, whom those believing in him would receive; for the Holy Spirit was not yet given, because Jesus was not yet glorified.

The results of coming to Christ are set out with Jesus' summarization of teaching found in a number of Old Testament passages, together with an interpretive comment from the apostle John.

New life in Jesus Christ

When we come to Christ, we receive new life. God's people have the living water within them: **'He who believes in me, as the Scripture has said, out of his heart will flow rivers of living water'** (7:38). Notice the three components of this verse.

1. 'He who believes in me...'

A living, personal faith in Christ is the condition of new life. 'The right way of a thirsty soul's coming to Christ for refreshment is by believing...,' observes Hutcheson. 'It must be the root from which the rest must spring ... for nothing we have can be right or acceptable without faith laying hold on Christ and his righteousness.'[7] 'Without faith it is impossible to please him [God]' and 'Whatever is not from faith is sin' (Heb. 11:6; Rom. 14:23). This is not 'faith' in the abstract — any sort of faith in any kind of god or any type of redemption — it is *saving* faith, faith that knows what Jesus' exclusive claims are, that accepts what God's Word says as to who Jesus is and what he has done, and from the heart trusts him, alone, as the Saviour and Lord of one's life. Anything else is an illusion and a false hope.

2. 'As the Scripture has said...'

The necessity of coming to Christ is laid upon our consciences by the full authority of the Word of God. What the Lord subsequently cites is no single text of Scripture, but a doctrine drawn from a number of places (see Isa. 12:3; 43:20; 44:3; 55:1). In the background is the frequent declaration in the Old Testament that waters will flow from Zion to the blessing of a renewed humanity (Ezek. 47:1-12; Zech.14:8). The fact that the Son of God constantly cites Scripture in support of his teaching is a timely corrective for a day when many churches, preachers and theologians ask us to believe propositions that are often framed without reference to Scripture, or even formulated contrary to the clear teaching of Scripture.

3. 'Out of his heart will flow rivers of living water'

It is clear enough that it is from the heart of the believer that 'living water' pours forth. This has been challenged in recent years by a so-called 'Christological' interpretation that insists that it is Christ's heart in view here — this on the ground that the standard view would require seeing the believer's heart as the ultimate source of living water, which it obviously cannot be. This, however, holds sound exegesis

hostage to a false premise. It is clear from what
follows (in verse 39) that the heart that brings forth
living water (in verse 38) is only able to do so because
of the work of the Holy Spirit. Any ambiguity is
exploded by John's commentary, which shows that
the experiential fruit of coming to Christ is to overflow with newness of life. Christ is indeed the ultimate source of the living water, but, in Christ, believers well up with the living water he gives to the soul.
This is the fruit of being 'born again' (3:3). It grows
within us as a 'fountain', and never ceases because it
springs up to everlasting life (4:14). Therefore, it can
be said of the believer that 'From the abundance of
the heart, the mouth pours forth praise' (cf. Matt.
12:34; Luke 6:45). There is light where there was
spiritual darkness, 'beauty for ashes, the oil of joy for
mourning, the garment of praise for the spirit of
heaviness' (Isa. 61:3).

New life through the Holy Spirit

'But this he spoke concerning the Spirit,' that is,
he spoke of what the Holy Spirit would do in believers, subsequent to the glorification of Christ. John
writes from a post-John 20/Acts 2 perspective and
wants it clearly understood that the living water is a
metaphorical bridge between the water poured out at
the Feast of Tabernacles and the work of the Holy
Spirit in the post-Pentecostal church. The giving of
the Holy Spirit and his gifts was reserved for the time
after Christ had actually died, risen and ascended
into heaven, so demonstrating that salvation and
newness of life are the fruit of Christ's mediatorial
sacrifice for sin.

The invitation and you
(John 7:40-52)

As usual, Jesus got mixed reviews: **'There was a division among the people because of him'** (7:43). This is the invariable effect when the truth of God is brought to bear on the human conscience (cf. 2 Cor. 2:14-16).

Three responses (7:40-44)

7:40-44. Therefore many from the crowd, when they heard this saying, said, 'Truly this is the Prophet.'

Others said, 'This is the Christ.'

But some said, 'Will the Christ come out of Galilee? Has not the Scripture said that the Christ comes from the seed of David and from the town of Bethlehem, where David was?'

So there was a division among the people because of him. Now some of them wanted to take him, but no one laid hands on him.

Some said, **'Truly this is the Prophet,'** clearly with reference to the promise of Deuteronomy 18:15-19 (7:40). They appeared to stop short of explicitly identifying Jesus as the Christ (Messiah), in spite of the fact that 'the Prophet' is clearly one and the same with the Messiah.

A second group explicitly proclaimed, **'This is the Christ'** (7:41a). This does not prove they had any more of a living faith in Jesus as Messiah than the first group. Since 'the Prophet' and 'the Christ' were actually one and the same person, the fact that they could be divided on the basis of these titles indicates a certain lack of comprehension on both sides — reminding us perhaps of the way the Corinthian church divided over Paul, Apollos, Peter and Christ, as if they were somehow opposed to one another (1 Cor. 1:12), when they were completely united.

The third group could not accept that Jesus was the Messiah. Believing that Jesus originally came from Galilee, they advanced the otherwise quite proper argument that the Christ had to come from **'the seed of David and from the town of Bethlehem'** (7:41b-43; cf. 2 Sam. 7:12-16; Ps. 89:2-3; Isa. 9:7; 55:3; Micah 5:2). They simply did not know that Jesus had been born in Bethlehem and was of Davidic descent (2 Sam. 7:12-13; Matt. 2:1: Acts 2:30; Rom. 1:3; 2 Tim. 2:8; Rev. 5:5). Some were angry enough to want to **'take him'**, but were prevented from doing so, not by purely circumstantial realities, but, as Hutcheson puts it, by 'the overruling and restraining power of God'.[8]

Rejected by the establishment (7:45-52)

7:45-52. Then the officers came to the chief priests and Pharisees, who said to them, 'Why have you not brought him?'

The officers answered, 'No man ever spoke like this man!'

Then the Pharisees answered them, 'Are you also deceived? Have any of the rulers or the Pharisees believed in him? But this crowd that does not know the law is accursed.'

Nicodemus (he who came to Jesus by night, being one of them) said to them, 'Does our law judge a man before it hears him and knows what he is doing?'

They answered and said to him, 'Are you also from Galilee? Search and look, for no prophet has arisen out of Galilee.'

The scene now shifts to a meeting of the Sanhedrin, the council of the Jewish leadership. The dynamic of their discussion is most interesting, in that it reveals something that is true of all seemingly monolithic establishments — namely, that they are constantly frustrated by lack of compliance on the part of others and dissent within their own ranks.

The officers responsible for carrying out the wishes of the authorities failed in their task because they were overwhelmed by Jesus' words and, no doubt, the crowd's reaction to Jesus. Their excuse, **'No man ever spoke like this man!'** (7:46), betrays that sense of the inherent evil of the task that often arises in the consciences of the agents of persecution when confronted by palpable holiness. That did not impress the Pharisees, who promptly and contemptuously berated both their police (as those who were **'deceived'**) and the people (**'This crowd that does not know the law is accursed'**).

When Nicodemus, a member of the council, courageously reminded them that the law did not judge a man without a trial, they turned on him with an implicit suggestion of insincerity. Was Nicodemus himself from Galilee? He would have to be to close his mind to the fact that **'No prophet has arisen out of Galilee'**! (7:52). For them, it was an 'open and shut' case. No other facts were needed. Jesus was an impostor!

What will you do with Jesus?

The wrath of the Pharisees and the confusion of the people all conspire to challenge John's readers with the question as to what they themselves have done, or will do, with Jesus and the claims of the gospel.

Some had already come to Jesus Christ as their own Saviour. They had drunk of the living waters. They knew what it was to be dead in trespasses and sins and to thirst for a new life and new righteousness. They had come to repentance and faith, had received forgiveness of sin and been clothed in the robes of Christ's righteousness. Sinners saved by free grace, they understood also that the message of life must be proclaimed in word and deed to a parched and lifeless world.

Others would have read this account — as many do today — and found no desire within their hearts for the living water that is Jesus the Saviour. To them, this comes as an earnest call to come to Christ without delay.

Ho! Everyone who thirsts,
Come to the waters;
And you who have no money,
Come, buy and eat.
Yes, come, buy wine and milk
Without money and without price.
Why do you spend money for what is not bread,
And your wages for what does not satisfy?
Listen carefully to me,
And eat what is good,
And let your soul delight itself in abundance.
Incline your ear and come to me:
Hear, and your soul shall live...
(Isa. 55:1-3).

19. 'Go and sin no more'
John 7:53 – 8:11

Jesus frequently used the circumstances of the moment to teach the people about himself and the truth of God. He meets a woman at a well and describes himself as the giver of living water. Someone mentions God's gift of manna in the wilderness and he identifies himself as the living bread. Now, in connection with the famous incident of the woman taken in adultery (7:53 – 8:11), Jesus takes occasion from the sunrise over Jerusalem to speak of himself as the light of the world. This, at any rate, is the connection made by the flow of our standard English Bible texts.

There is, however, a general and long-standing consensus that 7:53 – 8:11 was not originally part of John's Gospel. It appears in no manuscript before the fifth century and is not commented on as part of John by any of the Church Fathers. It was nevertheless clearly known in the church from the earliest days, for Eusebius records that Papias, who was a student of the apostle John, is known to have expounded it, though not in connection with John's Gospel.[1] It has certainly been received as canonical Scripture for most of two millennia. Most commentators today follow Calvin,[2] who did not believe it belonged to John, but taught that it was true and edifying and therefore ought to be expounded.

It certainly fits theologically, if not chronologically, between John 7 and 8, and provides a dramatic illustration of what it meant for Jesus to be the light of the world in a very practical situation. As such, it forms a dramatic introduction for the 'light of the world' discourse (8:12-59) — which was no doubt the motivation of the scribe who inserted it in John's Gospel in the first place. From the light of the dawn we are led to witnesses bringing a sin to the light, and on to the light of new life for the woman who is told to go and sin no more. Jesus confronts the spiritual darkness with the light of God, and brings that light to hitherto darkened souls. The woman taken in adultery is the practical example illustrating the revelation of Christ as the light who alone can truly enlighten any human soul.

The passage dealing with the woman taken in adultery would appear to record an authentic historical incident in the ministry of Jesus. It is obvious, however, that Jesus is the one who is really on trial. The woman might have been in danger of being executed, but it is not clear that, under the Roman hegemony, the Jews had any power to put adulterers to death, whatever the requirements of the Mosaic law. She had been caught *in flagrante delicto*, to be sure, but her role was more that of a pawn in a larger scheme to trap Jesus (8:6). The passage unfolds in three phases: there is a dishonest question (7:53 – 8:6), a searching response (8:7-9) and a gracious admonition (8:10-11).

A dishonest question
(John 7:53 – 8:6)

7:53 – 8:6. And everyone went to his own house. But Jesus went to the Mount of Olives.

Now early in the morning he came again into the temple, and all the people came to him; and he sat down and taught them.

Then the scribes and Pharisees brought to him a woman caught in adultery. And when they had set her in the midst, they said to him, 'Teacher, this woman was caught in adultery, in the very act. Now Moses, in the law, commanded us that such should be stoned. But what do you say?' This they said, testing him, that they might have something of which to accuse him.

But Jesus stooped down and wrote on the ground with his finger, as though he did not hear.

Spiritual darkness frequently hides behind a cloak of apparent light. Here are some **'scribes and Pharisees'** — the leading luminaries of Jewish society — coming to the famous itinerant teacher, Jesus of Nazareth, with an apparently serious question about the punishment of a crime, as defined in the law of Moses.

Even if we had not been explicitly told of the subterfuge (8:6), we would have a strong clue in the conspicuous absence of the other party to the sin. Where was *the man*? God's law prescribed death for both the man and the woman in the case of adultery (Lev. 20:10; Deut. 22:22-24). Why did they only bring the woman? No prizes for the answer to that one! These people were not interested in equal justice before the law. In fact, they were not interested in 'justice' at all! This was an exercise in duplicity.

The question as to whether she should be executed, then, was not so much designed to kill her as to elicit from Jesus an answer that might be taken down and used in evidence against him. Jesus was known for his compassion for such women (Luke 7:36-50). Clearly, they wanted him to come out with something more lenient than the penalty of the law of Moses. If he did, they could accuse him of heterodoxy. On the other hand, if he agreed to a stoning, he might lose some support from the people, whose interests could be assumed to be the other way.

Jesus was not about to fall for such an obvious, if not ham-fisted, ruse.[3] He just stooped down, wrote on the ground with his finger and acted as if he had heard nothing at all. His action has occasioned ingenious speculations by the commentators, including the suggestion of an allusion to the 'finger of God' writing the Ten Commandments at Sinai. But this is surely a case of over-elaboration obscuring the obvious. Jesus was simply letting them stew for a bit! Writing in the dirt was no more than a dramatic doodle to heighten the tension. Let them wonder what he would say. Let them speculate about the deeper meaning of his action — that was just a diversionary tactic, setting them up for a *coup de grâce* that was about to be administered in plain language! If there is a lesson here, it is to resist being drawn into making a rushed judgement, and to avoid telegraphing a response until it can made with maximum effect. Body language is an important part of this. Jesus did not leap into the fray. He used an apparently unresponsive silence to seize the initiative from his interrogators. When he did eventually open his mouth, they were on the run.

A searching response
(John 8:7-9)

8:7-9. So when they continued asking him, he raised himself up and said to them, 'He who is without sin among you, let him throw a stone at her first.' And again he stooped down and wrote on the ground.

Then those who heard it, being convicted by their conscience, went out one by one, beginning with the oldest even to the last. And Jesus was left alone, and the woman standing in the midst.

Jesus' apparent unresponsiveness only made the men more insistent that he answer. He then raised himself up, said, **'He who is without sin among you, let him throw a stone at her first,'** and promptly returned to his doodling in the sand. The result was that they were **'convicted by their conscience'** and left the scene **'beginning with the oldest even to the last'**.

It should first be said that, contrary to popular opinion, Jesus was not here abrogating any law of God respecting sexual sin. He was in fact upholding that law. He was insisting upon rules of evidence and equal justice. His question exposed the involvement of the men in the sin of the woman's conspicuously absent male partner. They had chosen to cover his sin, while bringing her under the penalties of the law, and were therefore guilty as accessories after the fact. Could they throw the first stone at the woman, which the law required of witnesses in capital crimes

(Deut. 13:9-10; 17:7), while letting the man go scot-free? They were as guilty as he, for they had connived at his sin.

Another popular notion connected with this incident is the idea that anyone who was ever guilty of sexual sin, even if only in his thought-life (Matt. 5:28), is disqualified from condemning that sin in others. The law stands, even if the judge and the prosecutor are personally lawless. The point here, however, is that anyone involved in the same *particular* sinful act cannot condemn the others involved without himself being subject to the same penalty. The judge and prosecutor perish with the condemned if they are party to the same particular criminal act in which the prosecution is brought. 'No man, therefore,' says Calvin, 'shall be prevented by his own sins from correcting the sins of others, and even from punishing them, when it may be found necessary, provided that both in himself and in others he hate what ought to be condemned; and in addition to all this, every man ought to begin by interrogating his own conscience, and by acting both as witness and judge against himself, before he come to others. In this manner shall we, without hating men, make war with sins.'[4]

The men knew that Jesus had seen right through them and that he understood the law of God. Hence their embarrassed withdrawal, from the oldest, who were quicker on the uptake when it came to their own sins, to the youngest, who eventually saw their hypocrisy for what it was.

A gracious admonition
(John 8:10-11)

8:10-11. When Jesus had raised himself up and saw no one but the woman, he said to her, 'Woman, where are those accusers of yours? Has no one condemned you?'

She said, 'No one, Lord.'

And Jesus said to her, 'Neither do I condemn you; go and sin no more.'

Only the woman remained. It was therefore entirely in accord with the law of Moses for Jesus to say to her, **'Woman,'** — *gynai*, the term of respectful formal address to a lady (cf. 2:4) — **'where are those accusers of yours? Has no one condemned you? ... Neither do I condemn you...'** There is not one shred of abrogation of the law in these words.[5] Jesus was observing the law precisely as to the letter and the spirit. Without accusers, there was no charge to answer. Jesus refuses to condemn in the legal sense of passing sentence[6] and consequently upholds the integrity of the law.

She was, of course, not innocent. Just as peace is more than the absence of war, innocence is more than the absence of illegality. She was an adulteress. Jesus knew that, and so did she. If she was not a condemned criminal, she was still a counselling case. Sexual sin is always the death of trust, of family and of society itself. The oceans of misery that daily wash across the face of our adulterous generation bear irrefutable testimony to this truth.

Accordingly, **'Go and sin no more,'** is free grace proclaiming a benediction of forgiveness upon personal repentance and a resolve to live a holy life. Forgiveness is not the cold excision of responsibility for past, present and future spiritual and moral failure. Forgiveness comes to a heart warmed by mercy from on high and awakened to the blessing of newness of life in fellowship with the Lord.

If you, LORD, should mark iniquities,
O LORD, who could stand?
But there is forgiveness with you,
That you may be feared

(Ps. 130:3-4)

He is the light we need for our darkness.

Most of us are technically 'legal', but none of us is innocent. There may be no witnesses to charge us in a human court, but before heaven we are condemned already, unless and until we embrace the same Saviour who said to the woman, 'Go and sin no more.' Jesus unmasks the hypocrites, corrects the unbelieving and calls both to sincere repentance, to saving faith and to new obedience. Nevertheless, observes Charles Simeon of Cambridge, 'The admonition given to the woman is equally addressed to every true believer. And here must I suggest a caution against a common, but fatal error. If persons abstain from some particular sins which they have before committed, they are ready to think that they have done all that is required of them. But to turn from gross iniquities is a small matter; and to perform some particular duties is a small matter. Pride and self-complacency may carry us thus far: but the grace of God must carry us much farther. We must lay the axe to the root: we must put away "our *besetting* sin": and must become "new creatures", and "be renewed *in the spirit of our minds*". Mark this expression: it conveys a more complete idea of sound conversion than almost any other ... contemplate it: enter into it: beg of God to reveal to you its true import.[7] We need Christ. We need to know him in the power of the resurrection. Then, in his enabling and prevailing grace, we will go and sin no more with resolve, delight and victory.

20. The light of the world

John 8:12-29

The 'light of the world' discourse (8:12-59) builds upon the 'living water' teaching of 7:37-52. The context is the Feast of Tabernacles, although it may be that by this time the feast had concluded and the crowds had dispersed to their homes.[1] Jesus continued to face the questions of the Jewish leadership. In what looks like a further instalment of the conversation broken off in 7:52, Jesus makes the startling pronouncement that he is **'the light of the world'** who will provide his followers with **'the light of life'**. This inevitably engenders further objections from the Pharisees and occasions one of the most luminous passages in which Jesus identifies himself and his mission.

The first main section of the discourse (8:12-29) focuses on Jesus' authority to make the claim to be the light of the world, and is addressed to the Pharisees. The second section (8:30-59), to be covered in our next chapter, is addressed to those Jews who in the broadest sense believed him, and deals with their, and his, relationship to Abraham, the great father of Israel.

In the passage under consideration in this chapter, Jesus defines his identity (8:12), his authority (8:13-20) and his message (8:21-29).

Identity: the light of the world (John 8:12)

8:12. Then Jesus spoke to them again, saying, 'I am the light of the world. He who follows me shall not walk in darkness, but have the light of life.'

The Feast of Tabernacles not only made use of the imagery of water, as we have seen, but also that of light (cf. the connection of light and water in Zechariah 14:7-8; and notice the parallels between 7:37-38 and 8:12). On the evening of the day on which the water had been drawn from the Pool of Siloam, the Court of the Women was brightly illuminated with 'four huge lamps'[2] for a 'festal liturgy'[3] involving rejoicing with singing and dancing. A festive brilliance lit up the whole city, so enhancing the sense of the divine favour through the days of celebration. God is light, and in him is no darkness at all (1 John 1:5; cf. Exod. 13:21-22; Ps. 27:1; 119:105; Prov. 6:23; Isa. 49:6; 60:19-22; Rev. 22:5). It was with this still fresh in the memory of the people that Jesus identified himself as 'the light of the world'.

The revealed resource

John has already identified Christ as 'the light of men' and 'the true Light which gives light to every man' (1:4,9). This is not to say that 'every man' is saved, but only to emphasize that whatever 'light' a man may have is not self-generated. The point is that all 'light' is truly from God through Jesus Christ.

'I am the light of the world' is a stupendous claim. The contrasting character of the darkness determines its scope and significance. It is, says Calvin, 'a beautiful commendation of Christ ... for, since we are all blind by nature, a remedy is offered, by which we may be freed and rescued from darkness and made partakers of the true *light*.'[4] He is, in his person and work, the revelation of the light that alone can dispel the darkness. He is the revealed resource of the true Light without which the darkness — whether of ignorance, wickedness, misery, alienation from God and man, or condemnation and a lost eternity in hell — will prevail in the experience and destiny of an unregenerate humanity.

The required response

If this is to come to anything in our lives, we will have to follow Jesus. **'He who follows me,'** Jesus says, will experience deliverance from the darkness. Following Jesus is a matter of 'wholehearted discipleship, not ... casual adherence'.[5] Full-orbed faith — acknowledging, accepting and trusting Jesus as Messiah and Saviour — put into obedient practice is the *sine qua non* of this entrance into light. People in a dark tunnel eagerly scramble towards the light at the end of it. The existence of the light invites them to freedom. Only foolishness, delusion or a death-wish would lead someone to retreat further into the blackness of darkness. Yet that is what many sinners choose to do. Even when 'the light has come into the world ... men loved darkness rather than [come to the] light, because their deeds were evil' (3:19).

The resultant renewal

Those who do follow Jesus **'shall not walk in darkness, but have the light of life'**. When the night is pitch black and only one person in a group has a light, there is then only one way to escape walking in the darkness, and that is to stick close within the orbit of the light. Jesus is the light 'of life'. He is life in himself, and he renews with eternal life the dead souls of those who will trust him as their Saviour. 'But to you who fear my name,' says the Lord, 'the Sun of Righteousness shall arise with healing in his wings' (Mal. 4:2). 'Then the righteous will shine forth as the sun in the kingdom of their Father' (Matt. 13:43).

Authority: sent by the Father
(John 8:13-20)

Needless to say, Jesus' claim to be 'the light of the world' received mixed reviews from the Jews. Here we need to enter a caution. We are so used to running the Pharisees down that we almost instinctively paint their negative reactions to Jesus in the most lurid and contemptible colours, and dismiss them as uniformly perverse and unworthy people. But it is surely legitimate for anyone to ask by what authority a man makes such far-reaching and exclusive claims for himself. After all, Jesus claimed to be far more than one good teacher among many. He did not merely maintain that he was *a* light for the world. Had he done so, it is doubtful whether many people would have objected. Few, then as now, have much trouble with admitting that others have some light to shed on life's challenges. The indefinite article threatens no one.

The problem with Jesus, however, is that he uncompromisingly proclaims that he is *the* light of the world. This allows us no room for manoeuvre. If he is correct, then a host of other erstwhile luminaries are put in the shade, if not to flight. To believe him implies the radical rethinking of old commitments, and commands a new discipleship based upon the recognition that he is who he claims to be — the Son of God and the promised Messiah. The question as to what authority he had for such claims accordingly bears some examination. Two main objections are put to Jesus.

First objection: 'Your witness is not true' (8:13-18)

8:13-18. The Pharisees therefore said to him, 'You bear witness of yourself; your witness is not true.'

Jesus answered and said to them, 'Even if I bear witness of myself, my witness is true, for I know where I came from and where I am going; but you do not know where I come from and where I am going. You judge according to the flesh; I judge no one. And yet if I do judge, my judgement is true; for I am not alone, but I am with the Father who sent me. It is also written in your law that the testimony of two men is true. I am one who bears witness of myself, and the Father who sent me bears witness of me.'

When the Pharisees say, **'You bear witness of yourself: your witness is not true,'** they are no doubt alluding to the Mosaic requirement for at least two witnesses (Deut. 17:6; 19:15). The admissibility of any evidence depends, not merely on the witness himself, but on corroboration by another credible witness. Some commentators suggest there may also be an allusion here to what Jesus said in 5:31 ('If I bear witness of myself, my witness is not true'),[6] although that would imply a rather flat-footed evasion of Jesus' explication, in 5:32-47, of the fourfold witness supporting his testimony (John the Baptizer, the miracles, the Father and the Scriptures). People who were determined to ignore Jesus' previously, and publicly, stated arguments would hardly be inclined to remind him of what he had already said in that connection. So it is more likely that these Pharisees, even if they were aware of the statement recorded in 5:31-47, were confining their objections to what he had said on this particular occasion, and were, if anything, concealing any prior knowledge they might have had of his stated position. Jesus appears to accept their objection at face value, at least at first (see comment on 8:17-18), and proceeds to supply a twofold answer.

1. The unique validity of Jesus' testimony

Jesus begins by asserting that his witness is uniquely valid, whether or not he has another witness and whatever anyone may think (8:14-16). He advances two reasons for this.

The first is *the inherent validity of his self-testimony*, based upon his origin and destiny and, by implication, his mission (8:14). He says, **'Even if I bear witness of myself, my witness is true, for I know where I came from and where I am going.'** This does not deny the rules of legal validity which Jesus acknowledged in 5:31, but just says that he knows who he is, whereas they do not. And what is it about his self-knowledge that leaves them without any excuse for not believing his testimony? Surely it is simply that he is God, and that, for those with eyes to see and ears to hear, the evidence is irrefutable that he is who he claims to be! His testimony, observes Ridderbos, 'is not presumptuous but has inner validity'.[7] He came from heaven and goes to heaven. Now he proclaims the message of salvation. He is, in his character, his words and his works, his own self-revelatory evidence. The fact that many will not accept this does not invalidate his testimony, but proves them to be possessed of a profound blindness in their souls.

Secondly, Jesus appeals to *his union with the Father* (8:15-16). They judge **'according to the flesh'** — that is, according to outward appearances (7:24),[8] or, worse still, earthly standards.[9] He had not come to judge anyone in that way, but if and when he did judge them, his judgement would be true, **'for,'** he says, **'I am not alone, but I am with the Father who sent me'** (cf. 5:27). He is one with the Father — and from eternity to eternity — and judges in perfect conformity to the Father's will (5:30). Here, the earlier assertion of certain self-knowledge (8:14) is applied to their consciences in terms of a quiet warning of the perils of resisting the claims of God himself. With a commanding gentleness of expression, Jesus informs them as to who it is with whom they are dealing, and implicitly invites them to reconsider their attitude to him.

2. His testimony was not in fact unsupported

Jesus also points out that his testimony did, in fact, fulfil the law's requirement of at least two witnesses (8:17-18; Deut. 17:6; 19:15). He calls the law of Moses **'your law'**, not because it is not also his law, but to rub it into their consciences that they, for all their professed devotion to God's law, ignore the law when it suits them (cf. 5:45; 10:34; 15:25). This would seem to imply that these Pharisees were aware of Jesus' explanation of his authority in 5:31-47 and knowingly rejected it anyway. If this was so, it would also explain why Jesus forbore to elaborate on his defence at this point.

The other witness was implied in 8:16, but is here explicitly identified: **'I am one who bears witness of myself, and the Father who sent me bears witness of me.'** How the Father continued to bear that testimony is, as we have noted, detailed in 5:31-47 and consisted in the *works*, including the miracles, he had given Jesus to do (5:36), and the *Word* — the Scriptures, also given by God — which testifies of Jesus (5:39). The facts were plain enough, and still are. The problem is not evidence, but a heart of unbelief that is determined to deny the truth, come what may. Ridderbos' comment hits the nail on the head: 'If only they were a different kind of people and understood with whom in his self-witness they were dealing, they would not aim the law against him but understand that precisely in him they are confronted, in an unprecedented and most unexpected way, with the law's demand for truth and justice; and then not reject him but accept him.'[10]

Second objection: 'Where is your Father?' (8:19-20)

8:19-20. Then they said to him, 'Where is your Father?'
Jesus answered, 'You know neither me nor my Father. If you had known me, you would have known my Father also.'
These words Jesus spoke in the treasury, as he taught in the temple; and no one laid hands on him, for his hour had not yet come.

The question, **'Where is your Father?'** was not a naïve appeal for his father — whether Joseph or God — to step forward and give a formal deposition. These Pharisees were anything but naïve. They knew exactly what Jesus was saying, that he was claiming a personal solidarity with God, as a divine Son to a divine Father. This they just would not accept. Their question, then, was far more than a misunderstanding; it was a summary dismissal of the testimony of the Father, as cited by Jesus.

Jesus' answer is, as John Brown puts it, 'worthy of his divine mission'.[11] He wastes no time in arguing details, but gets straight to the heart of the matter, which is their relationship to his Father and, indeed, the truth of the gospel itself: **'You know neither me nor my Father. If you had known me, you would have known my Father also.'** Jesus identifies himself as one with the Father

and also hints at his mediatorial role as the only
way to the Father (5:38; 14:7-9; Matt. 11:27). Whatever 'God' people may think they know and believe
in, he is not the true God, the God of the Bible,
unless and until he is known as the God and Father
of the Lord Jesus Christ and approached through
faith in Christ as Saviour and Lord. Had these
Pharisees understood the Scriptures and the power
of God, the advent of the promised Messiah would
have been answered in their hearts with excitement
and anticipation, as indeed it had been, failings and
all, by the fishermen, tax-gatherers, and the like,
who did become Jesus' disciples.

What people do with Jesus says something about
their true relationship to the living God, whatever
they may say and however cleverly they may be able
to elaborate their theology. Jesus is 'the image of the
invisible God', and 'the brightness of his glory and
the express image of his person' (Col. 1:15; Heb.
1:3). There is an inescapable element of the self-
evident in this, the response to which indicates the
soul's disposition to the overtures of his grace. 'The
divine nature did so evidently shine in the Son,'
observes George Hutcheson, 'that whosoever knew
what a deity was might have seen it in him; and
whosoever took up his deity were thereby forthwith
led to know the deity of the Father... And herein
God's gracious condescension is to be seen, who,
since his divine nature could not be comprehended
nor taken up by us, was pleased to reveal and
manifest himself in his own Son ... clothed with our
flesh, and to hold out this mirror unto us in that
word which is near unto us, and which doth prevent
our anxious thoughts about ascending up to
heaven, or descending down unto the deep, Romans
10:6-8.'[12]

Jesus' hearers were not persuaded, but **'No one
laid hands on him, for his hour had not yet**

come' (8:20). This assumes that 'The animus against Jesus in some circles had not abated, but had increased, and was biding its time. But the right "hour" (*hora*) would be determined by God himself.'[13]

Message: believe or die!
(John 8:21-29)

This concluding section of 'the light of the world' discourse pulls together all the main threads of a teaching session that probably extended through a long morning (cf. 8:2). Earlier themes are taken up — where Jesus is from, where he is going, and the identity of both Jesus and the Father — all illuminating the central proclamation that Jesus is the light of the world to the end that many might hear and believe in him, even if some were determined to resist him to their last breath.

What they must do (8:21-24)

8:21-24. Then Jesus said to them again, 'I am going away, and you will seek me, and will die in your sin. Where I go you cannot come.'

So the Jews said, 'Will he kill himself, because he says, "Where I go you cannot come"?'

And he said to them, 'You are from beneath; I am from above. You are of this world; I am not of this world. Therefore I said to you that you will die in your sins; for if you do not believe that I am he, you will die in your sins.'

The Lord begins with a pronouncement of eternal danger that should, now as then, shake all who hear it to the very depths of their being: **'I am going away, and you will seek me, and will die in your sin. Where I go you cannot come'** (8:21; cf. 7:33; 13:33;

16:28) The point is simply that once he is gone, it will be too late for them to come to him for salvation. This is not to be taken as a sentence of death upon these particular hearers, for the implication is clearly that they should lose no time in coming to him in faith, believing that he is the promised Messiah.

Even after the Jews fail to respond with anything better than their standard mocking incomprehension (8:22), Jesus leaves the door open for any who will hear: **'Therefore I said to you that you will die in your sins; for if you do not believe that I am he, you will die in your sins'** (8:24). In other words, Jesus is saying, 'If you die and go to hell, it will only be because you have not believed "that I am he".' The 'he' is added by our translators to make plain in English what the original 'I am' suggested to John's readers — namely, that he is the divine Son, the living Word of God (1:1,14; cf. Exod. 3:14; Isa. 43:10).

It is interesting that Jesus first refers to people as dying in their 'sin' (singular — 8:21) and then in their 'sins' (plural — 8:24). This encompasses everything from sin as a characteristic condition of life to the particular sins which incur guilt in the course of life. Some find it easy to excuse many of their sins (plural) as extraneous errors, mistakes and slips, while drawing comfort from the idea that their general condition and way of life are moral and decent, and therefore not 'in sin'. Jesus leaves no such hiding-place. Guilt of one of many 'sins' is as deadly as guilt of 'sin' as a comprehensive generality (cf. James 2:10).

The one whom they must believe (8:25-26)

8:25-26. Then they said to him, 'Who are you?'

And Jesus said to them, 'Just what I have been saying to you from the beginning. I have many things to say and

to judge concerning you, but he who sent me is true; and I
speak to the world those things which I heard from him.'

Jesus' meaning was not entirely lost on his hearers.
The language was not so ambiguous that they can be
held to ask an honest **'Who are you?'** Had they
heard nothing about Jesus' origins or his teaching
and his activities? Everybody had an opinion about
Jesus precisely because they knew, or thought they
knew, who he was and what he had done. They were
confused on certain points, to be sure, but they were
certain in their rejection of the man and his message.
This was an irritated and evasive dismissal. They had
caught enough of Jesus' drift to know they did not
accept it. It was as if they said, with a wave of the
hand, 'Who do you think *you* are?'

Jesus replies with a sharp assertion that he is
exactly what he had told them about himself **'from
the beginning'** (8:25). It was preposterous for them
to affect any incomprehension on this point. Jesus
was not about to let them get away with such dis-
honesty. Unlike their Saviour, however, Christians
are too ready to shrink from opposing people to their
faces when they trot out facile excuses to justify a
lofty indifference to the gospel, as if scepticism and
unbelief occupied the moral and spiritual high
ground.

If they entertained such a notion, Jesus dispelled
it with his majestic, but withering riposte: **'I have
many things to say and to judge concerning you,
but he who sent me is true; and I speak to the
world those things which I heard from him'** (8:26).
His meaning would seem to be as follows: he could
answer their question as to his identity with greater
rigour, justifying his position with compelling arguments that would rebuke their unbelief, but would for
the present confine his response to the affirmation
that the truth of what he had said depended, not on

their persuasion of the validity of his arguments, but 'upon the fact that the one who sent him is true, the true and only God'.[14] In these words of Jesus we hear the voice of the offended God — offended because his revelation of himself in his Son is so wilfully brushed aside, when everything about his person and his ministry shines forth so brightly with the glory of his Father. In the end there is no excuse. Although we must be persuaded in our own minds concerning the truth as it is in Jesus, the fact remains that we have no grounds for being unpersuaded in the face of the evidence. What was true for the people of old is even more true for us today. Human incomprehension of the identity of Jesus and the nature of the gospel is more than mere intellectual confusion or ignorance. The gospel offends because it searches and challenges the deepest commitments and darling sins of sinners, finds them wanting, and calls them to repentance towards God and faith in Jesus Christ. Christ threatens the citadel of self. The rest is your personal history. Did you surrender and come to him in saving faith? Or did you dig in, determined to fight to the last breath of your godless life?

When they will understand (8:27-29)

8:27-29. They did not understand that he spoke to them of the Father. Then Jesus said to them, 'When you lift up the Son of Man, then you will know that I am he, and that I do nothing of myself; but as my Father taught me, I speak these things. And he who sent me is with me. The Father has not left me alone, for I always do those things that please him.'

The fact that they **'did not understand'** does not excuse their incomprehension, but is an indictment of their intransigence. They could not see either because they would not see, or because they could not see. They stared the 'express image' of the Father in the face (Heb. 1:3) and still saw only the son of Joseph. This is more than an intellectual problem. It is an essay in the blinding power of sin. 'Were the doctrine never so clear,' remarks Hutcheson, 'yet Satan will keep men from understanding it, either by their ignorance or malice.'[15] The interplay of sin and Satan and unrenewed human nature 'puts up the shutters', so to speak, and blots out the light (1 John 2:11; cf. Acts 26:18). Beyond that is the possibility of the judgement of God, which can, and does, judicially blind certain people to the truth of God (12:40; quoting Isa. 6:10)

That said, there still was much more to be revealed about Jesus. Most importantly, he still had to die by crucifixion, and that awful cross would be the definitive fulcrum of everyone's personal history, as well as that of humanity as a whole. **'When you lift up the Son of Man, then you will know that I am he,'** says Jesus (8:28a). This is not to say that at the crucifixion the Jews would all believe in Jesus. The point is that the cross reveals Jesus as the Saviour of sinners. It is because of the cross that those lost and blind sinners who are saved actually come to believe in Christ. In his death he is exalted a Prince and a Saviour. The irony is that the very act of murder that Jesus' enemies were planning, and succeeded in executing at Calvary, becomes the means of bringing life to untold millions yet unborn. What they thought was the end of a local Galilean heretic turns out to be the unleashing of an unstoppable flood of grace for the entire world.

There is, of course, a certain ambiguity in Jesus' words. Will they know him in a saving way, or under judgement? That is left open precisely to invite a change of heart. When they do see Jesus dying on the cross, and later hear of the empty tomb, and still later witness the events of the Day of Pentecost, will they recall what Jesus said on this occasion and put two and two together? Will they then repent and believe, or further harden their hearts against him? This is what remains to be seen. Jesus sows a seed in their consciences that may yet germinate to new life in their souls. If not, they would one day 'awaken to the terrifying realization that this One whom they despised was, nevertheless, whatever he claimed to be. Too late this truth would crash in upon them, in the hour of death and at the final judgement.'[16]

This great event will definitively demonstrate Jesus' unity with the Father. Jesus no doubt emphasizes this now, ahead of time, because his death — including his great agonizing cry on the cross expressing his sense of being forsaken by God (Mark 15:34) — will seem to many to demonstrate the opposite, namely that he and the God of Israel are not one and that a godless impostor has perished in his sin. Yet the truth is that the cross is the decisive moment in both the incarnate Son's devotion to the Father and the Father's purpose to save his people from their sins.

1. Jesus does not act independently (8:28)

'I do nothing of myself' indicates his perfect harmony with the Father, something both rooted in the essential (ontological) unity of the Trinity and expressed in the various (economic) ministries of Father, Son and Holy Spirit in human history. As the incarnate Son, Jesus can say, **'But as the Father taught me, I speak these things'**, because he subordinated himself, in taking a truly human nature, to the discipline and sacrifice of obedience, to the point of death, even the death of the cross (Phil. 2:8).

2. God the Father did not leave Jesus alone (8:29)

It is true that Jesus was forsaken by his Father in that he bore alone the punishment of the Father upon the sin of sinners. It is true that in that dark and fearful passage, Jesus was deprived of the consoling fellowship of the Father. In making atonement for sin, Jesus was alone. There was no rod and staff to comfort him when he passed through that valley of death. That, however, is only the exception that proves the rule, for the underlying permanent reality for Jesus is expressed in the declaration: **'And he who sent me is with me. The Father has not left me alone, for I always do those things that please him.'** The Father loves Jesus all the more because of his willingness to die for lost people. God in his love gave his only begotten Son to die on the cross, and God receives him into glory at his right hand in a love enhanced by the joy he has in Jesus' perfect obedience.

This is the one who is the light of the world! And he must be your light and mine, if we are not to remain in the darkness for all eternity. 'If we follow Christ on earth,' notes John Brown of Edinburgh, 'we shall follow him to heaven.'[17] The confession of the believer in Jesus is that the Lord is his light, his only true light and his everlasting light.

> The LORD is my light and my salvation:
> Whom shall I fear?
> The LORD is the strength of my life:
> Of whom shall I be afraid?...
> Wait on the LORD;
> Be of good courage,
> And he shall strengthen your heart;
> Wait, I say, on the LORD!
>
> (Ps. 27:1,14).

21. 'The truth shall make you free'

John 8:30-47

How many times have you heard politicians, pundits and propagandists use the words, 'The truth shall make you free' — usually to provide an incentive for supporting their proposals and points of view? It is their particular understanding of the truth that they have in mind. Rarely, if ever, is the content of Jesus' teaching about truth and freedom brought into the picture. In the public arena, these words are usually no more than a self-serving slogan. It is therefore appropriate to ask what truth and whose freedom those who quote Jesus have in mind.

When Jesus spoke these words, however, he was not talking about any old truth. He was not talking about somebody else's facts, or about truth in the abstract. He was talking about his truth, the truth which is God's light, the truth which is essential to salvation, the truth without which men and women will die in their sins (8:24), the truth which he is in himself — the absolute truth of the gospel of the Son of God.

The issue here comes to a practical focus in the opening verse of this section: **'As he spoke these words, many believed in him'** (8:30). What were these people believing? What kind of faith did they have? What view of truth did they hold? What did they believe about Jesus and his teaching? The passage addresses such questions and makes plain that Jesus is the truth that sets people free (8:31-36), that Jesus reveals God's truth (8:37-41) and that Jesus is the sinless Son of God (8:42-47).

Jesus is the truth
(John 8:30-36)

8:30-36. As he spoke these words, many believed in him.

Then Jesus said to those Jews who believed him, 'If you abide in my word, you are my disciples indeed. And you shall know the truth, and the truth shall make you free.'

They answered him, 'We are Abraham's descendants, and have never been in bondage to anyone. How can you say, "You will be made free"?'

Jesus answered them, 'Most assuredly, I say to you, whoever commits sin is a slave of sin. And a slave does not abide in the house for ever, but a son abides for ever. Therefore if the Son makes you free, you shall be free indeed.'

Since it is clear that the entire passage is of a piece — the record of one extended interchange between Jesus and the Jews who in some sense 'believed' him (8:30-31)[1] — it is equally clear that whatever 'faith' these people had in Jesus was very far short of a living, saving faith in him. It would be a great mistake to take the use of the expression, **'believed in him'**, in 8:30 and simply assume this to be indicative of an evangelical conversion to Christ. The fact that Jesus goes on to explain something of what it means to believe in him, and then ends up roundly rebuking them for their unbelief, tells us just how superficial their acceptance of Jesus really was (cf. 2:23-24). It is worth noting, in passing, that the easy way people today will 'accept Jesus' and go on living as if nothing had happened is subject to the same strictures that Jesus applies to these Jews. The issue may be summed up in this way: 'So you think you have accepted Jesus! But has Jesus accepted you?' There is more to *saving* faith than a flutter of emotional or intellectual approval. There must be knowledge of his claims about himself, heart acceptance of these claims and personal *trust* in him as Saviour *and* Lord.

Freed by the truth (8:31-32)

Jesus immediately defines the character of the true disciple. There is no 'easy-believism' from Jesus! Notice the parallelism in his explanation:

A	B
If you abide in my word,	... you are my disciples indeed.
A	B
And you shall know the truth,	... and the truth shall make you free.

The first test of the validity of professed faith is very practical. Abiding in Jesus' word means an active, continuing personal obedience to his revealed will (cf. 5:38). Such folk take the Bible seriously as the rule of faith and life. Christ and his Word are central to their lives, and observably so. Hence they may be called 'disciples indeed'. Furthermore, they will grow in their experiential knowledge of the truth, and this in turn will convey a freedom they had not otherwise enjoyed. None of these elements — perseverance, truth or freedom — is abstracted from Jesus, his teaching and his mission. This freedom, for example, is not political or economic freedom, nor is it a merely personal sense of being a liberated individual.

This is gospel freedom — freedom from sin and its consequences, and freedom to be holy people in Jesus Christ. Let others 'proudly vaunt of their free will,' says Calvin, 'but let us, who are conscious of our own slavery, glory in none but Christ our Deliverer. For the reason why the Gospel ought to be reckoned to have achieved our deliverance is, that it offers and gives us to Christ *to be freed* from the yoke of sin.' Furthermore, 'We ought to observe that *freedom* has its degrees according to the measure of their faith; and therefore Paul, though clearly *made free* still groans and longs after *perfect freedom* (Rom. 7:24).'[2]

Accordingly, it is a gross misappropriation of this text to apply it to political or economic liberty, or to a heightened knowledge of facts that are in themselves true. Discipleship to Jesus is the heart and soul of the matter, and the progression is from abiding in Jesus' word, through growing in the knowledge of Jesus' truth, to enjoying an ever-expanding measure of Jesus' freedom.

Sons not slaves (8:33-36)

Some of these erstwhile 'believers in Jesus' immediately objected to his tying true freedom to discipleship towards him. After all, they objected, they were already free, on account of being **'Abraham's descendants'** and had **'never been in bondage to anyone'** (8:33). Now they were not talking about political freedom, since they had been under the heel of foreign powers for centuries. It was spiritual freedom in Jehovah that they assumed was already and always theirs as a people. They were offended by the suggestion that they might actually be slaves and in need of true freedom! They were Jews. They were God's people. They were never slaves! Jesus knew that this said more about the Jews' national pride than their heart-commitment to God. So he came straight to the point and defined their problem in terms of the related themes of sin, sonship and adoption.

1. Sin (8:34)

What makes someone a slave? Sin does! The bottom line is that **'Whoever commits sin is a slave of sin'** (cf. Rom. 6:16). Jesus' expression, 'commits sin', refers to the continuing, committed practice of unrenewed human nature, the point being that freedom is not secured by an external ecclesiastical connection, but by the work of God in the salvation of the sinner. The Jews were trusting in 'a misplaced appeal to being the seed of Abraham, as though that by itself guaranteed freedom from the bondage of sin'.[3] Forget your labels ('Abraham's descendants', 'C of E,' or whatever denomination you belong to) and apply sound theology to your soul! Whether Jews or Gentiles, we need a Saviour, and that means coming to Jesus in faith and committing to follow him in practical obedience.

2. Sonship (8:35)

Jesus now takes a slightly different tack. What freedom of tenure does a slave have in his master's house? The answer is that he has only a limited and temporary tenure. Why? Because he is not a son, but a slave. Only a son **'abides for ever'** (cf. Gal. 4:21-31). The slave would therefore have to become a son in order to enjoy the true freedom of the house. In spiritual terms, this is what sinners really need in relation to God and their destiny in time and eternity. To be 'Abraham's descendants' after the flesh is no substitute for being a true child of God. Merely 'going to church' is no substitute for knowing the Lord. Any slave to sin can give a show of religion, but only a true believer will 'dwell in the house of the LORD for ever' (Ps. 23:6).

3. Adopted to be free (8:36)

How does a slave become a son? By adoption! Jesus drives home the point about true freedom first made in 8:32: **'Therefore, if the Son makes you free, you shall be free indeed,'** this time with reference to the adoption effected by his saving work (cf. Rom. 8:14-17). The point is that 'the Son' thereby confers sonship on those who have hitherto been the slaves of sin. By identifying himself as 'the Son' (of God the Father), he implies what he will later make explicit, namely that they have another father altogether (8:44), while calling them to come to him as the one who can set them free. He alone can give this gift of freedom which, once received, makes the child of God 'free indeed' — really, absolutely, richly, profoundly, everlastingly free! (2 Cor. 3:17; Gal. 4:6-7).

Jesus reveals God's truth
(John 8:37-41)

8:37-41. 'I know that you are Abraham's descendants, but you seek to kill me, because my word has no place in you. I speak what I have seen with my Father, and you do what you have seen with your father.'

They answered and said to him, 'Abraham is our father.'

Jesus said to them, 'If you were Abraham's children, you would do the works of Abraham. But now you seek to kill me, a man who has told you the truth which I heard from God. Abraham did not do this. You do the deeds of your father.'

Then they said to him, 'We were not born of fornication; we have one Father — God.'

We can almost hear the reaction of Jesus' hearers. 'How can you say any of Abraham's descendants are not free? Was he irrelevant? Does freedom depend entirely upon you? How dare you question our spiritual parentage! Who are you to say such things?'

Who is your spiritual father? (8:37-38)

Jesus concedes that they were descended from Abraham in a physical sense. The real question, however, was whether they were the spiritual children of Abraham. The test for that was how they acted. It was not who the father was that pointed to who were his children, but 'What the children "do" points to who their father is.'[4]

1. The evidence: what they were doing and why (8:37)

They aimed to **'kill [him]'** (cf. 5:18; 7:19,25). They
were doing this because Jesus' word had **'no place'**
in them. True spiritual children of Abraham would
welcome the Messiah, who is the true seed of Abraham, but they were doing the very opposite. What
conclusion would you draw from that?

2. The principle: our actions reveal our true paternity (8:38)

Jesus explains: **'I speak what I have seen with my
Father, and you do what you have seen with your
father.'** Jesus has one father; they have another.
Whether they admit it or not, their father is not
Abraham, still less God himself. Their father is the
devil! (8:44). All their religion is no more than a cover
story concealing hearts that are far from God.

Whose father is God? (8:39-41)

The Jews miss the 'proleptic allusion to the devil'[5]
and remain adamant that Abraham is their father.
Jesus, however, presses home the point that true
children of Abraham would do **'the works of Abraham'** (8:39). What did Abraham do? He listened to
the **'man'** who told him **'the truth ... from God'**
(8:40). He did not try to kill the messenger who
revealed the truth of God to him.

Jesus is saying plainly that he reveals God's truth,
the truth from his Father God. Their resistance
arises from their pre-commitments, which in turn
were born of a darker spiritual paternity than they
will admit. They are in a state of denial — denial of
the bearer of truth, the truth itself and the God of
truth. Nevertheless, when Jesus says, **'You do the
deeds of your father'** (8:41a), they are quite capable

of grasping that he is saying, not only that Abraham is not their father, but that God is not their Father either, and that they have no real heart for him and no willingness to hear his voice. To this, they put up more defensive denial. They are not illegitimate (**'born of fornication'**), but surely have **'one Father — God'** (8:41b,c). They could easily have quoted Scripture to support this. Had God not said, 'Israel is my son, my firstborn'? (Exod. 4:22). You can almost hear them thinking, 'Would this man from Nazareth deny the very Word of God?' What they could not stomach was the rather obvious proposition that a man who lives like the devil can hardly be regarded as a true child of God.

Jesus is the sinless Son of God
(John 8:42-47)

8:42-47. Jesus said to them, 'If God were your Father, you would love me, for I proceeded forth and came from God; nor have I come of myself, but he sent me. Why do you not understand my speech? Because you are not able to listen to my word. You are of your father the devil, and the desires of your father you want to do. He was a murderer from the beginning, and does not stand in the truth, because there is no truth in him. When he speaks a lie, he speaks from his own resources, for he is a liar and the father of it. But because I tell the truth, you do not believe me. Which of you convicts me of sin? And if I tell the truth, why do you not believe me? He who is of God hears God's words; therefore you do not hear, because you are not of God.'

Our Lord is relentless in his pursuit of resistant consciences and hardened hearts. He will not let them get away with the assertion of their rightness with his Father, when this is an illusion, sustained by the utter denial of the facts. Jesus does not deny the truth that Israel is God's firstborn — he simply insists on distinguishing the true Israel from the false. He then proposes a test and applies it both to them and to himself.

The test: loving Jesus (8:42)

'If God were your Father,' says Jesus, **'you would love me, for I proceeded forth and came from God; nor have I come of myself, for he sent me.'** A genuine filial love for God could not but issue in a recognition of, and love for, the one he had promised in Scripture and had now sent in the flesh. Love for God sets up an experiential recognition system. That is the effect of the work of God in the heart. Old Testament believers readily received Jesus as the Christ — the disciples themselves are cases in point. 'Whoever believes that Jesus is the Christ,' John will later write, 'is born of God, and everyone who loves him who begot also loves him who is begotten of him' (1 John 5:1). Just as you cannot truly love Christ if you hate other believers, you cannot truly love God if you hate Christ.

The link between the Father and Jesus extends from his eternal generation to his incarnation and to his mediatorial mission. He is **'from God'** in all these senses, although the precise reference of Jesus' language here is properly limited to the last of these, his functional submission to the Father as the Servant of the Lord. Jesus is the express image of the Father. It is impossible to love the Father and not be drawn to the Son, for it is in the Son that we uniquely and truly see the Father (cf. 14:7-11,23-24).

The test applied to the Jews: the blinded sons of Satan (8:43-45)

Why does their failure to love Jesus prove that they do not love God as their Father? Jesus analyses this in terms of a three-part spiritual and constitutional complex.

1. Rationally, they were incapable of understanding Jesus (8:43)

They were **'not able to listen'** to his word. Their
instinctive reaction to Jesus, based on their predisposition, was one of incomprehension. They drew a
blank as far as the true meaning of his word was
concerned. James Fisher, in his famous catechism
explaining the *Shorter Catechism*, asks 'Wherewith is
the *understanding* corrupted?' and answers, 'With
darkness and blindness, so that we cannot know and
receive the things of the Spirit of God, 1 Cor. 2:14.'[6]

*2. Relationally, they were actually at one with their 'father the
devil' (8:44)*

They were, so to speak, on Satan's wavelength. They
wanted to do **'his desires'**. Just look at the evidence:

Satan **'was a murderer from the beginning'**
(cf. 1 John 3:8; Rom. 7:11). Did they not desire
to kill Jesus?
Satan **'does not stand in the truth, be-
cause there is no truth in him'**. In rejecting
Jesus' word, were they not rejecting the truth of
God?
Satan **'is a liar and the father of it'**. Did
they not buy the lie that denies and contradicts
God at every turn?

3. Religiously, they did not believe Jesus (8:45)

The truth was offensive to them. They had hearts of
unbelief. 'How doth the Spirit of God, in scripture,
express man's estate of sin and misery, into which he
hath fallen?' asks Fisher's *Catechism*. He gives the
answer: 'By a state of darkness, Eph. 5:8; a state of
distance, Eph. 2:13; a state of condemnation and
wrath, John 3:18; a state of bondage, or captivity,

Isa. 49:24-25; and a state of death, both spiritual
and legal, Eph. 2:1.[7] Far from being children of God,
then, they were the blinded sons of Satan, and, as
the English proverb so aptly puts it, 'There are none
so blind as those that will not see.' This is the very
nature of the sin of unbelief, which is the heart and
soul of the problem of fallen humanity.

The test applied to Jesus: the sinless Son of God (8:46-47)

Jesus has already said that if they loved God, they
would love him. Concomitant with that would be
their acceptance of his word as truth. They, however,
reject Jesus as if he were a liar. Jesus accordingly
presses his truthfulness upon them by asking two
leading questions: **'Which of you convicts me of
sin? And if I tell the truth, why do you not believe me?'** (8:46). This is not so much an invitation
to press charges against him, as it is a majestic
assertion of his sinlessness before God and man.
That he is legally beyond reproach is certainly true.
But the focus here is *their unbelief* in the face of *his
unimpeachable holiness*. If Jesus is indeed sinless,
why does anyone not believe him? The only ground
for disbelieving Jesus is that his claims are pretensions built upon a lie.

Our response is not negotiable. **'He who is of God
hears God's words; therefore you do not hear,
because you are not of God'** (8:47). This is the
crack of doom for any heart that rejects God's Word
and God's Son. 'You are not of God,' ought to shake
us to the core and send us fleeing to Christ so that
we may become 'of God'. To be forced to admit on the
day of our death that we have believed the lie in
denying Jesus and dismissing God's Word will be a
shock that lasts for all eternity. Christ is the truth
who sets sinners free in time and in eternity. 'If you

abide in my word, you are my disciples indeed. And you shall know the truth, and the truth shall make you free.'

> Make me a captive, Lord,
> And then I shall be free;
> Force me to render up my sword.
> And I shall conqueror be.
> I sink in life's alarms
> When by myself I stand;
> Imprison me within thine arms,
> And strong shall be my hand.
>
> (George Matheson, 1842-1906)

22. 'Before Abraham was, I AM'

John 8:48-59

It is a basic rule in the game of rugby football that you play the ball and not the man. Tackling a man without the ball is regarded as something of a dirty trick, and as such is appropriately penalized. The same is supposed to hold true in the discussion of serious issues, but we have all noticed at some time in our lives that when someone is losing an argument his words become more strident and his attacks more personal. The *argumentum ad hominem* — the argument against the person — is a neat way of knocking someone out of the game without, so to speak, honestly playing the ball.

Having exhausted the more gentlemanly forms of debate, Jesus' hearers turn to out-and-out name-calling and end by taking up stones to kill him. Far from silencing Jesus, however, this occasions one of the most sublime passages in Jesus' self-revelation, as he proclaims himself to be the giver of life (8:48-51), the one promised in the Scriptures (8:52-56) and God come in the flesh (8:57-59). Notice the objection-answer dialogue format of the interchange.

The giver of life
(John 8:48-51)

8:48-51. Then the Jews answered and said to him, 'Do we not say rightly that you are a Samaritan and have a demon?'

Jesus answered, 'I do not have a demon; but I honour my Father, and you dishonour me. And I do not seek my own glory; there is one who seeks and judges. Most assuredly, I say to you, if anyone keeps my word he shall never see death.'

People do not take kindly to being informed they are 'not of God' (8:47). That is why the world is never a very healthy place for prophets and preachers. Their job, after all, is to tell people where they stand with the Lord. To many, this just seems so much arrogance and bigotry. People are generally quite comfortable with their version of truth and their hope of heaven — polls show, for example, that 78% of Americans expect to go to heaven, while only 4% think they even risk going to hell! Any who have the temerity to challenge that kind of assurance may find they are taking their lives in their hands! That, of course, was precisely what Jesus was doing.

Objection one: 'Are you not a Samaritan and demon-possessed?'

Invective now poured from the lips of these children of Abraham and erstwhile 'believers in Jesus' (cf.

8:30). **'Do we not say rightly that you are a Samaritan and have a demon?'** (8:48). We all recognize the use of ethnic slurs — every nation seems to find its own *bête noire* among other peoples. Theologically, the Samaritans were essentially a sub-Jewish cult holding to only selected portions of the Scriptures. Calling Jesus 'a Samaritan' was tantamount to charging him with the rejection of the orthodox, Jewish view of the law of Moses. Add to that the idea of madness through demon-possession (cf. 7:20; 8:52; 10:20), and then ask why anyone should give credence to the views of such a man? Blacken the man's name, and his arguments follow him to the scrap-heap of discredited ideas! Besides, surely only Satan could inspire anyone to suggest the Jews were not the children of God?

Answer one: 'I am from God and I bring eternal life'

Jesus will not let such calumnies stand. Name-calling is never merely name-calling. This was an assault upon the very character of God. Accordingly, Jesus offers a brief but comprehensive rebuttal.

1. He honours the Father

Jesus ignores the 'Samaritan' epithet, or rather subsumes it under the charge of diabolical motivation, and simply asserts his commitment to the Father's glory. He in effect appeals to the Father and, by implication, also invites them to assess the evidence. To this he adds a rebuke that carries an air of impending judgement about it: **'... and you dishonour me'** (8:49).

2. The Father will vindicate him

The danger of dishonouring Jesus is now made apparent. **'And I do not seek my own glory,'** he says; **'there is one who seeks and judges'** (8:50). Jesus is the servant of his Father. Jesus humbles himself in submission to the Father. But let no one be lulled by his gentleness into thinking that contempt for him will escape the notice of the one who does seek his own glory, namely the Father himself! They may reject Jesus today, but tomorrow they will answer to the God who loves his incarnate Son! The same applies to the ocean of blasphemy that washes around us in our own time. From 'Christ' to 'Jesus' and 'My God', and worse, millions execrate the Son of God and his Father every day with hardly a thought as to what they are doing. Ask yourself what you would think if your name were used as the currency of contempt, and your character daily dismissed with such easy hauteur. Were you to be belittled in this manner, would you laugh it off, and say these folk are really all good people anyway? No, it would offend you deeply to be abused in such a way! Now, do you think God should be less concerned about his honour than you are about yours? Behind the effortless name-calling heaped on Jesus, there is a world of disdain for God, for his Son and for the claims of the gospel — hearts that resist the pleadings of grace and truth. Understand, then, that you must 'repent' or 'perish', for he who 'shows mercy to thousands' will 'by no means [clear] the guilty' (Luke 13:5; Exod. 20:6; Num. 14:18).

3. He is the giver of life

'Most assuredly I say to you, if anyone keeps my word he shall never see death' (8:51). Jesus had not come to promote himself, or establish some movement or school of thought, but to give life from the dead to other people! He has the words of eternal life (6:63,68). To keep his word necessarily includes a believing acceptance of Christ himself, personal trust in him as the Saviour he declares himself to be, as well as commitment to practical obedience to the comprehensive content of the Word of God. The fruit of this is to receive the new life 'which physical death cannot extinguish'[1] and which will be established in its completion at the resurrection in the last day (6:39-40,44,54; cf. Rom. 8:10; 1 Peter 1:23).

Far from having any basis upon which to criticize Jesus, his hearers had the most impressive reasons for believing his message and committing themselves to him. What is different today? Nothing at all! The same Jesus addresses the same spiritual need. The same power of God to save and transform comes to the same devastated lives and unbelieving hearts, and calls them to repentance, faith and newness of life. Furthermore, two millennia of real Christianity give evidence of the efficacy of his grace and the persistence of his love for sinners. Still, the wicked would rather be turned into hell than have Jesus to be their Lord (Ps. 9:17; cf. Isa. 28:15; Rev. 6:15-16).

The promised one
(John 8:52-56)

8:52-56. Then the Jews said to him, 'Now we know that you have a demon! Abraham is dead, and the prophets; and you say, "If anyone keeps my word he shall never taste death." Are you greater than our father Abraham, who is dead? And the prophets are dead. Whom do you make yourself out to be?'

Jesus answered, 'If I honour myself, my honour is nothing. It is my Father who honours me, of whom you say that he is your God. Yet you have not known him, but I know him. And if I say, "I do not know him," I shall be a liar like you; but I do know him and keep his word. Your father Abraham rejoiced to see my day, and he saw it and was glad.'

You know how it is in a dispute. Whatever you say in your defence may immediately be thrown back at you as a further ground for rejecting your argument. Jesus rebutted the charge of being motivated by a demon by asserting that he is the giver of life — and what demon gives life? But his defence only adds grist to the objectors' mill, and they press their objections with even greater vigour: **'Now we know that you have a demon!'** they triumphantly exclaim.

Objection two: 'Are you greater than Abraham?'

Their argument goes like this: 'You say you have life to give. But Abraham, our greatest patriarch, is dead, as are the prophets. **Are you greater than our father Abraham, who is dead?** How can you give life, when they couldn't get it for themselves? Obviously you think you are greater than Abraham. Since that is patently absurd, you must be a crazy man, possessed by a demon!' (8:52-53).

Abraham was the bench-mark of their whole religious system and national existence. To their way of thinking, it was unbounded arrogance for Jesus to claim that he is divine and a redeemer, and so place himself above that great man of God. It is as simple as that. They just see Jesus as going against all they have held true in the past, and they cannot grasp that he 'does not wipe out their past or position himself *against* it but is its secret and its fulfilment (cf. vss. 56ff.)'.[2] They cannot even begin to think it through. They just splutter with outrage, as if to say. 'Who do you think you are???!!! You are out of your mind!'

Answer two: 'Abraham rejoiced to see my day!'

The unspoken, underlying motive for this expostulation is the, to them, unthinkable implication that Jesus is indeed the divine Messiah. It is for this reason that Jesus replies in terms of his submission to God his Father.

Negatively, *Jesus denies all self-seeking motives* (8:54a). They miss the point if that is what they think he is doing. Self-praise is no honour, even for the incarnate Son of God. There is no glory apart from the glory of God. Jesus submits absolutely and entirely to the will of the Father. This is transparent in every aspect of his earthly ministry.

Positively, *he affirms that the honour he does have is from God* (8:54b). They miss this entirely, yet it too is transparently obvious in the ministry of Jesus. Is it

so difficult to tell when a man's life is being honoured
by God? But those who hate the work of God will
deny all evidences of his grace with their last breath.

Further driving home his point, Jesus declares
that *he, not they, truly knows God and keeps his
word* (8:55). Jesus is not, like even the great prophet
Isaiah, a man of unclean lips (Isa. 6:5). Jesus is unimpeachable in his obedience to the law of God. Possessed by a demon, indeed? All they have ever seen
in Jesus is perfect righteousness.

Finally, Jesus comes to the climax of his argument
— and sublime it is in its evocation of the promise
and fulfilment of the true Messianic hope of Israel.
He reveals that their **'father Abraham rejoiced to
see my day, and he saw it and was glad'** (8:56). The
question is: when did Abraham rejoice? When he was
alive on earth two millennia before, or as an observer
from heaven in the days of Jesus' life on earth?
Ridderbos is surely right when he notes that 'The
focus is on Jesus' contemporaneity with the *historical*
Abraham, not on that of the *heavenly* Abraham with
the historical Jesus (v. 58).[3]

It is true that relatively little of the Messiah and
the gospel age to come was revealed to the patriarchs
and prophets (Luke 10:24). They were nevertheless
given a certain prophetic anticipation of the promise
of God and, irrespective of the precise nature of
Abraham's 'seeing' of Jesus' day, 'The fact remains,'
as Carson puts it, 'that Jesus identifies the ultimate
fulfilment of all Abraham's hopes and joys with his
own person and work.'[4] What was new to the Jews
was not the notion that Abraham anticipated the age
of the Messiah. The rabbinical schools had taught
this, in one way or another. What was new — and
devastating in its claim — was that this Jesus of
Nazareth was the one for whom the patriarch hoped,
and in anticipation of whom he rejoiced. This was
nothing less than a full-blown self-identification of

Jesus as the Messiah! They understood only too well the implications of what Jesus was saying, and it troubled them greatly. Jesus had placed them with their backs up against the wall and had left them no escape. They must accept him as Messiah or reject the God of Abraham!

God incarnate
(John 8:57-59)

8:57-59. Then the Jews said to him, 'You are not yet fifty years old, and have you seen Abraham?'

Jesus said to them, 'Most assuredly, I say to you, before Abraham was, I AM.'

Then they took up stones to throw at him; but Jesus hid himself and went out of the temple, going through the midst of them, and so passed by.

You can almost see them rolling their eyes, looking at each other in disbelief and spluttering the Aramaic equivalent of 'Can you believe this fellow?' Confronted by sublime, but unpalatable, truth, people will end all discussion and retreat into an affected superiority, expressed in banalities masquerading as substantive arguments.

Objection three: 'You can't possibly know Abraham!'

So they say to Jesus, **'You are not yet fifty years old, and have you seen Abraham?'** (8:57). Jesus had not said that he and Abraham were contemporaries, that is, that they had lived on earth at the same time and known one another in the way that people know those living around them. Neither had he said that Abraham saw with his eyes what Jesus was doing now. Jesus had been talking about Abraham's faith and his anticipation of the promised

Messiah. That did not matter! Never mind dealing
honestly with what he actually said! By crassly
twisting Jesus' words, they sought to render his
claims absurd, and so lampoon his real argument
into the oblivion of the unbelievable.

Answer three: 'Before Abraham was I AM'

Had our words been butchered in this way, we would
have been hurriedly going back over all that we had
said to set the record straight and make sure everybody knew we had been misrepresented. Jesus,
however, moves right ahead. He takes his cue from
what they have just said and makes an even more
startling claim: **'Most assuredly, I say to you,
before Abraham was, I AM'** (8:58). Jesus is not only
saying that he existed before Abraham, but that he is
the divine Son, one in essence with the great 'I AM'
(Exod. 3:14; Isa. 41:4; 43:10,13).[5] Jesus was indeed
before Abraham. But Jesus transcended time, for he
was God! What they 'hold to be the height of folly is
in fact the final and deepest reality underlying their
conflict over Abraham'.[6]

That is why they **'took up stones to throw at
him'** (8:59a). They understood clearly that he was
claiming to be the *divine* Son of God. The mob
deemed that to be blasphemous, and in their outrage
attempted to take the law of God into their own
hands (cf. Lev. 24:16). They failed, for **'Jesus hid
himself, and went out of the temple, going
through the midst of them, and so passed by.'**

In closing...

The very heart of the gospel is in Jesus' words in this exchange with his critics. He is the giver of life, the promised Messiah, and all in virtue of his being God come in the flesh. His claims are absolute, inescapable and exclusive. It is him, or nothing. It is his way, or the byway — there is no middle way, no other way. That is what infuriated many of his hearers, and still does. The implications could not be more profound.

1. Jesus challenges, head on, the spirit of the age

At the dawn of the third millennium since Christ's first advent, we live in an age of radical individualism. Not only do men do what is right in their own eyes, but they demand that everyone acknowledge that their choices constitute 'what is right' for them, notwithstanding the fact that, in terms of substance, different people's standards of 'what is right' utterly contradict one another. No one may tell another that he is wrong; still less that he is bound for a lost eternity. Absolutes are gone. All is relative and one opinion is as good as another. Ours is a 'pro-choice' culture — not simply in reference to abortion (with which that term is most recognizably associated), but with respect to personal ethics as a whole. Ultimate questions are resolved by the sovereign individual, in his own interest, and woe to any who declare that he is accountable to the God and Father of the Lord Jesus Christ! So this generation repeats the prevailing sin of the period of the judges — with the same predictable and disastrous results (Judg. 21:25; cf., Prov. 14:12).

2. This is the day in which sinners are called to new life in Jesus Christ

What Jesus said then holds true for us now. We live in the 'day' that Abraham 'rejoiced to see', though he saw it only in the anticipation, in faith, of promises yet to be revealed. We live in the day between the first and second comings of Jesus Christ, the day of what Charles Simeon called 'the meridian light of Gospel'. So the great practical question is: 'What will you do with this day, this light, this Saviour?' Abraham rejoiced to see it, but millions today are totally indifferent. We have so much more of its light than he did, but people still choose the darkness, still take up stones to kill Jesus and, in many parts of the world, his followers also.

There is another way. It is to receive Jesus for who he is and what he has done — the Son of God who took our humanity and died as the substitutionary sacrifice for the sin of sinners, that they might believe in him and not perish, but have everlasting life. The believing response is beautifully foretold by the prophet Isaiah when he says:

And it will be said in that day:
'Behold, this is our God:
We have waited for him, and he will save us.
This is the LORD;
We have waited for him;
We will be glad and rejoice in his salvation'
(Isa. 25:9).

23. Light for the blind
John 9:1-41

It was no accident that Jesus' disclosure that he was
'the light of the world' (8:12) was followed by the
miraculous healing of a man who was blind from
birth. The power of the light of the world to dispel the
darkness — both spiritual and physical — was most
visibly attested by the opening of unseeing eyes. The
significance of this transcends the marvel of the healing itself, because, whereas there are no healings of
blindness recorded in the Old Testament, there are
promises of such healing associated with the prophecies of the Messiah (Isa. 29:18; 35:5; 42:7). In the
New Testament such healings are the most frequent
of Jesus miracles — there are seven of them — and
these unmistakably highlight his divine and Messianic office.

The healing of the man born blind, then, speaks to
us about the victory of light over darkness. Jesus is
indeed the light of the world. This comes out in two
ways in our passage. First of all, Jesus healed the
man on the Sabbath. The Pharisees objected because
this transgressed their conception of the use of that
day. They could not see the light in Jesus' action,
because of their darkened insistence upon a legalism
of their own invention. Secondly, we see that Jesus
brought the man to faith and so healed his spiritual

blindness — and that after the man had been rejected by the Pharisees.

The passage poses three main questions: why was
the man blind? (9:1-7); how did he regain his sight?
(9:8-34); and what was the purpose of the healing?
(9:35-41).

Why was the man blind?
(John 9:1-7)

The basic premise was that the man had been **'blind from birth'** (9:1). In our scientific age, we tend to seek the reasons for such conditions in medical diagnoses and the like — in so-called 'secondary causes' — and it is distinctly unfashionable to look for a 'primary cause' behind the observable cause-and-effect phenomena. Those who believe there is a God, who is sovereign over his creation, inevitably ponder the relationship between observable events and his secret will. Invariably, this manifests itself in the tendency to make a simple ethical connection between the two, and so ascribe the event to the blessing or the judgement of God, as the case may be.

Jesus, for example, was once asked if certain people who died in the collapse of a tower were greater sinners than the rest of the people in Jerusalem. He decisively rejected any such notion, but declared that unless we repent, we shall 'all likewise perish' (Luke 13:5). He was saying, of course, that the fact of death is the more significant event than the precise manner of death. Mishaps befall the righteous and the wicked, apparently indiscriminately (Eccles. 9:2). God does have his particular will for each person, to be sure, but that is largely hidden from us, and we have no warrant to assume that one person's misfortune is God's judgement upon some particular sin. In the present instance, the disciples fall into the same trap. **'Rabbi, who sinned,'** they ask Jesus, **'this man or his parents...?'** (9:2).

This problem is not just ancient history. I was once offered the suggestion by a church member, on hearing that another member had fallen terminally ill, that 'Maybe he's not one of the elect.' The person who made this comment did not intend to be cruel, any more than did the disciples, but this was the inevitable effect of assuming a direct cause-and-effect relationship between health/illness and faith/sin. An ounce of faith does not equal an ounce of health. Jesus first speaks to this question (9:3-5) and then acts on his answer by restoring the man's sight (9:6-7).

The reasons for his blindness

9:1-5. Now as Jesus passed by, he saw a man who was blind from birth.

And his disciples asked him, saying, 'Rabbi, who sinned, this man or his parents, that he was born blind?'

Jesus answered, 'Neither this man nor his parents sinned, but that the works of God should be revealed in him. I must work the works of him who sent me while it is day; the night is coming when no one can work. As long as I am in the world, I am the light of the world.'

Jesus first disposes of the disciples' false assumption. The man's blindness was *not* a judgement on personal sin, whether his own or that of his parents (9:3a). Calvin notes that while 'every man is ready to censure others with extreme bitterness, there are few who apply to themselves, as they ought to do, the same severity,' and concludes, 'They are false teachers, therefore, who say that all afflictions, without any distinction, are sent on account of sins; as if the

measure of punishments were equal, or as if God
looked to nothing else in punishing men than to what
every man deserves.'[1] Carson notes, 'That a specific
illness or experience of suffering *can* be the direct
consequence of a specific sin, few would deny (e.g.
Miriam's revolt, Num. 12; ... cf. 1 Cor. 11:30). That it
is invariably so, numerous biblical texts flatly deny
(e.g. Job; Gal. 4:13; 2 Cor. 12:7).'[2]

This is not to say that there were no intelligible
reasons for the man's handicap. Jesus advances a
threefold explanation.

Firstly, the man's need was the arena in which
God's redeeming work would be seen for what it is.
He was blind in order that **'the works of God should
be revealed in him'** (9:3b). This is no less true in our
experience. Our afflictions offer the widest scope for
God's loving and transforming grace.

Secondly, his blindness emphasized *the urgency of
Jesus' ministry*. Jesus had work to do **'while it is
day'** — that is, while he was still with the disciples.
God **'sent'** Jesus for the work of his kingdom on
earth, and he had a deadline for this work — the
coming **'night ... when no man can work'** (9:4).
Jesus is focusing on his ministry and the darkness
that would descend on the disciples in the immediate
aftermath of his death. Nevertheless, the same principle applies to all Christian ministry throughout the
present age. Every man has his own 'day', and human history has its 'day' (cf. 2 Cor. 5:10; Heb. 9:27).
Hearing the gospel is the most urgent need of a world
that is constantly in the state of passing away.

Thirdly, the man's blindness occasioned *Jesus'
self-revelation in his earthly ministry as* **'the light of
the world'** (9:5; see the exposition of 8:12-29,
pp.320-37). This is not to say that the risen Jesus,
though absent bodily from this world, is not still the
light of the world. His light did not cease to shine
with his death, but it shines by different means. The

point is that his ministry among us as 'the man
Christ Jesus' (1 Tim. 2:5) is circumscribed by his
true humanity. He was born, he lived and he died. So
while he is bodily present, he has his time to work
and he manifests himself as the one and only 'light of
the world'. The scandal and the sadness in this is
that so many were oblivious to the most brilliant
revelation of divine light the world has ever seen. It
will only be surpassed when Jesus comes again in
glory at the end of the age (cf. Luke 17:23-24).
Meanwhile, the healing of the blind man proves him
to be that unique light, and 'invites sinners to employ
him as such',[3] by coming to him in faith.

The healing of his blindness (9:6-7)

9:6-7. When he had said these things, he spat on the ground
and made clay with the saliva; and he anointed the eyes of
the blind man with the clay. And he said to him, 'Go, wash in
the pool of Siloam' (which is translated, Sent).
So he went and washed, and came back seeing.

Jesus makes a mud-pack of spittle and clay and
applies it to the blind man's eyes. Speculations
abound as to what this means. Did saliva have
curative powers? Was he alluding to man's creation
from the dust? (Gen. 2:7). Was he somehow, as
Calvin suggests, rather unconvincingly, intensifying
the blindness so as to magnify the cure?[4]
An examination of the text itself, however, offers a
simple and satisfying explanation. It is not the mud-
pack that is central to the miracle, but the washing
of the man's eyes in the Pool of Siloam: **'So he went,
and washed, and came back seeing'** (9:7). Siloam is
the key: no mud-pack, no washing in Siloam; no
washing in Siloam, no exposition of the point Jesus
is making by healing him. It is evident that Jesus

wanted the man to have something to wash off his eyes in the Pool of Siloam. Siloam means 'sent' and is the same as 'Shiloh', in connection with which we have the Messianic promise in Genesis 49:10:

The sceptre shall not depart from Judah ...
Until Shiloh comes,
And to him shall be the obedience of the people.

Carson notes that "As it [Siloam] was called 'Sent', so Jesus was supremely the sent one... Moreover, in Isaiah 8:6 the Jews reject the waters of Shiloah; here they reject Jesus."[5] In other words, Jesus orchestrates the healing so as to make a tangible connection between the theology of Shiloh/Siloam (see also the exposition of John 7:37-39, pp.299-306) and his office as the promised Messiah. The mud-pack is no more than a tool; the water of Siloam is the central symbol, and Jesus the Messiah is the substance — the light of the world, come to take sinners from darkness into his marvellous light (1 Peter 2:9). The 'deeper meaning is surely this', says Hendriksen, 'that for spiritual cleansing one must go to the true Siloam, i.e., to the One who was *sent* by the Father to save sinners'. [6] When the man **'came back seeing'**, no one present was speculating about the powers of Jesus' spittle, for they understood that Jesus himself was responsible for the miracle.

How did the man come to see?
(John 9:8-34)

9:8-12. Therefore the neighbours and those who previously had seen that he was blind said, 'Is not this he who sat and begged?'

Some said, 'This is he.' Others said, 'He is like him.' He said, 'I am he.'

Therefore they said to him, 'How were your eyes opened?' He answered and said, 'A man called Jesus made clay and anointed my eyes and said to me, "Go to the pool of Siloam and wash." So I went and washed, and I received sight.'

Then they said to him, 'Where is he?' He said, 'I do not know.'

The people who knew the man well were both astonished and disbelieving. Some thought he was the same man. Others thought he was someone like him. He clinched the matter by declaring, **'I am he.'** Then, in answer to their question as to how he had regained his sight, he told the story of what Jesus had done. When asked where Jesus was to be found, he could not say, no doubt because the Lord was deliberately retreating from potential confrontation with the authorities at this point (9:8-12; cf. 8:59).

The Jewish church leadership soon enter into the picture, however, and controversy does erupt, although Jesus remains in the background until after the man had been cast out of the synagogue (9:35). There is no reason to doubt the man's neighbours' good intentions. They took him to the synagogue to consult the clergy regarding his miraculous healing. Little did they suspect that their own spiritual leaders would evaluate the man's situation (9:13-17), examine his parents (9:18-23) and then excommunicate him (9:24-34).

Evaluation (9:13-17)

9:13-17. They brought him who formerly was blind to the Pharisees. Now it was a Sabbath when Jesus made the clay and opened his eyes.

Then the Pharisees also asked him again how he had received his sight. He said to them, 'He put clay on my eyes, and I washed, and I see.'

Therefore some of the Pharisees said, 'This man is not from God, because he does not keep the Sabbath.' Others said, 'How can a man who is a sinner do such signs?' And there was a division among them.

They said to the blind man again, 'What do you say about him because he opened your eyes?' He said, 'He is a prophet.'

The Pharisees interviewed the man, and two main issues were identified. The first was the miracle itself. The other was the fact that Jesus had healed the man on **'a Sabbath'** (9:14). The significance of the latter is that Jesus had clearly broken some rules on Sabbath observance — not *biblical* rules, mind, but the laws of rabbinical teaching.[7] This was to lead to divided opinions among the Pharisees.

Some reasoned that since Jesus had not kept 'the Sabbath' according to their rules, he could not be from God (9:16). They might have cited Deuteronomy 13:1-5, which prescribes death for prophets who do miracles but use their resultant influence to lead the people away from the righteousness of God. They would have done better, observes Calvin, instead of asserting that it could not be a work of God because it violated the Sabbath, to ask 'if a work of God was a violation of the Sabbath'.[8]

Others argued that the miracle, being genuine, indicated that Jesus could not be **'a sinner'** — that is, a man destitute of any real religion (9:16; cf. Mark 2:16). This, if seemingly less legalistic than the other view, still misses the point that Satan and his false prophets have sometimes performed 'lying wonders' and 'unrighteous deception' (2 Thess. 2:9,10). They, at least, did not dismiss Jesus as a charlatan. What both groups failed to do was see the conjunction and consistency of revealed truth and miraculous attestation in Jesus' ministry.

This, in his naïve way, was exactly what the formerly blind man did. When asked his opinion of Jesus, he answered, **'He is a prophet'** (9:17). His eyes were opened in more ways than one! He saw Jesus for who he was: a true prophet, speaking the truth of God and doing the works of God!

Examination (9:18-23)

9:18-23. But the Jews did not believe concerning him, that he had been blind and received his sight, until they called the parents of him who had received his sight. And they asked them, saying, 'Is this your son, who you say was born blind? How then does he now see?'

His parents answered them and said, 'We know that this is our son, and that he was born blind; but by what means he now sees we do not know, or who opened his eyes we do not know. He is of age; ask him. He will speak for himself.'

His parents said these things because they feared the Jews, for the Jews had agreed already that if anyone confessed that he was Christ, he would be put out of the synagogue. Therefore his parents said, 'He is of age; ask him.'

Still looking for a way to justify their scepticism, the Pharisees called in the parents. Maybe the man had not really been blind from birth. Think of all the naturalistic explanations put up in the last two millennia to explain away the miracles of Jesus. Was the 'transfiguration' a function of the angle of the sun making him brighter than usual? Were there stones just under the water upon which he 'walked' on the Sea of Galilee? They would make God a liar and Jesus a con-artist rather than believe that God can be God!

The parents confirmed that the man was their son and had been born blind, but, **'because they feared the Jews'**, stayed on the fence as to Jesus' role or status. John gives the precise reason: **'The Jews had agreed already that if anyone confessed that he was Christ, he would be put out of the synagogue'** (9:22). This was not the last time that church sanctions would be used to suppress the truth, as a million martyrs continue to cry from 'under the altar' of their sacrifice (Rev. 6:9-11). The parents took the line of least resistance — their son could speak for himself (cf. Ps. 27:10).

Excommunication (9:24-34)

9:24-34. So they again called the man who was blind, and said to him, 'Give God the glory! We know that this man is a sinner.'

He answered and said, 'Whether he is a sinner or not I do not know. One thing I know: that though I was blind, now I see.'

Then they said to him again, 'What did he do to you? How did he open your eyes?'

He answered them, 'I told you already, and you did not listen. Why do you want to hear it again? Do you also want to become his disciples?'

Then they reviled him and said, 'You are his disciple, but we are Moses' disciples. We know that God spoke to Moses; as for this fellow, we do not know where he is from.'

The man answered and said to them, 'Why, this is a marvellous thing, that you do not know where he is from; yet he has opened my eyes! Now we know that God does not hear sinners; but if anyone is a worshipper of God and does his will, he hears him. Since the world began it has been unheard of that anyone opened the eyes of one who was born blind. If this man were not from God, he could do nothing.'

They answered and said to him, 'You were completely born in sins, and are you teaching us?' And they cast him out.

Excommunication is a necessary sanction if the true church of Jesus Christ is to maintain a faithful separation from the world. It is essential that those who deny Christ and openly flout the righteousness of God should be put out, or kept out, of the membership of the church, for that membership signifies membership in Christ (cf. 1 Cor. 5:1-8). When this becomes a tool of policy in the hands of ungodly church leaders in the interest of error rather than truth, it means that what was a church is well on the way to becoming what Scripture calls a 'synagogue of Satan' (Rev. 2:9; 3:9). Behind the pious language of the Pharisees, this is what was happening in the Jewish church of Jesus' day.

1. Rejection required (9:24)

The authorities called the man back in, not to gather more evidence, but to secure his agreement that Jesus was a wicked man: **'Give God the glory! We know that this man is a sinner.'** 'Give God the glory,' as in Joshua 7:19, means, 'Tell the truth before God,' rather than 'Praise the Lord!' Since they

could not face admitting Jesus to be who he claimed
to be, they must reject him as a 'sinner' — an ungodly man. That is why those who would live for
Jesus and faithfully tell the world about God's law
and the gospel of saving grace can expect to be called
bigots and extremists. Why? Because Jesus challenges the root of man's rebellion and demands the
unconditional surrender of both heart and hand, and
this is highly offensive to those whose commitments
are in the opposite direction.

2. Rejection rebuked (9:25-33)

Unlike his parents, the man would not be intimi-
dated. He first responds by saying he does not know
whether or not Jesus was a sinner, and then effectively answers the question by stating the obvious:
**'One thing I know: that though I was blind, now I
see'** (9:25). It is as if he says, 'You have to be kidding! You ask me to condemn the man who restored
my sight?'

This must have taken the wind out of their sails,
for all they could manage was a rehash of their
earlier question (see 9:15). This was even more unbelievable to the man. He had told them — had they
listened? Must he say it again? Then came the
clincher: **'Do you also want to become his disciples?'** (9:27). He knew very well they did not. He
was lampooning their pretended interest in Jesus'
miracle-working. He was exposing their true interest,
which was not in the facts, still less in his health, but
only in getting somebody to say something against
Jesus.

This infuriated the Jews. The man may be **'his
disciple'** — they cannot bring themselves to utter
Jesus' name — but they are **'Moses' disciples'** (9:28).
The invocation of Moses' name, not for the first time
(cf. 8:5), seeks to set up an invidious comparison

between the two. They are not to be mentioned in the same breath! After all, they argue, they know that **'God spoke to Moses'**. In contrast, they do not know **'where he is from'** (9:29). Since they clearly knew where Jesus came from physically (6:42; 7:27), this language is figurative, and therefore roughly equivalent to modern usage as in the expression: 'I don't know where you're coming from.' They saw no reason to believe Jesus' words had been given to him by God.

The irony is, of course, that, so adamantine were they in their rejection of Jesus' claims that they could not even grasp the true significance of Moses (5:45-46; 6:32). They were not true disciples of Moses, for, as Calvin says, 'They have turned aside from the end of the Law... If Christ be the soul of the law (Rom. 10:4), what will the Law be when separated from him, but a dead body? We are taught by this example, that no man truly hears God, unless he be an attentive hearer of his word, so as to understand what God means and says.'[9] Men who, in the face of scriptural exposition and the mighty works of God, give way to apoplectic outbursts and murderous rage are incapable of rational discourse, far less receptivity to the self-revelation of the Son of God. They know neither 'the Scriptures, nor the power of God' (Matt. 22:29).

The response of the man born blind is unaffected in its simplicity. He marvels at their incapacity to put two and two together! They **'do not know where he is from; yet he has opened my eyes'** (9:30). The word-play is delicious. His (physical) eyes are opened, but their (spiritual) eyes are closed! He even takes them through the logic of the situation:

Major premise

God does not hear sinners (cf. 9:24), but he does hear those who worship and obey him (9:31). God answers believing prayer.

Minor premise

The opening of congenitally blind eyes was unheard of **'since the world began'** (9:32). What actually happened, only God could do. In fact, notes Carson, 'One of the signs of the dawning of the messianic age is the restoration of sight to the blind (Isa. 29:18; 35:5; 42:7).'[10]

Conclusion

'If this man were not from God, he could do nothing' (9:33). Jesus is 'from' God (cf. 9:29). In the blind man's case, 'seeing' was believing. That the hand of God was in this miracle was plain as a pikestaff.

3. Rejection resorted to (9:34)

The Pharisees would listen no more. They were not about to be lectured by one such as he. Now they wrote him off as **'completely born in sins'** — a cruel reference to his blindness from birth — and **'cast him out'**, that is, removed him from membership in the synagogue. He was to be regarded as an unbeliever and a reprobate. When churches and clerics depart from the truth of God's Word, church discipline merely serves their interest in retaining their institutional power.

What was the purpose of the healing? (John 9:35-41)

Solemn excommunication by a faithful church is indeed judicial exclusion from the kingdom of God (1 Cor. 5:5; Titus 3:10). But was the man rendered odious in God's sight by his summary excommunication by a corrupt church? That the answer is 'No,' is now made plain by Jesus threefold answer.

Spiritual blindness is curable (9:35-38)

9:35-38. Jesus heard that they had cast him out; and when he had found him, he said to him, 'Do you believe in the Son of God?'

He answered and said, 'Who is he, Lord, that I may believe in him?'

And Jesus said to him, 'You have both seen him and it is he who is talking with you.'

Then he said, 'Lord, I believe!' And he worshipped him.

Rejection by the synagogue was not proof that the man was saved. The formerly blind man was now on his own. That might soon have turned into a root of bitterness, had the man who got him into this trouble not sought him out. Notice, then, how Jesus dealt with him once he had been cast off by the 'organized religion' of the time.

1. The Saviour reaches out (9:35)

Jesus found the man and asked him, **'Do you believe in the Son of God?'**[11] This is one of many
Christological titles used in John's Gospel. Whether
'Son of God', 'Son of Man', or simply 'the Son', the
thrust is the same and no one would mistake Jesus'
meaning. He was alluding to the divine Messiah
promised in the Scriptures. The man had never seen
Jesus but, on the basis of his healing, had affirmed
him to be a 'prophet' (9:17) and 'from God' (9:33),
notwithstanding the cost of these convictions (9:34).
Jesus now brings the nature of his commitment to a
precise and personal focus. *Who* has healed him?
And *what* is the import of what he has done? To
affirm Jesus to be a good man is one thing, but to
trust him as the Redeemer is another. The miracle is
the lead-in, for temporal physical deliverance is
emblematic of eternal spiritual deliverance. None of
the works of God is to be abstracted from the gospel
of salvation through Christ. Jesus shows us the way.
Even the 'cup of cold water' given in Christ's name
cannot be given in his name unless explicitly connected with his larger purpose of grace. People who
have received physical help from Christ and from his
people will still die and face an eternal destiny.
Welfare, even of the most exalted kind, puts no one
in heaven. The blind man's restored vision did not
save him. Belief in the Lord Jesus Christ is the sole
instrument of being saved (3:16; Acts 16:31).

2. The Saviour sought (9:36)

The man is not sure, so he asks who the 'Son of God'
is. Compare Saul, on the Damascus road, asking,
'Who are you, Lord?' (Acts 9:5). The man asked the
question that the Pharisees refused to countenance
even for a moment. They hardened their hearts

against the Lord. The man's heart was melted to the point where he sought the answer with an open face.

3. The Saviour revealed (9:37)

As he did with the woman at the well (4:26), Jesus here identifies himself in the simplest and most majestic manner: **'You have both seen him and it is he who is talking with you.'** This stops short of explaining the whole gospel way of salvation, including the cross, the atonement and the resurrection, but it does reveal Jesus explicitly to be the Messiah and implicitly calls for personal commitment. He is not yet the crucified and risen Saviour, and so the man is not called upon to believe him in the terms of Christ's accomplishment of redemption. He is simply called to trust Jesus for who he is, the promised divine Messiah, and so trust him for whatever the future would unfold in due time.

4. The Saviour believed (9:38)

And so he does. **'Lord, I believe!'**, is a confession of faith in Jesus as the Messiah, the Redeemer of Israel. The fact that he **'worshipped him'** seals his conviction that Jesus is the divine Son. His comprehension of the person and work of Christ had at least as far to go to maturity as did that of the Twelve, and we know how confused their grasp of things could be even after Jesus' resurrection. The fundamental fact is that he trusted Jesus as the Son, and shared in substance the confession of Peter: 'You are the Christ, the Son of the living God' (Matt. 16:16).

Judgement remains for the unbelieving (9:39)

9:39. And Jesus said, 'For judgement I have come into this world, that those who do not see may see, and that those who see may be made blind.'

Jesus' purpose in coming into the world is 'not ... to condemn the world, but that the world through him might be saved' (3:17). The world was 'condemned already' and needed no extra push from him (3:18). Nevertheless, a necessary consequence resulting from the accomplishment of his saving work is the judgement of those who will not believe. He had before him a man, blind both physically and spiritually, who had come to faith and saw, both physically and spiritually, the truth about Jesus. On the other hand, he had seen the church leaders, who thought they could see the truth, reject him and his message. The blind came to see the true light, and the 'enlightened' were shown to be blind!

Reflecting on this paradox, he observes that his purpose of salvation cuts both ways. His coming means that **'Those who do not see may see, and that those who see may be made blind.'** There is a 'wrath to come', and we must 'flee' from it (Matt. 3:7). There is a punitive blindness that deepens the darkness of those who continue to reject the Lord. That is the judicial entail of the process by which the gospel comes to the lost, and the lost respond, either to believe and be saved, or to disbelieve and remain lost. There is none so blind as he who will not see. The Word of God divides the lost humanity to which it comes with the message of salvation in Christ (2 Cor. 2:14-16). The blind will see, but many will love darkness rather than light (3:19).

'Do you want to see?' (9:40-41)

9:40-41. Then some of the Pharisees who were with him
heard these words, and said to him, 'Are we blind also?'
   Jesus said to them, 'If you were blind, you would have no
sin; but now you say, "We see." Therefore your sin remains.'

It appears that **'some of the Pharisees'** had observed his conversation with the man born blind.
They did not mistake his meaning, and asked, one
supposes in incredulous and offended tones, **'Are we
blind also?'** Did Jesus mean to put them in the
same category as 'this crowd that does not know the
law' and is 'accursed'? (7:49). It was unconscionable!
How could he think such a thing?
   Jesus did not mistake their meaning. They believed they really could see and that if anyone had
the problem it was he and his followers. Well, says
Jesus, here is the real issue: **'If you were blind, you
would have no sin; but now you say, "We see."'**
That is to say, 'If your problem were just that you
cannot see, but (like the man born blind) you know it
and yearn for healing, there would be no sin in that.
Realizing your need and acting on it is the beginning
of the solution. But your problem is that you do not
admit you are blind, but insist that you can see.'
   In spiritual terms, they sinned because they
actually did *see* what Jesus was saying and *did not
like* what they saw! They did not sin in ignorance, but
against knowledge, against truth and against light.
'Therefore your sin remains,' he adds. There is no
hope of comfort or forgiveness, unless and until you
admit yourself to be blind and apply to the light of
the world for healing. The challenge remains. You
think you see? You think you are right with God? But
do you really see? Have you received Christ? Will you
receive Christ? Then come to him. He is the true
Light. He saves. He saves today!

24. The Good Shepherd

John 10:1-21

Apart from watching a televised sheepdog trial like the BBC programme *One Man and his Dog*, or maybe seeing a shepherd at work on a trip into the country-side, people in urbanized societies have no exposure to the art of shepherding sheep. The Scriptures, reflecting the setting into which they were given, frequently employ the imagery of sheep and the shepherd to portray various aspects of the character of both God and humankind, and their relationships one to another. Psalms 23 and 80 speak of God as the Shepherd of Israel. Psalm 119:176 and Isaiah 53:6 describe people as sheep that have gone astray, while Isaiah 56:9-12 and Ezekiel 34 address the failure of God's ministers to watch over his sheep.

The last-mentioned chapter also prophesies the coming Messiah: 'I will establish one shepherd over them, and he shall feed them — my servant David. He shall feed them and be their shepherd' (Ezek. 34:23). This theme is taken up by Jesus in John 10, where he identifies himself as 'the good shepherd', who looks after his sheep, dies for his sheep and has authority over his sheep. In doing so he sets himself in sharp contrast to the Pharisees and the way they were pas-toring their sheep — in particular, the way they had treated the man who had been blind from birth, after Jesus had miraculously restored his vision (9:13-34).

Illustration: shepherd and sheep (John 10:1-5)

10:1-5. 'Most assuredly, I say to you, he who does not enter the sheepfold by the door, but climbs up some other way, the same is a thief and a robber. But he who enters by the door is the shepherd of the sheep. To him the doorkeeper opens, and the sheep hear his voice; and he calls his own sheep by name and leads them out. And when he brings out his own sheep, he goes before them; and the sheep follow him, for they know his voice. Yet they will by no means follow a stranger, but will flee from him, for they do not know the voice of strangers.'

John calls Jesus' description of the shepherd an 'allegory' (Gk. *paroimia*), or, as in our translation, an **'illustration'** (10:6). This is just to say that it was not a narrative parable (Gk, *parabole*) of the kind encountered in the Synoptic Gospels, but more an extended metaphor in which selected allusions to a particular setting, in this instance to the shepherd's craft, are used to illustrate particular aspects of the truth that Jesus wishes to convey. His leading concern is to distinguish the true shepherd from the false — that is, the shepherd as opposed to the sheep-stealer. This, as already noted, implies an immediate application to the preceding event — there is hardly a pause for breath between 9:41 and 10:1[1] — in which a human 'sheep', the man who was born blind, was healed by Jesus but given nothing but grief by his ostensible 'shepherds', the Pharisees. Jesus actually cared for that particular sheep. The Pharisees did not. Who, then, is the real shepherd?

Jesus points out two main criteria by which to tell the true shepherd from the false.

The first has to do with *the approach to the sheep* (10:1-2). For their safety at night, the sheep were kept in a walled enclosure. This was sometimes connected to the house, but was often a separate structure out in the hills. There would be a 'doorkeeper' to keep an eye on things in the small hours (10:3). The true shepherd **'enters ... by the door'**, while the man who **'climbs up some other way'**, seeking to avoid detection, **'is a thief and a robber'**.

The second criterion is that of *voice recognition* (10:3-6). In the West, sheep have an adversarial relationship to the shepherd. He uses dogs to chase them into the fold and tends to follow the flock. If he calls, it is to the dogs rather than the sheep. In the Middle East, the shepherd leads the sheep and he calls them to follow him. They recognize his voice, as opposed to those of impostors who would seek to rustle them.

Jesus goes on to provide his own interpretation (10:7-18). That fact offers us a lesson in resistance to the kind of over-interpretation that dogs the exposition of parables. Here we know for sure that we must not look for more meaning in the details than Jesus is willing to furnish. Calvin's caveat still stands as a model of interpretive restraint: 'Let us rest satisfied with this general view, that, as Christ states a resemblance between the Church and a *sheepfold*, in which God assembles all his people, so he compares himself to a *door*, because there is no other entrance into the Church but by himself. Hence it follows that they alone are good *shepherds* who lead men straight to Christ; and that they are truly gathered into the *fold* of Christ, so as to belong to his flock, who devote themselves to Christ alone.'[2]

Interpretation: Saviour and sinners (John 10:6-18)

10:6. Jesus used this illustration, but they did not understand the things which he spoke to them.

Jesus' hearers were none the wiser for hearing his **'illustration'** (10:6). We need not think ourselves superior to them. They could hardly have been expected to grasp instantly such an enigmatic allegory, especially in view of their scepticism about Jesus. Jesus intended to explain it in detail, and so lead them into the main themes of his teaching about himself, and their need of him as their Saviour-shepherd. He makes two main points.

'I am the door' (10:7-10)

10:7-10. Then Jesus said to them again, 'Most assuredly, I say to you, I am the door of the sheep. All who ever came before me are thieves and robbers, but the sheep did not hear them. I am the door. If anyone enters by me, he will be saved, and will go in and out and find pasture. The thief does not come except to steal, and to kill, and to destroy. I have come that they may have life, and that they may have it more abundantly.'

Jesus is emphatic and his meaning is unmistakable: **'Most assuredly, I say to you, I am the door of the sheep'** (10:7). Whitacre, following Beasley-Murray and others, suggests that Jesus here introduces a scene change, taking us from the village sheep-fold with its doorkeeper (cf. 10:3) to the field in summer, where there 'is neither roof nor door, but thorns along the top of the rock walls protect the sheep from wild animals, and the shepherd himself sleeps in the entrance, providing a door'.[3] Jesus then absorbs that seasonal function of the shepherd as a gate for the sheep into his composite picture of himself as the Shepherd of his people. There is one, and only one, entrance into God's fold. There is one, and only one, Saviour worth knowing — hence Paul says, 'For I determined not to know anything among you except Jesus Christ and him crucified' (1 Cor. 2:2). This is the central offence of the gospel message — the exclusive claim of the crucified Christ to be the one and only Saviour. The implications of this are staggering, and Jesus does not conceal them from his audience as he unfolds a six-part picture of what it means for him to be the door to eternal life.

1. All other self-proclaimed 'messiahs' and putative ways of salvation are false (10:8a)

Such people are **'thieves and robbers'**. Jesus does not have in mind here those whom God sent ahead of him to prophesy his coming (Moses, Abraham, Isaiah, Elijah, John the Baptizer, etc.). The ban is, however, absolute on all other religions and the purveyors of their false teachings. All who deny that Jesus is the *divine* Messiah who has come *in the flesh* are liars and antichrists (1 John 2:18-23; 4:2-3). Whether modern Judaism, Islam, Hinduism, Buddhism, Mormonism, Unitarianism, anti-supernatural 'liberal' Christianity, secular saviours, or a myriad of cults and heresies — all are illusory paths to truth and to heaven, and as such deny Christ and the gospel. Unpalatable as this is to those who trust in such false hopes, these constitute the broad way that leads to eternal, and even temporal, destruction (Matt. 7:13).

2. The elect of God are not deceived and will accept no substitutes for the one and only Saviour of sinners (10:8b)

The sheep **'did not hear them'**. All attempts by false shepherds to deceive the true sheep will in the end fail (Mark. 13:22). There is a barb in these words, for hearers who were not responding to Jesus with understanding and enthusiasm would not escape the dual implication that they were being told that they were not really God's flock and that the teachers they followed were false shepherds! Indeed, they were 'like sheep having no shepherd' (Matt. 9:36; cf. Ezek. 34:12).

3. All who believe in Jesus 'will be saved' (10:9a,b)

To be 'born again' is to be placed beyond the reach of eternal death (3:3,16-17). To come to Christ in faith is to be delivered from danger, to be taken from death to irreversible newness of life.

4. All who believe in Jesus have true freedom (10:9c).

The sheep will **'go in and out'**. That is to say, believers will operate in an essential security as they live their lives from day to day. The Lord is the constant Shepherd of his sheep (Ps. 23:4-6; cf. Ps. 80).

5. All who believe in Jesus will grow in grace (10:9d)

The Christian life will not only be secure but expanding. It will be one of spiritual growth. 'Such also as do thus come to God,' observed George Hutcheson over three centuries ago, 'will find such satisfaction and spiritual refreshment for making them grow in grace as they shall not need to complain, or betake themselves to other comforts; for he shall "find pasture." '[4]

6. The issue is one of abundant life versus certain death (10:10)

Christ, as Philip Henry, the father of the more famous Matthew, noted, is 'a living door'. He adds, 'This is peculiar to him. No other door is so besides him; as he is the "living way", Heb. 10, so he is the living door, the door to life and the door that hath life. Other doors are dead things. Now it is true he was dead, but he is alive, and lives for evermore, and thence it follows, Rev. 1:18, "and have the keys of hell and of death".[5] The false religious teacher, like a thief, comes **'to steal, and to kill, and to destroy'**, whereas Jesus comes to give **'life'**, and to give it **'more abundantly'**.

'I am the good shepherd' (10:11-18)

10:11-18. 'I am the good shepherd. The good shepherd gives his life for the sheep. But a hireling, he who is not the shepherd, one who does not own the sheep, sees the wolf coming and leaves the sheep and flees; and the wolf catches the sheep and scatters them. The hireling flees because he is a hireling and does not care about the sheep. I am the good shepherd; and I know my sheep, and am known by my own. As the Father knows me, even so I know the Father; and I lay down my life for the sheep. And other sheep I have which are not of this fold; them also I must bring, and they will hear my voice; and there will be one flock and one shepherd. Therefore my Father loves me, because I lay down my life that I may take it again. No one takes it from me, but I lay it down of myself. I have power to lay it down, and I have power to take it again. This command I have received from my Father.'

Jesus is not only the door of the sheepfold. He is also the Shepherd! More than that, he is, literally, 'the Shepherd the good' (ὁ ποιμὴν ὁ καλός / *ho poimen ho kalos*). Both the choice of the adjective and its position are significant. *Kalos* is preferred to the more common *agathos* ('good'), because it means 'beautiful' or 'excellent' in reference to character. The position of the adjective adds emphasis. What makes for this excellent character is set forth along four lines.

1. Self-sacrificial death (10:11-13)

Jesus is **'the good shepherd'** who **'gives his life for the sheep'**. A hired hand can be the most faithful of servants, but a **'hireling'** only works for money and has no particular commitment to his sheep. He **'sees the wolf coming and leaves the sheep and flees'**, with predictably disastrous results for the flock. He is the opposite of the Good Shepherd who will never let his sheep be snatched out of his hand (10:28).

2. Personal relationships (10:14-15)

Jesus knows his sheep and they know him. If the Pharisees are strangers and robbers in their relationship with the flock of God (10:5,8), Jesus is the Shepherd who shares an experiential mutual knowledge with his sheep (10:3-4). 'Christ,' observes Thomas Manton, 'hath a particular and exact knowledge of all the elect, their individual persons, who they are, where they are, and what they are, that shall be saved; he taketh special notice of them, that he may suitably apply himself to them.'[6] When someone comes to Christ, with repentance towards God and faith in him as Saviour, that exhaustive, loving knowledge Jesus has for his own finds its echo in the response of the believing heart. Jesus says, **'I ... am known by my own.'** The true sheep know that they

know Jesus. He is the decisive experiential reality in
their lives. This mutual knowledge of the Good Shepherd and his sheep in turn rests on two things: the
mutual knowledge of the Father and the Son and the
sacrificial death of the Son for the sheep.

There is a chain of personal intimacy from the
Father to the Son and to the redeemed (15:9-11;
17:21). God's love is settled on particular people: his
only-begotten Son and, in and through him, the
people born again to newness of life. The renewed
mention of Christ's death in connection with this
chain of intimacy emphasizes that the atonement
was intended to apply to particular individuals.
Jesus says, **'I lay down my life for [my] sheep.'**
Carson comments most aptly, 'However clearly this
Gospel portrays Jesus as the Saviour of the world
(4:42), the Lamb of God who takes away the sin of
the world (1:29,36), it insists no less emphatically
that Jesus has a peculiar relation with those the
Father has given him (6:37ff.), with those he has
chosen out of the world (15:16,19). So here: Jesus'
death is peculiarly for his sheep, just as we elsewhere
read that "Christ loved the church and gave himself
up for her" (Eph. 5:25).[7] Commenting on John 10:15,
Thomas Manton observes, 'Though Christ's death be
sufficient for all, yet the efficacy and the benefit of it
is intended only to believers — to those that enjoy it
by faith — not only applied, but intended only. Mark,
I say, that not only the efficacy of it is to believers,
but the efficacy is intended to believers... There was
the intent of God and Christ, that Christ should die
only for those of his own flock; and therefore many
times, where you find the expressions of God's love
very general, you shall see the intention of it is re-
strained to those that believe. As John 3:16 ... God
intended him to the world of believers: whoever
amongst them do believe, let him be whatever he will,

or whatever he was, he should not perish[8] (see also
Rom. 3:22; John 17:9,20).

3. Cosmic claims — Jesus gathers one great flock (10:16)

The 'sheepfold' of 10:1 represents believers among
the Jews. Jesus, however, has **'other sheep ... not
of this fold'**. These, he will **'bring'** in so that there
will be **'one flock and one shepherd'**. In this way,
the Lord serves notice of what becomes a major
theme of the New Testament — the salvation of the
Gentiles, who will hear his voice through his servants, the apostles, evangelists and ministers of the
gospel (11:51-52; 17:20; Matt. 28:19-20; 1 Cor. 12;
2 Cor. 5:14-21; Gal. 3:28; Eph. 2:11-22; 4:3-6).
Jesus is saying, 'Watch for the future emergence of
my flock among all the nations of the world and see if
what I am saying is not true.'

4. Obedience to death — Jesus submits to the Father's will (10:17-18)

Although the shepherd-sheep relationship illustrates
the work of Jesus, it does only limited justice to the
actual scope of his redemptive mission. Jesus, as the
Good Shepherd, is unique in several ways.

First of all, *what he does is in obedience to the
Father's will,* and it is for this reason that he may
say, **'Therefore my Father loves me'** (10:17a).
Specifically, Jesus lays down his life **'that [he] may
take it again'** (10:17b). In other words, the great
transaction in which he is the pivotal actor is death
and resurrection on behalf of his sheep. Jesus' shepherding is redemptive. He dies to live, that those
condemned to death may be saved to eternal life (cf.
3:16-17). He does so within the orbit of the Father's
love, even though, as will be revealed on the cross, this
involves the Father's forsaking him in the moment of

his bearing our iniquities (see Isa. 53:4-6,10-12; Matt. 27:46).

Secondly, *he lays down his life voluntarily* (10:18a). He does not merely risk his life, like an earthly shepherd. He willingly surrenders to death. He does so for the reason that his death actually effects the salvation of his sheep. He takes on himself the only thing that can harm them — the sin that calls forth the righteous judgement of God against them.

Thirdly, *he is able to take up his life again* (10:18b). His death is not an end in itself. He must rise from the dead and live. The efficacy of his sacrifice depends upon this. Paul will later admit that 'If Christ is not risen, your faith is futile; you are still in your sins!' (1 Cor. 15:17). The resurrection is the proof that the cross sufficed to save sinners, for it demonstrates the power of the sinless Jesus to be the sin-bearer who satisfies the full extent of divine justice against the sin of sinners.

Here Jesus makes clear that his death is not merely a martyr's death, but a unique once-for-all substitutionary sacrifice. The distinction is rarely paid the attention it should receive. Martyrs are those whose lives are taken by others, because they have witnessed (the Greek is *martureo*, hence our English 'martyr') for a cause unacceptable to their persecutors. In one sense, Jesus was a martyr for his own cause. Men killed him to extinguish his message and memory. The reality is that all of that was merely the occasion for a death required by God as the penalty of sin that was not his own. Jesus freely gave himself to meet the demands of divine justice: **'This command I have received from my Father'** (10:18c).

The wrath of man was therefore made to praise God in the most profound manner possible (Ps. 76:10). Those who crucified the Lord of glory thought they were doing one thing, when all the while, God was doing another. The death they inflicted on Jesus secured life for a multitude that no man can number. 'It pleased the LORD to bruise him' (Isa. 53:10).

Disharmony
(John 10:19-21)

10:19-21. Therefore there was a division again among the Jews because of these sayings.

And many of them said, 'He has a demon and is mad. Why do you listen to him?'

Others said, 'These are not the words of one who has a demon. Can a demon open the eyes of the blind?'

The divided response of Jesus' hearers is thoroughly understandable. Some said, **'He has a demon and is mad'** (10:20), while others, evidently in the minority, observed that **'These are not the words of one who has a demon,'** and asked, **'Can a demon open the eyes of the blind?'** (10:21). They at least acknowledged that Jesus must, in some sense, be from God.

There is never any neutrality in human response to the claims of Jesus Christ. There is always a **'division'** (Σχίσμα / *schisma*) along that greatest of fault lines in human life — the antithesis between God and Satan, truth and error, righteousness and evil, darkness and light (cf. 7:43; 9:16). The disharmony between the two reactions to Jesus is the difference between those who see the conformity between his message and his actions, and those who dismiss the evidence of their eyes and ears and declare him to be the very opposite of what he claims to be and to do. Nothing has changed. Jesus still divides people. The preachers of the gospel are still, as Paul puts it, 'the fragrance of Christ among those who are being saved and among those who are perishing. To the one we are the aroma of death leading to death, and to the other the aroma of life leading to life' (2 Cor. 2:15-16).

The wonder of the gospel is that we 'silly sheep', to use an expression of Charles Simeon's, have been arrested in large numbers by the grace of the Lord Jesus Christ and brought to saving faith in him. Then, says the Cambridge preacher, 'Let it be your delight to hear your Shepherd's voice, and to follow his steps: then shall you be separated from the goats in the day of judgement, and receive from the Chief Shepherd the portion reserved for you.'[9]

25. 'Tell us who you are!'

John 10:22-42

People are always 'reading' one another. What we say and do always suggests questions, and often proposes conclusions, in the minds of others as to our character, motives and intentions. This is natural and inevitable. It comes as no surprise, then, to find that the things that Jesus said and did have caused many people to wonder who he was and what he was seeking to achieve.

During his earthly ministry, Jesus was often deliberately vague and for a while refused to declare himself explicitly. The question put to him by the Jews, **'How long do you keep us in doubt?'** (literally, 'Until when will you hold [i.e., in suspense] our soul?'), arose in the context of that ambiguity.

The Bible as a whole leaves no doubt whatsoever as to the identity and mission of Jesus Christ. He is explicitly revealed as the incarnate Son of God, who died a substitutionary death for sinners and rose from the dead on the third day for their justification (Rom. 4:25). In response to these claims of Scripture, the questions still flow — although frequently in the attempt to escape the truth that Jesus really is the Son of God and the coming Judge of every human being.[1] In his rounding out of the account of what is known as the 'Good Shepherd' discourse, the apostle John records the Jews' question and offers answers that have never been excelled for their clarity. Jesus, says the apostle, is the promised Messiah (10:22-30), the Son of God (10:31-39) and the Saviour of sinners (10:40-42).

The promised Messiah
(John 10:22-30)

10:22-24. Now it was the Feast of Dedication in Jerusalem, and it was winter. And Jesus walked in the temple, in Solomon's porch. Then the Jews surrounded him and said to him, 'How long do you keep us in doubt? If you are the Christ, tell us plainly.'

After Jesus had identified himself as the 'Good Shepherd', and so had implicitly pointed to his Messianic character, his hearers became divided in their opinions of him. Some thought him demon-possessed and therefore someone to be ignored. Others suspected that he might actually be from God. None of them appears to have accepted him as the Messiah (10:20-21). Still, the question lingered on: 'Who are you, Jesus?'

Some time after the healing of the blind man, the **'Feast of Dedication'** took place. This festival — also known as the Feast of Lights, or Hanukkah — was a commemoration of the rededication of the temple and the revival of Jewish nationhood under Judas Maccabaeus in 164 B.C. For eight days in December, the Jews remembered how their worship had been restored to them and how God was the light and hope for his people. At such a time, the twin themes of Messianic hope and national deliverance were not far from Jewish minds. One day, Jesus was walking in **'in the temple, in Solomon's porch'**, when **'the Jews surrounded him'** and confronted him with the

question: **'If you are the Christ, tell us plainly'**
(10:24).

Many people no doubt asked this question most
sincerely. Nicodemus, for example, had approached
Jesus with a transparently genuine interest in
knowing more about him. In this instance, however,
it is abundantly clear from Jesus' reply that the
questioners were more concerned to trip him up and
find an excuse to do him harm. An outright claim
that he was 'the Christ' — that is, the Messiah, the
Anointed One of prophetic Scripture — using the very
word, would have given them all the ammunition
they needed.

Jesus and his enemies (10:25-26)

10:25-26. Jesus answered them, 'I told you, and you do not
believe. The works that I do in my Father's name, they bear
witness of me. But you do not believe, because you are not
of my sheep, as I said to you.'

Jesus accordingly answered with the greatest care,
and yet with enough clarity to let his hearers draw
their own conclusions as to who he was. He did not
give a 'yes' or 'no' answer. Why? Because it would not
have been helpful in the circumstances. They had
mistaken notions as to what the Messiah should be
like. Jesus' own time had not come (7:6-8), and he
was deliberately holding back from precipitating the
final crisis that such a self-revelation would certainly
have triggered. He therefore took an indirect approach and referred them to their own knowledge of
his ministry among them.

First of all, we must note once again that *people
did not reject Jesus for lack of evidence.* **'The works
that I do in my Father's name,'** he tells them,
'they bear witness of me' (10:25). Jesus pointed

them to what they had seen and heard of his ministry, and in effect confronted them in their consciences with the double fact that they had already
rejected this as evidence that he was 'the Christ', and
were only willing, so to speak, to give him enough
rope with which to hang himself.

What Jesus had already *said* in his public ministry had shown them the general drift of his teaching
(cf. 9:35-41; 8:58). **'I told you,'** he says, indicating
that the answer they pretended to be seeking had
already been clearly given.

What Jesus had *done* — most recently the healing
of the man born blind (9:1-7) — had attested his
authority. There was in fact no lack of evidence upon
which to come to a sound conclusion, but still, said
Jesus, **'You do not believe.'**

From the start, then, Jesus confronted them with
their unbelief! He made them face up to the insincere
motives that lay behind their asking him if he were
truly the Messiah. Instead of making it easier for
them to feel more justified in persecuting him, he
made it more difficult for them to escape their guilty
consciences and their dissembling attitudes. Jesus
did not allow them to hide behind their hypocritical
affectation of sincerity. He did not call them names.
He did not accuse them head-on of hypocrisy. He
rather outflanked it by going to the fundamental
issue, which was their actual response to his ministry hitherto. The problem was not a lack of evidence.

We must note, in the second place, that a condition of *unbelief*, not an insufficiency of objective
evidence (which included undeniable miracles of
healing), was the reason for their rejection of Jesus.
**'But you do not believe, because you are not of
my sheep, as I said to you'** (10:26). Earlier he had
told them, 'I know my sheep, and am known by my
own' (10:14). 'They pretended that they only
doubted,' remarks Matthew Henry, 'but Christ tells

them that they did not believe. Scepticism in religion is no better than downright infidelity. It is not for us to teach God how he should teach us, nor prescribe to him how plainly he should tell us his mind, but to be thankful for divine revelation as we have it.[2] They were not merely in need of more explanation — they were in an unbelieving condition of heart. They were therefore spiritually blind to the character of Jesus and his ministry. Their allegiance was in another direction. They were not Jesus' 'sheep' (10:15).

Jesus and his followers (10:27-29)

10:27-29. 'My sheep hear my voice, and I know them, and they follow me. And I give them eternal life, and they shall never perish; neither shall anyone snatch them out of my hand. My Father, who has given them to me, is greater than all; and no one is able to snatch them out of my Father's hand.'

What, then, are Jesus' sheep like? John notes five leading characteristics.

1. They truly know Jesus

'My sheep hear my voice' (10:27a). There is what we may call a 'recognition of acceptance' in the true followers of Jesus. That carries with it an experiential challenge for each of us. Do you know that you know Jesus? Or is this all a mystery to you? Answer honestly and you know where you stand!

2. They are known by Jesus

'I know them' (10:27b). We may easily claim to know some famous people from afar. We may even have been introduced to a celebrity. But that does not

mean the celebrity knows who we are. Jesus actually
foreknew those whom he predestined and subsequently called and justified (Rom. 8:30). His personal
knowledge of his sheep is the basis for his calling
them in the first place.

3. They follow Jesus

'They follow me' (10:27c). As we noted in the previous chapter, whereas our shepherds drive the sheep
with the help of dogs, the shepherds of the Middle
East lead the sheep from the front. The picture is one
of attachment and devotion. So, observes Hutcheson,
'It is an undeniable and special evidence of Christ's
sheep, that they give themselves up to his teaching
and direction, and do incline their heart and ear to
take notice of what he says.'³

4. They receive eternal life from Jesus

**'... I give them eternal life, and they shall never
perish; neither shall anyone snatch them out of
my hand'** (10:28). Those whom God saves, he also
keeps. The entail of this in the experience of the
redeemed is that they persevere in the faith. They do
not cease to be saved. They will never perish. They
will always be in the Lord's hand. People who profess
to be Christians, and people who appear to the outward view to be Christians, can and do fall away into
apostasy. The truly saved — regenerated by the Holy
Spirit and converted to Christ through a living faith
— 'never perish' and, whatever the ebbs and flows of
their Christian experience, endure to the last and
receive the crown of life. The (Arminian) insistence
that those who are truly converted to Christ and are
saved can be unconverted and unsaved again, founders on this word of Jesus alone (but do also consult Ps.
18:32; 37:31; 73:24; 138:8; Prov. 10:30; Mark 16:16;

John 4:14; 11:26; Rom. 8:38-39). 'That a righteous
man may fall is evident,' observes Elisha Coles, 'and
as evident it is, that he cannot fall finally; for though
he fall seven times in a day, as often does he rise
again, Prov. 24:16, and this, because the "Lord
upholdeth him with his hand," Ps. 37:24, and again,
the "Lord upholdeth all that fall," Ps. 145:14, that is,
either he stays them when they are falling, or so
orders and limits the matter, that they may not fall
into mischief as others do; and to be sure he will set
them on their feet again.'[4]

5. Their security is guaranteed by God

**'My Father, who has given them to me, is greater
than all; and no one is able to snatch them out of
my Father's hand'** (10:29). 'Who then can steal from
God?' asks Carson.[5] The Lord's sheep are therefore
able to give glory to God as the one who 'is able to
keep [them] from stumbling, and to present [them]
faultless before the presence of his glory with exceeding joy...' (Jude 24).

Jesus and his Father (10:30)

10:30. 'I and my Father are one.'

What makes this all so certain? It is the unbreakable
solidarity between the Father and the Son. This
union seals all that Jesus taught and did. Without
saying in explicit terms, 'Yes! I really am the promised Messiah!', Jesus pointed to the conclusion the
evidence demanded!

This is confirmed by a closer look at Jesus' language. He and his Father are **'one'** (the neuter ἑν /
hen) in purpose, but distinct persons (which would
require the masculine *heis*). There is also more than

a hint of the unity of essence that subsists between the First and Second Persons of the Godhead. There is no comfort here for the Arians (who today include most sub-Christian cults and pseudo-Christian theological liberals), who deny that unity and end up with a merely human Jesus. Carson is quite correct to note that 'John's development of Christology to this point demands that some more essential unity [than that of purpose and action] be presupposed, quite in line with the first verse of the Gospel... The Jews had asked for a plain statement that would clarify whether or not he was the Messiah. He gave them far more, and the response was the same as in 5:18; 8:59.[6] His unique oneness with the Father declared that all the power of God undergirded and ensured the success of his mission.

The Son of God
(John 10:31-39)

10:31. Then the Jews took up stones again to stone him.

Although Jesus' statement in 10:30 does not *require*
the conclusion that he is the divine Son of God, it is
quite clear that the Jews did not miss the implication
of what he had said. They **'took up stones again to
stone him'**, to punish him for what they believed
was blasphemy (cf. Lev. 24:16). The charge had to be
that Jesus claimed oneness and equality with God,
which was true. They had not missed that point.
What they would not accept was that the promised
Messiah was the Son of God and was God the Son!
To them, Jesus' claim was setting him up as a distinct god and almost a rival to Jehovah.

Not for the first time, Jesus faced a self-
righteously indignant crowd bent on putting him to
death (cf. 8:59). There was no pretence at a proper
trial.[7] For all that, Jesus was able to forestall the
lynch-mob by offering another of his brilliant replies.
His opening is classic. He deflected their wrath by
reminding them of the miracles he had done
(10:32-33). Then, having hooked them, he had time
to show them from the Scriptures how the charge of
blasphemy was unfounded (10:34-38).

Consider the miracles (10:32-33)

10:32-33. Jesus answered them, 'Many good works I have shown you from my Father. For which of those works do you stone me?'

The Jews answered him, saying, 'For a good work we do not stone you, but for blasphemy, and because you, being a man, make yourself God.'

Jesus stood his ground and called for some consideration of his ministry as a whole. **'Many good works,'** he declared, **'I have shown you from my Father. For which of those works do you stone me?'** (10:32). There is no wheedling here, no abject pleading for his life. Jesus' words breathe the air of authority. He does not back down. He faces them down with a searching insistence on an examination of the facts. Did they not remember the miracles he had done ('from my Father', by the way)? Which of these justified a stoning? Were they opposed to good works? Did they think God was opposed to miracles such as they had seen? How do such (God-given) good works square with a charge of blasphemy? Think about it! Would such miracles not lead to the opposite conclusion — namely, that the one who performs them is from God and acts in the power of God?

Were they impressed by this reasoning? 'Though wicked men carry on open war with God,' says Calvin, 'yet they never wish to sin without some plausible pretence.'[8] Jesus' good works are ruled irrelevant, on the grounds that he is guilty of **'blasphemy'**, for, they tell him, **'You, being a man, make yourself God'** (10:33). Again, they clearly understood Jesus' claim to be the divine Messiah. In their view, this was inexcusable and fully deserved death by stoning, which was the penalty of the law (Lev. 24:16). They would not admit that his miracles and ministry were of such a quality as to attest infallibly the truth of his self-identification as the Son of God.

Consider what the Scriptures say

10:34-39. Jesus answered them, 'Is it not written in your law, 'I said, "You are gods" ' ? If he called them gods, to whom the word of God came (and the Scripture cannot be broken), do you say of him whom the Father sanctified and sent into the world, "You are blaspheming," because I said, "I am the Son of God"? If I do not do the works of my Father, do not believe me; but if I do, though you do not believe me, believe the works, that you may know and believe that the Father is in me, and I in him.'

Therefore they sought again to seize him, but he escaped out of their hand.

Jesus immediately addresses this most serious charge. He first appeals to Scripture, and then to the evidence of their eyewitness observations.

1. The appeal to Scripture

Jesus begins with a quotation from Psalm 82:6: **'I said, "You are gods." '** In this passage, Asaph is probably referring to Israel's judges, although something of the mantle of this dignity appears to descend on all 'the children of the Most High'. The point is that they are God's vicegerents on earth. In their limited and derivative way, they act for God, and the Lord is not above calling them by his name.

Jesus' argument is from the lesser to the greater. If God calls some men 'gods', surely the man who gives sure evidence of being his Son cannot be censured for identifying himself in this way. The argument goes like this:

- since Israel's judges are called 'gods' by the psalmist (10:34);
- and since God called them 'gods' because they acted for him according to the law (**'the word of God'**) which he had given to Israel, his first-born son (10:35a,b; cf. Exod. 4:21-22);
- and since **'the Scripture cannot be broken'**, that is, the words of the psalm are not to be explained away (10:35c);
- and since Jesus is the one **'the Father sanctified and sent into the world'**, that is, who fulfils the promise of God (10:36a);
- then it follows that he cannot justifiably be charged with blasphemy when he identifies himself as **'the Son of God'** (10:36b).

This argument does not in itself prove that Jesus is the Son of God — that is what the appeal to the evidence does. What it does do is give pause to those who would cry 'blasphemy' whenever the language of divinity is used of one who is clearly a man. They need to think it through and assess the full-orbed evidence of his words and his works.

2. The appeal to the evidence

He then confronts their consciences with hard facts to which they are witnesses (10:37-39). Look at the evidence! Did he actually do the works of his Father? If not, do not believe him. If he did, then, even if you do not believe what he says, **'Believe the works,'** says Jesus, **'that you may know and believe that the Father is in me, and I in him.'** They would condemn him with a label — 'blasphemer'. He challenges them with what they have seen with their own eyes and read in their own Scriptures!

All this was to no avail. They did not change their minds and **'sought again to seize him, but he escaped out of their hand'** (10:39). Perhaps this, too, was but another evidence of his divine sonship, for once again, his hour had not yet come (cf. 8:59).

The Saviour of sinners
(John 10:40-42)

10:40-42. And he went away again beyond the Jordan to the place where John was baptizing at first, and there he stayed. Then many came to him and said, 'John performed no sign, but all the things that John spoke about this man were true.' And many believed in him there.

Jesus withdrew beyond the Jordan to the place where his public ministry began with his baptism by his forerunner, John. This was significant on two counts.

It signalled that the close of Jesus' itinerant public ministry was near. There only remained his visit to Bethany, on account of the illness of Lazarus, before his final journey to Jerusalem and the road to the cross.

It also sealed, in the minds of not a few, the fact that John's testimony had indeed been true, namely that Jesus was the promised Messiah, the Lamb of God who would take away the sin of the world. In that secluded place, **'Many believed in him'** (10:42), whereas, in Jerusalem, they had rejected him and even sought to kill him. Matthew Henry has a wonderful comment on this: 'Where the preaching of the doctrine of repentance has had success; as desired, there the preaching of the doctrine of reconciliation and gospel grace is most likely to be prosperous... The Jubilee-trumpet sounds sweetest in the ears of

those who in the day of atonement have afflicted
their souls for sin.[9]

The great issue remains. Who do people say that
this Jesus is? A great teacher? A motivator of followers? A great moralist? A prophet? A blasphemer? Or,
the Messiah, the Son of the living God? Years later,
the apostle John sets out the issue with challenging
clarity: 'Who is a liar but he who denies that Jesus is
the Christ? He is antichrist who denies the Father
and the Son. Whoever denies the Son does not have
the Father either; he who acknowledges the Son has
the Father also' (1 John 2:22-23).

26. The resurrection and the life

John 11:1-37

Jesus has already declared that one of his reasons for coming into this world was that his lost sheep might 'have life, and ... have it ... abundantly' (10:10). He came to give life to dead people and, having made them alive, he promised to give them a continuing and growing experience of that new life. The general perspective behind all of this is that death and hell are the twin realities in the human condition presupposed by the coming of Christ and his revelation of the gospel. 'And as it is appointed for men to die once, but after this the judgement, so Christ was offered once to bear the sins of many. To those who eagerly wait for him he will appear a second time, apart from sin, for salvation' (Heb. 9:27-28).

Why did the human race need this Jesus, who variously describes himself as 'the bread of life', 'the light of the world' and 'the good shepherd'? The answer is that without him, fallen man is 'condemned already' (3:18), must soon die and be plunged for ever into a lost eternity! The 'wages of sin is death' and it is Jesus alone 'who delivers us from the wrath to come' (1 Thess. 1:10).

The immediate context of the events recorded in John 11 is the conclusion of Jesus' public ministry and the brief interlude he spent in Transjordan as he waited for the final Passover week in which he was to die upon a cross in Jerusalem. His last and most dramatic miracle — the raising to new life of Lazarus, when the latter had been dead for four days — acts as a bridge between the two and sets out the heart of the redemptive promise of the gospel, at one and the same time looking back to Jesus' earlier teaching about the gospel of the kingdom and forward to his self-sacrificial death for sinners. The chapter's core teaching is that life comes through Jesus, who *is* 'the resurrection and the life' (11:25a); that life will surely come to believers at the moment of death (11:25b); and that life also comes to believers while they are still in this world (11:26). This theme is developed in the unfolding narrative of the death and resurrection of Lazarus and its after-effects. There are four parts to the story: death (11:1-16), grief (11:17-37), life from the dead (11:38-44) and atonement for sin (11:45-57). The last two will be the subject of the next chapter.

Death
(John 11:1-16)

We are so used to the marvels of modern medicine that we have forgotten the apprehension with which earlier generations greeted sickness of most kinds. They knew that illness is merely death deferred. So, when **'Lazarus of Bethany'** became ill, the sense of urgency with which his sisters sent word to Jesus is entirely understandable.

Death feared — 'Lazarus ... is sick'

11:1-3. Now a certain man was sick, Lazarus of Bethany, the town of Mary and her sister Martha. It was that Mary who anointed the Lord with fragrant oil and wiped his feet with her hair, whose brother Lazarus was sick.
    Therefore the sisters sent to him, saying, 'Lord, behold, he whom you love is sick.'

Lazarus was the brother of the Mary and Martha first mentioned in Luke's Gospel (Luke 10:38-42). John offers some background information on these ladies, by mentioning an incident which at this point in the narrative was still in the future — the one in which Mary anointed Jesus' feet with spikenard (12:1-8). This would seem to indicate that John's readers were already well acquainted with this story from Jesus' life.

When Lazarus fell ill at Bethany in Judea, some
two kilometres from Jerusalem, Jesus and his disciples were in another 'Bethany' — Batanea in the
Tetrarchy of Philip — 150 kilometres to the north-
east.[1] The sisters wasted no time before sending word
to Jesus: **'Lord, behold he whom you love is sick'**
(11:3). This appeal is strikingly different from the way
most people ask for help. For example, someone who
has been done a favour will acknowledge it with an
emphatic, 'I owe you one' — meaning that he will
return the favour when called upon to do so. Help is
then sought as the *quid pro quo* for some past kindness. Here, however, there is no appeal in terms of
how much Lazarus loved Jesus, or how often they
had entertained him in their house. The sisters rest
their plea on Jesus' love for Lazarus! 'Our love to him
is not worth speaking of,' says Matthew Henry, 'but
his to us can never be enough spoken of.'[2] 'In this is
love, not that we loved God, but that he loved us and
sent his Son to be the propitiation for our sins'
(1 John 4:10). He owes us nothing, but his love is
everything. Our love is merely the fruit of love received. 'We love him because he first loved us'
(1 John 4:19).

Death deflected — 'this ... is not unto death' (11:4-6)

11:4-6. When Jesus heard that, he said, 'This sickness is
not unto death, but for the glory of God, that the Son of
God may be glorified through it.' Now Jesus loved Martha
and her sister and Lazarus. So, when he heard that he was
sick, he stayed two more days in the place where he was.

Since we know that Lazarus did die, Jesus' response
to the messenger calls for explanation. **'This sickness is not unto death,'** he says, **'but for the glory
of God, that the Son of God may be glorified**

through it' (11:4). For the sisters, who would have received the message some days later, this implied several things: first of all, Lazarus was not going to be taken from them by death, whatever happened with his sickness; secondly, God and his Son would be glorified in some signal way through the events in Lazarus' immediate future; and, thirdly, they could meanwhile trust God for the outcome, for, as John adds, **'Jesus loved Martha and her sister and Lazarus'** (11:5).

This was no doubt puzzling to the sisters, even more so after Lazarus did die, but it served to strengthen their faith and to lay the groundwork for the miracle to follow. Jesus deliberately delayed his trip to Bethany for **'two more days'**, surely so that he could arrive after Lazarus had died and, furthermore, was incontrovertibly known to be dead. Then no one could say that he 'only' healed Lazarus' illness. Even the Lord's delays are a vital element in both the revelation of his glory and the blessing of his people. He never works quite fast enough for us, of course, but his timing always perfectly serves his purposes.

Death confronted — 'Lazarus is dead'

11:7-16. Then after this he said to the disciples, 'Let us go to Judea again.'

The disciples said to him, 'Rabbi, lately the Jews sought to stone you, and are you going there again?'

Jesus answered, 'Are there not twelve hours in the day? If anyone walks in the day, he does not stumble, because he sees the light of this world. But if one walks in the night, he stumbles, because the light is not in him.'

These things he said, and after that he said to them, 'Our friend Lazarus sleeps, but I go that I may wake him up.'

Then his disciples said, 'Lord, if he sleeps he will get well.' However, Jesus spoke of his death, but they thought that he was speaking about taking rest in sleep.

Then Jesus said to them plainly, 'Lazarus is dead. And I am glad for your sakes that I was not there, that you may believe. Nevertheless let us go to him.'

Then Thomas, who is called the Twin, said to his fellow disciples, 'Let us also go, that we may die with him.'

The time comes and Jesus tells the disciples they are to return to Judea (11:7). This necessitates their confronting that most unpalatable of subjects — death — and in more ways than one.

1. The threat of death (11:8-10)

The disciples wondered aloud if Jesus should go to Judea, given the threats against his life. They did not want to go. They were afraid. Jesus, however, was in no doubt: **'Are there not twelve hours in the day? If anyone walks in the day, he does not stumble, because he sees the light of this world'** (11:9-10). This rather enigmatic answer does not reward over-meticulous exegetical dissection. It approximates roughly to the modern, 'A man's got to do what a man's got to do.' More specifically, we are reminded of 9:4 where Jesus says he must get on with the work God gave him 'while it is day', for 'The night is coming when no one can work,' and 'As long as I am in the world, I am the light of the world.' The death that the disciples saw as a threat was, for Jesus, the very purpose of his going to Judea.

2. The grip of death (11:11-15)

Jesus also indicated that Lazarus had died. He used the language of sleep, something common in the Bible with reference to the death of believers (see

Gen. 47:30; 2 Sam. 7:12; Matt. 27:52; Acts 7:60; 1 Thess. 4:13). The disciples at first misunderstood, but Jesus told them **'plainly'** that Lazarus had died. Jesus also noted his satisfaction that he was not with Lazarus, because this circumstance would strengthen their faith. How? By demonstrating his sovereignty in revealing both the death of Lazarus and his resurrection ahead of time. They had only to walk down to Bethany and witness the evidence that proved Jesus to be who he claimed to be! In this way he does the groundwork for their eventual understanding of his own death and resurrection, which is less than two weeks away. Lazarus is a living parable of what Jesus will do, irreversibly, for all believers in the resurrection in the last day, as a result of his own death and resurrection.

3. The acceptance of death (11:16)

Thomas responds, **'Let us also go, that we may die with him.'** John Calvin, although he sees this as 'the language of despair', recognizes that Thomas 'does not refuse to die with Christ'. This, however, 'proceeds from inconsiderate zeal; for he ought rather to have taken courage from faith in the promise'. [3] It is not to be dismissed, then, as glum resignation to a dark prospect. So much has been made of Thomas' famous 'doubting' in 20:24-29 that we can lose sight of the genuine earnestness of his devotion to Christ. There is, to be sure, a mixture of both 'the spirit of devotion and despondency'.[4] But Thomas is surely as sincere as was Peter in his much more extravagant protestations of loyalty unto death. After Jesus' arrest, they both saved their lives, the one by denial and the other by flight. There is certainly an element of resignation in Thomas' attitude, but, according to his light, he was surrendering his life to Jesus and thought himself ready to share his fate. He had some way to go, to learn, as Paul did, what it meant to be willing to 'die daily', to be able to wish, with utter submission to the sovereign will of the Lord, 'rather to be absent from the body and to be present with the Lord', and so constantly to have his life 'hidden with Christ in God' (1 Cor. 15:31; 2 Cor. 5:8; Col. 3:3).

Grief
(John 11:17-37)

11:17-19. So when Jesus came, he found that he had already been in the tomb four days.

Now Bethany was near Jerusalem, about two miles away. And many of the Jews had joined the women around Martha and Mary, to comfort them concerning their brother.

As he had planned, Jesus arrived in Bethany after Lazarus was well and truly dead and buried (cf. 11:39), but when the mourners were still in attendance upon the bereaved. This set the scene for the climactic miracle of his earthly ministry. Much has been made by the commentators of a Jewish superstition, actually attested to no earlier than the third century A.D., to the effect that the soul hovers over the corpse for three days after death. Jesus' arrival on the fourth day, so we are told, is designed to preempt any suggestion that Lazarus might not have been 'really' dead, had Jesus raised him in days one to three. Hendriksen is correct to say that John 'makes special mention of this *fourth* day in order to stress the magnitude of the miracle',[5] but he does not explain why that would not make Jesus' resurrection on the third day of lesser magnitude! No doubt Jesus took his time so as to ensure that everyone knew Lazarus to be dead, but there is no evidence connecting this with a Jewish fable not known to be believed at the time, however appealing the idea may seem. What is of real significance is the time and

place — the week before Jesus' own death and resurrection, Passover week, and the proximity of the great
metropolis, Jerusalem, the city of the Great King,
where he would lay down his life for lost sinners.

The dual focus of the narrative is not the death of
Lazarus as such, but the ministry of Jesus to his
sisters, Martha and Mary.

Jesus comforts Martha (11:20-27)

11:20-27. Then Martha, as soon as she heard that Jesus
was coming, went and met him, but Mary was sitting in the
house.

Now Martha said to Jesus, 'Lord, if you had been here,
my brother would not have died. But even now I know that
whatever you ask of God, God will give you.'

Jesus said to her, 'Your brother will rise again.'

Martha said to him, 'I know that he will rise again in the
resurrection at the last day.'

Jesus said to her, 'I am the resurrection and the life. He
who believes in me, though he may die, he shall live. And
whoever lives and believes in me shall never die. Do you
believe this?'

She said to him, 'Yes, Lord, I believe that you are the
Christ, the Son of God, who is to come into the world.'

On hearing of Jesus' approach, Martha immediately
went off to meet him, while Mary, always the quieter
of the two, remained in the house (cf. Luke 10:38-42).
This leads to an exchange between the two that not
only comforts the grieving sister, but does so in
terms of an explicit doctrine of resurrection life in the
experience of believers in Christ. This unfolding of
Martha's need and Jesus' provision of comfort is a
kind of acted-out three-point funeral sermon pointing
from death to life in Christ for both the living and the
dead in every age.

1. The need of comfort: sorrow (11:21-24)

Martha already is a disciple of Jesus. **'If you had been here...'** (11:21) shows that she believed Jesus would have healed Lazarus had he arrived in time. But her words, **'Even now I know that whatever you ask of God, God will give you,'** indicate no more than a flickering hope that the promise of Jesus' earlier message ('This sickness is not unto death,' 11:4) somehow might come to fruition. She is obviously struggling emotionally with the whole idea. She does not quite believe Jesus can raise Lazarus *now*. This is confirmed when, in response to Jesus' assurance that Lazarus will **'rise again'**, she says that she knows he will rise **'in the resurrection at the last day'** (11:24; 5:28-29; cf. Old Testament teaching on resurrection in Ps. 16:9-11; 17:15; 49:15; 73:24-26; Job 19:25-27; Isa. 26:19; Dan. 12:2).

2. The ground of comfort: resurrection (11:25-26a)

'Jesus' concern', observes Carson most aptly, 'is to divert Martha's focus from an abstract belief in what takes place on the last day, to a personalized belief in him who alone can provide it... There is neither resurrection nor eternal life outside of him.'[6] Accordingly, Jesus applies the doctrine of the resurrection in terms of its beginning, its end and its middle as it has impact on the lives of his people.

Eternal life from Jesus Christ (11:25a)

'I am the resurrection and the life,' says Jesus. This is the fifth of seven **'I am'** statements (see 6:35; 8:12; 10:9; 10:11; 14:6; 15:5). He is in himself the very embodiment, and indeed accomplishment, of resurrection life. His resurrection precedes and secures the life he will give. Jesus is the source of new life. Ridderbos observes that 'Just as that which is truly food and drink, light and life are given only in him and can only be known from him (cf. 4:10,14; 6:33,48,53-58; 8:12, etc.), so also he is "the resurrection and the life"; all who face the recurrent death situations of life and wrestle with questions of death and life can find an answer only through faith in him.[7] New life begins with Jesus.

Eternal life after physical death (11:25b)

Jesus declares that **'He who believes in me, though he may die, he shall live.'** The death in view here is that of the body. At the moment of death, there will be a continuance of life for the believer. The *Shorter Catechism* asks, 'What benefits do believers receive from Christ at death?' and answers, 'The souls of believers are, at their death, made perfect in holiness, and do immediately pass into glory; and their bodies being still united to Christ, do rest in their graves till the resurrection' (Question 37).

Eternal life in this life (11:26a)

There is still more, because Jesus adds that, in the meantime, **'Whoever lives and believes in me shall never die.'** Calvin asks, 'Why then is Christ *the resurrection*?' and answers, 'Because by his Spirit he regenerates the children of Adam, who had been alienated from God by sin, so that they begin to live a new life.[8] The believer is no longer under the dominion of sin and death, even though his body will die one day soon. Hence Paul will say, 'And if Christ is in you, the body is dead because of sin, but the Spirit [who "dwells in you"] is life because of righteousness' (Rom. 8:10,11); and will write to the Corinthians, 'Even though our outward man is perishing, yet the inward man is being renewed day by day' (2 Cor. 4:16). 'What is still more,' observes Calvin, 'death itself is a sort of emancipation from the bondage of death.[9]

3. The appropriation of comfort: saving faith (11:26b-27)

To understand Jesus' proposition that believers never die is one thing. To experience its power to comfort is another thing altogether. Accordingly, Jesus issues to Martha a gentle call to faith. **'Do you believe this?'**, he asks, the 'this' in his question being his claim to be 'the resurrection and the life', with all that this implies for those who trust themselves to him for life and eternity. This elicits one of the sweetest confessions of personal faith in the whole of Scripture. **'Yes, Lord,'** says Martha, **'I believe that you are the Christ, the Son of God, who is to come into the world.'**

The *nature* of her faith is indicated by the verb, which is in the perfect tense *(pepisteuka)*, thereby connoting a settled conviction as to the truth of Jesus' words, including the personal trust in him called for in his claims. Faith is 'the substance of things hoped for', and 'the evidence of things not seen' (Heb. 11:1). Martha believed Jesus, and believed *in* Jesus.

The *content* of her faith confirms this very clearly. Martha acknowledges four things about Jesus:

1. He is **'Lord'** — the one to whom allegiance is properly due;
2. He is **'the Christ'** — the Messiah promised through the prophets;
3. He is the **'Son of God'** — the divine Son (cf. 1:14,34,49; 20:31);
4. He is the one **'who is to come into the world'** — the incarnate God, who took our human nature (cf. Phil. 2:5-8; 2 Cor. 8:9).

The *consistency* of her faith was yet to be tested and it is important to note that she later wavered for a moment on the likelihood of Lazarus' being restored to life (11:39). George Hutcheson observes, 'In times of great strait saints may expect to have frequent and sore tossings... Saints who have their confidence fixed, when impediments are at a distance, may yet be in hazard of staggering when it comes to the push, and faith is to grapple with these impediments.'[10]

Jesus weeps for Mary (11:28-37)

11:28-37. And when she had said these things, she went her way and secretly called Mary her sister, saying, 'The Teacher has come and is calling for you.'

As soon as she heard that, she arose quickly and came to him. Now Jesus had not yet come into the town, but was in the place where Martha met him. Then the Jews who were with her in the house, and comforting her, when they saw that Mary rose up quickly and went out, followed her, saying, 'She is going to the tomb to weep there.'

Then, when Mary came where Jesus was, and saw him, she fell down at his feet, saying to him, 'Lord, if you had been here, my brother would not have died.'

Therefore, when Jesus saw her weeping, and the Jews who came with her weeping, he groaned in the spirit and was troubled. And he said, 'Where have you laid him?' They said to him, 'Lord, come and see.' Jesus wept.

Then the Jews said, 'See how he loved him!' And some of them said, 'Could not this man, who opened the eyes of the blind, also have kept this man from dying?'

Martha went into the house and tried to arrange for a private conversation between Jesus and her sister, but the visitors noticed Mary leaving and, incorrectly assuming that she was going to mourn at Lazarus' tomb, they followed her, thereby putting themselves in the position to be witnesses of the raising of Lazarus (11:28-31).

1. Compassion felt (11:32-34)

When Mary met Jesus, she said exactly the same as Martha had. Had Jesus been there, she believed, Lazarus would have been healed. There was no reproach in this, just sorrow. Mary was weeping, the (professional) mourners were weeping, and Jesus, seeing this, **'groaned in the spirit and was troubled'** and asked to be taken to the tomb. Debate has centred on the nature of Jesus' groaning. Was it a purely compassionate grief, or an outraged sorrow mingled with compassion? The Greek *ebrimaomai* usually carries an element of anger or sternness (Matt. 9:30; Mark 1:43; 14:5) and this suggests the latter. Death is, to be sure, the wages of sin — the universal consequence of Adam's fall into sin. It is none the less an outrage, an abnormality imposed even upon those whom God loves and is determined to save. Jesus does not regard death as a normal part of life, but as an enemy that bids to bring people down to a lost eternity.

2. Compassion expressed (11:35)

Jesus too was overwhelmed with grief. John records simply that **'Jesus wept.'** This briefest of Scripture sentences is short in words but long in love. The verb *(dakryo)* is found only here, but the noun form occurs with reference to Jesus in Hebrews 5:7: 'who, in the days of his flesh, when he had offered up prayers and supplications, with vehement cries and tears ... was heard because of his godly fear'. Because of these tears, notes Hendriksen, God will 'wipe away every tear' from the eyes of his people (Rev. 7:17).[11]

Jesus weeps all the way to the cross, moved by the plight of undone sinners and determined to save them to the uttermost (Heb. 7:25).

3. Compassion observed (11:36-37)

Jesus' public display of emotion impressed the mourners in two ways. They saw that he deeply loved Lazarus, and they opined that he, **'who opened the eyes of the blind'**, might also have **'kept this man [Lazarus] from dying'**. This was all true, as far as it went, but it betrays the fact that they had not begun to grasp who Jesus really was and did not see that he was more than a caring man who worked the occasional healing miracle. There is just the hint, also, that, in this instance, Jesus might have done better than he did. We do much the same when, in the face of some similar personal loss or bad experience, we ask half-plaintively and half-accusingly why the Lord has let this happen to us.

The bottom line is that they believed Lazarus to be beyond all hope. Perhaps they had not heard of Jairus' daughter or the son of the widow of Nain (Mark 5:22-43; Luke 7:11-15). In any event, they had no expectation that Jesus could do anything other than merely mourn for his departed friend. This was coping without hoping, closure without confidence, grief without glory and resignation without redemption. They needed both a resurrection and a life. They needed the one who is 'the resurrection and the life'.

27. The raising of Lazarus
John 11:38-57

Jesus had known all along why he had come to Bethany and had even given a few hints of this along the way (cf. 11:4,11,14-15,23). Everything was now in place — the dead Lazarus, his grieving family, plenty of witnesses and a Saviour determined to give him back his life. Christ approaches the tomb, says Calvin, not 'as an idle spectator, but as a champion who prepares for a contest ... for the violent tyranny of death, which he had to conquer, is placed before his eyes'.[1]

   The significance of the raising of Lazarus cannot be overestimated. What is at stake is the viability of Jesus' message and ministry. Having committed himself to the proposition that Lazarus' sickness was 'not unto death' (11:4), Jesus must follow through or fail utterly and for ever. Once raised, Lazarus becomes a living parable of Jesus' own resurrection. The central point at issue is the power of Christ to give newness and eternality of life to all who will trust themselves to him.

Life from the dead
(John 11:38-44)

In the previous chapter, we noted that John 11 may be divided into four parts, each highlighting a particular theme associated with the Lord's miraculous raising of Lazarus: death (11:1-16), grief (11:17-37), life from the dead (11:38-44) and atonement for sin (11:45-57). At this juncture, we turn to the last two of these sections.

As these unfold, we shall notice how life for Lazarus resulted in death for Jesus. We shall also see how the high priest Caiaphas, in his unwitting prophecy (11:51-52), links the death of Jesus to the salvation of the people of God, and so, in spite of himself, points us to the centrality of the cross in their redemption. The first of these sections (11:38-44) elaborates the theme of life from the dead in terms of Jesus' purpose, his prayer and his power.

Purpose (11:38-40)

11:38-40. Then Jesus, again groaning in himself, came to the tomb. It was a cave, and a stone lay against it.

Jesus said, 'Take away the stone.'

Martha, the sister of him who was dead, said to him, 'Lord, by this time there is a stench, for he has been dead four days.'

Jesus said to her, 'Did I not say to you that if you would believe you would see the glory of God?'

The three main elements in this section all teach us, as Ridderbos points out, that Jesus, 'as the One sent by the Father, was moved to resist the demonstration of human impotence in the face of death as though it had the last, decisive word in the world'.[2] These are as follows:

1. *Complaint* — By **'groaning in himself'** Jesus demonstrates his compassion on account of the depredations of death in general, and the loss of Lazarus in particular.
2. *Command* —Jesus' order to **'Take away the stone,'** indicates his commitment to overthrow death in Lazarus' case.
3. *Challenge* — Jesus' response to Martha's disbelieving demurral, **'Did I not say to you that if you would believe you would see the glory of God?'**, points to the manifestation of divine glory in the impending miracle.

This seventh and last great sign in his public ministry[3] has the purpose of rolling back the border of death so clearly as to reveal something more of Jesus' glory as the Messiah and, in the event, paradoxically to pave the way for his own death as that which will secure permanent newness of life for all who believe in him (cf. 3:16).

Martha's insistence that, after four days, Lazarus' body would be decomposing amounted to an active discouragement for Jesus to fulfil that purpose, but also serves to accentuate the 'impossibility' of the miracle that was about to happen. Jesus sweeps her objection aside. With just a little faith she will see God's glory! Has he not told her already that he *is* 'the resurrection and he life'? (11:25). Lazarus will be raised, so that in the light of Jesus' own death on the cross and subsequent resurrection from the grave, his purpose of redemption could be understood in

terms of its full scope for human life and destiny.
Jesus means to 'kill death dead'. Lazarus would be a
foretaste and pledge of the real thing which would
soon follow.

Prayer (11:41-42)

11:41-42. Then they took away the stone from the place
where the dead man was lying.
   And Jesus lifted up his eyes and said, 'Father, I thank you
that you have heard me. And I know that you always hear
me, but because of the people who are standing by I said
this, that they may believe that you sent me.'

The stone was rolled away and Jesus prayed, for all
to hear. We must ask, especially since Jesus claimed
to be the Son of God, why he prayed at all. After all,
he already knew the outcome. Indeed, we know that
he had planned it all from before the foundation of
the world (Eph. 1:4).
   So why does Jesus pray here? The answer lies in
his distinct role as the only Mediator between God
and man (1 Tim. 2:5). As the incarnate Son, Jesus
submits to the Father. In his human nature, Jesus
depends upon his Father. He learns obedience in the
things that he suffers (Heb. 5:8). Even now, he lives
for ever to make intercession on behalf of his people
(Heb. 7:25). 'Christ's use of prayer in this miracle,'
notes Hutcheson, 'doth nothing cross [does not
contradict, GJK] what was marked on [verses] 22,25,
of his doing these things by his own power; for as
God, he is a principal efficient, as man, he is the
instrument of the Godhead, and as Mediator, he acts
as the Father's servant. And albeit he had spoken
before of his own power as God, yet he chooseth
rather to take this way before the people, to manifest

that he was owned and approved by God, and not
contrary to him, as the Jews gave it out."[4]

Power (11:43-44)

11:43-44. Now when he had said these things, he cried with
a loud voice, 'Lazarus come forth!' And he who had died
came out bound hand and food with grave-clothes, and his
face wrapped with a cloth. Jesus said to them, 'Loose him,
and let him go.'

With the voice of authority, Jesus calls loudly, again
for all to hear. The very succinctness of the account
emphasizes the electric character of the moment.
Jesus had laid his entire ministry and message on
the line. Had Lazarus not come forth, his claims
would have declined to mere pretensions and we
should never have heard of him. Putative 'messiahs'
who fail to deliver on their promises have rightly
ended up in historical oblivion.

To many a mind, of course, the only trouble with
resurrections is that, desirable as they no doubt are
to everyone, they just cannot happen. 'Dead men do
not rise in a closed universe,' is Bruce Milne's apt
way of summarizing an attitude common in our day.[5]
But this is precisely why the raising of Lazarus was
so striking in his day. Resurrections were no more
routine then than they are now. The few that are
recorded in Scripture were given to attest the credentials of those who were instrumental in their
taking place. As such, they bore eloquent testimony
to the two great days, at that point both still in the
future, when Christ would rise (the third day after
his death) as the firstfruits of those who would rise at
his coming (the last day of world history). There is
nothing natural about rising from the dead, just as
there is nothing natural about redemption itself.

Both require the supernatural work of God in both body and soul. The temporary resurrection of Lazarus was a foretaste of the permanent resurrection of Jesus and all whom he saves.

'Loose him, and let him go' (11:44) is Jesus' benediction upon the rest of Lazarus' life. There is no discussion of his experience in dying, being dead and rising to renewed life. How those who, in our day, speculate about so-called 'near-death experiences' would have loved some insights from Lazarus! Today, Lazarus would have a £5 million book deal and a lucrative tour of the world's TV talk-shows. John is silent on the details. The focus is wholly upon the giver of life. So, having robbed the grave of his dear friend, the Lord commands the removal of death's trappings — the **'grave-clothes'** that bound him **'hand and foot'** — and sends him out, without further comment, to enjoy his new freedom. It is a kind of living parable of redemption itself. 'Newness of life' is the inevitable and happy fruit of being united to Jesus 'in the likeness of his resurrection' (Rom. 6:4-5).

Atonement
(John 11:45-57)

Attention now shifts to the various responses to Jesus' raising of Lazarus in and around Jerusalem. Out of this emerges one of the most astounding pieces of unwitting prophecy the world has ever known, namely that **'Jesus would die for the nation'** (11:51). In this way, John links resurrection with atonement and gives a theological framework that paves the way for his account of the death and resurrection of Jesus as the Saviour of all who will believe in him (20:31).

Divided opinion (11:45-46)

11:45-46. Then many of the Jews who had come to Mary, and had seen the things Jesus did, believed in him. But some of them went away to the Pharisees and told them the things Jesus did.

People were often divided over Jesus, his message and his miracles (cf. 6:14-15; 7:10-13,45-52). The same is true today, as are the reasons for it (2 Cor. 2:15-16). The principal point of mentioning this here is to show how the authorities came to the final decision to put Jesus to death.

Discussion, nevertheless, has centred on the meaning of *epistuesan eis auton* (**'believed in him'**). Was this a true saving faith in Jesus (3:16-18,36;

6:35-40; 7:38; 11:25-26; 12:44-46; 14:12; 17:20), or merely a mental persuasion without heart devotion? (cf. 2:23; 7:31; 8:30-38; 12:42). The context (11:4,52) would seem to indicate that many, if not all, of the mourners did indeed become committed believers in Christ at that time.[6] That some perhaps did not truly believe in Jesus should not obscure the fact that he was steadily changing the hearts of men and women wherever he went, already preparing the ground for the explosion of grace that would come with the apostolic ministry less than two months later. What is absolutely clear is that the rate at which people were turning to Jesus, whatever the precise quality of their commitment, frightened the religious establishment and impelled them towards a final show-down with Jesus himself.

Determined opposition (11:47-54)

11:47-54. Then the chief priests and the Pharisees gathered a council and said, 'What shall we do? For this man works many signs. If we let him alone like this, everyone will believe in him, and the Romans will come and take away both our place and nation.'

And one of them, Caiaphas, being high priest that year, said to them, 'You know nothing at all, nor do you consider that it is expedient for us that one man should die for the people, and not that the whole nation should perish.'

Now this he did not say on his own authority; but being high priest that year he prophesied that Jesus would die for the nation, and not for that nation only, but also that he would gather together in one the children of God who were scattered abroad.

Then from that day on, they plotted to put him to death. Therefore Jesus no longer walked openly among the Jews, but went from there into the country near the wilderness, to a city called Ephraim, and there remained with his disciples.

The religious élite hastily convened a 'council' (Gk, *sunedrion*) — the Sanhedrin (11:47a). This, the highest judicial authority in the country, consisted of the **'chief priests'** (mostly Sadducees), the more conservative minority (**'Pharisees'**) and some elders drawn from the aristocracy. Under the Romans, they were responsible for internal affairs.

1. The problem defined (11:47b-48)

The question put to the council accepts that Jesus had performed **'signs'** and, accordingly, that he claimed to be the Messiah. Three things ought to be noted.

First of all, while reviewing the situation, *they apparently saw no necessity for any re-evaluation of their previous views* of Jesus and his ministry on the basis of the mounting evidence of his miracles. They consistently cast him in the role of an impostor and viewed him as a threat to their own position and privileges.

Secondly, *they did not see any blessing from God* in Jesus' signs, nor did they appear to discern the work of God in the lives of the people who were being added to his following.

Thirdly, *they analysed the problem in political rather than religious terms*. If Jesus gathered more followers, they reasoned, the Romans would take away their **'place'** (the Temple) and **'nation'** (the Jewish political entity). In other words, seeing political instability and potential rebellion centring around a charismatic messiah-figure, the Romans will disperse the Jews and eliminate their present leadership.

The modernity of this is striking. One sees echoes of it in the reaction of the political establishment in the USA to the rising influence of the so-called 'Christian Right', which first swung the balance for the Reagan presidency and has since consolidated as a powerful influence for public righteousness on such issues as abortion and homosexuality. Sound religious principle scares liberal politicians stiff in every age.

2. The solution proposed (11:49-52)

Caiaphas, **'high priest that year'** (and every year from A.D. 18–36), was contemptuous of such fears. They knew **'nothing at all'**! A modern equivalent of his response would have been something like this: 'Give me a break! You people are clueless!' But Caiaphas went on to propound a very simple solution: **'one man should die for the people'** — that is, Jesus should be permanently removed from the scene (11:50). Pragmatism came before principle and expediency above justice. Worse still, God and Scripture did not figure at all in his reasoning. There was no appeal to truth, no evidence of spiritual commitment to the God of their fathers, but only policy and politics, power and position, which must be maintained by hook or by crook! Power-religion was in the saddle in the Jewish church. There was, in fact, no place for truth.

The enemies of God and truth can scheme and plot all they like. The overarching reality, to which they are always oblivious, is that 'He who sits in the heavens shall laugh; the LORD shall hold them in derision' (Ps. 2:4).

On the one hand, Caiaphas' scheme did not save his place and nation. He should have feared God rather than the Romans. 'In the space of forty years,' notes Simeon, 'God executed upon them the most signal vengeance: he inflicted upon them the judgement he had warned them of: and made use of the

Roman armies "miserably to destroy those murderers, and to burn up their city" (Matt. 21:38-41;
22:7).[7] The application thunders into the present
age: 'Of how much worse punishment, do you suppose, will he be thought worthy who has trampled
the Son of God underfoot, counted the blood of the
covenant by which he was sanctified a common
thing, and insulted the Spirit of grace? ... It is a
fearful thing to fall into the hands of the Living God'
(Heb. 10:29,31).

On the other hand, Caiaphas would have been
horrified to discover that what he meant for evil, God
meant for good (cf. Gen. 50:20). His murderous policy
for dealing with the problem of Jesus, most ironi-
cally, turns out to be an unwitting prophecy of God's
plan that **'Jesus would die for the nation'** (11:52)
— not Caiaphas' nation as it then was, but the 'holy
nation' (1 Peter 2:9) of all who in every place would
call upon the name of the Lord Jesus Christ. Neither
does Jesus die according to Caiaphas' idea of substitutionary sacrifice, for Jesus' sacrifice is not to
maintain the status quo, but for sin. It is not to save
a corrupt regime, but to redeem lost sinners. It is not
to preserve a godless élite, but to call out God's elect.
Furthermore, far from destroying his mission, that
rain of blows on the dying Jesus ushers in a reign of
grace for a dying world! He will **'gather together in
one the children of God who were scattered
abroad'** — not the exclusively Jewish Diaspora of the
Old Testament, but 'the church, which is his body,' of
the New Testament, redeemed by his blood 'out of
every tribe and tongue and people and nation', the
'elect' gathered in the last day 'from the four winds,
from the farthest part of earth to the farthest part of
heaven' (Eph. 1:23; Rev. 5:9; Mark 13:27).

3. The results arising (11:53-54)

The response of the Jewish leadership was to plot the death of Jesus. The response of Jesus was to withdraw to a quiet place with the disciples — a village called 'Ephraim' (possibly the Ephrain, or Ephron, of 2 Chronicles 13:19), a dozen miles from Jerusalem, there to await God's time for the final confrontation with his enemies (12:23).[8]

Decided anticipation (11:55-57)

11:55-57. And the Passover of the Jews was near, and many went from the country up to Jerusalem before the Passover, to purify themselves.

Then they sought Jesus, and spoke among themselves as they stood in the temple, 'What do you think — that he will not come to the feast?' Now both the chief priests and Pharisees had given a command, that if anyone knew where he was, he should report it, that they might seize him.

This would have been the Passover of A.D. 30, the third of Jesus' ministry (cf. 2:13-25; 6:4). Large numbers gathered from all over the country, and the world, and many arrived early in order to ensure their ceremonial purification according to the provisions of Mosaic law (Exod. 19:10-15; Num. 9:9-14; 2 Chr. 30:17-18; cf. John 18:28).

Apparently, Jerusalem was buzzing with talk of Jesus. The word was out that the authorities planned to arrest him and, in view of this development, the speculation was that he might not appear at the Passover. The scene was set for the climactic crisis of Jesus' ministry.

The road to the cross

The mystery of God's providence and the richness of his grace do not divert the evil blade from Jesus' breast, but make it achieve the very results its perpetrators would most wish to thwart! Remarkable as this is, is it not even more astounding that this course of events — the road to the cross and the establishment of Messiah's kingdom — had already been long anticipated in the Jews' own Scriptures?

1. The rulers had taken counsel together 'against the LORD and against his Anointed' (Ps. 2:1-3).
2. Nevertheless, God will make even 'the wrath of man to praise [him]' (Ps. 76:10; cf. John 11:51-52).
3. He will be 'numbered with the transgressors' and bear 'the sin of many' (Isa. 53:12).
4. The promised Messiah will 'sprinkle many nations' (Isa. 52:15).
5. He 'will feed his flock like a shepherd' (Isa. 40:11).
6. He will rule at God's 'right hand' and will come to 'execute kings in the day of his wrath' (Ps. 110:1,5; 98:9).

The irony of the raising of Lazarus is that it precipitates the judicial murder of Jesus. The supreme wonder, however, is that the death of Jesus secures new life for the world and that this is effected not because Jesus suffers the wrath of man, but that he satisfies the just wrath of God against sin that is not his own. The raising of Lazarus from the dead, then, anticipates the raising of sinners to newness of life through faith in Christ and calls the whole world to repentance towards God and faith in the Lord Jesus Christ.

The doctrine of a literal bodily resurrection is not merely incidental to Christian faith. Still less is it a legend adapted to a more supernaturalistic age, or a metaphorical construction of the human mind fitted to some need of the transcendent in a life otherwise doomed to end for ever in a few short years. The apostle Paul will later make clear that the denial of bodily resurrection is the denial of the gospel of Christ. Paul will declare, with blazing honesty, that 'If Christ is not risen, then our preaching is empty and your faith is also empty ... you are still in your sins! ... If in this life only we have hope in Christ, we are of all men the most pitiable' (1 Cor. 15:14-19). An existential hope that cannot reach beyond the grave is no more than a psychological crutch. A dead Christ cannot make for a live faith!

> He mindful of his grace and truth
> To Israel's house has been.
> The great salvation of our God,
> All ends of earth have seen.
>
> Because he comes, he surely comes,
> The Judge of earth to be!
> With justice he will judge the world,
> All men with equity.[9]

28. A unique gift

John 12:1-11

We love to receive gifts. We also like to give gifts. Some gifts may be no more than tokens, others very substantial. Occasionally, a gift may be a unique expression of love and esteem. Mary's gift to Jesus of **'costly oil of spikenard'** was certainly no routine present. Indeed, in content, mode of expression and ultimate meaning, it was unique and so noteworthy, says Scripture, that she is remembered for it wherever the gospel is preached (Matt. 26:13). What she did, says Jesus, was 'a beautiful thing' (Mark 14:6, NIV). Yet there is no miracle here, and no extended discourse from Jesus. The air of the domestic pervades the scene, but with the fragrance of a devotion of heavenly sweetness.

Mary's gift to Jesus reminds us that he himself is the most remarkable gift of all to us. For all who will receive him, he is the gift of new and eternal life! In one of his most startling sayings, Jesus told his disciples, 'If you then, being evil, know how to give good gifts to your children, how much more will your heavenly Father give the Holy Spirit to those who ask him!' (Luke 11:13). His argument is that if imperfect, sinful people can be kind and give gifts to their loved ones, what kind of a gift-giver should we expect God to be? What price, then, the Father's gift of his only begotten Son? God's gifts are the best of all, and in Christ he has promised to give us all things.

The gift given
(John 12:1-3)

12:1-3. Then, six days before the Passover, Jesus came to Bethany, where Lazarus was, who had been dead, whom he had raised from the dead. There they made him a supper; and Martha served, but Lazarus was one of those who sat at the table with him.

Then Mary took a pound of very costly oil of spikenard, anointed the feet of Jesus, and wiped his feet with her hair. And the house was filled with the fragrance of the oil.

After the raising of Lazarus, Jesus had withdrawn to Ephraim/Ephron (11:54). He may have stayed there for several weeks — we do not know for sure. During this period, perhaps on a special visit there, or maybe on his way to the Passover, he stopped in Jericho with Zacchaeus (Luke 18:35 – 19:10). In any event, he arrived in Bethany, 'six days before the Passover', that is on a Friday. He would then have rested on the Sabbath (Saturday), with the meal at which the anointing occurred taking place at the close of the Sabbath on 'Saturday' evening. He made his 'triumphal entry' to Jerusalem the next day ('Palm Sunday', 12:12-16). The Passover was on the Thursday following, as was the Last Supper, and Jesus was crucified on the Friday.[1] He stood at the threshold of the climactic last week of his earthly ministry.

Which anointing?

This account is one of four in the Gospels recording an anointing of Jesus. Integrating these variously differing reports into the chronology of Jesus' ministry has occasioned considerable debate. The best solution traces these reports to two distinct anointing events.

The first (Luke 7:36-50) takes place earlier in Jesus' ministry when he was still welcome in a Pharisee's home. The woman is unnamed and evidently one who had been living a sad and wicked life and who had now come to conviction of sin. She anoints the Lord, and Jesus declares her sins forgiven on account of her faith.

The other three (12:1-11; Matt. 26:6-13; Mark 14:3-9), although different in certain respects, appear to describe the same event. The Synoptics don't name the woman, locate the supper at the home of Simon the Leper, seem to place it after the triumphal entry, make no mention of Judas Iscariot and have Jesus' head anointed rather than his feet. These are all rather easily harmonizable, as Carson shows quite handily.[2] There are, of course, numerous similarities, but what is of most significance is the common theme running through all three accounts, namely, the character of the gift as a preparation for the burial of Christ (Matt. 26:12; Mark 14:8; John 12:7).

Mary of Bethany

The occasion, then, was the Saturday before Palm Sunday. The place was the house of Simon the Leper, whose very title suggests that he had been healed of the illness (Matt. 26:6; Mark 14:3). The company included Lazarus, **'whom he had raised from the dead'**, and his sisters Mary and Martha.

Mary's gift was a precious perfume called **'spikenard'**. The NIV's 'pure nard' is a better rendering of
nardou pistikes — *pistikes* more probably deriving
from the Greek word *pistos* (genuine/pure) than from
the Aramaic *pistaqos* (spiked — referring to the form
of the plant).[3] Nard came from India and, if Judas'
estimate is accurate, a pound of it might have sold for
about **'three hundred denarii'** — perhaps the
equivalent of a year's wages for a labourer!

The guests would have been reclining at table, in
the fashion of the time. Mary, in what can only have
been a most dramatic intervention, proceeded to
anoint Jesus with this costly perfume — on **'the
feet'** says John, on 'his head' say Matthew and Mark.
There is no call to see the one as exclusive of the
other. Reporters often differ in their accounts of the
same event without transgressing essential accuracy.
She then wiped it off with her tresses, perhaps
knowingly emulating the woman who had done this
to Jesus earlier in his ministry.

A fragrance filling the world

Jesus will interpret this a few minutes later, but from
the beginning we know it to be an act of devotion,
redolent of Christ's own love for his people. Anointing
with oil is, in Scripture, always a mark of the notable
blessing of God (Ps. 23:5; 133:2). 'Mary's action
expresses', observes Ridderbos, 'what she did not
have the words to voice, but it "filled the whole
house" with the fragrance of her love and as such
would continue to spread through the preaching of
the gospel in the whole world (cf. Mark 14:9; Matt.
26:13).'[4]

The gift questioned
(John 12:4-6)

12:4-6. But one of his disciples, Judas Iscariot, Simon's son, who would betray him, said, 'Why was this fragrant oil not sold for three hundred denarii and given to the poor?' This he said, not that he cared for the poor, but because he was a thief, and had the money box; and he used to take what was put in it.

If Judas was the spokesman, there were others present who agreed with him (Matt. 26:8; Mark 14:4). How dare Mary waste the whole of such an expensive asset in one gesture of devotion, when there were poor people who might benefit from the price it would fetch! It all sounds so pious. It assumes that riches must never be enjoyed, and that private property is not held at the discretion of its owner — principles also taught in God's Word. The existence of poverty is certainly a *prima facie* argument against what is today called 'conspicuous consumption'. On the other hand, it has always been a convenient screen for a variety of less altruistic ends, such as self-righteousness or, as in Judas' case, the abuse of trust and the theft of other people's money. Ethics were not exactly on Judas' mind, for the first church treasurer of the Christian era was a thief who had already calculated how much he could skim off from the collections donated by the Lord's followers! Pious Judas was ready to sell Mary's perfume for 300 denarii, ostensibly in the interests of the poor, but really for himself. Within a week he would take just sixty denarii ('thirty pieces of silver') for the sale of Jesus, and the poor did not figure in that transaction at all! Matthew Henry sums it up with characteristically Puritan pithiness: 'Here is charity to the poor made a colour for opposing a piece of piety to Christ, and secretly made a cloak for covetousness'[5]

Mary's love for Jesus was a mystery and an embarrassment to Judas. Selfish people cannot fathom the unselfish. 'That the native language of love is generosity', says Hendriksen, 'was something that Judas could not comprehend.'[6] The 'natural man' does not have a clue when it comes to spiritual things (1 Cor. 2:14). His heart is in the wrong place. He lives in a different world in his soul. He cannot see past himself.

The sheer hypocrisy of Judas is breathtaking. Mind you, he had his brethren fooled, at least as far as we know. John writes with hindsight. He was oblivious to this at the time. Jesus, who 'knew what was in man', also knew 'who would betray him' (2:25; 13:11), yet he did not expose Judas' hypocrisy, but let it run its course all the way to Gethsemane, and so to the cross. What this incident does illustrate, however, is the general reality, to use Hutcheson's assessment, that 'Very gross hypocrites may be near to Christ in outward profession, and may be entrusted in eminent employments, for Judas ... is one of his disciples.'[7] Judas was not the last church bureaucrat to be one of the devil's moles in the kingdom of God on earth.

The gift accepted
(12:7-8)

12:7-8. But Jesus said, 'Let her alone; she has kept this for the day of my burial. For the poor you have with you always, but me you do not have always.'

One wonders how Mary felt, with all these men around her disapproving of her supremely loving and generous gift. There is nothing more discouraging to discipleship than the frowns of fellow-believers. What a humiliation — to give of your heart and soul, only to be greeted with a cold disapproval!

In such situations, however, Jesus is a majority of one. In several ways he takes up her case and silences the gainsayers.

1. *He rebukes the critics* with a firm, **'Let her alone.'** Mark records him as saying, 'She has done a beautiful thing to me' (Mark 14:6, NIV). The meaning is that Mary's keeping the perfume for this occasion and for the purpose which Jesus delineates in the next breath is a good thing. It was not a 'waste' (Matt. 26:8). Furthermore, it is a sin to discourage anyone in his or her service to Christ, and especially so when the discouragement is coming from leading people in the Christian ministry, as were the Twelve.

2. *He hints at the true significance of Mary's action* when he says, **'She has kept this for the day of my burial.'** It is not certain that Mary was clear on this in her own mind. Yet it is by no means impossible that, unlike the disciples, she took seriously Jesus'

predictions of his coming death — matters with which she could not but be acquainted. She at least grasped the tendency of Jesus' ministry as something that could only lead to a final clash with the authorities. It is also not at all impossible that she understood that the Messiah foretold by the prophet Isaiah had to suffer and die. Not everyone in Jewry was in denial of Scripture truth. The anointing itself is evidence that she discerned the approach of Jesus' death, whether or not she thought it to be just around the corner. Jesus, of course, knew the moment was at hand and took the opportunity to point just a little more explicitly to the coming shock.

3. *Jesus disposes of Judas' objection*: **'The poor you have with you always, but me you do not have always.'** This will always seem callous to anyone who has no grasp of the true significance of the death, burial and resurrection of Christ and, not least, who disregards the teaching and example of Jesus himself, who owned no property, had only the clothes on his back and displayed a compassion for the poor beyond that of any of his contemporaries (cf. Luke 9:58). When Jesus says these words, we know he is beyond reproach and cannot be charged with an uncaring attitude towards the poor. Jesus did not mean to say that the poor did not matter, or to stifle a genuine concern for their real needs. His point was that his followers would always have plenty of scope for ministry to the poor and should throw themselves into it. At that moment, however, they stood at the hinge of history. Jesus would not always be with them. The significance of that, although they had little or no grasp of it at that point, was that salvation itself was about to be secured for the world that Jesus had come to save. The death anticipated in Mary's sumptuous gift was the one death that could pay the penalty for sin for everyone who will be redeemed and reconciled to God from all generations,

past, present and future, of humankind! There was more — much more — to what was going on than what met their eyes.

4. Finally, we know from the Synoptics that 'Wherever [the] gospel is preached in the whole world, *what [Mary] has done will also be told as a memorial to her'* (Matt. 26:13). The fulfilment of this prophecy is with you as you read your Bible, and even as you read this book at this moment in your life. Mary stands as a believer who, at that crucial point in Jesus' ministry, understood the trials he wrestled with better than did the inner circle of disciples!

What is your response?
(12:9-11)

12:9-11. Now a great many of the Jews knew that he was there; and they came, not for Jesus' sake only, but that they might also see Lazarus, whom he had raised from the dead. But the chief priests plotted to put Lazarus to death also, because on account of him many of the Jews went away and believed in Jesus.

Three responses to Jesus

People can be interested in Jesus for widely varying reasons and to quite divergent ends. John identifies three main categories of response.

Some were merely *curious* about both Jesus and Lazarus (12:9). This was a carnal, not a spiritual interest. Jesus might as well have been a magician for most of them.

The ecclesiastical leadership was *downright hostile* and aimed to kill them both (12:10). Matthew Henry succinctly contrasts their attitude to the raising of Lazarus with the gracious purpose of God: 'God will have Lazarus to live by a miracle, and they will have him to die by malice.'[8]

Many **'went away and believed in Jesus'** (12:11). This is what still sends a chill down the spines of God's enemies — as witness the tolerance of the ecclesiastical and political authorities for all who deny the claims of the Bible, in contrast to the vigour with which they seek to marginalize and even suppress those who affirm and proclaim these truths.

What about you?

This challenges us as to what will be our response to Jesus, his teaching and his mighty acts. Here, we are helped by the very character of Mary's gift, because it provides evidence of the impact that Jesus had made upon her. Her response to Jesus is a window on the nature of saving faith itself. As such, it shows us the way to a believing response to Jesus.

1. It was a loving gift

'Mary was perhaps the best listener Jesus ever had,' observes Hendriksen. 'The one who ... anointed the Lord's feet was the same one who previously had been sitting at the Lord's feet (Luke 10:39).' Mary had absorbed his teaching. She had observed his ministry. She had experienced his love for souls, not least in the raising of her brother from death to life. She loved him who first loved her (1 John 4:19). Mary answered love with love. This invites us to ask ourselves, 'What shall I render to the LORD for all his benefits toward me?' (Ps. 116:12).

2. It was a generous gift

Her gift was, so to speak, 'fit for a king'. She acknowledged Christ to be her sovereign. Her gift was a tribute to his lordship. Again we are invited to ask ourselves a leading question: 'Will I offer burnt offerings to the Lord my God with that which costs me nothing?' (see 2 Sam. 24:24). What, if any, are the gifts of *your* Christian service?

3. It was a discerning gift

Mary anticipated Jesus' death and burial. She believed, and her active exercise of faith enabled her to discern. Contrast this with Peter, who, though a believer, was in such a state of denial on this point that he could not accept Jesus' own predictions of his death: 'Far be it from you, Lord; this shall not happen to you!' (Matt. 16:22). Mary had spiritual discernment. She wanted to comfort and encourage the Lord, and also to confess faith in him in the special way she did. Again a question is posed to our consciences: 'Do you believe?' (Matt. 9:28).

4. It was a timely gift

Lazarus had been raised. Simon had previously been healed. Jesus was about to enter into the climax of his sufferings for sinners. This was the time for Mary's gift, for he would not be with them much longer. This presses some urgency upon us. When should we call upon Jesus? When he is near! (Ps. 145:18; Isa. 55:6; Heb. 10:22; James 4:8). Call upon him 'while it is still called "Today",' for 'Now is the day of salvation' (Heb. 3:13; 2 Cor. 6:2).

'God's Anointed should be our Anointed,' observes Matthew Henry. 'Has God poured on him the oil of gladness above his fellows? (Ps. 45:7). Let us pour on him the ointment of our best affections above all competitors. By consenting to Christ as *our* king, we must comply with God's designs, appointing him *our head* whom he has appointed (Hosea 1:11).'[10] Christ is the true gift. Our gifts to him are the fruit of receiving him as Saviour and Lord. The story of Mary's unique gift is written, says John, 'that you may believe that Jesus is the Christ, the Son of God, and that believing you may have life in his name' (20:31).

29. The seed must die

John 12:12-36

We all too easily assume that it is more difficult to be a follower of Jesus in our increasingly neo-pagan world than it must have been in the days when Jesus and the apostles walked the earth. However, even a little reflection on the text of the New Testament shows that it was in fact very difficult to be a Christian at that time.

While Jesus was with them in the flesh, his disciples were constantly confused about what he was doing and where he was going with his mission. They were especially perplexed by his predictions of approaching death (Mark 8:31-33; 9:31-32; 10:32-34). Indeed, they could not face it all. Consequently, Jesus' 'triumphal entry' to Jerusalem was more to their liking. Here, as they saw it, was public recognition, even acclamation, that not only was more appropriate to the Messiah, but augured better things for the future.

As events unfolded, however, the 'triumphant' part stopped with the 'entry' and gave way to the very thing they could not face — the death of their leader. The triumph itself was fleeting and premature. Jesus was certainly hailed as Israel's king but, in the context, it was the right thing for the wrong reasons. It, therefore, did not last and issued in the derisory legend nailed with Jesus to the cross on which he was to die just a few days later.

The passage under consideration in this chapter encompasses the inherent tension between the triumphal entry and the cross, and illuminates it in terms of prophetic fulfilment, prediction and challenge. It forms a kind of pedagogic *hors-d'œuvre* for the Lord's teaching at the Last Supper.

Prophetic fulfilment — triumphal entry (12:12-19)

The transitional passage (12:9-11) sets the context for Jesus' entry to Jerusalem and so shows him, as it were, 'marching towards the sound of the guns'. The plotters plot, the spies keep watch and the crowds are electric with anticipation of the coming clash. The tension, then, is between the louring sky of Pharisaic intrigue and the bright prospect of Messianic promise and fulfilment. And that is how John's account begins — with the fulfilment of one particular prophecy by Jesus in his entry to Jerusalem on what would be a week of comprehensive fulfilment of divine promise.

Revelation (12:12-15)

12:12-15. The next day a great multitude that had come to the feast, when they heard that Jesus was coming to Jerusalem, took branches of palm trees and went out to meet him, and cried out:

Hosanna!
'Blessed is he who comes in the name of the LORD!'
The King of Israel!

Then Jesus, when he had found a young donkey, sat on it; as it is written:

> Fear not, daughter of Zion;
> Behold, your King is coming,
> Sitting on a donkey's colt.

The crowd, hearing of Jesus' approach, went out on the Bethany road to greet him, bearing palm branches. The commentators point out that palms were 'the symbols for victorious and beneficent rulers',[1] and 'since the Maccabees ... a recognized symbol of the Jewish state'.[2] They therefore cast the 'triumph' of the 'triumphant entry' more in terms of a nationalistic triumphalism than a spiritual homage to the biblical Messiah. In Scripture, however, palms signified joy in the prosperity of the children of God (Lev. 23:40; cf. Ps. 92:12) and it is perhaps more likely that the nationalist anti-Roman angle, though ever-present in Jewish minds, is still somewhat overestimated by the commentators and that what we are seeing is simply the exuberance of more or less pious Jews rejoicing in the annual Passover — with the added element, to be sure, that Jesus was believed by some to be the promised Messiah.

Two components of John's account link this event with Old Testament predictive prophecies of the Messiah. One wonders how many of those present really grasped the applicability of these points to Jesus. As with Caiaphas' unwitting prophecy, the full meaning would only come out with hindsight, as further events confirmed to more and more people that Jesus was indeed the promised Christ.

1. *Jesus is greeted with enthusiasm* by a large number of people. Their exultant cries consist of three distinct parts:

'Hosanna' is a transliteration of the Hebrew (הוֹשִׁיעָה נָּא) from Psalm 118:25 and means literally, 'Give salvation now!' This is a kind of slogan

summing up the theme of the Hallel psalms
that were sung in connection with Passover (Ps.
113-118).

**'Blessed is he who comes in the name of
the LORD!'** is from Psalm 118:26 and follows on
quite naturally from 'Hosanna!' Psalm 118 is a
distinctly Messianic psalm, always sung at the
Passover. The immediate context is in Psalm
118:22: 'The stone which the builders rejected
has become the chief cornerstone' — that stone
being the Messiah. Whether they knew it or not,
they had the 'chief cornerstone' among them,
and were about to witness his sufferings and
death in order to give the salvation called for in
their 'Hosannas'!

The words acclaiming Jesus as **'The King of
Israel!'** did not come from any psalm, but, as
Milne points out, 'show how the crowd were understanding it'.[3] The nationalist and political
dimension emerges. They had some very earthly
expectations of their Messiah-King. The Jews
should have recognized in all of this that Jesus
was the fulfilment of the promise of the Messianic psalms. The events of the next five days
demonstrated, however, that the vast majority
did not.

2. *Jesus rides on the colt of a donkey* (although
John leaves to the Synoptics the details of the manner in which it was secured — see Matt. 21:1-3;
Mark 11:1-7; Luke 19:29-35) and that not only fulfils
prophecy, but quietly counters the approach that
would have preferred his entry on a white horse at
the head of an army. This is a very deliberate fulfilment of the prophecy of Zechariah 9:9 and the Messianic anticipations in the whole of that book.
Zechariah prophesied the glory of Israel and her

Shepherd-King, and his worldwide reign (cf. the reference to Psalm 72:8 in Zechariah 9:10).

Response (12:16-19)

12:16-19. His disciples did not understand these things at first; but when Jesus was glorified, then they remembered that these things were written about him and that they had done these things to him.

Therefore the people, who were with him when he called Lazarus out of his tomb and raised him from the dead, bore witness. For this reason the people also met him, because they heard that he had done this sign.

The Pharisees therefore said among themselves, 'You see that you are accomplishing nothing. Look, the world has gone after him!'

The misreading of Christ's triumphal entry was fairly comprehensive across the community.

1. The *disciples* made nothing of it until after Jesus was **'glorified'**, that is, raised from the dead (12:16; cf. 2:22). Only then did the scales fall from their eyes. This is true of so much Christian experience. We often fail to see the 'obvious'. In the worst-case scenario, there are none so blind as those who do not want to see.

2. The *people*, having learned of the raising of Lazarus, were there to see the miracle-worker and seem to have been looking for another **'sign'** (12:17-18). This was the perennial interest of the Jews and continues today in the thirst of many for appearances of the Virgin Mary and for instantaneous healings from life-threatening illness (cf. Mark 8:12; 1 Cor. 1:22).

3. The *Pharisees* — or at least the 'hawkish' ones (here apparently rebuking the more 'dovish' members

of their order) — came closest of all to understanding what was happening. They saw 'the world' running after Jesus. They saw their influence being eroded before their eyes, and they could not see how a 'wait-and-see' attitude was doing anything to stop the rot (12:19). As far as they were concerned, Jesus had been too successful already and they did not intend the triumphal entry to go on to a triumphant conclusion. They wanted Jesus eliminated — and soon!

Summing it up...

Summarizing the event and the various responses, it must be said that, although Jesus was further revealed to be the promised Messiah and was greeted with a measure of enthusiasm by a large number of people, the fact remains that this was an illusory triumph. Even the disciples did not read the evidence correctly. The cheers were largely frothy exuberance based upon ignorance and confusion.

All the same, the Pharisees had reason to be worried. The instinct of unbelief rarely fails to detect the approach of righteousness and always tries to nip it in the bud. Jesus' real triumph was yet future. Some probably thought, especially after his death on the following Friday, that this Sunday had seen the final triumph and high-point of his short career. The irony is that the triumphal entry precipitated his death by execution; and, irony of ironies, that his death on the cross secures the true triumphs of his resurrection, ascension, kingly rule (Eph. 1:22) and his, yet future, coming again.

Prophetic prediction — death on a cross (12:20-33)

If riding on a donkey in fulfilment of Scripture prophecy (Zech. 9:9) failed to remind the people that the Messiah they should expect was not a political leader but a suffering servant, Jesus soon drew their attention more explicitly to the real state of things by prophesying both the purpose and the manner of his death.

The purpose of Jesus' death (12:20-28a)

The first exchange was triggered by a question from some Gentile worshippers. This resulted in Jesus' setting out the goal of his impending death and a prayer for his Father to glorify his own name in what must transpire.

1. The Greeks' question (12:20-22)

12:20-22. Now there were certain Greeks among those who came up to worship at the feast.

Then they came to Philip, who was from Bethsaida of Galilee, and asked him, saying, 'Sir, we wish to see Jesus.' Philip came and told Andrew, and in turn Andrew and Philip told Jesus.

The occasion of Jesus' first statement was the request of some Greeks for an introduction to Jesus.

These would have been uncircumcised Gentile
proselytes to Judaism (cf. Acts 10:1-2; 13:16; 17:4),
who could worship in the temple, but were permitted
only into the Court of the Gentiles.[4] Their only recorded words — **'Sir, we wish to see Jesus'** — do
not tell us what they wanted of him, but they approach him respectfully and with apparent sincerity,
and we may surmise from the Lord's answer that,
like so many others at the time, they wanted to know
if he were really the Messiah. The underlying drama
in the juxtaposition of 12:20-22 and 12:19 is the
spectacle of marginalized Gentile proselytes seeking
Jesus, while establishment Jewish ecclesiastics were
plotting his death! It is the shape of things to come,
for in the end the world of the Gentiles would follow
after Jesus, while Judaism rejected its own Scriptures and Messiah, and went its own way, a fossilized
parody of its true Old Testament self.

2. Jesus' answer (12:23-26)

In responding to the Greek converts, Jesus teaches
both them and his disciples, once again, about his
approaching death, linking it to the salvation and
discipleship of his hearers.

Jesus' time had come (12:23)

12:23. But Jesus answered them, saying, 'The hour has
come that the Son of Man should be glorified.'

There are three significant components in this declaration, variously connecting to his mission, his person
and his work.

Firstly, he says that his **'hour'** had arrived. That is
to say, *his mission was about to come to fruition.*
Hitherto, his 'hour' had always been in the future
(2:4; 4:21,23; 7:30; 8:20). From here to Calvary it is
presented as imminent (12:27; 13:1; 17:1). All along

the way, the initiative is clearly with Jesus. He does the will of his Father. He precipitates the final crisis. His timing is sovereign. He acts; his enemies react. Jesus is the hinge of redemptive history. He opens the life-gates by his death in space-time history so that the redeemed may have eternal life in heaven itself!

Secondly, he again identifies himself as **'the Son of Man'** and so *gives a window on his person.* He does so more than eighty times in the Gospels.[5] As we have noted earlier, this title is apparently drawn from Daniel 7:13, which describes a divine being who comes to God the Father ('the Ancient of Days') and receives dominion over the earth and an endless kingdom. The very rarity of this designation in the Old Testament, coupled with the fact that it is Jesus' favourite way of referring to himself during his earthly ministry, all the more highlights his Messianic character and claims (cf. 1:51; 3:13-14; 6:27,53,62; 8:28; 9:35; 13:31).[6]

Thirdly, in speaking of his being **'glorified'**, *he alludes to his work as the God-man.* The centre-piece of this 'hour' is Jesus' glorification. What is the glorification of the Son of Man? It is clear that Jesus is speaking of his death and its fruits. There may be an allusion here to Isaiah 52:13, where the Suffering Servant of the Lord is to be 'exalted and extolled and be very high'. Lenski sums it up succinctly: 'In the one word δοξασθῇ [*doxasthe* — 'glorified'] he sums up everything — the passion as something glorious, the exaltation following, and the future adoration by the hosts of believers the world over and in heaven.'[7]

Jesus' death was necessary (12:24)

12:24. 'Most assuredly, I say to you, unless a grain of wheat falls into the ground and dies, it remains alone; but if it dies, it produces much grain.'

Using the illustration of the planted seed and the harvested crops, Jesus emphasizes the absolute necessity of the atonement for sin (cf. Gen. 2:16-17; Luke 24:26; Rom. 3:23-25; 5:12-21). Seeds, of course, are not dead — something the ancients knew perfectly well — but unless they are buried in the soil they will produce no new life (cf. Mark 4:3-9,26-32; Matt. 13:24-30). This is the heart of the illustration. Jesus must die and be buried in order to bring new life to the world. Had he stayed buried, he would have achieved nothing, just as seeds that do not germinate produce no crop. The illustration is very apt, because it stresses the necessity of his death for anyone to enter into life (cf. 1 Cor. 15:36-38). 'In the request of the Greeks,' remarks Hendriksen, 'Jesus sees *his seed*, i.e., numerous spiritual posterity.'[8] He is the substitute for the sinners he intends to save. He is '*the* Seed', through whom and in whom all who believe become his seed — Abraham's seed, and heirs according to the promise' (Gal. 3:16,19,26-29).

Discipleship involves sharing in Jesus' death (12:25-26)

12:25-26. 'He who loves his life will lose it, and he who hates his life in this world will keep it for eternal life. If anyone serves me, let him follow me; and where I am, there my servant will be also. If anyone serves me, him my Father will honour.'

From his own fruitful death, Jesus moves to his followers' fruitful lives. There is a connection between the two, and it consists in the latter's sharing in the death of their Saviour. In the case of the disciples of Jesus also, death is a necessary element in their entrance into life. They do not die *for* their sins, of course, but in Christ, who has died for their sins, they die *to* their sins (cf. 1 Peter 2:21-25). Christ's example forms a template for Christians as they live their lives. This implies a certain pattern of discipleship.

First, *we must have the right attitude to life* (12:25). Just as Jesus did not cling to his earthly life, so we must not love it as if it were the be-all and end-all of our existence. Indeed, says Jesus, **'He who hates his life in this world will keep it for eternal life,'** while he who loves it will lose everything. Parallel contrasts appear in Jesus' teaching in Matthew 10:37-39; 16:24-26; Mark 8:34-38; Luke 9:23-26; 17:32-33. 'Remember Lot's wife,' he warns in the last of these passages. 'Whoever seeks to save his life will lose it, and whoever loses his life will preserve it.' If you live for the passing things of this life, your life will surely pass with them. This is at the root of so much depression and suicide in modern life. Having nothing but 'life under the sun', the modern unbeliever finds his hope and joy in life only coextensive with his temporal successes and comforts in this world. Deny it as he may while in the sunshine of his life, he is confronted soon enough with its essential meaninglessness as the things he lived for fade away, his faculties decline and his erstwhile idols leave him to a lost eternity.

The true love of life discerns the true life to love. Here we have no continuing city. The Christian's citizenship is in heaven. It is better to be absent from the body and present with the Lord. He who believes in the Son has eternal life — already, here and now. This puts our present life in proper perspective. Christ is the Christian's life, whether he lives or dies, and this means he lies loose to the things of this world, even though he loves every sunrise and enjoys God's good gifts throughout his days. Thus Martin Luther, in his hymn 'Ein feste Burg' (as translated by Thomas Carlyle) could bear testimony:

And, though they take our life,
Goods, honour, children, wife,
Yet is their profit small,
These things shall vanish all:
The city of God remaineth.

Secondly, *we must follow the right pattern for life*
(12:26a). Jesus says, **'If anyone serves me, let him
follow me.'** The word διακονῇ (from *diakonein*, to
serve) indicates a willing commitment to service. How
will this service be effective? By following Jesus
closely. The verb ἀκολουθείτω (*akolentheo* means literally 'to go along behind') is a present active imperative. They must keep following him constantly and
closely. This strikes modern 'easy-believism' a mortal
blow and is a wake-up call for those who think that a
'decision' for Jesus on some past day, a vague attachment to Judaeo-Christian values and a modicum
of church-going and clean living are evidence of a
saving knowledge of Christ. Devotion is where discipleship starts, not where it ends! The mark of a real
Christian is that Jesus can say of him, **'Where I am,
there my servant will be also.'** He refers to the
Christian life — taking up the cross, being faithful
even to death and coming at length to heaven itself
and the crown of life (Rev. 2:10).

Thirdly, *we must look for the right satisfaction from
life* (12:26b). This will be found in the believer's
affirmation by God the Father: **'If anyone serves me,
him my Father will honour.'** Although God's re-
wards are as much unmerited gifts of grace as the
obedience to which he attaches them (Eph. 2:10), it
remains the case that God honours only faithfulness
in his servants and will despise those who despise
him (1 Sam. 2:30). The encouragement to continue in
enthusiastic discipleship reaches from here to eternity and God's welcome into glory: 'Well done, good
and faithful servant; you were faithful over a few

things, I will make you ruler over many things. Enter
into the joy of your lord' (Matt. 25:21).

3. Jesus' prayer (12:27-28a)

12:27-28. 'Now my soul is troubled, and what shall I say?
"Father, save me from this hour"? But for this purpose I came
to this hour. Father, glorify your name...'

All that Jesus has said depends upon the death he is
still to die. For his followers to follow him, he must
lead from the front. The horror of paying the wages of
sin sinks in and troubles his innermost being. His
true humanity shrinks from death, as we all instinctively do, but the heart of the incarnate Son of God
contemplates with trembling the prospect of the
wrath of the Father against sin not his own. Here is a
foretaste of Gethsemane (cf. Mark 14:36).

From a grammatical viewpoint, Jesus' words,
'**"Father, save me from this hour"?**' could be read
as either a potential prayer, or as a positive prayer.
The former is to be preferred for, as R. C. H. Lenski
points out, 'The context not only forbids this [latter]
sense but actually annuls it. For the Greek ἀλλὰ [*alla
/ 'but'*] negatives the idea of such a prayer: "But no
— for this very reason I came to this hour." Then
follows the prayer that Jesus does make.... As in
Gethsemane [Mark 14:36 — 'Take this cup away
from me'], Jesus merely thinks of the possibilities
obtaining in his case, namely that even now, though
the hour has come, he might ask the Father to deliver him completely from it. In plain human fashion,
true man that he was, he looked at that possibility,
allowed us to hear his thoughts, and then at once
dismissed them from his mind — he had come to
suffer and he was resolved to suffer.[9]

It was not easy for Christ to die for us. He did not
rebel against his mission, but demonstrated to those

around him something of his willingness to be obedient to the death of the cross (cf. Phil. 2:6-8). 'His desires of his own safety,' says Thomas Manton, 'were moderated, and submitted to the conscience of his duty, and he preferreth the honour of God, and seeks to advance it above his own case.'[10] He accordingly affirms his commitment to his death and prays that the Father would glorify his name through it (12:28).

Applying the Lord's example to us, Manton remarks that 'A love to our private interests hinders us from seeking the glory of God: Rom. 15:3, "For even Christ pleased not himself"; John 12:27-28, "For this cause came I to this hour: Father glorify thy name." Every Christian should be thus affected; let Christ dispose of him and his interests as it seemeth good to him.'[11] This also means cultivating 'an indifferency of mind with respect to future events, leaving them to be disposed according to the will and wisdom of God, for his own glory and our good... For Christ consulted not with his own ease, but God's glory; as he respected not the innocent inclinations of his human nature, but the glory of his Father.'[12]

The manner of Jesus' death (12:28b-33)

The last phase in this prediction of Jesus' death begins with the voice of God the Father and ends with the voice of God the Son. Sandwiched between these are the voices of confused humanity. Nothing could more graphically highlight the sovereignty of God in initiating the plan of salvation than the juxtaposition of these various voices. God speaks into uncomprehending human history. His Son Jesus comes to his own and his own receive him not. But the lost will be saved. Hearts will be changed. Lives will be transformed. God's free grace reaches into blinded souls by the gospel of his Son.

1. The voice from heaven (12:28b,c)

12:28. ...Then a voice came from heaven, saying, 'I have both glorified it and will glorify it again.'

The answer to Jesus' prayer was immediate. For the third time in his ministry — the others were at his baptism and the transfiguration (Mark 1:11; 9:7) — God spoke from heaven. As in the later case of Paul on the Damascus road, the people in general heard the sound but could not make out the words (Acts 9:7; 22:9). It was nevertheless sufficient to impress them that something supernatural had occurred. We are not told whether John reports the words as one who did hear them, or, as is more probable, received them from Jesus at another time. The point is that they constitute a divine testimony to the person and work of Jesus as the promised Messiah. God declares that he had already glorified his name through the incarnation and earthly ministry of Jesus, including his miracles and, as Calvin says, 'promises that the death of Christ will be glorious', so offering in advance a radically different perspective of the cross from the natural view that regarded it as a shameful and offensive thing.[13]

2. The voice of the people (12:29)

12:29. Therefore the people who stood by and heard it said that it had thundered. Others said, 'An angel has spoken to him.'

Opinions in the crowd as to the source of the voice / sound were divided between the naturalists (those who said it was thunder) and the supernaturalists (those who thought it was an angel). Both were evidently unwilling to believe that God himself had spoken and to link it with what Jesus had just said about his oneness with the Father. Calvin calls the former 'deaf' and the latter 'dull' (cf. 2 Cor. 4:4; Eph. 2:2). He aptly notes that this remains the common response to the claims of God in this world, for, he says, 'God speaks plainly enough in the Gospel, in which is also displayed the power and energy of the Spirit, which ought to shake heaven and earth; but many are as little affected by the doctrine, as if it only proceeded from a mortal man, and others consider the word of God to be confused and barbarous, as if it were nothing else than thunder.'[14]

3. The voice of Jesus (12:30-33)

12:30-32. Jesus answered and said, 'This voice did not come because of me, but for your sake. Now is the judgement of this world; now the ruler of this world will be cast out. And I, if I am lifted up from the earth, will draw all peoples to myself.' This he said, signifying by what death he would die.

Seeing the scepticism and indifference around him, Jesus states four things for the record about the voice they had heard.

Firstly, *God spoke audibly for the sake of the hearers* — and, we might add, modern readers of Scripture — and not for Jesus' sake alone (12:30). Indeed, Jesus had settled the matter of his death with his prayer (12:27-28). God spoke to *them* so that later many would remember and believe, and all, whatever their faith or the lack of it, would be without excuse.

Secondly, *God* in this way *gave notice of judgement to come and the destruction of Satan* (12:31). Here again, Jesus puts in a pre-emptive strike on the offence of the cross. His death would seem to be more a judgement upon him and defeat for his message and mission than a judgement on the world. But there is a great reversal in Jesus death. He does indeed accept the judgement due to those for whose sins he atones. But this means defeat for Satan (Matt. 12:29; Luke 10:18) and judgement for that world which determinedly rejects him to the last breath (Heb. 2:3). It is by 'the blood of the Lamb' that Christ's followers will overcome Satan (Rev. 12:11). The fact of Christ's death and resurrection judges each generation until all is sealed in the last judgement (2 Cor. 2:14-16). Will you 'repent' or 'perish'? (Luke 13:3,5).

Thirdly, *it presages Jesus' death by crucifixion* (12:32a,33). The means by which Satan is cast out and sinners saved is Christ's death by crucifixion. His being 'lifted up' (see also 3:14) ties his death, resurrection and ascension together. Death and glory are linked in his exaltation as the risen Saviour (Phil. 2:8-9; Heb. 1:3).

Fourthly, *the voice of God portended the salvation of the nations,* Jew and Gentile alike, for Jesus will draw **'all peoples'** to himself (12:32). 'By "all men" (παντας) Jesus does not mean every individual man, for some, as Simeon said (Luke 2:34) are repelled by Christ, but this is the way that Greeks (verse 22) can and will come to Christ, by the way of the cross, the only way to the Father (14:6).'[15]

Prophetic challenge — trust in the light (12:34-36)

The final exchange between Jesus and the people begins with a theological question and ends with a challenge to faith — the role of all theology, rightly understood and applied!

Who is this 'Son of Man?' (12:34)

12:34. The people answered him, 'We have heard from the law that the Christ remains for ever; and how can you say, "The Son of Man must be lifted up"? Who is this Son of Man?'

The crowd was perplexed. They had the notion that the Messiah, once come to his people, would stay for ever. Their mention of **'the law'** no doubt refers to Scriptures that they associated with the Messianic kingdom, and which stressed the enduring nature of that kingdom and the Davidic king who would rule over it (e.g., Isa. 9:7; Ezek. 37:25; Ps. 72:17; 89:35-37).[16]

But Jesus, who identifies himself as the 'Son of Man' (Messiah) says that he will die. Surely this is no triumphant, victorious Messiah, but a mere man put to death, perhaps under God's curse? This is, of course, still the leading question that everyone must answer in responding to Christ and the gospel. Was he a man inspiring his followers by his death, to be sure, but just a man who died and stayed dead? Or was he who he claimed to be — the Son of God who died and rose again as the Redeemer of God's elect? Is Jesus just Jesus, or is he the Christ, the Son of the living God?

Believe in the light (12:35-36)

As with the Greeks' earlier question (12:20), Jesus does not answer the people's specific question (had he not already answered that by word and deed?), but instead points them to **'the light'** — surely a clear reference to himself as the 'true Light' that has come into the world (1:9; cf. 12:46). He offers a three-fold appeal to their minds, hearts and consciences:

1. The light is with you (12:35a)

12:35. Then Jesus said to them, 'A little while longer the light is with you...'

It is difficult to imagine that Jesus' hearers had not heard of his healing of the man who was blind from birth and his self-designation as 'the light of the world' (9:1-7; cf. 3:19; 8:12; 11:9). He had attracted their attention precisely because they knew so much of what he had taught and done. Jesus' language reasserts his earlier claims and tells them, 'I am the light. I am with you for a little while longer. Therefore take advantage of the privilege of my presence with you.'

2. Shun the darkness (12:35b-d)

12:35. '... Walk while you have the light, lest darkness overtake you; he who walks in darkness does not know where he is going.'

Pious Jews knew very well that walking in light was a biblical expression for living in faith as a committed disciple of the living God (Ps. 56:13; 89:15; Isa. 2:5). Conversely, to walk in darkness was to be lost, a rebel against God, and under his chastising hand (Ps. 82:5; Prov. 2:13; Isa. 59:9; Lam. 3:2). It is a fearful thing to be lost, not to know where you are going and, in fact, to be heading for a lost eternity. Jesus had earlier taught that 'the condemnation' is that 'The light has come into the world, and men loved darkness rather than light, because their deeds were evil' (3:19). So shun the darkness if you love your soul and want a future.

3. Believe in the light (12:36)

12:36. 'While you have the light, believe in the light, that you may become sons of light.'
    These things Jesus spoke, and departed, and was hidden from them.

They should put their trust in Jesus without delay and so become **'sons of light'** (cf. Eph. 5:8; 1 Thess. 5:5; 1 John 1:7). Even his subsequent departure and his becoming **'hidden from them'** emphasizes the urgency of believing, lest the light be withdrawn. 'Such as neglect opportunity ... are justly deprived of that light, and punished with darkness of ignorance and wandering in sinful courses, and of afflictions and judgements...' says Hutcheson, 'and that is sadder than if they had never enjoyed the light'.[17] The Seed must die (12:23-24; cf. Gal. 3:16). Why should you who hear his voice today not turn to him and live?

30. Why Jesus was rejected

John 12:37-50

It is commonly assumed today that education will definitively solve society's problems. If we are insistent, earnest, clear and persuasive enough and, not least, spend large amounts of the taxpayer's money on doing so, then people will listen, learn, change their ways and the politicians' promised paradise will come to pass. This is, at any rate, the official eschatology of Western secularism at the beginning of the twenty-first century. An excursion through any of our cities, or a review of statistics for crime, family breakdown, educational performance, etc., will tell you how well this theory is standing up to the facts.

Good education is a good thing, of course, and does pay certain dividends in those who take advantage of it. But that is the rub! The 'garbage in, garbage out,' principle works at both ends of the equation: the education must be good and the response to it must be positive. For Christians, the question becomes most pointed with respect to the progress of the gospel of Jesus Christ. The Word of God can be preached, taught and lived with the utmost passion, clarity, love and exemplary obedience, and yet, as Jesus himself has said, 'When the Son of Man comes, will he really find faith on the earth?' (Luke 18:8). The best message in the world

will not change everyone who hears it. When the
books are closed on human history, there will be a
hell and it will have a population. As Jesus says,
'For many are called, but few chosen' (Matt. 20:16).
Some hear and trust in Christ, while others do not.

This was true in the response of people to Jesus'
ministry on earth. For all the excitement over his
entry to Jerusalem and the vast crowds attending
his meetings, there were in the end few real disciples who truly believed in him as the promised
Messiah. Jesus was not 'successful' in his mission,
in any conventional sense of the term. Why was this
the case? What is it that led people to reject Jesus
Christ and his gospel of saving grace? Jesus
answers this in 12:37-50, discussing successively
the facts of unbelief (12:37-43) and those of living
faith (12:44-50).

The facts of unbelief
(John 12:37-43)

The text brings out four facts about the rejection of Jesus Christ. These, as we shall see, are as pertinent to our day as ever they were two millennia ago.

Fact one: many dismiss the evidence (12:37)

12:37. But although he had done so many signs before them, they did not believe in him...

Many people simply would not accept the evidence! The proof was there, before their very eyes! Jesus' many miraculous signs attested and confirmed him to be the one he claimed to be. Jesus is a historical figure and the Christian faith is a historical movement. They are neither mere verbal fabrications, nor the hopeful constructions of 'man's search for meaning'. They are not myth and legend, but solid fact. The people, however, did not want to know. They had decided that they knew better. The Greek ἐπίστευον (*episteuon*) is an imperfect, meaning, 'They were not believing.' This indicates an ongoing spirit of rejection, 'an unwillingness to accept Jesus with a genuine, living faith'.[1] They are, therefore, without excuse, as are those who follow them in the same sceptical attitudes today. Lack of evidence, then, is not the real problem, but a willingness to believe is. 'A wicked and adulterous generation seeks after a

sign, and no sign shall be given to it except the sign
of the prophet Jonah' (Matt. 16:4) — that is, the
resurrection of Jesus. But they will stumble at that
also in due course.

Fact two: prophecy is fulfilled in their not believing (12:38)

12:38. ... that the word of Isaiah the prophet might be fulfilled, which he spoke:

> Lord, who has believed our report?
> And to whom has the arm of the LORD been revealed?

John quotes the prophet Isaiah to show that the
widespread rejection of Jesus had been prophesied
centuries before (Isa. 53:1 from the Septuagint). The
'report' (ἀκοῇ / *akoe* — literally, 'that which is
heard') that is not believed refers to the words of
Jesus in preaching and teaching. The **'arm'** (ὁ
βραχίων / *ho brachion*) of the Lord represents the
miraculous signs that Jesus did. In the end, neither
words nor works persuaded the majority of the Old
Testament people of God to follow Jesus. Two decades later, the majority of Jews responded in the
same manner to the apostles' ministry, leading Paul
to cite the same text in explanation of their unbelief
(Rom. 10:16). The same is true today, as Christians
wait hopefully for the fulfilment of another prophecy, namely that before this world is done, 'All Israel
will be saved' (Rom. 11:26-27, which also cites Isa.
59:20-21).

The force of the Greek ἵνα (*hina* — **'that'** in the
sense of 'in order that') is to establish that God
planned it this way, and that is confirmed in 12:39-40
with even greater rigour. The interface of divine predestination and human responsibility is inevitably

mysterious, but the former in no way eliminates the latter. Unbelief is a choice, and these people chose to reject Jesus for reasons of their own. That they did so within the orbit of God's foreordination does not excuse their determined rejection of Christ.

Christians find the rejection of Jesus and the gospel hard to take. Surely, we would like to think, people can see the love of Christ and the beauty of his message of new and eternal life. Rejection discourages us, all the more because it is so undeserved. Perhaps it raises doubts as to the truth and the power of God himself. Well, God is not thwarted by human rejection. God's plans are not set aside. He will not be disappointed or denied. His plan and purpose are being worked out. There will be unbelief towards Christ while the world lasts. This is prophesied in the Old Testament and recorded in the New, and it will only be completely extinguished on the great day of the Lord's return.

Fact three: many cannot believe (12:39-41)

12:39-41. Therefore they could not believe, because Isaiah said again:

> He has blinded their eyes and hardened their hearts,
> Lest they should see with their eyes,
> Lest they should understand with their hearts and turn,
> So that I should heal them.

These things Isaiah said when he saw his glory and spoke of him.

Unbelieving Israel not only did not accept Jesus as the Messiah, but **'could not'** believe in him! Their eyes were blinded and their hearts hardened! Yes, God hardens hearts! Remember Pharaoh (Exod. 7:3;

8:32; 9:12). John quotes Isaiah 6:9-10, a passage also used in Matthew 13:14-15 (cf. Mark 4:12; Luke 8:10) and Acts 28:26. A similar passage (Isa. 29:10) is cited in Romans 11:8, also in explanation of Israel's recurrent unbelief towards the Lord.

This is a fearful teaching, because it shows that unbelief is not merely a bad choice, which it always is, but it can also be a judgement of God in which what begins as rebellion intensifies until it becomes nothing less than a state of reprobation.

1. Rejecting Jesus meant a progressive experiential hardening

Those unwilling to believe become progressively unable to believe. They convince themselves ever more intensely that any alternative is unthinkable, whatever the evidence. Adolf Hitler, in his bunker, with Germany in ruins, could not accept reality and fantasized endlessly of last-minute victory, until, of course, only suicide was left to keep him from the facts (although that, surely, plunged him into an even more profound and permanent reality).

You do not have to be a Hitler to have a hardened heart. Ordinary people can be as irrationally devoted to their fantasies. Speaking of those who are openly committed to the rejection of God's moral law, Paul notes that people become 'futile in their thoughts' and 'professing to be wise' become 'fools' (Rom. 1:21-22). Furthermore, as their practice of all sorts of moral evil becomes more public and shameless, he says, 'God gave them over to a debased mind, to do those things which are not fitting' (Rom. 1:28). What could more accurately describe our amoral, deconstructionist world? For example, it is no accident that the homosexual activists' Gay Pride Week is held at Easter. Why? Because, in a perverse parody of new life through the crucified and risen Saviour, Jesus Christ, they are consciously claiming a resurrection for the homosexual lifestyle and its practitioners. That it is actually a proven death-style (as are 'lifestyles' involving heterosexual sin, theft, murder, envy, lying, etc.) only serves to underscore the experiential and intellectual impact of a hardening of the heart against the revealed truth of God.

2. This is also a judicial hardening

God makes it so as a punishment for determined rebellion. When human wickedness burgeoned in the ancient world, God declared, 'My Spirit shall not strive with man for ever' (Gen. 6:3). This issued in two major restraints upon the capacity of the human race to sin. One was the shortening of his lifespan. The other, a little more drastic, was the flood in the days of Noah. The principle remains applicable in every human life. When God hardens a heart, he is in effect saying, 'My Spirit will no longer strive with that person.'

We understand that as it applies in our relationships with people who injure us in some way. We may give someone a second chance, maybe a third, but after that the offender is usually dismissed as incorrigible. Yet many object to God's writing anyone off, unless he or she is a mass-murderer or an embezzler of pension funds.

The evidence of Scripture is, however, that God is longsuffering, with a patience in dealing with sinners that we at our best do not remotely approach. John notes that Isaiah said these things in connection with seeing 'his' glory, surely a reference to the vision of God's glory in Isaiah 6, at the time he was equipped and commissioned to go out and speak of the coming of the Servant of the Lord. God is sovereign. He is glorious in holiness. He is full of love and grace. He sends his Servant to save sinners. The fact that we have not burned up in the blaze of his righteous justice is entirely due to his mercy (Lam. 3:22; Mal. 3:6). His judicial hardening of proven reprobates should not come as a surprise. It is not as if the Lord has not demonstrated his longsuffering and his faithfulness.

If this finds us uncommitted to Christ and indifferent or opposed to the things of God, it should send us trembling to Jesus Christ for salvation before it is too late. That is the silver lining on the cloud. Hear the Lord now, believe him and you will be saved! (cf. Heb. 3:7-8,13,15).

Fact four: Some say they believe but are silenced by fear (12:42-43)

12:42-43. Nevertheless even among the rulers many believed in him, but because of the Pharisees they did not confess him, lest they should be put out of the synagogue; for they loved the praise of men more than the praise of God.

Unbelief often masquerades as faith. Thomas Halyburton (1674-1712), later one of Scotland's choicest Christians, recounted the days when he wrestled with the claims of Christ upon his life. He had a kind of belief, but he also held back. He was about fifteen years old at the time and Scotland was in the last throes of the attempt by the Roman Catholic James II/VII to maintain his throne and establish the ascendancy of Rome in the land. Halyburton had recurrent daydreams of an 'Irish cut-throat' who would hold a dagger to his chest and say, 'Quit your religion, turn papist, and you will live: hold it, and you are dead!'[2] He was afraid to confess Christ, for fear of persecution. As it turned out, it was almost ten years later that he, in his own estimation, came to Christ in faith. His fears had been an excuse for inward resistance to Christ. These exposed the fact that whatever he said he believed, he did not know Christ in the power of the resurrection. So it seems to have been with those 'rulers' who 'believed', but kept their mouths shut for fear of the Pharisees.

1. The necessity of confessing Christ (12:42)

Telling no one but yourself that you believe in Jesus is arguably just a subtle version of rejecting him, whatever the true state of your soul. Were these rulers true believers? Perhaps — but how would anyone know? A secret believer is unidentifiable as a believer. It is possible, as Matthew Henry says, that 'some are really better than they seem to be'. But, as he also remarks, there is here some cause 'to question the sincerity of that faith'.[3] In Scripture, it is open public confession of Jesus as Saviour that is the crux of the matter of evidencing true faith: 'If you confess with your mouth the Lord Jesus and believe in your heart that God has raised him from the dead, you will be saved ' (Rom. 10:9).

2. The snare of loving the praise of men (12:43)

'See the power of the world in the smothering ... of convictions,' says Matthew Henry.[4] They **loved the praise of men more than the praise of God**. Your faith is a great theory until it costs you something. Compare Moses, who 'forsook Egypt, not fearing the wrath of the king; for he endured as seeing him who is invisible' (Heb. 11:27). These supposed believers were more concerned about their reputation with their peers, and their privileged positions, than to hazard them on an open commitment to Christ. Perhaps some were numbered among those who did commit themselves after Pentecost (Acts 6:7).

Meanwhile, cowardice is not evidence of discipleship and silence is not confession of faith.

These, then, are the facts of unbelief as they concerned the hearers of Jesus just days before his arrest and crucifixion. There is, as the preacher said, 'nothing new under the sun' (Eccles. 1:9).

The facts of living faith
(John 12:44-50)

The last paragraph of the chapter looks very like a last word from Jesus to the Jews, a 'concluding summary' of his public ministry and its implications for their lives.[5] Hereafter, he teaches his disciples (chs. 13-16), intercedes for his people (ch. 17) and dies and rises again for the salvation of sinners (chs. 18-21).

Calling this a 'summary', however correct as a formal description of content, misses the vital point that it is at once a self-revelation of Jesus as the Messiah and a powerful plea for people to come to him in saving faith. Jesus **'cried out'**. He preached with passion to the minds and consciences of his audience. Too many modern preachers never work up a sweat in the pulpit. They give what Martyn Lloyd-Jones, borrowing from the titles of an American writer's books on various Christian subjects, called 'quiet talks'.[6] Small wonder their people are no more excited than they are about the message and the faith. In this vignette, Jesus shows that what you believe is a matter of life or death and that the preacher ought to proclaim this with a warmth appropriate to the theme. Urgency and love for souls drive his every syllable. They must hear if they are to live (Isa. 55:3; John 5:25). And, 'How shall they hear without a preacher?' (Rom. 10:14).

Jesus stresses three main points about true and living faith: it is in him as the Mediator, the light for the world, and the giver of everlasting life. Note, in the sub-divisions of these points, the way he reveals himself as the God-man, the incarnate Son of God.

Living faith is in Christ as Mediator (12:44-45)

12:44-45. Then Jesus cried out and said, 'He who believes in me, believes not in me but in him who sent me. And he who sees me sees him who sent me.'

Believing in Jesus and seeing Jesus, he says, is not believing in and seeing him only, as if he were a great leader and the founder of a new movement, but believing in and seeing **'him who sent me'**. This one expression encompasses a whole theology of mediation. Jesus acts for God as the only Mediator between God and men (1 Tim. 2:5).

- Jesus was sent by the Father (7:27-29; 8:16-18,42; 13:20; Matt. 10:40; Luke 9:48; 10:16).
- Jesus subordinated himself to the Father's will (3:31-36; 5:19-27; 6:37-40; 8:28-29).
- Jesus is one with the Father (10:30,38; 16:15), and there is a perfect unity of love between the Father and the Son in their intention to save a people for themselves (14:21; 15:9; 16:27).

When Philip later asks Jesus to show them the Father, Jesus replies in similar terms to 12:45: 'He who has seen me has seen the Father' (14:9-11). There is no better view — indeed, no other view — of God than that which we see in the face of Jesus Christ (2 Cor. 4:6). He and the Father are one, and no one comes to the Father but by him (6:37; 14:6).

Living faith is a darkness-to-light experience in Christ (12:46)

12:46. 'I have come as a light into the world, that whoever believes in me should not abide in darkness.'

The reason for Jesus' coming was to bring people from spiritual darkness — potentially eternal darkness — into the light of salvation, that is, reconciliation to God through his own atoning sacrifice for sin (Acts 26:18; Rom. 2:19; 2 Cor. 4:6; Eph. 5:8; 1 Peter 2:9). This reaffirms two important truths:

* Jesus reveals his Father-God to the world (1:18; 2 Cor. 4:6). He is the supreme revelation of God — 'the brightness of his glory and the express image of his person' (Heb. 1:3).
* Jesus is light for a lost world (3:19; 8:12; 12:35; Luke 1:79). To reject him is to remain in darkness.

The alternative to knowing Jesus as the 'true Light', then, is to 'abide in darkness'. He did not come to condemn, but to save (3:17). Coming to Christ in faith is coming to the light. 'Believers in Christ,' notes Hutcheson, '... ought to shine as lights, being illuminated by him who is the light of the world, Phil. 2:15.' Furthermore, 'as children of light, Eph. 5:8 ... they shall by faith be translated out of the kingdom of darkness ... Col. 1:13, and shall daily partake of that light of direction, refreshment, and consolation that is in him... And if men would in the first place cherish faith, their light and consolation would grow more.'[7]

Living faith issues in everlasting life in Christ (12:47-50)

This whole passage addresses the fact that most of Jesus' hearers rejected him. They heard his words, they saw his works, but still they did not believe. How does this fit in with his mission? Two main points are made as he closes his message to the Old Testament people of God.

1. The lost are judged by the Word of God (12:47-48)

12:47-48. 'And if anyone hears my words and does not believe, I do not judge him; for I did not come to judge the world but to save the world. He who rejects me, and does not receive my words, has that which judges him — the word that I have spoken will judge him in the last day.'

Since his coming is devoted to seeking and saving the lost (Luke 19:10), where does that leave those who, in such large numbers, reject the gospel?

- Jesus does not judge the unbelieving *now*, for he did not come to judge but to save. People seem to get away scot-free, in spite of treating him with indifference or contempt. He remains the longsuffering Servant of the Lord, who 'all day long' stretches out his hands 'to a disobedient and contrary people' (Rom. 10:21).
- Jesus' words will be the measure of his judgement in the last day (Rom. 2:16; 2 Tim. 4:1).

Millions reject the Word of God without a thought of accountability and judgement. Daily life-experience seems to suggest they are in little danger; such people would later ask Peter, 'Where is the promise of his coming? For since the fathers fell asleep, all things continue as they were from the beginning of creation' (2 Peter 3:4). These are days of grace, but the reckoning will dawn one day.

2. Jesus speaks the word of life (12:49-50)

12:49-50. 'For I have not spoken on my own authority; but the Father who sent me gave me a command, what I should say and what I should speak. And I know that his command is everlasting life. Therefore, whatever I speak, just as the Father has told me, so I speak.'

The authority and finality of Jesus' words rest upon the Father, whose words they are. We need to grasp two fundamental truths:

- Jesus has authority to require faith, because God commands his message and mission (12:49; cf. 3:11; 8:26; 14:10).
- Jesus has authority to give everlasting life (12:50; cf. 3:16; 6:63).

Jesus is saying, in effect, what Paul later applies to the Greeks in Athens, when he says that God 'now commands all men everywhere to repent' (Acts 17:30). He is appealing to those who are rejecting him that they should come to the light that they might have life. 'And this is the testimony: that God has given us eternal life, and this life is in his Son' (1 John 5:11). 'You have given him authority over all flesh, that he should give eternal life to as many as you have given him. And this is eternal life, that they may know you, the only true God, and Jesus Christ whom you have sent' (John 17:2-3). The message is the same today, and will remain so while the world lasts: 'Believe on the Lord Jesus Christ, and you will be saved, you and your household' (Acts 16:31).

Notes

Preface
1.William Hendriksen, *A Commentary on the Gospel of John* (London: Banner of Truth, 1959 [first published1954]), vol. I, p.3.
2. D. A. Carson, *The Gospel according to John* (Leicester: IVP, 1991).
3. Herman Ridderbos, *The Gospel of John: A Theological Commentary* (Grand Rapids & Cambridge: Eerdmans, 1997).

Introduction
1. D. Martyn Lloyd-Jones, 'Singleness of Heart,' *Banner of Truth*, issue 438 (March 2000), p.13.
2. Rodney A. Whitacre, *John* (Downer's Grove, Ill.: IVP, 1999), p.18, citing Robert Fortna, *The Fourth Gospel and its Predecessor: from Narrative Source to Present Gospel* (1988), p.xii.
3. Perhaps the most persistent modern myth connected with the authorship of John is the ascription of authorship to a different John — 'John the elder' — on the basis of a quotation from Papias recorded by Eusebius, in which he mentions the two Johns side by side (*Ecclesiastical History*, Book III, xxxix). Papias refers to the 'discourses of the elders' — evidently meaning the New Testament Scriptures — and some have made a connection between that expression and the title of the second John ('the elder'), so as to propose him as possibly the real author of the Fourth Gospel. This combination of ambiguity (calling one John an 'elder' does not mean the apostle John was not one) and *non sequitur* (the fact that the 'discourses' were by 'elders' does not imply they were not written by apostles) flies in the face of plain biblical and historical evidence and has surely only been entertained seriously because of a disposition to dismiss Scripture when a flimsy argument can be employed to erode its claims.
4. Bruce Milne, *The Message of John* (Leicester: IVP, 1993), p.16.
5. Eusebius, *Ecclesiastical History*: Book V, xx, 5-6.
6. Irenaeus, *Against Heresies*, iii, 1.2.
7. See Carson, *Gospel According to John*, p.72 for a comprehensive survey that convincingly demonstrates Johannine authorship against all comers.
8. Eusebius, Book III, chs xxiii, xxxi.

9. Milne, *The Message of John*, p.25.
10. Carson, *Gospel According to John*, pp.82-7.
11. Robert H. Gundry, *A Survey of the New Testament* (Grand Rapids:1970), p.81.
12. Those miracles unique to John are:

1. Water into wine (2:1-11)
2. Healing the nobleman's son (4:46-54)
3. Healing the paralytic at Bethesda (5:1-15)
4. Healing the man born blind (9:1-12)
5. Raising Lazarus (11:17-44)
6. Miraculous catch of fish (21:1-12).

Two others, the feeding of the 5,000 (6:1-15), and Jesus walking on the sea (6:16-21), are also found elsewhere.
13. Gundry, *Survey of the New Testament*, p.105.
14. Milne, *The Message of John*, p.21.
15. Gundry, *Survey of the New Testament*, p.110.
16. See Carson, *Gospel According to John*, pp.87-95 for a helpful survey of the field.
17. Carson, *Gospel According to John*, p.89.

Outline
1. This outline is adapted and expanded from one first suggested by W. Graham Scroggie in *Charlotte Chapel Record* (Edinburgh, Scotland), vol. XX, 3 (March 1926), p.44.

Chapter 1 — Who is Jesus?
1. Leon Morris, *The Gospel according to John* (Grand Rapids: Eerdmans, 1971), p.73.
2. As above, p.76.
3. The Jehovah's Witness heresy — really just recycled Arianism — regards Jesus as a created angel. This arises from the blunder of taking Hebrews 1:5 to mean that Jesus is an angel and then understanding that as requiring the rewriting of John 1:1. This interpretation in both cases has no support whatsoever in the Greek text.
4. W. G. T. Shedd, *Dogmatic Theology* (Grand Rapids: Zondervan, 1969 [first published 1888]), vol. 1, p.315.
5. John Calvin, *Commentary on the Gospel according to John*, vol. I, p.26. (All quotations from Calvin on John in this exposition are from the 1979 reprint by Baker Book House of the volume in the Calvin Translation Society edition.)
6. Matthew Henry, *A Commentary on the Whole Bible* (Iowa Falls: n.d.), vol. 6, p.849.
7. George Hutcheson, *An Exposition of the Gospel according to John* (Grand Rapids: Sovereign Grace Publishers, 1971), p.10.

8. Octavius Winslow, *The Glory of the Redeemer in his Person and Work* (New York: 1868), p.35.

Chapter 2 — The true Light
1. R. C. H. Lenski, *The Interpretation of John* (Minneapolis: Augsburg Publishing House, 1943), p.48.
2. As above, p.49.
3. Morris shows convincingly why this rendering is to be preferred. He notes, 'John does not normally speak of men at large as "coming into the world". This is a description he reserves for Christ. Moreover, this verse stands at the head of a section dealing with the incarnation, where a statement about the incarnation rather than one about men in general seems required' (*Gospel according to John*, p.95).
4. Calvin, *Commentary on John*, vol. I, pp.38-9.
5. Hutcheson, *Exposition of John*, p.15.
6. Morris notes that John uses the verb form (*pisteueiv* — to believe) ninety-eight times and never uses the noun (*pistos* — faith). The construction 'believe *in*' appears thirty-six times. This indicates his desire that we understand 'faith' to be a doing, active experience of trusting in and living for Jesus as Saviour and Lord, and do not reduce it to 'a faith' in the sense of a static, nominal attachment to a school of thought or an institution (*Gospel according to John*, p.99, note 75).
7. J. A. Motyer, article on 'Name' in *The New Bible Dictionary* (Leicester: IVP, 1975), p.862.
8. Carson, *Gospel according to John*, pp.125-6.
9. Charles Simeon, *Expository Outlines on the Whole Bible*, (Baker, 1988 [first published 1847]), vol. 13, p.197.
10. As above, p.200.
11. As above, pp.201-2.
12. *The Book of Psalms for Singing* (Pittsburgh: Crown and Covenant, 1973), No. 27A.

Chapter 3 — God became man
1. John Murray, *Collected Writings* (Edinburgh: Banner of Truth, 1977), vol. II, p.133.
2. Morris, *Gospel according to John*, p.103.
3. Simeon, *Expository Outlines*, vol. 13, p.204.
4. Rodney A. Whitacre, *John* (Leicester: IVP, 1999), p.59.
5. Calvin, *Commentary on John*, vol. I, p.50.
6. Carson, *Gospel according to John*, p.139.

Chapter 4 — The Lamb of God
1. Philip Henry, *Christ all in all, or what Christ is made to believers* (Swengel, Pa: Reiner Publications, 1970 [first published 1691]).

2. Hendriksen, *Commentary on John,* vol. I, p.99.

3. Thomas Manton notes, 'When he cometh to destroy men, he cometh as a lion; but when he cometh to destroy sins he cometh as a lamb' (*Works,* Worthington, PA: Maranatha Publications, 1975, vol. 3, p.338).

Chapter 5 — They followed Jesus

1. See Hendriksen, *Commentary on John,* vol. I, pp.18-20 for a thorough discussion of this point.

2. Carson, *Gospel according to John,* p.157.

3. As above, p.156.

4. Morris, *Gospel according to John,* p.160.

5. As above, p.158.

6. M. Henry, *Commentary,* vol. 5, p.867.

7. Hutcheson, *Exposition of John,* p.29.

8. Morris, *Gospel according to John,* p.165.

9. Hendriksen, *Commentary on John,* vol. I, p.109.

10. P. Fairbairn (ed.), *The Imperial Standard Bible Encyclopaedia* (Grand Rapids: Zondervan, 1957), vol. IV, p.341 (Article on 'Nazareth' by Robert Buchanan).

11. Carson, *Gospel according to John,* p.161. (For other instances of this, Carson cites 2:4; 6:70; 9:3; 11:4,11 and 13:10-11,38.)

12. Morris, *Gospel according to John,* p.169. Compare Carson, who genuflects towards current scholarship by waltzing us around a minimalist exegesis of sonship, and then quietly slips in his personal conviction of full divine sonship in the last two sentences of comment. He affirms that Jesus' sonship to the Father involves a 'metaphysical, not merely a Messianic relationship' (*Gospel according to John,* pp.161-2). This allows far too much to the anti-supernaturalists, because it admits their divorce of biblical Messianism from a necessary true divinity. The promised Messiah in Scripture *is* none other than the divine Son, Second Person of the triune God, and inseparably so.

13. Lenski, *Interpretation of John,* p.174.

14. Carson sees the parallel as between Jesus and Jacob, not Jesus and the ladder, and says that John 'clearly' understands Genesis 28:12 in this way (*Gospel according to John,* p.163). It seems to me that this is plucked out of the air, because the parallels, begun in 1:47, have Nathanael as the 'Israelite indeed' (i.e., a true son of the patriarch Jacob) seeing the vision in which Jesus is the ladder/Mediator between God and man. The disciples and the future New Testament church, in other words, are the new Israel in Jesus, the Son of Man and the only Mediator between man and God.

15. Lenski, *Interpretation of John,* p.175.

16. M. Henry, *Commentary,* vol. 5, p.870.

17. For full discussions of the meaning of 'Son of Man' see Hendriksen, *Commentary on John,* vol. I, pp.203-7, and Lenski, *Interpretation of John,* pp.177-82.
18. Lenski, *Interpretation of John,* p.181.
19. Hutcheson, *Exposition of John,* p.31.

Chapter 6 — Water into wine
1. It is worth pointing out that the Greek *oinos* is always, in the New Testament, *fermented* wine. In the United States especially, efforts have been made to establish the theory that wherever *oinos* (or some other scriptural word for wine) is used favourably, as in John 2, it must refer to unfermented grape juice, and wherever it is used unfavourably, as in connection with the sin of drunkenness, the wine is necessarily fermented. On this basis, total abstinence from alcoholic beverages has been propounded as a biblical requirement for Christians and a pledge to that effect has often been imposed as a condition for church membership. Apart from the meanings of the words for wine, which allow no such imposition of prohibitionist presuppositions upon the exegesis of the text, a plain reading of John 2 alone is sufficient to explode this so-called 'two wines' theory.
2. 'Mariolatry' is the term used to describe the complex of dogma and devotion centring on Mary that is promulgated by the Roman Catholic Church. This includes the Immaculate Conception (that she was born without sin), the Assumption (that she ascended bodily to heaven on the third day after her death), her perpetual virginity, and her worthiness to be worshipped and prayed to as a mediatrix more merciful than Christ.
3. Calvin, *Commentary on John,* vol. I, p.84.
4. Hutcheson, *Exposition of John,* p.33.
5. Morris, *Gospel according to John,* p.185.
6. Hutcheson, *Exposition of John,* p.35.

Chapter 7 — Cleansing the temple
1. Turner quoted in Morris, *Gospel according to John,* p.194.
2. For a discussion of this, see Hendriksen, *Commentary on John,* vol. I, p.123.

Chapter 8 — 'You must be born again!'
1. Calvin, *Commentary on John,* vol. I, p.107.
2. As above, p.108.
3. The AV's 'Verily, verily' accurately renders the Greek *Amen, amen,* even if the language is somewhat archaic. Modern renderings somehow fail to capture this solemn emphasis.
4. For a thorough discussion of this, see Murray, *Collected Writings,* vol. 2, pp.182-3.
5. Hendriksen, *Commentary on John,* vol. I, p.134.

6. See Shedd, *Dogmatic Theology*, vol. II, pp.491-537, for a lucid statement of this distinction.
7. See John Murray, *Redemption Accomplished and Applied* (London: Banner of Truth, 1961), p.79f., for a discussion of the order of salvation.

Chapter 9 — Amazing love
1. Calvin, *Commentary on John*, vol. I, pp.122-3.
2. Murray, *Collected Writings*, vol. 1, p.79.
3. From the hymn, 'There is a green hill far away.'
4. John Brown of Edinburgh makes a very striking comment on this point, when he writes, 'Only the hopelessly lost [in hell, GJK] know what the salvation of Christ delivers *from*. Only the blessed in heaven know what the salvation of Christ exalts *to*... Eternity will ever be disclosing new horrors in the one, new glories in the other' (*Discourses and Sayings of Our Lord*, London: Banner of Truth Trust, 1967, vol. 1, p.33).
5. Calvin, *Commentary on John*, vol. I, pp.124-5.
6. Sir James Young Simpson (1811-70) discovered the anaesthetic properties of chloroform. He is commemorated by a statue in Princes Street, Edinburgh. He was a member of the Free Church of Scotland. The quotations are from his published testimony entitled *My Substitute*.

Chapter 10 — A witness for Christ
1. For a thorough exposition of this theme, see Geerhardus Vos, *Biblical Theology* (Grand Rapids: Eerdmans: 1948), pp.335-54. Vos points out that although, in John 1:21, John denied being Elijah 'in that realistic Jewish sense' (i.e., the original Elijah returned from the dead), he 'would not have denied being so in the symbolic sense affirmed by Jesus' (*Biblical Theology*, p.338f.).
2. Simeon, *Expository Outlines*, vol. 13, p.272.
3. See Hendriksen (*Commentary on John*, vol. I, p.149, footnote) and Lenski (*Interpretation of John*, p.286ff.), who attribute this to John the Baptizer; *versus* Morris (*Gospel according to John*, p.242ff.) and Carson (*Gospel according to John*, p.212), who regard it as an apostolic reflection some fifty years after the event. Take your pick!
4. Hendriksen, *Commentary on John*, vol. I, p.149.
5. Calvin, *Commentary on John*, vol. I, p.139.
6. Morris, *Gospel according to John*, p.247.
7. *Heidelberg Catechism*, 1 (1975 translation by the Christian Reformed Church, Kalamazoo, Michigan).
8. Carson, *Gospel according to John*, p.214.

Chapter 11 — The living water
1. Carson, *Gospel according to John*, p.215.

2. There is no doubt that Jesus *planned* to go through Samaria *precisely* for the purpose of ministering to the Samaritans. Jesus always knew exactly what he was doing and for what reason. The argument that when this text says that he **'needed'** to go through Samaria, it does not require the interpretation that this represents the 'compulsion of divine appointment' rather than simple geography (Carson, *Gospel according to John,* p.216), is contradicted by the common practice of devout Jews of the time who took the long way round Samaria rather than breathe the air of a region of notorious heretics. The divine predestination of the events often lies behind the language of circumstantial contingency, but in this case, 'the compulsion of divine appointment' is too obvious to be explained away.
3. Carson notes that rabbinical teaching held that Samaritan women were to be regarded as perpetually ceremonially unclean (*Gospel according to John,* pp.217-18).
4. Morris, *Gospel according to John,* p.260; Carson, *Gospel according to John,* p.218; Hendriksen, *Commentary on John,* vol. I, pp.161-2.
5. Calvin, *Commentary on John,* vol. I, p.148.
6. Hutcheson, *Exposition of John,* p.60.
7. Calvin, *Commentary on John,* vol. I, p.150.
8. Carson, *Gospel according to John,* p.221.
9. As above.
10. As above, pp. 221-2.
11. Calvin, *Commentary on John,* vol. I, p.165.
12. Morris notes the view that Jesus is here using the divine I AM with respect to himself — 'I who speak to you, I AM' — as he certainly does later in John 8:58; cf. Exod. 3:14 (*Gospel according to John,* p.273, citing Stauffer, *Jesus and His Story,* London: 1960, p.152). This is an attractive thesis, but is not clearly required by the language of 4:26. Carson is probably correct when he says that 'This instance of *egi eimi* (lit. "I am") is not theologically loaded' (p.227).

Chapter 12 — Fields white for harvest
1. Carson, *Gospel according to John,* p.228.
2. Simeon, *Expository Outlines,* vol. 13, p.306.
3. As above, vol. 13, p.307 (footnoted).
4. Lenski, *Interpretation of John,* p.333.
5. Calvin, *Commentary on John,* vol. I, p.169.
6. R. L. Dabney, *Discussions: Evangelical and Theological* (London: Banner of Truth Trust, 1967) vol. I, p.575f.
7. Carson, *Gospel according to John,* p.230.
8. Simeon, *Expository Outlines,* vol. 13, p.313.
9. *The Book of Psalms for Singing,* No. 126A.

Chapter 13 — Prophet without honour
1. Carson notes that there are 'about ten' proposed solutions to this problem (*Gospel according to John*, p.235).
2. Morris, *Gospel according to John*, p.290.
3. M. Henry, *Commentary*, vol. 5, p.918.
4. Carson, *Gospel according to John*, p.241. Hendriksen describes it as meaning 'house of mercy' (*Commentary on John*, vol. I, p.189).
5. Morris lists the manuscripts including verses 3-4 as A, C3, K, L, *Theta*, f1, f13 and Tertullian; and those omitting these verses as p66, p75, *Aleph*, B, C*, D, W, 33, 157, *f, l, q*, and syrc. (*Gospel according to John*, p.302, note 14).
6. For an example of this phenomenon, see G. Richard Fisher and M. Curt Goedelman, *The Confusing World of Benny Hinn* (Personal Freedom Outreach, St Louis, Mo: 1997).
7. See Morris, *Gospel according to John*, p.302, note 17, and Carson, *Gospel according to John*, pp.242-3 for solid comments on this point. The crucial question when making any parallels of this nature is whether there is, to use Carson's expression, any 'interlocking symbolism' between the two. Do the events in view give warrant for making the connection in the manner proposed, or is this merely a superficial and speculative association?
8. See Hendriksen, *Commentary on John*, vol. I, p.193.
9. Carson, *Gospel according to John*, p.245.
10. Hutcheson, *Exposition of John*, p.77.
11. As above, p.78.
12. Hendriksen, *Commentary on John*, vol. I, p.196.
13. M. Henry, *Commentary*, vol. 5, p.925.

Chapter 14 — Jesus and the Father
1. See the exposition of John 2:23 – 3:15 (Chapter 8 — 'You must be born again!', pp.122-39).
2. Calvin, *Commentary on John*, vol. I, pp.198-9.
3. Carson notes that Jewish tradition cited Elijah as an exception, for he 'served as a representative of God in raising the dead' (*Gospel according to John*, pp.252-3). Elisha also served in this way (2 Kings 4:34).
4. When Jesus spoke of 'hearing his word', he was certainly not referring to the direct quotations highlighted in red-letter editions of the Bible. These red letters drive an unwarranted and dangerous wedge between the words Jesus spoke in his earthly ministry and the rest of God's Word to mankind. One might note, for example, that chapter upon chapter of Leviticus consists of direct quotations from God, and these are no less the words of God than any Jesus uttered while on earth. The same may be said for the inspired utterances of the prophets and historians who were

carried along by the Holy Spirit to express the words of God in words of their very own.

5. Hutcheson, *Exposition of John*, p.83.

6. Carson notes that this 'stress on realized eschatology is typically Johannine'. He regards the last half of verse 24 as 'perhaps the strongest affirmation of inaugurated eschatology in the Fourth Gospel', but adds, 'Nevertheless, it does not mean the Evangelist has adopted the error of Hymenaeus and Philetus (2 Tim. 2:17-18), who insisted the resurrection had already taken place. John still anticipates a final resurrection' (*Gospel according to John*, p.256).

7. Hutcheson has a fine comment that remains unsurpassed in the three and a half centuries since he penned it: 'This property of life is common to each person of the blessed Trinity, to the Father and to the Son; yet the Father is first in order of having it, and doth communicate it to the Son; for of both it is said, he "hath life in himself", and that the Father "hath given" it to the Son, which is to be understood of his communicating it, in communicating his nature with him, by eternal generation; and as for the human nature [of Christ], this [life] is only gifted to it, in this respect, that by the grace of the personal union the human nature is assumed into the unity of the person with him, who hath this life by eternal generation' (*Exposition of John*, p.84).

8. Morris, *Gospel according to John*, p.324.

9. As above, p.328.

10. Hendriksen, *Commentary on John*, vol. I, p.208.

11. Morris, *Gospel according to John*, p.330.

12. Carson, *Gospel according to John*, p.263. 'Hillel affirms that the more study of the law, the more life, and that if a man gains for himself the words of the law he has gained for himself life in the world to come (*Pirke Aboth* 2:7).'

13. Carson, as above.

Chapter 15 — The food that lasts

1. Morris, *Gospel according to John*, p.340.
2. Carson, *Gospel according to John*, p.272.
3. M. Henry, *Commentary*, vol. 5, pp.942-3.
4. Carson, *Gospel according to John*, p.287.
5. M. Henry, *Commentary*, vol. 5, p.948.
6. As above.

Chapter 16 — 'I am the bread of life!'

1. See p.222.
2. These are:

1. The bread of life (6:35; also see 6:41,48,51)
2. The light of the world (8:12)
3. The door (10:7,9)
4. The good shepherd (10:11,14)
5. The resurrection and the life (11:25)
6. The way, the truth, and the life (14:6)
7. The true vine (15:1,5)

3. Morris, *Gospel according to John*, p.365.
4. Carson, *Gospel according to John*, p.289.
5. As above, p.293. 'Prevenient grace' (or 'preceding' or 'operating' grace) is the term given to that 'inward, secret, and wonderful operation of God upon man' by which he 'attains faith', comes to an insight of God, and by which power is given him to will the good' (A. A. Hodge, *Outlines of Theology*, Grand Rapids: Eerdmans, 1949, p.97). Arminian theology modifies this in such a way as to evade the biblical doctrine of the bondage of the human will (so-called 'total depravity'). It posits that God gives a certain grace to all human beings that gives them a totally free, unaided (by God) choice to decide for Christ and be saved. This has no biblical basis, but flows from an unwillingness to accept (1) that man's 'free' will is actually not able to turn to the Lord *by itself*, and (2) that a man without a completely free will can still be held responsible for being lost. Augustinian prevenient grace preserves the sovereignty and sufficiency of grace as that which saves lost and helpless sinners. Arminian (Wesleyan) prevenient grace confers universal ability to decide to be saved upon all sinners, who, having thereby been granted autonomy from God in the matter, may be held fully responsible should they reject the gospel. This latter position, however, fails to see that human responsibility is not inconsistent with human inability. Man does exercise free agency of a kind, but within the spiritual and moral parameters of his fallen nature. Salvation is *all* of God's free and sovereign grace, which both precedes and accompanies the operation and co-operation of the human will in the act of believing in Christ for salvation and the subsequent exercise of faith and obedience in the ongoing experience of living the Christian life.
6. Hutcheson, *Exposition of John*, p.121.
7. Morris seems to be of this opinion (*Gospel according to John*, pp.372-3).
8. Hendriksen, *Commentary on John*, vol. I, p.243.
9. Hutcheson, *Exposition of John*, pp.126-7.
10. Carson sees the crucifixion as included in Jesus' reference to his ascension, by making a connection between 'ascending' to heaven and being 'lifted up' on the cross (*Gospel according to John*, p.301). This is purely speculative, however, and is to be

rejected. Jesus is simply serving notice that, if they stumble at what he is now saying, they will be doubly embarrassed by his future ascension, which will prove him to be the true bread from heaven!

11. Carson, *Gospel according to John*, p.302.

12. For a luminous exposition of this see W. G. T. Shedd, *Sermons to the Natural Man* (New York: Scribner, 1873), pp.358-78 ('The Exercise of Mercy Optional with God').

13. Carson suggests that this is an 'advance explanation' preparing 'the true believers to face the attacks of unbelievers, without finding their own faith threatened' (*Gospel according to John*, p.302). This may be so — everything Jesus said has a didactic dimension for others — but it should not take our eyes off the point that Jesus was making to the wavering disciples themselves about their spiritual danger.

14. Carson (*Gospel according to John*, p.304), Hendriksen (*Commentary on John*, vol. I, p.248) and Morris (*Gospel according to John*, p.390) all accept the critical text. They recognize, however, that 'Holy One of God' is an unusual expression, used elsewhere of Jesus only once, and from the mouth of a demon (Mark 1:24/Luke 4:34). It is certainly a confession of deity, and is implicitly Messianic.

Chapter 17 — Indications of spiritual need

1. For the chronology of this event see Carson, *Gospel according to John*, p.305 and Hendriksen, *Commentary on John*, vol. I, pp.188-9 (cf. vol. II, p.3).

2. The Greek word used here is *kairos*, which refers to God's appointed times. This is distinguished from *chronos*, which refers to the extent of time, and *hora*, which refers to the time of Christ's death on the cross.

3. Morris, *Gospel according to John*, p.405.

4. Morris points out that the rabbinical teaching long believed that Leviticus 12:3 — the command to circumcise on the eighth day — overrode any prohibition that could be argued from the Fourth Commandment (*Gospel according to John*, p.408).

5. Morris notes that some may have expected the Messiah to appear suddenly, almost out of nowhere, on the basis of Daniel 9:25; Malachi 3:1 and certain texts in the apocryphal books of 4 Ezra and 2 Baruch (*Gospel according to John*, p.412, note 50). Jesus' own people in Nazareth rejected his ministry on more prosaic grounds, when they asked, 'Is this not the carpenter, the son of Mary...?' (Mark 6:3).

6. Calvin, *Commentary on John*, vol. I, p.301.

7. As above, p.302.

8. As above, pp.304-5.

9. Hendriksen, *Commentary on John*, vol. II, p.20; Calvin, *Commentary on John*, vol. I, p.305.

Chapter 18 — The living water

1. Carson, *Gospel according to John*, p.321. 'The water and the light of the Tabernacles rites pass into memory, year after year; his claim to provide living water and light for the world is continuously valid.'
2. As above, p.322.
3. Hutcheson, *Exposition of John*, p.150.
4. Commentators debate whether this 'last day of the feast' was the seventh day of the feast proper, or the eighth day, when, in later centuries at least, there appear to have been closing ceremonies, as attested by 2 Maccabees 10:6 and Josephus, *Antiquities of the Jews*, III, x, 4. Hendriksen discusses the issue at some length (*Commentary on John*, vol. II, p.21ff.). Since the data are inconclusive and a decision one way or the other has no material impact on what Jesus did, it seems a rather idle question.
5. Carson, *Gospel according to John*, p.326.
6. As above, p.327.
7. Hutcheson, *Exposition of John*, p.151.
8. As above, p.154.

Chapter 19 — 'Go and sin no more'

1. Hendriksen has a very clear discussion of this (*Commentary on John*, vol. II, pp.33-5). See also Carson, *Gospel according to John*, pp.333-4, Milne pp.123-4 and Ridderbos, *Gospel of John*, p.285ff. for additional useful comments.
2. Calvin, *Commentary on John*, vol. I, p.319.
3. Why so many commentators think this a 'clever' stratagem is something of a mystery. It might have fooled some rash and undiscerning zealot into a rush to judgement, but not an experienced and discerning teacher (or politician), far less the Son of God!
4. Calvin, *Commentary on John*, vol. I, p.321.
5. Few things offend modern susceptibilities as much as the notion that adultery should be subject to legal sanction (never mind the penalty of death). Calvin's comment is worthy of serious reflection: 'They who infer from this that adultery ought not to be punished with death, must, for the same reason, admit that inheritances ought not to be divided, because Christ refused to arbitrate in that matter between two brothers (Luke 12:13). Indeed, there will be no crime whatever that shall not be exempted from the penalties of the law, if adultery be not punished; for then the door will be thrown open for any kind of treachery, and for poisoning, and murder, and robbery. Besides, the adulteress, when she bears an unlawful child, not only robs the

name of the family, but violently takes away the right of inheritance from the lawful offspring, and conveys it to strangers. But what is worst of all, the wife not only dishonours the husband to whom she had been united, but prostitutes herself to shameful wickedness, and likewise violates the sacred covenant of God, without which no holiness can continue to exist in the world' (*Commentary on John*, p.323). God had his reasons for the Mosaic law of adultery. They are not mysterious at all, and we would do well, without reinstating the Mosaic death penalty, to see that the equity of that law is again enshrined in the law of the land.

6. Ridderbos, *The Gospel of John*, p.291. Jesus 'speaks not as a rabbi giving an opinion in a matter concerning the law but as one who has power "on earth to forgive sins" (Luke 5:24) and "to set at liberty those who are oppressed" (Luke 4:18)'.
7. Simeon, *Expository Outlines*, vol. 13, p.434.

Chapter 20 — The light of the world
1. Morris, *Gospel according to John*, p.435.
2. Carson, *Gospel according to John*, p.337; cf. Milne, *The Message of John*, p.127; Morris, *Gospel according to John*, pp.436-7.
3. Ridderbos, *The Gospel of John*, p.292.
4. Calvin, *Commentary on John*, vol. I, p.324.
5. Morris, *Gospel according to John*, p.438.
6. Milne, *The Message of John*, p.127.
7. Ridderbos, *The Gospel of John*, p.294.
8. *The New International Dictionary of New Testament Theology* (Grand Rapids: Zondervan), vol. 1, p.680.
9. Carson, *Gospel according to John*, p.339; Hendriksen, *Commentary on John*, vol. II, p.43; Milne, *The Message of John*, p.129.
10. Ridderbos, *The Gospel of John*, p.297.
11. J. Brown, *The Discourses and Sayings of Our Lord*, vol. 2, p.33.
12. Hutcheson, *Exposition of John*, p.164.
13. Carson, *Gospel according to John*, p.341.
14. Ridderbos, *The Gospel of John*, p.303.
15. Hutcheson, *Exposition of John*, p.158.
16. Hendriksen, *Commentary on John*, vol. II, p.48.
17. Brown, *Discourses and Sayings*, vol. 2, p.29.

Chapter 21 — 'The truth shall make you free'
1. See Hendriksen, *Commentary on John*, vol. II, pp.50-52 for a thorough and persuasive exposition of the unity of this section. Instead of adopting the view that the Jews' faith in 8:30-31 *must* be saving faith, and using that assumption as a ground for dividing the passage that follows (since it is clearly addressing unconverted people), we ought to apply the unity of the passage

to the understanding and definition of the kind of 'faith' in Jesus these people professed to have. The people who think they 'believe in him' in 8:30-31 are the very same ones who are exposed in 8:44 as children of their father the devil and who go on in 8:59 to pick up stones to kill him.

2. Calvin, *Commentary on John*, vol. I, p.342.
3. Ridderbos, *The Gospel of John*, p.310.
4. As above.
5. Carson, *Gospel according to John*, p.351.
6. James Fisher, *The Westminster Assembly's Shorter Catechism explained* (Philadelphia: A. Walker, 1818), vol. 1, p.80 (This is his thirty-third 'Question and Answer' on Question 18 of the *Shorter Catechism*).
7. As above, vol. 1, p.76 (This is Fisher's eighth 'Question and Answer' on Question 17 of the *Shorter Catechism*).

Chapter 22 —' Before Abraham was, I AM'

1. Carson, *Gospel according to John*, p.355 (quoting G. R. Beasley-Murray).
2. Ridderbos, *The Gospel of John*, p.319.
3. As above, p.321.
4. Carson, *Gospel according to John*, p.357.
5. Ridderbos is not prepared to say this is an explicit 'self-identification [by Jesus] with the divine "I",' on the ground that it is as ambiguous as the usage in 8:24 (*The Gospel of John*, pp.322-3). But Carson points out that whereas it is indeed doubtful that 'I am he' in 8:24 and 28 proves or requires such a self-identification, in 8:58 the meaning is clearly absolute (*Gospel according to John*, p.358). Ridderbos tries to make Calvin agree with him, in spite of the Reformer's insistence that it not only refers to Exodus 3:14, but encompasses the whole ministry of the Son of God, including his character as the incarnate Christ, who is the same yesterday, today and for ever (Heb. 13:8). The 'efficacy which belonged, in all ages, to the grace of the Mediator', says Calvin, 'depended on his eternal Divinity; so that this saying of Christ contains a remarkable testimony of his Divine essence' (Calvin, *Commentary on John*, vol. I, pp.362-3). Ridderbos wants to say that it is *no more than* a reference to 'Christ's power and grace ... common to all ages,' but in fact Calvin says it encompasses *both* his eternal divinity and his Messianic ministry.
6. Ridderbos, *The Gospel of John*, p.322.

Chapter 23 — Light for the blind

1. Calvin, *Commentary on John*, vol. I, pp.364-5.
2. Carson, *Gospel according to John*, p.361.
3. Hutcheson, *Exposition of John*, p.187.
4. Calvin, *Commentary on John*, vol. I, p.370.

5. Carson, *Gospel according to John*, p.365.
6. Hendriksen, *Commentary on John*, vol. II, p.76.
7. See Carson, *Gospel according to John*, p.367 for citations.
8. Calvin, *Commentary on John*, vol. I, p.375.
9. Calvin, *Commentary on John*, vol. I, pp.384-5.
10 Carson, *Gospel according to John*, p.375.
11 'Son of *God*' is a Received/majority text reading. Bibles dependent on critical texts have 'Son of *Man*', on the supposition that 'God' is a later copyist's gloss.

Chapter 24 — The Good Shepherd

1. For an extensive discussion of the connection between chapters 9 and 10, see Hendriksen, *Commentary on John*, vol. II, pp.97-103 (cf. Carson, *Gospel according to John*, p.383).
2. Calvin, *Commentary on John*, vol. I p.395.
3. Whitacre, *John*, p.257.
4. Hutcheson, *Exposition of John*, p.205.
5. P. Henry, *Christ All in All*, p.199.
6. Manton, *Complete Works*, vol. 12, p.153.
7. Carson, *Gospel according to John*, p.387.
8. Manton, *Complete Works*, vol. 3, p.333.
9. Simeon, *Expository Outlines*, vol. 13, p.502.

Chapter 25 — 'Tell us who you are!'

1. One thinks of the various 'quests' for the 'historical Jesus' undertaken (principally) by German liberal theologians over the last two hundred years. These theological contortions, all of course in contradiction of one another, are essentially the fruit of denying the real Jesus revealed in the Scriptures. See Fred H. Klooster, *Quests for the Historical Jesus* (Baker, 1977), for a lucid and manageable account of the various answers of theological liberalism to John 10:24.
2. M. Henry, *Commentary*, vol. 5, p.1036.
3. Hutcheson, *Exposition of John*, p.212.
4. Elisha Coles, *The Sovereignty of God* (Baker, 1979 [c. 1678]), p.276.
5. Carson, *Gospel according to John*, p.393.
6. As above, p.395.
7. As above, pp.395-6. Carson points out that the Romans would not have allowed execution by stoning (they preferred crucifixion) and, in any case, tended to reserve capital punishment to cases in which they had a direct interest.
8. Calvin, *Commentary on John*, vol. I, p.418.
9. M. Henry, *Commentary*, vol. 5, p.1042.

Chapter 26 — The resurrection and the life

1. Hendriksen, *Commentary on John*, vol. II, p.137; Carson, *Gospel according to John*, p.407.
2. M. Henry, *Commentary*, vol. 5, p.1044.
3. Calvin, *Commentary on John*, vol. I, p.432.
4. Hendriksen, *Commentary on John*, vol. II, p.144.
5. As above, p.146.
6. Carson, *Gospel according to John*, p.412.
7. Ridderbos, *The Gospel of John*, p.396.
8. Calvin, *Commentary on John*, vol. I, 435.
9. As above, p.436.
10. Hutcheson, *Exposition of John*, p.234.
11. Hendriksen, *Commentary on John*, vol. II, p.155.

Chapter 27 — The raising of Lazarus

1. Calvin, *Commentary on John*, vol. I, p.442.
2. Ridderbos, *The Gospel of John*, p.403.
3. The seven 'signs' recorded in John are:

   1. Water into wine (2:1-11)
   2. Healing the nobleman's son (4:46-54)
   3. Healing the lame man (5:1-18)
   4. Feeding the multitude (6:1-15)
   5. Walking on water (6:16-21)
   6. Healing the man born blind (9:1-41)
   7. The raising of Lazarus (11:1-57)

4. Hutcheson, *Exposition of John*, p.235.
5. Milne, *The Message of John*, p.168.
6. Calvin (*Commentary on John*, vol. I, p.448), Hendriksen (*Commentary on John*, vol. II, p.161) and Morris (*Gospel according to John*, p.563) all believe the faith was genuine. Carson (*Gospel according to John*, p.419) is guardedly positive on this point.
7. Simeon, *Expository Outlines*, vol. 13, p.541.
8. Carson, *Gospel according to John*, p.423.
9. *The Book of Psalms for Singing*, no. 98A.

Chapter 28 — A unique gift

1. The chronology is very involved and cannot be discussed here. For full discussions see Carson, *Gospel according to John*, pp.427, 455-8; Hendriksen, *Commentary on John*, vol. II, pp.221-7.
2. Carson, *Gospel according to John*, pp.426-7.
3. Lenski, *Interpretation of John*, p.839.
4. Ridderbos, *The Gospel of John*, p.415.
5. M. Henry, *Commentary*, vol. 5, p.1068.
6. Hendriksen, *Commentary on John*, vol. II, p.177.

7. Hutcheson, *Exposition of John*, p.244.

8. M. Henry, *Commentary*, vol. 5, p.1070.

9. Hendriksen, *Commentary on John*, vol. II, p.180.

10. M. Henry, *Commentary*, vol. 5, p.1068.

Chapter 29 — The seed must die

1. Ridderbos, *The Gospel of John*, p.422.

2. Milne, *The Message of John*, p.180.

3. As above.

4. Hendriksen, *Commentary on John*, vol. II, p.193.

5. See Hendriksen, *Commentary on John*, vol. II, pp.204-5 (and note 119) for the tally.

6. Morris, *Gospel according to John*, pp.172-3. The Son of Man comes with 'the clouds of heaven' — something attributed in Scripture only to God (Ps. 104:3; Isa. 19:1) — and so identifies himself as divine and human at the same time, prefiguring the person of Christ as the incarnate Son of God.

7. Lenski, *Interpretation of John*, p.862.

8. Hendriksen, *Commentary on John*, vol. II, p.195.

9. Lenski, *Interpretation of John*, p.870; cf. Carson, *Gospel according to John*, p.440 — he favours the 'positive prayer' interpretation.

10. Manton, *Complete Works*, vol. 13, p.137.

11. As above, vol. 21, p.12.

12. As above, vol. 21, p.442.

13. Calvin, *Commentary on John*, vol. II, p.35.

14. As above.

15. *Robertson's Word Pictures* (as per *Bible Works for Windows 3.1*).

16. Carson, *Gospel according to John*, p.445.

17. Hutcheson, *Exposition of John*, p.260.

Chapter 30 — Why Jesus was rejected

1. Hendriksen, *Commentary on John*, vol. II, p.210.

2. T. Halyburton, *Memoirs of the Life of the Rev. Thomas Halyburton* (Edinburgh: c. 1845), p.46.

3. M. Henry, *Commentary*, vol. 5, p.1085.

4. As above.

5. Milne, *The Message of John*, p.192.

6. D. M. Lloyd-Jones, *Preaching and Preachers* (Hodder & Stoughton, 1971), p.16.

7. Hutcheson, *Exposition of John*, p.267.

A wide range of excellent books on spiritual subjects is available from Evangelical Press. Please write to us for your free catalogue or contact us by e-mail.

Evangelical Press
Faverdale North Industrial Estate, Darlington, Co. Durham, DL3 0PH, England

Evangelical Press USA
P. O. Box 84, Auburn, MA 01501, USA

e-mail: sales@evangelicalpress.org

web: http://www.evangelicalpress.org